Modern China Series

Critiques on Pan-Marketization

Rethink the Economic Reform in Modern China

Li Cunlin

Liu Hongfei

Tian Guang

North America Business Press

July 2018

NORTH
AMERICAN BUSINESS
PRESS

Seattle, WA
Atlanta, GA
Toronto, Canada

About Modern China Series

China, as one of the oldest civilized regions in the world, has emerged as something of a "new world" because it is working to embrace its own essence and heritage and link them to viable economic strategies. In the last 25 years, China has made tremendous strides by doing so. The country and her people have every right to take pride in these accomplishments. With these successes under their belt, many Chinese leaders and intellectuals anticipate continuing growth. China's plans and strategies, furthermore, are often based upon this premise.

There is tremendous interest in the US on the Chinese economy and business environment. China has emerged as a global super power, and scholars and businessmen in the US are keenly interested in learning how this is going to continue to affect them and how they can do business with China. In response to growing interest from international and Asian scholars, North American Business Press is pleased to announce our Modern China Series (MCS) books, which is first of such series in the US and has garnered tremendous interest both in the US and around the world. With our first book reaching stores in September 2011, this initiative is aimed at developing relationships between NABP and Chinese scholars who desire to promote their academic and applied business writings to the rest of the world.

We have had overwhelming demand for the Modern China Series from both authors who would like to publish in the series and people who would like to read the books. Currently, there are ten books published in the series and, additionally, we have a couple of dozen books that we are considering for the series. The books have been viewed by tens of thousands of people from the U.S. and the rest of the world.

We have published books relating to several areas revolving around the Chinese business environment. We have a few that focus on the best practices in marketing in China; a couple relating to "best practices" in doing business in China; and a few on the outlook of the Chinese economy. The market for the Modern China Series is huge. There are tens of thousands of scholars that are keenly interested in the continued growth of the Chinese economy and the implications that will have on the business world. Even more significant are the millions of businessmen that are interested in the impact that China will continue to have on the global economy. It is difficult to pin down the exact demand for the series, but it is very large.

We have big plans for growing the Moderns China Series. This has the potential to one of the most significant economic/business series ever produced. We are very selective with the books that we will add to the collection, but we encourage any scholars who think they have unique and interesting perspectives on China to submit their books to us. From the readers perspective, we are committed to producing high quality books on a regular basis so that readers should expect a steady stream of insightful books to be coming out for many years to come.

This initiative is headed by Dr. Robert Tian, a renowned researcher and academic, who spearheads our efforts in partnering with foreign authors and administering day-to-day operations of this series. Dr. Tian, a Vice-President with North American Business Press and Editor of this series, spends much of his time in Beijing, Shanghai, and other Chinese cities, focusing on developing and managing our interests with authors and universities. Below is the list for the books we have published:

1. Enterprise Strategy: New Horizon authored by Zhang Xiuyu
2. Governance of Private Enterprises in Modern China authored by Zhong Qin
3. The Art of War and Enterprise Strategy Management by Fu Shouzhi
4. Marketing Issues in Modern China edited by Robert Guang Tian et al.
5. The Footprints of the Academician authored by Fu Zhouzhi
6. Marketing and Economics in Modern China (I) edited by Xiaoguang Qi et al.
7. Marketing and Economics in Modern China (II) edited by Wang Tianjin et al.
8. An Islamic Heritage in China authored by Ma Zhanming
9. Environmental Anthropology in Modern China authored by Wang Tianjin et al.
10. Can China Rule the New World? Authored by Tian Guang and Chen Gang
11. Critiques on Pan-Marketization authored by Li Cunlin, Liu Hongfei, and Tian Guang

Critiques on Pan-Marketization

Rethink the Economic Reform in Modern China

Li Cunlin

Liu Hongfei

Tian Guang

North America Business Press

July 2018

Table of Contents

Preface

Be the Pioneers of Criticism on Pan-Marketization

In this book, we conceptualize Pan-Marketization phenomenon formatted during last 40 years in accordance with the economic reform in modern China, and make a systematic and even pungent criticism on the phenomenon from theory and practice perspectives. This type of critical study is of great theoretical and practical significance to correct some Chinese people's understanding on the function of the market, to prevent the disastrous spread of market behavior, to resist various erroneous thoughts on reform, and to firmly take the road of socialist market economy. Some ideological, theoretical and epochal views are addressed in this book.

We systematically put forward the theory of Pan-Marketization. Since the reform and opening up, China's market economy has developed rapidly, and the Chinese understanding of the market economy has evolved from the skeptical attitude at the beginning, to the basic recognition and then complete approval. Nevertheless, there are still some problems in the process of building socialist market economy, especially the Pan-Marketization phenomenon. The so-called universal marketization in China applies the principle of market trading to all fields, adjusts everything with the market mechanism, expands the role of market mechanism, and pushes the market operation to various fields of people's life. We hold that there should be a boundary and bottom line for marketization. Any marketization oriented reform beyond this boundary and bottom will inevitably lead to the overrun of market behavior, so that the whole society could be in a desperate situation.

We conduct a deep analysis of the Pan-Marketization phenomenon and its harmfulness in today's Chinese society. Under the disturbance of the trend of Pan-Marketization, disorder happens in the Chinese society, that is, no matter the issue belongs to the category of commodity trading or not, it is solved by means of buying and selling. We have summed up several typical phenomena of Pan-Marketization in the process of China's economic reform. For example, under the guidance of educational industrialization thoughts, universities run a variety of companies which are funded by the school, at the same time, they randomly collect fees from students. The marketization of education has made some parents overwhelmed. What's more, it misled the value pursuit and ideal faith of the faculty and staff, and decayed the quality of education. The general marketization of the medical service, push many public hospitals in the expansion of the operation scale by purchasing large and complex equipment, without considering the general economic capacity of the patients but charge a much more than the medical costs. In addition, the hospital's profit driven mechanism also misleads the value of medical workers, the prescription of excessive medical treatment continuously intensified the relationship between doctors and patients. Results find that the universities and hospitals, once considered as a pure land, have appeared very serious corrupted. We allege that Pan-Marketization thoughts are the important ideological source of the corruption phenomenon, which make the public power being abused by the authorities. If the marketization is eroded to the administration, the judicial field and the army, the power and money transactions and the right for sex transactions will be formed in a larger scope, thus cause more serious corruption.

We profoundly reveal the ideological roots of Pan-Marketization. The root cause of Pan-Marketization trend is mainly from the neoliberalism school in the West. In the 1980s, the ideas and theories of neoliberalism economics were very active in the western world, and had an enormous influence on the government decisions in the United States and Europe. The neoliberalism theory advocates privatization can improve efficiency, so its policy orientation is mainly concentrated in two aspects, one is to minimize the function of the government, and the other is to make the economic system privatized and liberalized. However, the implementation of the results did not reach the predetermined goal of the rulers, nor did it produce a paradise on earth, as depicted by Professor Freedman, a famous Nobel Prize winner of economics in US. It has also misled Russia to carry out a so-called shock therapy reform by implementing rapid marketization and privatization, the outcome of the radical marketization oriented reform in Russia damage the country's economy and we need learn the lessons from its extreme reform behavior. Unfortunately, some Chinese scholars failed to recognize that free market economy is not that much effective, which advocates the original accumulation of small scaled enterprises and small private ownership by dissolving large state-owned enterprises. Influenced by this trend of thoughts, marketization is fully introduced in China as the solution for modernization. As a result, individuals contract projects in education and scientific research units by so called market principles, the presidents, deans, and professors at universities are addressed as the bosses. A large amount of funds to be used in high precision and basic scientific research fields is nibbled out, and serious corruptions of academic research emerged. We accuse these phenomena are influenced by the neoliberalism thoughts.

We also make a proposal to control the spread of the Pan-Marketization phenomenon. We criticize ruthlessly the Pan-Marketization and concurrently put forward the theoretical thinking and policy assumption, to control the flood of Pan-Marketization. We suggest clarifying the boundaries of marketization theoretically, and we believe that the theory of market economy is quite correct. The establishment of a socialist market economy with Chinese characteristics is fundamental goal of reform but the key is that we should not narrowly understand market economy theory, nor should we implement market economy reform vulgarly. The marketization mechanism should be combined with China's specific national conditions, so that the market economy can develop within certain boundary. We have faith in that the field of public service, including hospitals and educational institutions, should not allow carrying out the market-oriented reform. The government administration department and the state armed forces are not supposed to have the market-oriented economic assessment mechanism. We propose to strengthen the state management function and mechanism. In the view of proponents of Pan-Marketization theory, the state management and regulation of economic matters is the old way of implementing the planned economy, only by vigorously promoting market economy can China develop well, only by regulating people's thoughts and behaviors according to market principles can China make it prosperous and strong. It is noticed that in a period, this theoretical view dominated way of economics and spread in the mainland of China. In those theorists' view that the Chinese society and even the entire human society can only be marketed, otherwise there is no way for development.

Under the misguidance of Pan-Marketization trend of thoughts, many sectors and industries that should not be marketed have been swiftly and radically marketized. Therefore, we propose an effective way to prevent Pan-Marketization trend by strengthening the ideology of state management. The state management concept refers to the central government and its responsible personnel as the managers of the state. In economic and social activities, the government behavior should be in accordance with the objective laws, to use as few resources as possible and to optimize the combination of resources to obtain the best social and economic effects, and moreover government should strive for the coordinated development of the economic and social environment to meet the people's substance needs and the growing demand for culture. Especially when dealing with severe economic and social crises, the national operation is necessary and powerful.

The government's function should change from leadership to management, and the government's behavior should change from leading decision to management decision. As the leader, planner and coordinator of the national economic system and its operation, the state government should regulate the market activities in two major fields:

on one hand, when the economic development and social orders are out of balance, the state should take the stable policy as the goal, take active intervention to restore the market balance and expand the social surplus. On the other hand, when the economy is balanced but is not in Pareto optimal condition, the state can directly or indirectly encourage the implementation of policy, to better utilize all the resources which can be freely distrusted by the society to obtain the improvement of Pareto status. We think that it is of great practical significance to criticize Pan-Marketization phenomenon. The reasons are as follows:

First, it is conducive to deepening the correct understanding of the socialist market economy, recognizing the essence and harm of Pan-Marketization, and consciously resisting the Pan-Marketization behavior. At present, the Chinese scholars have made various levels in terms of interpreting the causes of the negative phenomena caused by the Pan-Marketization, but are lack of the systematic analyses with no guidance value to the public. We reveal the ubiquitous phenomenon in China in a more systematic way, and deeply disclose its ideological root and its harmfulness. At the same time, we put forward some ideas for prevention and control of Pan-Marketization, which will undoubtedly enrich the theoretical system of socialist market economy and help the Chinese people to be more comprehensive and deeper in understanding the essential requirements of the socialist market economy.

Second, it helps to follow the direction of China's reform. At present, China has entered a new round of comprehensive deepening reform stage. The idea of the market adaptation scope that we proposed is conducive to the orientation of the reform direction and target, and bears a more important reference value for the comprehensive deepening reform. The reform of this round needs clear goals and objectives in the first place. It needs to be clear that which areas should carry out marketization oriented reform and which areas are not suitable to carry out the reform in the market to avoid blind reform or for the reform to reform, so that the reform can be truly put into practice and gain the effectiveness.

Third, our critiques on Pan-Marketization will help to establish a system of prevention and control of corruption. In present China, although under the leadership of Xi Jinping the official corruption trends have been stopped, the situation of anti-corruption still presents a complex and severe situation, and the institutional mechanism for the corruption phenomenon still exists in many fields. Collapse type corruption and family type corruption have become a new feature of corruption. We expose one of the ideological roots of the corruption phenomenon is the widespread Pan-Marketization trend of thoughts. As such, to get rid of Pan-Marketization thinking trend and to correct understand the marketization oriented reform are great significance to effectively prevent and deal with corruptions from the institutional level. Moreover, Pan-Marketization functions as the hotbeds for breeding corruption. It is therefore necessary to eliminate it thoroughly in all-round way in China.

Li Cunlin, Liu Hongfei, and Tian Guang

June 13, 2018

Acknowledgements

As the authors who have equally made the contributions to the book we are deeply indebted to many Chinese scholars for what they did to inspire it; we have referred hundreds of their articles and books published both in Chinese and in English. We thank Dr. Gao Jian, Dr. Liu Yu, Dr. Luo Kanglong, Dr. Ma Jianfu, Dr. Ma Rui, Dr. Ma Zhanming, Dr. Wu Hexian, Dr. Xu Zonglin, Dr. Zhang Hui, Dr. Zhao Peihua, Dr. Zheng Muqiang, Dr. Zhou Xinjun, and Professors Li Dekuan, Wang Tianjin, Yang Tingshuo, and Zhang Shaoping, for their insightful comments on and constructive suggestions to the initial manuscript, without their encouragements and supports this book may not be able to get published in time.

We thank our student Ms. Dai Qinqin who had participated in the project in the earlier stages and based on which we had published a book in Chinese on the same topic. Our students Mr. Hu Mingzhi, Ms. Li Wei, Ms. Lin Xiaoyan, Ms. Qian Shansha, Mr. Shao Huan, Ms. Xiong Huacui, Mr. Yang Lizhong, Ms. Yu Hong, Mr. Wan Yongan, Ms. Wang Ying helped us collected data and conducted some technique editing works. Ms. Lin Xiaoyan helped us translated considerable amounts of Chinese documents. Thanks also go to Professor Guan Yixin for his wonderful foreword for our book. Our gratitude also goes to Chairman Yang Qingwei from the Investment Association of China and Director Lee Donglin from the Ministry of Commerce of the People's Republic of China who have encouraged us regarding this book.

Finally, we would like to thank the First-Class Disciplines Foundation of Ningxia (Grant No.NXYLXK2017B09) for their support to the publishing of this book.

Foreword

The Crime and Punishment of Pan-Marketization

The book Critiques on Pan-Marketization, authored by Professors Li Cunlin, Liu Hongfei, and Tian Guang, summarizes the accomplishments and problems encountered in contemporary China's economic system reform during the last 40 years. It also reveals the principal reason behind the problems that lie in the fallacy of Pan-Marketization thoughts trend. The authors analyze the problems of social, economic, political and cultural aspects caused by deception and fallacy of the Pan-Marketization thoughts trend; offer the feasible solutions for various problems caused by that trend; and bring us the new understanding and more comprehensive thinking on the current economic system reform. After reading the manuscript, the current author ponders and feels infinite: when individuals and groups define a kind of existence as a necessity, and modify the impulses of religious belief beyond the objective law, the tragedy in the extreme way of breaking the inner contradictions that Fyodor Dostoevsky's Crime and Punishment portrayed seems unavoidable. On the road of this extraordinary pursuit, perhaps some people, just like Raskolnikov, have gone too far away.

China's economy has won the world's attention under the aura of miracles after 40 years of reform and opening up to the outside world. According to the current exchange rate, China’s GDP exceeded 13 trillion US dollars in 2017, second only to that of the United States, more than double of that of Japan which is ranked third in the world. If compared by purchasing power parity (PPP), China's GDP surpassed the GDP of the US in 2014. In addition, calculated according to constant prices, China's GDP in 2017 was about 225 times higher than that in 1978, and GDP per capita was about 154 times higher than that in 1978. By the end of March 2018, China's official foreign exchange reserves amounted to 3,142.8 billion US dollars, ranking as the first in the world. China has transformed from a planned economic system to an initially established market economic system over the past 40 years. The reform of the rural economy keeps developing; the state-owned enterprises reform continues breaking through the bottleneck; foreign trade increased year by year; non-state-owned economic components reached to higher level; and the gradual improvements of the macro control system have helped the Chinese economy become a significant part of the global economy. In 2012, the Joint Research Report "China in 2030: Building a Modern, Harmonious and Creative High-Income Society" by the World Bank and the Development Research Center of the Chinese State Council predicted that even if the economic growth of China slowed down it would be among the ranks of the highest income nations by 2030 and it would win also the title of the largest economy in the world by then.

However, cake not only needs to be big but also delicious. Moreover, it should be clear who is going to have it and how to make everyone happy. With the trend of Pan-Marketization thoughts, when all the reform and development results are attributed to the role of marketization, and when all reforms simplified to marketization, the so-called construction of a socialist economy with Chinese characteristics will completely transform China into a large market where nothing but only trading exists everywhere. Even many people consider the marketization process as the privatization of the whole society as it advocates adopting economic means to deal with all social issues that arise in the process of reform. It is characteristic result of such an inertia reform that various crises in many aspects of social, economic and political reform arose in the previous years, the income gap is continuously getting enlarged, and the unequal mode of distribution has distorted the most.

According to the Chinese National Bureau of Statistics, the Gini coefficient of national income in 2016 was 0.465. Moreover, the Domestic Financial Survey conducted by the Southwestern University of Finance and Economics in 2017 indicated that the savings rate for households in the 90-percentile income distribution group was 56.96%, and 76.85% of the operating income allocated to the households in the 90-percentile income distribution group showing that the operating income inequality was very severe. The gap of income has led to insufficient consumption from the poor and high savings from the rich. The poor families face lack of income to consume while the consumption of the rich families has reached saturation. The report also points out that, in 2016, the debt ratio of family property in China was 29.78%, of which the ratio of bank loans was 10.03%, and the average value of loans was 22.85 thousand RMB. The proportion of family education liabilities was 7.93% with a mean value of 12798 RMB. The ratio of average and median annual household income was about 2.9:1, the proportion of household income in top 10% was 74.9%.

Too much income disparity has hindered economic development, intensified social contradictions, threatened social stability, and led to mass incidents and serious psychological hatred. Moreover, the chaotic situation happens in medical services, education and other public service sections. The medical ethics and professional ethics are facing unprecedented challenges. The hospital is not to save lives, but to sell medical products and set tricks to make money from patients. Schools are not to teach and educate people, but to make money from students and parents by selling knowledge.

In his report at the 19th Congress of Communist Party of China, Xi Jinping pointed out that there are still many short boards in the construction of the people's livelihood. The task of poverty alleviation is difficult to be realized, the imbalanced development of urban and rural areas, and the gap of income distribution are still large, the masses are facing difficult problems in employment, education, medical treatment, living and pension. In fact, one of the major reasons for these unwanted phenomena is the widespread marketization of people's livelihood. Ideally, people’s livelihood should make education, medical and other industries to benefit the people, but it is operated in accordance with the market-oriented mechanism, ignoring the importance of many social issues, and only taking the economy as the guiding principle of all the schemes. For example, when marketization is taken as the guiding principle in all fields, the rural residents will be more disadvantaged in the enjoyment of public services, such as education and medical care, and as such the gap between urban and rural residents will also continue to expand.

Xi Jinping stressed that more challenging work needs to be done to reach the all-round development of economy and society. Idle talk will lead to the loss of the country and the vigorous development of the state. He also highlighted the one point of deployment and nine points of implementation. We need to take practical measures to push forward step by step in a comprehensive manner. As far as public health and social health care is concerned, we should vigorously promote the implementation of the health China strategy, design and complete the national health policy, provide the people with full cycle health service, deepen the reform of the medical and health system, establish the basic medical, health and medical insurance system with Chinese characteristics, maintain the high quality and efficient medical and health services. We should improve the system of modern hospital management, strengthen the construction of the basic medical and health service system and the team of general practitioners, and support the society to produce more effective medicine and to develop the health industry. At the beginning of the last decade of the 20th century, under the background of inspiring times, medical reform entered the market orbit. Unfortunately, nearly 30 years have passed, and health care reform is still in place of consoling the rulers with a constantly evolving stage. In the presence of various camps of interest groups, even a slight change in the reform is difficult. Radical marketization reform leads to a more difficult and more expensive medical treatment system. We do not know that system will disturb the Chinese people for how many years in the future.

In addition, Chinese people are not able to bear the great leap forward in education. The university enrollment expansion started in

1999, and after a few years of its popularity, the college students became familiar to the fact that they could not rely on their own efforts to change their fate by knowledge. Market oriented education results into uneven distribution of educational resources increasing the gap between urban and rural areas making regional differences fathomless. In fact, the proportion of students entering college examination from rural areas has increased year by year, and now it has exceeded 60%. However, from the perspective of admission, the proportion of rural students in ordinary universities, especially in key institutions, has been declining. Taking Peking University as an example, from 1978 to 1988, about 30% of Peking University students came from rural areas. From 1990s to 1990s, the data showed a decline trend, and from 2000 to 2010, the number of students from rural areas at Peking University has shrunk to less than 10%. Although some improvements have been made, it is still less than 20% by 2017. 'Graduation means unemployment' is a major social problem evolved by the marketization of education. It is a great hidden danger for social stability. The rural population is at the bottom of China's wealth ladder, and many families are heavily indebted to their children for going to university. They regard college as a chance to change their fate, get rid of the nightmare of poverty as this chance happens only once in a lifetime, however, availing of this chance makes them get entangled more and more deeper in the mire of poverty.

The marketization of education brings economic development for education industry. It led many students to the unknown future, and generated a feudal hereditary talent selection system in the Chinese society. The consequences of Pan-Marketization also include the loss of assets of state-owned enterprises, serious environmental pollution, lack of social honesty and corruption, and so on. This series of problems caused by Pan-Marketization, deepening and pushing to the edge of collapse, is torturing every Chinese conscience. Some of the so-called mainstream economists are still using economic terms to pack, to inflate the inevitability of corruption, and to make big comments on cakes. It seems to be deliberately concealing the other side of the coin and misleading the way of recognizing things. How can this idea or theory become a panacea for all the spirits and how to turn into some of the words in the mouth of some quack warlocks?

Keeping in view the problems faced by the reform of economic system in contemporary China and the profound reasons behind the problems, the Critiques on Pan-Marketization have carried out thoughtful theoretical reflection and empirical research. The authors intensely studied the fallacy influence of Pan-Marketization chemistry, the misguided market economy reform, and intensely analyzed a series of problems, such as social, economic, political and cultural ones caused by the absurd Pan-Marketization reform, and put forward specific suggestions to correct the fallacies of the Pan-Marketization trend thoughts bringing harm to the comprehensive development of economy and society.

The entire book is rigorously offers theoretical analysis, plentiful empirical materials, profound ideas and clear policy recommendations. The authors put four civilizations as the basic law of the development of human society in an all-round way. These four civilizations refer to material civilization, political civilization, spiritual civilization, and ecological civilization all of which combine to constitute a unified organism. Combining Marx's economic theory with western economic theory, Tian and his colleagues build a theoretical framework, analyze and discuss the current economic reform and the problems encountered in the reform of China's economy. China's reform and opening-up has become an entirely new view of the historical process of economic and social development all over the world, also declaring that the problems encountered in the marketization oriented reform illustrate that the market machine is not unconditionally applicable, nor is there any omnipotent theory and method for the Chinese people to copy. Building a socialist road with Chinese characteristics is the way out for the Chinese people to ensure the stability and sustainable development to maintain the stable economic and social establishment, and to realize the great rejuvenation of the Chinese nation.

Based on a comprehensive analysis of the reform of China's economic system along with the experience and lessons from opening to the outside world, the authors put forward the option of implementing the national operation strategy by emphasizing the strategic conception of making the soft power as the core to accelerate the integrated development of China's economy and society by focusing on the construction of a new socialist countryside and establishing the independent innovation as the foundation to develop the socialism with Chinese characteristics, and to build an innovative country based on innovative industrial and agricultural systems.

Currently, the economic and social development in China has entered a new era. President Xi Jinping has put forward the "One Belt and One Road" development strategy which uses historical symbol of the ancient Silk Road to uphold the banner of peaceful development, and to actively develop the economic relations with such countries that may be partners in this phenomenon. It relies on the existing bilateral and multilateral mechanism along with the existing and effective regional cooperation platforms, together with the relevant countries to create a political mutual trust, economic integration, cultural inclusion of the human community with common interests, common destiny, along with common responsibility. According to Xi Jinping, socialism with Chinese characteristics has entered a new era after a lengthy period of effort. It is necessary to fully and accurately implement the thought of socialism with Chinese characteristics in the new era. Based on the world situation, national conditions, and the conditions of the development of China, it is necessary to have a blueprint to build a well-off society in an all-round way. From basically realizing modernization, and then to building a socialist modern nation in an all-round way, China must persist in deepening the integrated reform to realize the great rejuvenation of the nation.

This book is about the "crime and punishment" of Pan-Marketization. It reveals the misleading of the so-called mainstream economics and the social, economic, political and cultural harms caused by Pan-Marketization. Moreover, this book would provide theoretical support for comprehensive understanding and rethinking marketization oriented reform in China. The authors have demonstrated that any types of reform in China must be adhered to the road of socialism with Chinese characteristics, and must be assembled to the economic, political and cultural aspects of Chinese characteristics. I applaud and congratulate to the authors and the publisher for such a wonderful work giving an ample opportunity to the reader to have a critical thought about Pan-Marketization.

Guan Yixin

June 16, 2018 in Beijing

Chapter 1

Rethink Economic System Reform in Modern China

The Chinese leadership launched reform and opening-up campaign in late 1970s. It brought great social and economic development in modern China. However, without a suitable guiding theory for the reform and opening up, there is a tendency to over stress the importance of marketization. This has generated some serious social issues that need the Chinese leadership to step forward to solve them. Although most profound changes created by the reform are positive, some economic, social, cultural and other phenomena failed to satisfy the public interests. This paper is to review the overall process of economic reform and to make an initial rethinking on reform by pinpointing the problems caused by Pan-Marketization oriented reform policy; it also looks at the policy process and gives some suggestions to overcome the problems caused by Pan-Marketization.

The reform and opening-up launched by the Chinese leadership in 1978 has brought a great-leap-forward development in modern China. People from the entire world could not help praising the miracles of economic and social accomplishments by Chinese people in the last thirty-four years. China has increased its comprehensive national power markedly and accumulated development strength through the policy of reform and opening-up. However, on the other hand, as the worldwide competition has escalated, China still faces some serious challenges.

How to seize opportunities and to meet challenges has become one of the hottest issues discussed in current China. It is expected that in the process of dealing with changing complexities, reform should absorb great thoughts both at home and abroad continuously, and should lead to more innovations. Without a suitable guiding theory, reform will lack the right guiding directions, high efficiency and good outcomes. Since China has a long history and a large population, the tasks of reform are arduous. Although the most profound changes in all fields occurred in the process of reform are positive, some economic, social, cultural and other by-products fail to satisfy the public interests.

The strategic goal of the 21st century declared by the Chinese authorities is to create a new nation with stronger comprehensive national power and to accomplish the great rejuvenation of the Chinese nation. To realize this strategic goal, it is necessary to explore the causes of problems and to repair defects came up during the process of previous economic system reforms. Pan-Marketization is one of such defects that need to be cleared up (Tian and Dai, 2012).

The Socialism with Chinese Characteristics

The reform and opening up of China made brilliant achievements in the first 5 years of the new century. Moreover, the new generation of collective leadership of Communist Party of China with Hu Jintao as the general secretary has sized up the situation and has put forward a scientific outlook on development, as well as introducing a ruling strategy of "being people-oriented and constructing a harmonious society", which has vitalized the national development greatly. During the 10th Five-Year Plan period (2001-2005) the national economy had maintained a sustainable and rapid development at the macro level. On March 14, 2006, the fourth session of the 10th National People's Congress approved the 11th Five-Year Plan for National Economic and Social Development. The economic development in the twelfth Five Year Plan period will have a decisive impact and exert a tremendous influence laying a solid foundation for promoting growth of economy in China.

The Great Accomplishments

According to the 11th Five-Year Plan for Chinese economic and social development formulated previously, the gross domestic product (GDP) of China should have reached ￥26.1 trillion RMB in 2010 with an annual growth of 7.5 percent, and the per capita GDP should have reached ￥19,270 RMB with an annual growth rate of 6.6% (National People's Congress, 2006). However, by 2007, China's GDP had reached ￥26.58 trillion RMB and per capita GDP exceeded ￥20,000 RMB (The National Bureau of Statistics, 2011). The data published by the National Bureau of Statistics of China showed that China's national economy took the lead in recovering from the international financial crisis in 2009. In 2009, China's GDP approximately reached ￥33.5 trillion RMB, 8.7% higher than that in 2008 but 0.9% point lower than that in 2007 at the comparable prices. In 2009, the total social investment in fixed assets was ￥22.5 trillion RMB, up 30.1% year-on-year, and with the growth rate 4.6% higher than that in the previous year. The retail aggregate of social consumer goods reached ￥12.5 trillion RMB , increased by 15.5% over the previous year, a real increase rate of 16.9% and 2.1% higher than that in the same period of previous year after adjusting for inflation (The National Bureau of Statistics, 2010). During the period of 11th Five-Year Plan, the Chinese economy maintained a relatively fast growth rate when the international financial crisis happened in the same period. China's GDP reached ￥39.8 trillion RMB with an average annual growth rate of 11.2%, and the national fiscal revenue increased from ￥3.16 trillion RMB to ￥8.31 trillion RMB (Wen, 2011). This was clear indication that the economic goals of the 11th Five-Year Plan were successfully achieved.

In 2006, China surpassed Italy, France and England becoming the fourth-largest economy with a GDP worth $2.229 trillion USD, while the United States maintained the strongest economic power in the world with a GDP of $12.455 trillion USD; Japan ranked second with a GDP of $4.505 trillion USD. Germany ranked as the third one followed by China (Xiao, 2006). In January 2009, China's National Bureau of Statistics announced that the GDP growth rate of China in 2008 was 13%. In 2007, the China's GDP was about $3.383 trillion USD, slightly surpassing the third largest economy, Germany, having

$3.321 trillion USD GDP in 2007. Vivek Arora, the chief representative of the International Monetary Fund in Beijing, publicly announced that China was already the third-largest economy following the United States and Japan in 2007 (Xin, 2009). On February 14, 2011, Japan's Kyodo News reported that the nominal GDP of the country in 2010 was $5.474 trillion USD, $0.404 trillion USD less than that of China, which means China had become the second-largest economy (Zhang, 2011).

Historical Process

The course of historic process has never been smooth for the Chinese people. After the Opium War launched by the British Army in 1840, China gradually became a semi-colonial and semi-feudal country. The development of Chinese nation suffered a significant setback. However, Marxism-Leninism was introduced to China from Russia, the first socialist country in the world, and those who were influenced by Marxism-Leninism in the early 1920s founded the Communist Party of China. The first-generation leadership group of the Party, with Mao Zedong as the representative, mastered the essence of Marxism-Leninism, comprehended the situation of Chinese society, and carried out a series of revolutionary actions led by the strategic thought of encircling the cities from the rural areas and seizing political power by armed forces. They led the Chinese people to practice and develop Marxism-Leninism within the Chinese context and established People's Republic of China in 1949. In the first Five-Year Plan of economic development period, Mao Zedong and his comrades worked hard to recover the national economy from wars. This laid a foundation stone for Chinese transformation from a backward agricultural country into an advanced industrial country.

In 1960, China encountered some difficulties and the leaders had a general feeling of insecurity in the process of socialist construction. In order to tide over the crisis, Mao economized on food and clothing together with his fellow citizens. He emphasized that we must settle down to build our modern industry, modern agriculture, modern science, modern culture, and modern defense (Mao, 1999a). Later, Mao and his team announced an ambitious plan to realize the modernization of agriculture, industry, military, and science in China. The goal of four modernizations inspired the whole nation and generated great power to overcome difficulties. At the same time, Mao Zedong spoke highly of the science and technology activities in the production initiated by the Chinese people across the country. He clearly pointed out that the innovation and technology revolution has now become a great movement. It is very urgent to sum up experience, to strengthen the leadership, to solve the problems in the movement and to guide the movement into a proper and scientific track (Mao, 1999b). Under the leadership of the Chinese Communist Party, the Chinese people united, overcame difficulties and worked hard for realization of the four modernizations proposed by the central government.

Since 1978, the second-generation leadership group of the Communist Party of China, with Deng Xiaoping as the representative, advocated emancipating minds to reform the rigidly planned economy and to open the door to the outside world. Deng Xiaoping led the Chinese people to continue the construction of the four modernizations put forward by Mao Zedong based on new historical conditions. Deng Xiaoping's theory states the contradiction, as well as the task and direction of the primary stage of socialism, and the program of making a fortune for the Chinese people by working hard. In about 20 years, Chinese people obtained high-speed development in socialist economic construction and solved the problem of food and clothing by the end of 2000. Chinese people who had been striving for food for thousands of years were wreathed in smiles.

In short, since 1840, under the guidance of Marxism-Leninism, Chinese people creatively established some significant thoughts, including Mao Zedong Thought, Deng Xiaoping's Theory, Three Represents, and the Outlook of Scientific Development, and formed the theoretical system of socialism with Chinese characteristics. These theoretical innovations are the core of all the party's policies, the essence of national development strategy and the soul of the Chinese nation. Without the guidance of correct theories, China would not have been able to taste the success that attracts worldwide attention. Obviously, it is a matter of significant importance for China to put forward innovational theory to keep developing constantly.

Socialist Theory with Chinese Characteristics

Marxism believes that human society is an organic unity of economy, politics, culture and the natural environment. In Marxism perspective, civilization is an organic unity of material civilization, political civilization, spiritual civilization and ecological civilization. Marxist classical writers provided some specific descriptions of a society that provides social members with the opportunity to fully display their creative ability instead of having their development constrained. In fact, human beings have concluded some basic rules of material civilization, political civilization, spiritual civilization and ecological civilization through experience and lessons of social practice. In addition, they have carried out a variety of activities to comply with objective law and have made excellent achievements.

The Chinese people have an especially deep understanding of the "Four Civilizations" in the process of modernization. On one hand, in the process of development in human society, the components of "Four Civilizations" are always closely connected with each other, which is also the universal law of human societal development. On the other hand, once political civilization and spiritual civilization have been formed, they have relative independence and historical inheritance, namely they have their own characteristics. Socialist material civilization, political civilization, spiritual civilization and ecological civilization are closely connected, and unified with the practice of socialist modernization. Owing to various reasons, many people seem to understand theoretically that socialist society is the one with comprehensive development of material civilization, political civilization, spiritual civilization and ecological civilization. However, in practice, some people do not act in accordance with the standard of social comprehensive development. As a result, they fail to reach the goals of social development outlined by Marxist classical writers.

On January 9, 2006, China held its new National Science and Technology Conference in the Great Hall of People in Beijing, the capital of China. As China's first grand meeting of science and technology in the new century, it not only provided a stage to display talents, but also offered an opportunity to develop strategies for modernized development. On the same day, the General Secretary of the Chinese Communist Party Hu Jintao stated that the country must adhere to the path of independent innovation with Chinese characteristics for turning China into an innovative country. Hu's statement was a summary of innovative concept in Chinese history, as well as a proposal of the Chinese historic task in the 21st century. The development of socialism with Chinese characteristics and the construction of an innovative country were not only a strategic objective, but also a challenge to the Chinese people. Hu emphasized that turning China into an innovative country within 15 years is an extremely arduous task, but, at same time it is an extensive and proud social change (Hu, 2006). The period from 2006 to 2020 is a significant historical stage for the Chinese socialist economy construction when the Chinese people took up the historic mission of national rejuvenation. The development of socialism with Chinese characteristics and the construction of an innovative country can be reflected in the following aspects:

Independent innovation as the foundation

Rapid development of science and technology in the 21st century is inevitable. The competition among countries is the competition of comprehensive national power which is formed by a country's politics, culture, economy, military, etc. The key method for a country to have stronger comprehensive national power is to achieve scientific and technological innovations almost completely based on independent intellectual property rights. Without independent innovation, it is difficult for a country to break through the limitation of the intellectual property rights barrier or to fundamentally solve the major strategic problems relevant to development and the country's security needs.

Independent innovation is the foundation of the independent development of national economy and society; it also represents the foundation of the indispensable lifeline of China's growth and development. Chinese people should increase the country's comprehensive innovation ability significantly from the aspect of a broad world vision. Only in this way can they have the competitive advantage in basic science and frontier technology research, and only in this way can they improve the key technology and core competiveness to enhance greatly comprehensive national strength. Eventually, innovation can help China become more powerful to seize opportunities to easily take on various challenges and to do its best to press forward on the socialist path.

Goal: to enrich Chinese people

The goal of Chinese socialist construction and economic system reform is to establish a powerful socialist economy and to create a well-off society that has never existed before and to build a harmonious society to benefit the Chinese people. It may take a long time to achieve this goal. In 1960, after suffering some setbacks, Mao Zedong expressed his understanding of China's development prospects to international friends and domestic comrades clearly: it will take 100 years or more to make China become a strong socialist economy (Mao, 1999c). After more than 30 years, the practice of reform and opening up has not only confirmed this profound understanding, but also further developed Mao Zedong's thoughts. Chinese economic construction experience and lessons in the second half of the 20th century indicated that three serious transformations must be carried out: switch from a planned economy to a market economy, switch from an agricultural society to an industrial one, and switch from a closed society to an open one.

In the process of building socialism with Chinese characteristics and establishing an innovative country, Chinese people carry out innovation practice independently and get benefits from the achievements. As such, Chinese people are delighted about the current economic and social situation. On the other hand, there is also something to worry about. Most people experience the happiness brought by the reform, and they sincerely support it. At the same time, they are dissatisfied with the widening income gap and inconvenient public services. The former economic construction had never met such problems. Therefore, we should use innovative thinking and explore methods to look for the answer. After all, the happiness of people is the true bond of cohesion of national power. Through active practice of reform and innovation, and through expanding the reform of the economic system, we can solve the deep-seated problems, safeguard the legitimate rights and interest of people, and share the results of the reform.

The courage to participate in world market competition

The competition of world business is like a cold war. The competitors need to occupy the commanding height of international economic competition with a high-spirited attitude and a fighting spirit. Compared with the high technology in developed industrial countries, the overall level of China's science and technology remain at a low level. It should keep bettering itself in the commercial competition of science and technology. China should apply the achievements of independent innovation in product manufacturing to occupy an important part of the industrial chain of world economic integration. Otherwise, it may lose its vitality eventually being eliminated by the market. China also should invest more capital in some specific areas of technology to catch up with other industrial countries.

In addition, in some scientific areas related to national development and security, China should try to seek a breakthrough in modern technology; focus on some significant fields; and expand its international market share in accordance with national conditions and strength. Nowadays, China is trying to step into the international business market by providing some products using independent intellectual property rights to meet the needs of the world market. China's products in high-tech fields (such as satellite launching and shipbuilding) and products of daily use (such as clothing, toys, hardware and sneakers) are being sold worldwide. As such, China has become the "world factory" of those products. China should keep developing brand-new, pertinent and practical technology to guarantee the competitive advantage in various levels of science and technology.

Preliminary Evaluation of Pan-Marketization

Innovation is the core of developing socialism with Chinese characteristics. Innovation relies on the sustainable and stable development of science and technology. Deng Xiaoping, the chief designer for China's reform and opening up road map, thought highly of the function of science and technology in economic and social construction, and put forward the thesis known as "science and technology are primary productive forces". The development of socialism with Chinese characteristics and building an innovative country are also a way to inherit and develop Deng Xiaoping theory. According to the concept of Deng Xiaoping, reform is to liberate productive forces and to arm various sectors with developed science and technology. This process is not easy and needs to clear out and change the old productive forces and backward ideologies.

Pan-Marketization ideology

Owing to the brief history of the socialist system, there exist some unavoidable defects. Meanwhile, even though the new system has been developing for less than 100 years, hostile forces that have existed for hundreds of years have never stopped impeding its development. Especially in the decade of 1990s, the socialist system had faced twists and turns in the world. Chinese communists have proposed new theories putting into practice to improve socialist society in its infancy. It was a very wise movement. The reform process of improving the socialist system is a process of liberating productive forces. The goal is to establish a socialist society with Chinese characteristics to guarantee the happiness of the people and the prosperity of the country.

Therefore, it is impossible for the economic reform of China to take marketization as its goal. The behavior that tries to use market mechanisms to regulate everything is a kind of "Pan-Marketization" behavior. This so-called Pan-Marketization behavior desires to apply free-market philosophy in all areas. Of late, in China, many elites or mainstream economists wantonly advocate western economic theory and operations and stir up Pan-Marketization thoughts by dominating the voice of public opinion. This stream ignores the history, reality and excellent traditional culture of Chinese society belittling Marxist doctrine and misleading policy-makers to equate "reform" with "marketization". It also adopts so-called "market-oriented operation" in all areas of people's lives trying to turn Chinese society into a big market in which all things can be traded. This thought was not prevalent for a long time, and the government has been trying its best to correct errors and to stop its dissemination.

The State Council and its ministries have issued several documents to forbid public industries degenerating into sources of income for a small number of for-profit institutions. Medical, security and other social welfare departments are not allowed to change. In the new era of world competition, how can marketization represent every aspect of a society? In the light of socialist theory, only the development of socialism with Chinese characteristics and innovative ability can improve comprehensive strength of China and defeat its enemies.

Promotion of Socialist Market Economy

In order to improve the socialist system comprehensively, Deng and his colleagues clearly point out that China's reform was not only limited to the economic system, but, it also involved the reform of the political system including the reform of the party and the state leadership system. Obviously, this reform is a huge project which not only involves fundaments, such as the economic system, but, also including the social superstructure system. The purpose of this reform is also to improve the completely socialist system, rather than to produce a reform with other properties. The reform of the party, the state leadership system, science and technology, education, culture, sports, health care, public health, environmental protection, ethnic and religious affairs and judicial system, etc. are all the same.

Such comprehensive reforms involving all areas of society view the self-improvement of the socialist system and the construction of a socialist harmonious society as goals of developing productive forces and achieving a common prosperity. Obviously, the purpose, content and method of reform cannot be all in one. In short, China's reform is not only to establish a socialist economic system, but also to build a harmonious socialist society with democracy, fairness and justice, sincerity, amity, vitality, stability and order, and harmonious relations between people and nature. However, in the process of the reform and opening up, some unexpected things happened and caused serious consequence.

It is very usual to reflect upon the reform efforts in the process of socialist construction. China used to be a country with an enormous population, a weak industrial base, and huge geographical differences. Modernization, therefore, is an unprecedented historical process that requires completing many tasks and overcoming complicated difficulties. The international environment around China has been very unstable for a long time. Because of the complex objective world, it is impossible for people to get a comprehensive understanding during a brief period. Therefore, it is very normal to see some different opinions and conflicts in the process of reform. In addition, some mistakes are unavoidable. It is very valuable that people praise wise policies, criticize errors and give out suggestions through the paper-based media and the Internet.

Early 1960s was a period of distress during which socialist construction of China met serious difficulties and many contradictions appeared in economic and social life. To the question of how to liberate from the distress, Mao Zedong explicitly pointed out that criticism and self-criticism is a way, perhaps the lone way, to solve contradictions among the people. He emphasized the significance of implementing democratic centralism inside and outside the party through letting the masses free to express their opinion. Mao also said that now we have many difficulties and it is impossible to overcome these difficulties without relying on the masses through arousing their enthusiasm. However, if we do not explain the situation to the masses and cadres and give them the chance to express their views, they will be afraid of us. As a result, it is impossible to arouse their enthusiasm (Mao, 1999d).

The Fallacies of Pan-Marketization

The well-known Chinese economist Liu Guoguang gave a short speech when he accepted the "World Marxist Economics Award" from the World Association for Political Economy Award Committee. He indicates that the goal of privatization forces in China is to replace public ownership with private ownership as the mainstay by premeditating to weaken the public sector of the economy and to strengthen the non-public sectors. They are opposed to attaching the adjective "socialist" with the word "market economy." They believe that there is no distinction between socialist market economy and capitalist market economy. Their intentions are obvious. Marxists and the Communist Party in China will thwart their malevolent schemes (Liu, 2011). Mr. Liu's position about the current development of the market economy is very clear. He is opposed to the interference with new liberalism or market fundamentalism, and he also points out the misleading statement of the so-called mainstream school of economics.

The undeniable fact is that, in the process of China's reform, some ambiguous concepts and arguments that confused right and wrong were once popular in the field of theory and practice. They advocated the full liberalization of the market, prices, and production factors such as land and labor, the sale of small and medium-sized state-owned enterprises and privatization of large and medium sized state-owned enterprises through the sale of shares. They also preached that we should replace the paternalism of Soft Budget Constraints with property rights reform theory (Han, 2006). Though, this stream claimed to be in line with Deng Xiaoping thought, in fact, it distorted the true meaning of economics and the blue print of constantly improving the socialist system proposed by the chief architect, Deng Xiaoping. This stream perpetrated a fraudulent "market-oriented" reform route. It decorated itself with a string of economic terms, especially the popular theories of certain types of economics schools in Western industrialized countries becoming the mouthpiece of those kinds of economics schools. As this stream proclaimed itself as Elite Theory, people have begun to ridicule it as mainstream economics.

The so-called mainstream economists always attempt to grasp the absolute right to speak, and to arbitrarily expand so-called market economy concepts to all areas of society. Based on the idea that people are rational, this school of thought has observed, analyzed, and explained all social phenomena, and has taught that "money is almighty", "all things are easy to be handled with money", "as long as both sides want to, any transaction is reasonable". Ignoring the resistance of people, with the use of ornate academic terms, some pretentious economic elites advocated solving all social problems in the reform process with economic means. They trumpeted "corruption is inevitable", the "High Salary Theory" and the "Bigger Cake Theory" and so on, essentially abusing and over-generalizing the functions of the market economy.

Practice under the direction of these types of theories would inevitably lead to the overrunning of Chinese society by the fallacies of Pan-Marketization. Unfortunately, during a period, this fallacy indeed has burst in like a flood and caused some setbacks in the overall economic and social development of China. It has done so because its disguised economic hypocrisy is very confusing. When this pseudo-economic theory, dressed in the cloak of science, overran the mainland of China, Pan-Marketization ideology overwhelmed every aspect of Chinese society. Under these misleading thoughts, some sectors and industries have taken marketization as the principle of daily operation, focusing on the exchange of interests and ignoring the real needs of society.

Common sense suggests that a sword has two sides. The implementation of any policy may have the risk of accidents. However, during a long historical period, the operators of some government agents seemed not to care about the practical consequences of reform as measured by marketization. They did not consider the benefits and risks of the implementation of reform by following the standard program of work. For example, could most Chinese people generally accept these reforms? Could that steadily raise the income of urban and rural residents and continuously improve their living condition? The operators just reformed all social sectors and industries with the use of Pan-Marketization economic theory. Obviously, such radical market-oriented reform was not a good approach to reform. It may have resulted in counterproductive and self-defeating situations. As mentioned earlier, Russia has implemented "Shock Therapy" reform which was derived from an extreme Pan-Marketization theory and was the product of western neo-liberal economics representatives. We should learn from the lessons of Russia and guarantee that Pan-Marketization ideology will never be widespread on the land of China again.

Pan-Marketization and Its Fraudulence

China's reform is the self-improvement of the socialist system. One of the important goals of reform is to establish a socialist market economy with Chinese characteristics that corresponds to the current national condition of China. However, those so-called mainstream economists and the so-called elites who manipulate the reform intend to equate the various reforms of the socialist system with the reform of Pan-Marketization. Under the guidance of the above concepts, they tend to desire to penetrate marketization into various fields of Chinese society with an aim to turn Chinese society into a big market in which all things can be traded. For example, in some areas where Pan-Marketization ideology has flourished, some reforms go to extreme which cause a huge loss of material and spiritual wealth in many fields, such as the economy and education, and which infringe on the interest of the Chinese people resulting into social instability or even disorder. Pan-Marketization ideology is fallacious, excludes the governmental management and regulation of the national economy, dismisses governmental management and regulation as "walking the old road of the planned economy", and preaches the handling of all matters with the rules of a market economy.

Key Issues and Questions

For the reform of state-owned enterprises, Pan-Marketization advocates some methods such as acquisition, holding, hosting and so on. As a management tool of economic activity, these methods do not have any errors. However, when we look at the actual situation in some areas of the country, things seem to be depressing. In some places, state-owned enterprises went to bankrupt and laid off many personnel. The state-owned enterprises were sold out which totally disintegrated the state-run system. Some individuals, small groups possess themselves of state-owned assets; and some overseas bosses control or purchase state-owned enterprises. For beneficiaries, it is certainly a windfall. However, the identity of those state-owned enterprise assets is the wealth saved by all the Chinese people by living frugally for decades. Such things do not only occur in several enterprises or several provinces, but also happen thousands of times during a period.

Under the clamor of Pan-Marketization ideology, there were seen some strange phenomena in certain places. It seemed that reform could be successful only by selling all the state-owned enterprises. Facing this extreme stream of marketization, people from all occupations who pursued national strength and prosperity had the right to question the practical effect of such market reforms, and to suspect the correctness of regarding market economic measures as the single means of production. The behavior of advocating a market economy as the wisest way of China's reform and excluding other economic adjustment methods can be referred to as "market player" views. At present, facing the problem brought by the economic behaviors of Pan-Marketization, China needs to rethink seriously about it.

Can we conclude that China already has the economic and social conditions of marketization? Is it true that China will stay in the primary stage of socialism for a long time? If it is true, why in such a period, the national efforts to promote comprehensive market-oriented reforms were doubted and opposed by grassroots? If the answer is no, then people have the right to ask. Since we already know that marketization leads to nowhere, why do we still take the risk? Where do those who preach Pan-Marketization would lead China to?

China's 12th Five-Year Plan has outlined a blueprint for future development. This outline pointed out that during the period of 12th Five-Year Plan, national and worldwide conditions would continue to undergo profound changes and the economic and social development of China presented stage characteristics. According to comprehensive judgments of the international and domestic situation, China would have a period of strategic opportunities, facing a rare historical opportunity, and facing predictable or unpredictable risks and challenges. Therefore, Chinese people should work together to resolve all conflicts effectively, and input more energy to promote China's reform and opening up for promote socialist modernization.

Depending on the major strategic thoughts proposed by the fourth-generation collective leadership of the CPC Central Committee led by Hu, China should establish a scientific concept of development to build a harmonious socialist and moderately prosperous society. Following the theme of the scientific concept of development and the main course of accelerating the transformation of economic development, China should redirect the reform and opening up to protect and improve people's livelihood. This will help to improve the ability to handle international financial crises, to promote the long-term stable and rapid development of the economy and society, and to lay the foundation of building a moderately prosperous society (Tian and Dai, 2012).

It is true that China's economy has developed rapidly and made significant progress in structural adjustment. What is more, science and technology education had been improved significantly; resource saving and environmental protection has achieved remarkable outcomes; people's living standards have been improved continuously; social construction has been significantly strengthened; and at same time reform and opening up has been deepened (National People's Congress, 2011). Historical experience and lessons have told us that if we did not despise or criticize fallacies, it was impossible for us to implement "12th Five Year Plan". Safeguarding the overall situation of stability and unity is not equal to accepting erroneous arguments. In fact, in the reform of China's socialist market economic system, many people try to use various facts to boycott the preaching of Pan-Marketization.

However, we cannot rule out the possibility that some people who worship money always want to grab ill-gotten gains from the market. We cannot deny all the people by providing vague understanding, especially those who beg god when facing troubles. In the final analysis, the market mechanism is not a panacea but has innate defects with it. The government should adjust the market mechanism according to people's need. Even in the country with the most developed market economy, the United State, the most popular economics textbook indicates that there are three distinct defects of the market mechanism (McConnell and Brue, 2001). The deficiencies of this mechanism limit people's thoughts and actions. It means that those people influenced by a wrong stream of information should consider objective limiting factors when doing evaluation. Apparently, reform cannot rely entirely on the market and Pan-Marketization ideology will be eliminated by the market itself.

Trade Principles are not Valid in the Public Service Sector

The development of socialism with Chinese characteristics, the establishment of an innovation-oriented country and the enhancement of overall national strength must involve all aspects of state affairs and should mobilize all positive factors. In other words, we should apply a variety of theories instead of one theory to guide economic development. According to the basic principles of Marxism, the country's economic development operates according to objective law. In addition, human beings should give play to their initiative in terms of objective laws. The other social fields also have their own social values and laws of development which means that people should behave under the rule of corresponding theories.

Undeniably, establishing a social market economy with Chinese characteristics that is compatible with the current national conditions of China is one of the most important objectives of the reform. The Constitution of the People's Republic of China (a modified version by the Second Session of the Tenth National People's Congress on March 14, 2004) Article 15 clearly stated that China should implement a socialist market economy. The guideline ensures the leading role of the planned economy supplemented by market regulation and implements a planned commodity economy.

Based on a serious reflection upon China's social and economic development theories before reform, this path of reform is finalized in the form of a constitution. Under the planned economic system implemented in the past, people's interpretations of market information are vulnerable to the impact of the subjectivity. As market activities can be easily dominated by people's narrow subjective interests, a market may be distorted and in this case, it is difficult for the laws of the market to play their roles.

Pan-Marketization regards seeking nothing but profits and maximum capital gains as the only principle to regulate various social relations between people. It disturbs the rational analysis and scientific thinking of the national situation. The marketization reforms in some places are trying to reduce the proportion of the state-owned economy and to enhance significantly the proportion of privatization. Many state-owned enterprises have been sold off resulting into the loss of state assets. If the governments do not stop or correct such practices, the ruling basis of the state power will be seriously eroded or even subverted. The long-term practice of building socialism has clearly shown that in fields such as the leadership system of the Communist Party of China and the nation, government agencies, ideology and theory, justice, military, ethnic and religious affairs, in-depth reforms cannot be fully accomplished by marketization.

Fields such as science and technology, education, culture, sports, health care, public health and environmental protection should not be totally privatized under the guidance of marketization theory. Similarly, the reform of many non-profit organizations and non-governmental organizations that have existed in Chinese society for a long time, should exclude the possibility of overall privatization advocated by marketization. Otherwise, overall privatization will weaken the ruling forces of Communist Party, excessively expand the rights of stakes, and harm the fundamental interests of the masses.

In fact, even in the economic field, for the sake of national security and social public interests, some public resources and public goods are impossible to be traded through market transactions, let alone privatization. The economic textbook used in American universities clearly states that the government controls the resource and capital of public products such as national armament (McConnell and

Brue, 2011). Can China privatize the defense industry? The answer is in negative, the same is to most of the countries all over the world. Furthermore, a real market economy necessarily requires a market environment with equal players playing a dominant role, open and transparent market rules, an orderly transaction process, and a fair market managed by laws. Privatization of key industries (such as the defense industry) will result in national subjugation and genocide. Therefore, it is impossible for the so-called private economic system of complete marketization to exist in contemporary human society.

Negative Effects of Extreme Pan-Marketization

In our real life, on the one hand, the degree of marketization is not enough, as the market is not free to do self-regulation, yet; on the other hand, there are many loopholes in the market allowing the possibility of marketization. A typical example is "anti-corruption by considerably increasing the officials' income". Compared with those countries that have established a market economic system for a long time, the wages of civil servants in China are relatively low. Normally, civil servants should have reasonable wages they deserve which correspond to their social status and contribution, and their wages should be raised to correspond with economic development. However, this does not mean that corruption will diminish because civil servants' income has increased. Anti-corruption by considerably increasing income is a principle of market transaction that advocates buying behavior free from corruption with high salaries. It is impractical to apply the trading principle in the political realm. Honest and incorruptible behavior can be not traded in the market, nor be bought with money. Political life should not focus on market principle but on politics, responsibility, and morality instead of money. Undeniably, Pan-Marketization ideology has brought a disaster to Chinese nation and country.

In the process of reform, the starting point of Pan-Marketization is to completely deviate from the direction of the interests of the state and the nation resulting in economic and social chaos. There are erroneous tendencies in some places thinking economic marketization is the economization of society and society marketization. Therefore, arguments such as "marketization of the medical system", "education industrialization" and "marketization of production" have flooded the society. It not only misleads civilians' thoughts, but also disrupts the thoughts of government administrators. Quirky things happen one after another, the market economy is twisted into several parts including "culture marketization", "education marketization", "technology marketization", "welfare marketization", "politics marketization" and even "defense marketization". In short, it seems that all things can be folded into money; some greedy speculators make their intentions come true.

What needs to be reflected upon and corrected is that some local executives misunderstand marketization as privatization of the whole society. Under the guise of marketization, some local governments give up many responsibilities that they ought to bear. The market is flooded with fake and shoddy products and deceit and lies. To earn more money, some public schools, hospitals and public welfare units confidently begin marketization reforms. What is worse, taking advantage of their power, some governments try to meet the interest of small groups. In some places, public resources are privatized by marketization operation. In official circles, under the direction of power capitalization and equivalent exchange, corruption and embezzlement of public funds occur frequently.

At the same time, the fundamental interests of the Chinese people are destroyed by marketization. Basic rights such as education, safety and health of grass-root people, especially the peasants, are hardly guaranteed. Under the influence of Pan-Marketization, social and national culture, and the masses of the people all take part in cultural transactions. Most Chinese people suffer much from marketization in education, health care and safety. In recent years, unreasonable sponsorship fees in the educational field have been the focus of discussion for the media and the public.

Surprisingly, even Master's and Doctor's degree, even man's soul and his conscience can be traded. Hazards such as toxic milk, products containing dye, explosions in coalmines, environmental pollution, food poisoning, and waste oil used in food, fake and shoddy products and so on, which should be regulated by the government, are threatening people's lives. It is worrisome that in the process of marketization, economic restructuring in some places is too abrupt. As there are no other alternative safety measures, many urban workers and rural farmers lost their original social benefits, including labor insurance, retirement benefits and rural farmers' subsidies that were available in the Communist period. When businesses fail in the city, employment opportunities are reduced, and many surplus laborers in rural towns cannot find jobs.

So-called Pan-Marketization threatens social stability; interferes with the normal order of socialist countries, all of which is very destructive to reform. Obviously, the Pan-Marketization argument has resulted in some radical policies and practices endangering China's development. Because of the widening gap between rich and poor, social conflicts often happen endangering the safety of the national system. However, the Communist Party of China is a political party that has been stressed by countless tests of hardship, and the Chinese are a people full of wisdom. As Deng Xiaoping once indicated that he would like to say: our socialist state apparatus is strong (Deng, 1993). Once it is found that there is a deviation from the direction of socialism, this state machine will rectify it. A key point of China's steady development is that the Party and people are using many ways to resist the storms of Pan-Marketization ideology. In addition, the country is implementing a prudent reform route. Changing outdated conventions is good for the steady development of reform.

The brilliant performance of China during the 11th Five Year Plan period not only enriched China but also benefited all human beings. As China's 11th Five Year Plan period is a critical period of building a moderately prosperous society, Chinese people must deal with situations that are more complex at home and abroad. We should seize the rare historic opportunities, meet the challenges and sum up experience. To implement the national economic and social development plan of the 12th Five-Year Plan, in addition to keep a stable and sustainable economic and social development situation, as well as to achieve the great rejuvenation of China, the leadership should criticize Pan-Marketization, clear out its significant risk and alter its radical policies of reform. Only in this way can China bring the blueprint of the12th Five Year Plan to fruition.

Conceive a New Economic Outlook

The practice of China's reform and opening up clearly tells people that it is impossible to grasp the complexity of modern society by relying solely on economic analysis in a country with a large population and different regional conditions. In other words, pure marketization may not be able to solve all the problem of modern society. Those rote practices of western economic theory and the radical arguments trying to influence the reform process may disturb China's harmonious social atmosphere. To bring order out of chaos and to understand the significance of building an innovative country, China needs to explicitly create and follow these development ideas.

To Innovate in the International Competition Environment

The results of the first "Five-Year Plan" after the founding of new China show that Mao Zedong and his comrades indeed led people to preliminarily change the old country and to begin to alleviate the poverty and blankness that appeared originally. In the national construction period of the "11th Five-Year Plan", the Communist Party of China with Hu Jintao as the General Secretary of the central collective leadership led the Chinese people to build a socialist society with prosperity all over the whole nation which provided ample food and clothing for the people. In 2010, the per capita disposable income of national urban residents reached ￥19,109 RMB, ￥8,616 RMB more as compared with the previous year (an increase rate of 82.1%). The actual growth rate was 59.0% after deducting for inflation, with an average annual increase rate of 9.7% in real terms. Per capita net income of rural residents rose from ￥3,255 RMB in 2005 Yuan to ￥5,919 RMB in 2010, an increase of ￥2,664 RMB. The nominal growth rate was 81.8%, and the average annual nominal growth rate was 12.7%. After deducting for inflation, the real average annual growth rate was 8.9% (Bureau of Statistics, 2011). The "11th Five Year Plan" managed to extend the coverage of basic endowment insurance to 257 million people, with an increase rate of 8.1%, exceeding the planned index which was coverage of 223 million people, with an increase rate of 5.1% (National People's Congress, 2011). The ruling idea of three generations of leadership is consistent, namely, to strive for the Chinese people's happiness and welfare.

The actual situation shows that China is flourishing currently. On the other hand, this is also presently a critical period of history. China must readjust its strategy according to changes in the international situation and according to changes in the domestic social and economic reality as well; otherwise the country will lose a historic opportunity. China's global strategy matter is of the most importance and cannot be ignored. China has completed a preliminary stage of industrialization, even with breathtaking development speed in some areas. It proves that the country has an enormous potential to be transformed into a world power. The history of the world repeatedly proves that the expansion of an emerging country often means that the decline of the dominant position of a previous generation's hegemony. China has declared repeatedly that the development road China has chosen is peaceful and never seeking for hegemony.

However, the world market space is limited, and the states who want world hegemony shall never allow the Chinese to become strong gradually. Small parts of the people in those countries will surely try very hard to contain China and to repeatedly warn of China's sharp rise. Therefore, China must have its own global strategic layout. The key points or value orientations of country are focused on maximization of the interests of the state. Therefore, there should be a new period of nationalist strategy. China will have grown into a developed country having international competitiveness within 50 years of its founding and will have completed the great revival of the Chinese nation if the country continues to have a correct nationalist strategy and if this strategy is implemented systematically.

Therefore, the important work for the present is to re-adhere to the vision of a socialist society with Chinese characteristics based on a complete repudiation of the arguments of Pan-Marketization, improving the innovation ability of the country with more abundant and high-impact national comprehensive strength, and showing a national revival on the 21st century international stage. The good news is that the outline of China's "12th Five-Year Plan" has shown some innovative ideas. These ideas are the Chinese people's crystallization of wisdom gathered by the leaders of the Central Committee, with Hu Jintao as the core focus. These ideas are filled with the philosophy of coordinated development by maintaining a strong inspiration of developing socialism with Chinese characteristics. This latter idea is more mature than the previous "Five-Year Plan" because it supplements theory with practice. It is certain to guide national economic development into a new world.

Uphold the Direction of the Socialist Market

Strong economic strength is still the foundation of innovative countries. China must firmly insist on the economic development without wavering, highlight the wise judgment that science and technology are of first importance above all else, produce high-tech and high value-added products, and participate in international economic competition to gain a position in the international commodity market. The United States is the most powerful economy in the world today. The leading national policy of the federal government is to produce high-tech products and to make profits from international trade. In 1965, the value of export and import trade accounted for only 4%-5%

of GDP. This proportion rose to 12%-14% by 1998 (McConnell and Brue, 2001). The U.S. exports are mainly aircraft, computers, automobiles, chemical products, machinery, etc. Most of the United States' agricultural products are also exported to international markets. The United States gets huge benefits from foreign trade, while strong economic strength is her fundamental tool to establish hegemony and a single polar world. China pursues the principle of peaceful development and maintaining world peace, and insists that it is a pipe dream to fulfill this mission without solid and strong economic strength. Therefore, to achieve the development of socialism with Chinese characteristics and to achieve the strategic goal of building an innovative country, China must take the road of independent innovation and strive to establish world-renowned brand-name products.

The strategic development plan to implement innovation in China is the specific condition for implementation of the initial stage of socialist countries. Economic construction of the country moves forward on a twisting and turning road. Under the guidance of the Marxist theory of scientific socialism, some methods that cannot generate economic benefits have been abandoned through continuous summary and reflection. China strongly focuses on the centralized planned economic system, single public ownership and single distribution according to work. These systems and policies in the past were regarded as the nature of socialism. The emergence of new things always begins with the denying of old things. Naturally, the negative process is painful. In the denial process, some people do not clearly know what socialism is.

What is the difference between socialism and capitalism? What is the essence of socialism? These questions have baffled people for an extended period. From the perspective of Marx's scientific socialism theory, the planned economy, distribution according to work and public ownership are indeed the basic characteristics of socialism, but these characteristics are highly theoretical and abstract. In social reality, experience and lessons tell us that we must partly correct these highly abstract characteristics when conducting socialist practice in the face of underdeveloped productivity. For example, a planned commodity economy can only take a market economy as the foundation; public ownership is only the mainstay, and co-develops with a variety of other common economics; distribution according to work co-exists with the other modes of distribution. The performance of the reform has proved that it is undoubtedly a wise way.

The aim of the Chinese people in choosing a socialist market economy is to seek integration into the world economy; it is the inevitable choice for people of all ethnic groups to realize a common prosperity. Examples such as the United States and other industrialized countries benefiting from international trade and international communication are worth studying and referencing. However, China has its own socialist goal as the country is in its primary stage of development. The socialist market economy that China has established or is still establishing never refers to the mechanical marketization across every nook and cranny of the country. An advanced state's social responsibility can never be abandoned by adopting Pan-Marketization.

As to market economy theory itself, its substantial expression in some respects is also purely about technology and it has great limitations to cover all societal issues. Therefore, we need to firmly make a critic review on the trend of Pan-Marketization. The correct theory can be developed only after wrong ones are destroyed. The goal of the socialist market economy brings prosperity and peace of the country and people. People should have a better guarantee of rights and interests, and should live safely in a beautiful country. However, the words and deeds of Pan-Marketization are a misunderstanding of the market economy. They distort marketization reforms that will eventually ruin them. The aftermath will be disastrous if we hold that the market principle is omnipotent and infinite. Taking marketing reforms one-step further into Pan-Marketization is a fallacious step.

To deeply understand the theory of an innovative country, we need to criticize and analyze Pan-Marketization in depth. This will involve some abstract concepts. This kind of difficulty in understanding the theory of an innovative country is caused by the Pan-Marketization arguments. That is because after the introduction of market economy theory in China, some voices of confusing terms of western economics have raised. Such a superficial title seems to be somewhat abstract theoretically, and a considerable number of people in society may have difficulty in understanding it. In the social ideology field, this is the exact situation because social reality is divorced from economic reality. The sentiments of Pan-Marketization are intense and its intention is obvious, but hidden beneath the surface are some old ideas in the western economic school.

However, the expansive income gap and deficiency of public services can explain what is right and what is wrong, and can reveal the representative essence of some seemingly mysterious western economic theory. People can also ponder on theories behind the representation of things, and gradually consider deep theoretical issues. It is very important to recognize that the dark side of the Pan-Marketization trend would be exposed undoubtedly after realization of the truth of the sort of economic development advocated by Pan-Marketization. People will naturally break the fetters of narrow self-interest, and strongly transform into pursuers of the common interests of all members of society. This is also the major premise of building a modern socialist country.

Maintenance of the Common Interests of the Community

Persons with lofty ideals at home and abroad have many recommendations about how to develop the socialist market economy with Chinese characteristics. However, the recognized core problem is how to make social change or social reconstruction. There are two points here that we must clearly indicate. First, the market economy is not equivalent to a market society. Former French Prime Minister Lionel Jospin gave a maxim that: "Yes to a market economy, no to a market society". The market economy is a kind of economic system having effective allocation of resources, but the principles of the market economy cannot penetrate and dominate complete social life. In recent years, mistakes, even significantly harmful errors, frequently have occurred in some areas of reform in China, such as the medical market-oriented reforms and the education industry reform. These errors have a direct relationship with the "pan-market" philosophy.

Second, the socialist market economy needs to be established on a society based on the principle of public ownership and distribution according to work. Modern sociological theory tells us that any economic system is embedded into the society that contains it, and if that society is not a good society, it is difficult for that society to normally operate even if there is a sound market economy. The socialist market economy China wants to establish must put an end to exploitation. Of course, a reasonable amount of capital gains should be protected by law and by social respect so that all members of society can enjoy the fruits of social development, commonly referred to the common interest.

Common interest is the national interest, and only an innovative country can maintain and develop this sort of national interest which is the true meaning of socialism. He Xin, a famous Chinese political economist, proposed a new socialism and a new nationalism in 2000 and 2009 respectively. These are the legacy and development of the Marxist theory of scientific socialism. Some points are quite insightful and have a very realistic significance to guide China to re-create a socialist society with Chinese characteristics. He argues that the future road China would travel on is not nationalism, conservatism, or liberalism. The single way leading to a harmonious society is socialism (He, 2010). In fact, there will be a more profound understanding of the idea of Marxist socialism based on common interests if China is able to build a public ownership and a planned economy. Grasping the common interest means socialism is at hand; if China grasps the common interest, she can grasp ownership relationships and structure, distribution relationships and other structural adjustment to ensure that the country will be neither divorced from reality nor disoriented.

In short, from the perspective of development, social equity and common prosperity must be the guiding principle for rebuilding the community of the Chinese nation. The market economy theory needs to be examined and enriched. Although the evolution process will endure a long time before becoming perfect, it still must be improved and upgraded continuously when difficulties appear in practice. Facing the fierce competition in international environment, there is no room for escape. Only the whole nation becomes stronger and more prosperous China can achieve the grand goal that was collectively planned by the national leadership.

Chapter 2

The Development History of Market Economy in the World

Market economy is different from the commodity economy existed in China 2000 years ago. Its external forms and underlying meaning are mutually incompatible with Chinese traditional culture. In recent history of the world, market economy has strongly supported the development of the industrial countries in creating a great amount of wealth within a short span of 200 years which is much greater than the total wealth created by feudal society for thousands of years. Within the framework of socialism, by implementing market economic system, the strength of China is increasing, and the standard of living is constantly improving. Now, China has become the second largest economic entity in the world. However, the Pan-Marketization argument confounds right and wrong, and advocates so-called economic theories which are unsuitable to China's basic conditions. It not only disrupts the rational development order of China's economy and society, but it also harms the basic interests of majority of the people. Studying the development history of market economy can help us clearly understand that the concept of Pan-Marketization is an indefensible flaw. We can improve the ability of discrimination and explore innovative ideas by tracing the source of Pan-Marketization.

History of Market Economy

The formation of market economy is based on large-scale socialization production, marketization and modern commodity economy. It is a resource allocation method. It is not only a form of social and economic operation, but also a form of social and economic development. Under the conditions of market economy, all factors of production enter into the market, with market as the basic form of resources allocation, and market mechanism as the basic means of allocating resources. Commodity producers and operators of goods produce and circulate products in accordance with the objective laws of the market economy.

In contemporary industrialized countries, the market economic theory which occupies the mainstream is closely linked with capitalism classical political economics. In the late 18th century, one of the industrialized countries, the United Kingdom, was in the eve of the Industrial Revolution. That special historical environment produced classical political economics which has a profound impact on contemporary capitalism with an Englishman Adam Smith as its representative. During the late 15th century to the 17th century, along with the world's great geographical discoveries, capitalist economic relations appeared and developed within the European feudal countries. As the production and development of capitalist economic relations demanded large monetary capital, the greedy and bloody primitive accumulation of capital lasted for several centuries. Mercantilism was the school of economics which represents the business interests of the bourgeoisie in the primitive period of capital accumulation, and the "pre-history" of bourgeois political economy. It has a profound effect on the formation of classical political economics.

Market economic theory was emerging in the United Kingdom. Its main early concept was systematically put forward by Adam Smith. The era of Adam Smith (1723-1790) was a stage during which handicraft workshop in the UK continued to occupy the main forms of production, and the economic status was classical liberal market economy stage. It was the second stage in the development of capitalism. The prior first stage was the era of primitive accumulation period of capitalism. It was the primary stage of capitalism and the heyday of mercantilism in economic theory. In 1767, Hager Reeve invented the improved textile machine in England. In 1771, Kerouac successfully invented textile machine which used horsepower firstly and hydraulic power later. As we all know, the emergence of the textile machine represented that manual techniques transited to machine production in the United Kingdom, and the clue of the development of the capitalist production mode. In 1778, Watt invented the steam engine representing the beginning of capitalistic industrial machine era.

Thus, capitalism began to develop rapidly from the British island to the European continent. The bourgeoisie gradually reached a dominant position in the UK. Before Adam Smith, the prevailing British mercantilism was an economics genre which represented the commercial interests of the bourgeoisie in the period of primitive accumulation of capital. For example, Englishman Thomas Mun (1571-1641) the representative of late mercantilism wrote two books, namely "On the Trade between England and the British East India Company" and "England's Treasure by Foreign Trade", and proposed that international trade was an important source of wealth in the United Kingdom, and summarized Trade Balance Theory (Man, 1996). In addition, the UK also expressed some academic thinking about the principles of market transactions, such as personal utilitarianism of Bentham promoting the idea that personal behavior was motivated by self-interest and self-love. Deeply influenced by mercantilism and personal utilitarianism, Adam Smith conducted a research on the basis of personal experience and put forward early market economic theory. Adam Smith stressed that the management of all economic activities and the coordination of social contradictions was directed by invisible hand. In *An Inquiry into the Nature and Causes of the Wealth of Nations*, Adam Smith had a classic formulation that we can present below:

As every individual, therefore, endeavors as much as he can both to employ his capital in the support of domestic industry, and so to direct that industry that its produce may be of the greatest value; every individual necessarily labors to render the annual revenue of the society as great as he can. He generally, indeed, neither intends to promote the public interest, nor knows how much he is promoting it. By preferring the support of domestic to that of foreign industry, he intends only his own security; and by directing that industry in such a manner as its produce may be of the greatest value, he intends only his own gain, and he is in this, as in many other cases, led by an invisible hand to promote an end which was no part of his intention. Nor is it always the worse for the society that it was no part of it. By pursuing his own interest, he frequently promotes that of the society more effectually than when he really intends to promote it. I have never known much good done by those who affected to trade for the public good (Hird, 2005).

The market economic thinking of Adam Smith can actually be described as a laissez-faire market economy universal theory. He advocated free competition without any form of state intervention. He lamented that if the management of the land was owned by the government, the society would not get a quarter of the existing production. The reason is that the government agency and agent management was negligence, wasteful and arbitrary (Smith, 1983). In 1930s, a British economist, Eric Roll wrote a very famous book titled *History of Economic Thoughts* and gave a comment about Adam and the essence of Smith's liberal economic theory as below: When Adam Smith applied the rules of the natural order in economic affairs, he became strong opponent of the government which interfered industrial or commercial matters in various forms. Each individual was trying his or her best to reap the maximum benefits.

Adam Smith strongly advocated the implementation of a laissez-faire policy. Did he really expect to maximize the economic and social interests? After a profound analysis, Eric Roll pointed out that Smith regarded the national non-intervention nature laws as the basis of economic policy, and he was to provide a theoretical basis for the main interests of the entrepreneurial class. In western society, it was always said that Adam Smith was on behalf of the interests of a single class. It was doubtlessly correct from either historical significance or subjective terms (Roll, 1981). Adam Smith advocated of the free economy and the anti-national management, which was very much in line with the needs of the emerging bourgeois. In Western economics textbooks, he was known as the Father of Economics.

In fact, as the pedigree of market economy theory, the laissez-faire theory Adam Smith advocated is untenable and childish. When establishing a scientific theory of communism, Marx had conducted an in-depth study on Adam Smith's theory. He pointed out ; on one hand, Smith was exploring the internal relations of the various sectors of the economy, or the hidden structure in the bourgeois economic system; on the other hand, he pointed out the contacts in competition and in the eyes of non-scientific observers who actually involved in the production process of the bourgeoisie (Marx and Engels, 1973). Adam Smith only saw the appearance of things, not the true meaning. The reality is, when everyone is seeking the best interests, they will tend to damage the interests of others. Not only the community as a whole cannot achieve maximum benefit, but also the society is likely to fall into chaos.

The era that Adam Smith said that the invisible hand guided all economic activities was the era during which the western capitalist primitive accumulation period had long been over and the past years was actually a bloody hell for most people and a paradise for few selfish people. Looking back the events happened in history, such as the brutal British Enclosure Movement, black slave plantation system, Western Gold Rush and the blood and sweat labor system in 18th and 19th century, the invisible hand sounds gorgeous. But this wantonly waving hand also produced endless human tragedy. History is a mirror that lights up the true colors of the laissez-faire market economy movement. Modern China must not allow the kind of beautiful Pan-market-oriented economic theory run amok.

From the views of the balance between individual and collective interests, as long as everyone contributes a little love, the world will become a better one. But if everyone becomes selfish, the society will certainly be disharmonious. As the ancient Chinese sage Confucius ever said: The highest purpose of political thought is that the world is shared by people. The society should select people of high moral character. All people have to emphasize on integrity and cultivate harmony atmosphere. So people not only take care of their own parents and bring up their children, but also try hard to feed the elderly until the end of their natural life span. The middle-aged people should do contribution to the society. The young children can successfully grow up. And the old man without wife, old woman without husband, and the child lost father when young, the old people without sub, and the disable people can get support. The men have occupations, and woman can get married timely. As a result, there would not be any thief, rebellion and evil won't happen, every household do not need to close the gate. It is called the ideal society.

The people all over the world are in the pursuit of common ground, and the realization of the ideal world should not rely on selfish behaviors, but the ideological guidance of the whole world as one community. And then the society can achieve harmonious development status. Now, the people become very selfish, only care about themselves and ignore the interest of other people…then intrigues and wars happen.

As people only care about themselves and their relatives, it results in wars and tragedies. In fact, a person should take the needs of others into account, and then he can achieve personal interests without infringing the interests of others. Another Chinese ancient sage the Mencius said: We should care about our own parents and others; take care of our own children but also others'. Then we can control the world easily.

Only the person who loves others as his or her family can get the endorsement and support of others. But according to Adam Smith, as long as the invisible hand plays a full role in suppressing the intervention of the state, the individual and society can get the maximum benefit at the same time. It does not work in reality. If each person becomes selfish and unscrupulous, it ultimately will lead to the damage to their own interests. If the interests of society as a whole is completely destroyed, how to achieve the purpose of individuals that gain the greatest benefits at the least cost?

The analysis of Adam Smith on the constitution of the value of the goods is correct. He said, labor was the yardstick to measure the value of all commodities exchange (Smith, 1983). He regarded labor as the only source of value. And the amount of labor contained in a commodity was the yard stick to measure this value. This labor theory of value is undoubtedly correct. Marx made a thorough research on Adam Smith's doctrine and also gave a fair evaluation about his historical position: Adam Smith developed political economy into some kind of overall. The scopes he included had been formed to some extent (Marx and Engels, 1973). Marx's political economy critically inherited and evolved on the basis of the classical political economy.

As China never experienced market economy but some different forms of commodity economy, so Adam Smith's theory including the mistaken views was consciously or unconsciously accepted in the country's reform and opening up process. It should be noted that the market economy is different from the commodity economy that existed in China 2000 years ago. Commodity economy is the primary form in which only existed commodity enters the market and sporadic places and markets for commodity exchange. Market economy is a product of production socialization: (1) all the factors of production such as capital, labor, land, information, and technology and so on enter the market; (2) it forms a nationally and globally unified, not divided market. Only in this way, the price signal is not blocked, and the price reflects the scarcity of resources; (3) market becomes the center of the resources allocation so that the law of value, supply and demand law, and competition law help to allocate resources and productivity to coordinate the relationship between supply and demand. As the market economy is very complex, people are looking for personal interests. There is no government stepped in to regulate the market. China's reform has proved that the rational allocation of various complex production factors, especially the national strategic resource reserves and production, must be under government's unified intervention and deployment.

Since the end of the 18th century and the early 19th century, the industrial system of the capitalist machine was basically established. At the same time, contradictions of social class were becoming increasingly acute. The classical economics founded by Adam Smith began to differentiate. One thought was the income constitution axiology which gradually developed into political economy defending for capitalist economy, and their representative was Say Jean Baptiste (1767-1832). Say lived in the era of the French bourgeoisie trying to seize power. The French utopian socialism criticized the shortcomings and contradictions of the bourgeoisie, and encouraged the struggle of the working class. The contradiction between the proletariat and the bourgeoisie became sharper. At the same time, some French economists and political activists such as Grainier were writing books to express their points of view. Say published *Introduction to Political Economy* in 1803 which was his masterpiece of advocating liberal economic views. Marx tartly said: after Grainier, Say Jean Baptiste published his vulgar book *Introduction to Political Economy* (Marx & Engels, 1972).

Say expanded some erroneous ideas of Smith and set up political economy for the defense of the capitalist economy. Marx sharply criticized that Say was the vulgarization of Smith's theory. (Marx & Engels, 1972) Say established economic views which fully advocated laissez-faire on the basis of theory of supply and demand, and production costs, against the state interfered product price and other economic activities in any ways. A central feature of Say's theory was that the effectiveness was the determinant of value. In his view, the value of all the production elements came from the value of their products. All elements have the necessary characteristics to create value: scarcity and indirect utility.

Say put forward a so-called theory of distribution from an argument that utility determined the value, and strived to promote the view "supply creates demand". He advocated that, under conditions of economic freedom, the phenomenon of insufficient supply of one product and excess supply of another at the same time would not exist forever (Say, 1983). Because of the self-regulation of the law of value, production was always conducted in accordance with the needs of the community, the general overproduction would never happen.

The internal contradictions of capitalism made the value of the commodity to become the abyss capitalists faced. And Say attempted to solve this dilemma encountered by capitalist production. Therefore, this argument was regarded as “Say Theorem” in the economic circles of the capitalists and a sacred dogma of modern western economics. Say’s ideas later became one of the foundations of bourgeois vulgar political economy theory. The British economist mentioned above, Eric Roll viewed Say Theorem and its disciples that they gradually abandoned the labor theory of value, and applied another different principle of interpretation. This principle excluded the remaining concepts. In technical terms, this meant that the development of a utility value theory will inevitably result in recognizing that capital was productive (Roll, 1981).

What is the core idea of Say’s theory? Marx criticized Say’s vulgar economic concepts from a deep level, especially the theory of distribution. Say opposed to the government’s intervention in production and products flow compelled by government (Say, 1983). Say’s theory tried to prove that the market economy has inherent stability, and governmental intervention in the economy should be abandoned. If Adam Smith's theory of free economics was to crusade against that feudalism impeded free economic competition, it reflected the historical trend of the development of the commodity economy in a period of rising capitalism. It has the role of promoting the progress of the development of the capitalist economy. Say theorem directly denied the contradictions of capitalist production and consumption and thought that supply would automatically create a demand. There was no possibility of widespread overproduction crisis, and the capitalist economy could be in balance forever.

The Evolution of Market Economy Theory

Adam Smith's free competition and laissez-faire theory was popular in the United Kingdom, the United States and other capitalist countries in the early 18th and 19th centuries. It was because the enterprises existing in such capitalist countries generally were of small scale. Any private enterprise was difficult to hold a monopoly in the market, so the set of theory was feasible under that historical circumstances. Owing to the widespread implementation of the Adam Smith's free-market economic theory, Western countries' social productivity was higher than ever before, achieving rapid development of science and technology, and a sharp increase in material wealth. However, by the mid-19th century, the development of capitalism had created many large enterprises whose monopoly had become increasingly evident. Then, the problem of the market economy also became prominent.

The characteristic of the market economy was that resources and wealth kept flowing from low efficiency to high efficiency. Therefore, it caused serious bankruptcy, unemployment, and polarization. Private ownership of capitalist with small business owners as the main society had large conglomerates, which is different from Adam Smith's new capitalist society. Capitalist exploitation is more brutal than ever before. Labor workers became the talking machine. This also meant that Adam Smith's theory of free competition failed. Because of the seriously unfair serious society, early western capitalist society was facing surging workers movement. The confrontation between employers and employees became fiercer and fiercer and the society tended to be turbulent. In this background Marx put forward the theory of the socialist economic system and socialist revolution aiming at promoting planned economy which advocated equal interests of the community as a whole.

What is the basis for doing it? Adam Smith demonstrated that the market economy was not a panacea, and had some limitations like any other economic system, such as: (1) competition in the market could not always be perfect competition, imperfect competition had greater proportion in economic activities; (2) The phenomenon of increasing returns to scale may lead to monopoly; (3) There were incomplete externalities and public goods in economic activities; (4) The allocation in the market economy could not be absolutely fair; (5) Owing to the presence of irrational individual economic behavior and transaction risk caused fluctuations in the economy. About the historical role of capitalist market economic system, the founder of the theory of communism, Marx made an objective evaluation that bourgeois society is most complex and the most developed production organization in the history. At the same time, he also issued a warning to the limitations of economic system that if the argument that bourgeois economic category contains a form which was suitable to all the other social forms was right. Then, this could only be understood in a certain sense. The final form of historical development was always built on the development of past historical forms. As historical development only self-criticizes under specific conditions, it always one-sidedly understands the past forms (Marx and Engels, 1962).

The success of the socialist market economy

The development of history is a continuous process, so is the economic system. It was no longer the private enterprises style economic structure in the 1870s (Hobsbawm, 1999). Now, United States still pursues Keynesianism which advocates massive government intervention in the economy. It is very different from the market liberal economy of Adam Smith. Some people developed the government intervention theory of the Keynesian theory and formed the Post-Keynesian school. The reason is that the capitalism in the 19th century was classical naive capitalism and primitive accumulation stage in the form of "free market capitalism”. In the 20th century, especially in the second half of 20th century, the capitalist economy had observed fundamental changes. Government interfered more and more in the economic affairs.

In the first half of the 20th century, some politicians and scholars in western capitalist countries reflected on the recession reasons and learned some successful experience from the emerging socialist countries in the post-World War II. The brilliant success of building socialism of the former Soviet Union, Eastern European countries and China, the early planned economy and the great power of the social security system, as well as the resolute struggle of the working class and the revolutionary party in capitalist countries shocked upper representatives of the capitalist countries. In the process of trying to come up countermeasures, the upper representatives in capitalist countries were forced to learn a lot of excellent management experience of socialism in the Cold War with the socialist camp. Under the control of executive power and the premise of the capitalist exploitation system, the Britain and other countries have carried out many social and political self-improvements aiming at demoralizing and conditionally easing the domestic revolt of the working class. The major capitalist countries get rid of the dying plight after getting the excess profits from information technology. The country's economy slowly recovered. Errors within the socialist camp also provided an opportunity for capitalism flourish.

In the 1930s and 1970s, market economy countries faced two global economic crises and suffered great losses. So, the market economy countries were forced to aware painfully that the market mechanism had its natural defects; the government must use the macro-economic control to operate the market. After the 1980s, on a global scale, the morphology of the market economy transited from a free market economy to a modern market economy, which is known as the control of invisible hand and visible hand. The invisible hand controlled the microscopic field and played the role of stimulator; on the other hand, visible hand controlled macro-areas, playing the role of coordinator.

According to the trend of the global economic system reform, the capitalist countries with the United States as the representative are trying to strengthen the governmental function, seeking effective interventions of government in economic operation. Although there are some conservative representatives in western countries who are stubborn and dogmatically insisting on the idea of Smith. Their intent is not purely for economic interests. They believe that the executive intervention is detrimental to social democracy and freedom. In short, the historical changes in the economic system show that the market economy has two sides. It is not only an invisible hand which promotes the development of human beings, but also an invisible "feet" which impedes the pursuit of personal interests.

The socialist countries with China as the representative have developed socialist market economy with Chinese characteristics by introducing market economy theories and implement methods through reform. Over a period of time, China made great efforts to shift from a planned economy to a new policy that Chinese government should timely develop and implement the most appropriate and comprehensive strategies according to the actual situation in China. In the process of establishing socialist system, China has explored some unique economic theories and economic policies, and the practice has proven that these theories and policies are effective and consistent with Chinese people's interests.

Neo-liberal Penetration in China

In *Das Kapital*, Marx pointed out that the most fundamental contradiction of capitalist system was the contradiction between socialized production and private ownership of the products. The intensification of this contradiction would cause economic crisis and production stagnation which lead to social chaos and world-wide turmoil and wars. The internal mechanism of the capitalist system only created and exacerbated the conflict, so, this system will inevitably die and be replaced by the new socialist system. History has proved Marx's brilliant thesis.

Neo-liberalism

During 1974 and 1975, the contradiction between large-scale socialized production and private ownership was re-intensified in the capitalist countries which led to cyclical new world economic crisis, namely the new economic crisis in the form of stagflation phenomenon in Western industrialized countries. Keynesian interventionist policies failed to rescue the economy, so the politicians and tycoons of the capitalist countries were eager to seek a solution to solve the dilemma. In 1978, the American economists, Rose and Milton published *Free to Choose* to criticize the Keynesian interventionist economic policy, and attempted to find out a solution which not only maintained the capitalist system, but also eliminated a new cyclical economic crisis. And then, many other scholars tried to find out solution from a new perspective, such as Friedman's monetarist policies, Lucas "rational expectation" theory and supply-side theory. This trend of thought is called Neo-liberal ideas in the West. As their representatives and believers gathered in the University of Chicago, it is also known as the "Chicago School" (He, 2004). These people advocated and interpreted the free economy of Smith and Say, and opposed to Keynesianism. Therefore, they were also known as the Post Keynesian revolution. After a period, neo-liberalism spread around the world and penetrated in China attempting to influence the reform and opening policy of China.

The neo-liberal “beautiful new world"

Neoliberal writings discussed money supply and monetary policy and utilized mathematical formulas such as monetary equation and the Cambridge equation to analyze the changes in the economy. The book *Free to Choose* published in 1979 was written by the former president of the American Economic Association, Friedman. Friedman was also an economics professor in the University of Chicago who worshipped free economic operation and Smith's invisible hand. He indicates that the hand is his imagination. In this way, voluntary actions of millions of people can be coordinated through the price system without the guidance center (Friedman, 1982). In the *Freedom to Choose* Friedman wrote: Voluntary transaction dominants economy, the inside has the potential to promote prosperity and human freedom. It may not take full advantage of its potential in these two areas, but as far as we know, the main organization form of prosperous and free society must be voluntary trade... free trade is a necessary condition for prosperity and freedom (Friedman, 1982).

Friedman is a neo-liberal monetarist leader. In his view, the fundamental flaw of the socialist system is the national plan which was contrary to the "voluntary transaction law". He strongly advocated liberal economy and opposed to the socialist system. He won the Nobel Prize in Economics. An economics professor named Gao Xijun who was from Taiwan, China, wrote a book called "The World of Economics" to make Friedman's monetary theory easier to understand. Gao Xijun described the Paradise Model of neo-liberalism as given below:

> *The government control is reduced to a minimum, people's incentive reaches the highest; consumers have enough information to make an informed choice. The manufacturers should be allowed to expand when in benefit, and allowed to bankrupt when in losses; there is no deficit in governmental budget, the money supply should be stably controlled; give cash when poor people apply for relief; give tax cuts when the rich create wealth; Personnel capital goods can flow freely in domestic without national intervention and limitation of other countries; In a fair competition, efficiency is more important than the fairness, freedom is more important than equality.*

This Beautiful New World is wonderful and extremely harmonious, and the road to this world is the free market economy. As how to enter it, Gao further commented: Adam Smith used the concept of invisible hand to point out that everyone directed the operation of the economic activity in the pursuit of self-interest. It resulted in consequences of self-interest and win-win price mechanism. But this 'invisible hand' was not as wonderful as described. Facing the Great Depression in 1930, the political sector - the visible hand - had no choice but interfere. On the one hand, it brought a change in the capitalism nature of the Western world; on the other hand, it made Keynesian theory popular for five decades (Gao, 1987).

The results of implementing neo-liberalism

In the 1980s, the neo-liberal economic thoughts were quite active in the Western world, and had a major impact on the governmental decision-making in the United States and European countries. Ronald Reagan and Margaret Thatcher ever applied neo-liberal thoughts in economic policies and actual economic and social affairs. Such policies focused on two points: firstly, minimize government function, advocate libertarianism; secondly, the economic system tended towards privatization and liberalization. However, the results of implementing neo-liberal economic policies did not reach rulers' expectation and did not produce paradise described by Professor Friedman. For example, to get rid of the "stagflation" of the economy, Margaret Thatcher government of the United Kingdom launched a privatization campaign attempting to stimulate British economy. But, during the implementation of this policy, the number of unemployed in Britain suddenly increased. Workers set off a strong strike to protest the capitalists' brutal exploitation of workers. In 1979, British Steel workers went on strike. During 1983 and 1984, coal miners set off a large wave of strikes. The social contradictions in Britain were suddenly intensified. The ruling class fell in a panic, and blamed each other for such situation. The strikes of coal miners led to a 1% decrease in gross national product of the United Kingdom and £ 4 billion losses in international balance of payment. The British government was forced to suspend the privatization process.

The substance of new system school

There is a genre of neo-liberalism called new institutionalism represented by North and Ronald Carrycase. North systematically put forward the theory of Institutional Change in the books Structure and Change in Economic History and System Innovation and United States Economic Growth. On the premise of economic man assumptions, North believed that all people were selfish and pursuing personal utilitarian and free competition. It was not only the basis of the system, but also the motivation of institutional transition. North said, "institutional equilibrium was such a state that when the bargaining power of the actors and the contract negotiations of overall economic exchange were given, there was no actor can get profit from using resources in re-establishment of the contract" (North, 1994). This argument was carried out in the situation of Pareto marginal optimal equilibrium which did not exist.

The Institutional Change Theory proposed by North has a clear purpose. He believes that the main clue of economic history is the history of institutional change. It is not only the process of institutional change, but also the process of political behavior. North attributes the economic growth of the Western world to the incentive mechanism provided by the capitalist system. He said, "The reason for the rise of the Western world is the development of an effective economic organization. Effective economic organizations need to build institutional facilities and determine the ownership of property, to continuously lead the individual economic efforts to become social activities" (North, 1988). He also specifically disclaimed that if a social ownership system clearly defined the exclusive right of everyone, then the community would be more innovative. And this process was a systematic innovation process. As the school of New System Economics speaks highly of capitalist system, it gained an acclaim from the capitalist world.

The other important thought of New System School is the Property Rights Theory. In 1937, Ronald Carrycase published an economic paper named The Nature of the Firm, and firstly proposed the concept of "transaction costs" establishing the initial theory of Property Rights System Change. Coase described the effectiveness of property rights contained embodied in the capitalist system. It enabled people automatically to know what to do and how to get benefit in the transaction process, and ultimately achieve maximum benefits. In 1960, Coase published another paper The Problem of Social Cost, and in 1988, he published Notes on The Problem of Social Cost. He systematically discussed the relationship between property rights, transaction costs and resource allocation which is called the Coase Theorem by his followers. Objectively speaking, the Property Rights Theory make up for the theoretical errors made by the capitalist political economists and played a role of stabilizing capitalist economic system. Coase clearly expresses his aim of studying property rights arrangement, "my dream is to create a theory which can help us analyze the determinants of the production's institutional structure" (Coase, 1990). Cease's statement about the changes in property rights system attempted to demonstrate that privatization can stimulate economic development. The theory of New System School has certain significance for China's economic reform. However, some Chinese academicians regard it as a treasure and deny its class nature and effectiveness attempting to change the structure of property rights in China. This approach is absurd, and the consequences are extremely bad.

The Shock Therapy of the New System School

The most powerful historical evidence of New System School's political tendency is that, during 1980s and 1990s, arguments about the change of ownership were spread to the former socialist countries in Eastern Europe to provide a theoretical basis for the privatization movement there. For example, some United States scholars who had very obvious ideological tendency continued spreading liberal economic ideology to the former Soviet Union and designed the so-called reform plan to improve economic efficiency, such as "Sachs Shock Therapy" and "Harvard 500 Days Program" to induce them to carry out the reform of property rights. However, the total privatization economic reform applied by the Gorbachev - Yeltsin government resulted in very serious consequence. The economy of Russia collapsed; the society fell into chaos; and people's living standard declined sharply. The property rights revolution in the former socialist countries in Eastern Europe also resulted in a decline in production, the depressed market, and economic and social chaos.

After nearly 20 years sweeping privatization reform, the original state-owned enterprises in the former Soviet Union and most Eastern Europe districts were destroyed. The national economy lost competitiveness in the world market and the domestic market. But Ronald Harry Coase was greatly praised by the Western countries. And in 1991, Coase won the Nobel Prize for Economics. North won the Nobel Prize for Economics in 1993. After the reform of property rights and economic privatization, Eastern Europe and the Russian have become a new market for Western transnational monopolies to find new living space. Russia's strong economy and industry has generally collapsed which provided a realistic possibility for the United States to implement the national missile defense system (NMD) and to dominate the world directly. This is the outcomes and goals of neo-liberal economy which China will never allow them to succeed in.

Disguised Ideological Tool

The historical facts show that the neo-liberalism's academic atmosphere is only appearance; it is essentially an ideological tool. Its most praiseworthy achievement in the Western world is to destroy the economies of the former socialist countries. This paper has introduced Say's theory that "supply automatically creates demand" and the government should not interfere with the economy. Say was called as the godfather of the liberal economics by Western economists. However, Say's theory has been refuted by some Western scholars. The

German economist Friedrich List (1789-1846) had systematically criticized the liberalism and exposed the true face of the Say's theory. He said, "Say does not have extensive knowledge of national policies and profound observation ability. He does not have political and philosophical vision, either. Based on the insights taking from others, he tries to find examples and facts that can support his views from the history, politics, and statistics as well as industrial and commercial relations" (List, 1961). List was not in favor of the socialist ideology that had been popular in Europe, but he was against Say's liberalism pseudo-science. His critique is undoubtedly correct.

There are insurmountable crises and contradictions within capitalism, although the Keynesian school of economics saved the capitalist economy for a brief period, in the 1970s, the Western capitalist economy suffered serious stagflation situation again. So, in addition to the monetarist school, another representative genre of the United States Post Keynesian revolution, the supply-siders appeared. This school thought that the error of Keynes was to deny the validity of Say's Law, and blindly implement expansionary fiscal and monetary policies to interfere the economy which resulted in stagflation. A representative of this school, George Gilder said, "The various changes of Say's Law are the basic rules of supply-siders ...... Say's Law is important because it focuses on the supply and the ability to stimulate capital investment" (Gilder, 1985). He appealed to abandon Keynesianism and be back to liberal economic route advocated by classical economics. Marx pointed out vulgar economics just use bourgeois agent's view to explain, systematize and defense (Marx, 1966). The purpose of Neo-liberal economics is to cover up the fundamental contradiction of the capitalist economy.

Features of western contemporary economic entities

From the 1870s to the 1930s, the production technology of the capitalist world has been tremendously improved. The industrial production grew rapidly and the scales of enterprises become larger and larger. Many joint-stock companies and monopoly organizations appeared because of the increasing concentration of capital and production. Capitalism transited from free competition stage to monopoly capitalism. The founder of the world's first socialist state, Lenin, in his famous book *Imperialism is the Highest Stage of Capitalism*, profoundly analyzed the subjective changes of capitalism. Lenin seized the opportunity to launch a war against imperialists, and established a new socialist country in the history of mankind. He turned Marxist theory into reality.

The strengthening capitalist monopolies and the intensified economic crises resulted in the profound changes of capitalist economic entities and the school of economics. Especially in the 1930s, the economic crisis of capitalist world led to a profound social crisis which forced Western economic powers to take some regulation policies of the new social system and gradually form a mixed economic system. Take the changes in the United States since 1930 as an example, the U.S. economy gradually changed to become a capitalist-oriented mixed economy. Both private person and government had economic influence in the market. The characteristic of most industrial sectors of the United States was that a relatively small number of large-sized enterprises rather than many small-sized competitive enterprises dominated the entire sector.

Pre-existing private ownership of the free-market capitalism has been changed. This form of market is called oligopoly by Lenin. At present, monopoly companies in the western countries have become large multinational companies. These super companies are dominating the economic lifeline of the world. The operation of Multinational Corporations is not purely economic. Administrative intervention has a strong impact on the company. In Germany, the famous Volkswagen AG and Lufthansa Airlines are multinational companies with national shares. Even in Britain, state-owned enterprises still occupy an eminent position in the national economy.

Neo-liberal economics penetrate China

When China is implementing reform, the developed Western countries are seeking to obtain high profits from global economic integration. Some multinational companies with political background invest in China, aiming at occupying the Chinese market instead of helping the China's social construction. Out of the global strategic considerations, some Western powers are trying to carry out value penetration by introducing neo-liberal economic views in China. This is not much surprising. In the entire history of the 20th century, the Western economic powers use a variety of ways to promote and implement capitalist system. For example, the United States has been selling its own values to the world. However, in fact those ideologies are not suitable to China.

Through several channels, the neo-liberalism prevailing in the United States, Britain and other countries were transited into China. Some advocates of the neo-liberal thoughts praise the change of ownership exaggeratedly. For example, a neo-liberal economics professor arbitrarily said, "the economy of every country with rapid growth is built on the base of private enterprise system. It means that most of the productive resources are owned by the private person and free from government intervention". He even advocated anarchism, "I think there is no corruption if there is no government control and regulation". He also arbitrarily commended that total elimination of government is equal to total elimination of corruption (Zhang, 2000). This so-called theory is totally inconsistent with the reality of contemporary capitalism, and cannot find any meaningful proof in the history of capitalism.

Modernized mass production is a complex cyclic process. The efficient operation of every link needs a variety of supporting conditions to guarantee. Privatization cannot solve all the problems. The privatization of each process is unable to achieve the multinational large-scale joint operations. In the social development process, certain social superstructure is always adjusted with a certain social and economic infrastructure. The situation of economic base determines the nature of superstructure, and in turn, the superstructure serves the economic basis. The modern mainstream economics is Anglo-American genre which develops ideologies and theories based on the economic activities in the United States, Britain and other industrialized countries. Many theoretical explanations and case studies are studying how to make industrialized countries become more prosperous and more profitable. There is no theory studying the economic activities in developing countries until 1960s. The new bifurcation theory named "development economics" observes and analyzes the market situation, investment opportunities, financial market and foreign exchange of developing countries from the perspective of outsider. Obviously, this theory is to provide advice for the industrialized countries to occupy the markets of developing countries.

Neo-liberalism influences China's reform

Since mid-1990s, China's economic reform concept has been significantly affected by "neo-liberalism" views, especially the so-called "property rights revolution" of new systematic. Some people on mainland China simplistically assert that the deficient performance of state-owned enterprises is because of unclear property rights. They think that changing the property rights system of state-owned enterprises in China will immediately improve the production efficiency of enterprises which lag in technology. A few people are trying to develop unrealistic "joint-stock reform" program to transfer the public property rights to private person. State-owned enterprise is to be decomposed and eroded. The property accumulated by some units for decades turn into private property instantly. Improving the efficiency of production is a complex process. Property rights reform is just a part of the process. The key to improve social productivity is the science and technology innovation. Science and technology are primary productive forces. Changes in property rights cannot be a substitute for inventions.

The most fundamental problem is that property rights are the most central element in the economic entity. The changes in the property ownership have a significant impact on the normal operation of the economic entity. After the complete change of property rights nature, the nature of the economic entity has also undergone a qualitative change. For example, in a period, under the instigation of the Pan-Marketization thoughts, some people advocate to trade market for technology in mainland China. To import the technology of the Western countries, some state-owned enterprises give up property rights and turn into a joint venture. Finally, these state-owned enterprises were merged by foreign enterprises. We can see that the contemporary capitalism is not the laissez-faire capitalism which is built based on so-called clear property rights, but capitalism which advocates foreign expansion, mergers, and monopoly. After China's state-owned enterprise turns into a wholly foreign-owned enterprise, the actual operation is not as the expectation in the plans of Chinese enterprise. As these state-owned enterprises lost market, it means that they also lost technology and rights of ownership. Among all the radical reform practices influenced by Pan-Marketization thoughts, the measurement of "clear property rights " is out of control resulting in the fact that the reform of old system to improve state-owned enterprise effectiveness do not reach expectation. The contemporary socialist reform must keep learning so that the people recognize the true face of neo-liberalism. Only in this way, the economic construction can get developed.

The loss of state assets

A few economic powers always want to impose their own values to the Chinese people. Under the cover of neo-liberalism, these countries admire laissez-faire economic policies and advocate that privatization of enterprise property rights is the only way to develop productive forces. It is easy for the people with philosophical knowledge to know that although the superstructure has a dynamic role on the economic base but there is no mutual relation between the superstructure and the economic base. Neo-liberalism is just a slogan and ideology that has never become an active and effective economic policy. The neo-liberalism theory of Economics Anglo-American genre was born in the Western industrialized countries. It is the abstract principle of economic and social activities in the United States and Britain. Most of the teachers and its advocators live in the industrialized countries, or receive education in those countries. As a result, these theories maintain economic interests of those countries. Thus, independently thinking people will see through neo-liberal's intention which is to replace socialism' opening up thought with capitalism liberalization and to bring socialist economy into the orbit of the capitalist economy. Some people in China are interested in analyzing China's social and economic life via capitalism theologies. The obvious conclusion they always reach at is that it does not conform to China's national conditions.

Table 2.1 Unemployment Rate of China Urban

Year / Item	1990	2000	2007	2008	2009
Urban registered unemployed people (million)	3.83	5.95	8.3	8.86	9.21
Urban unemployment rate (%)	2.5	3.1	4. 0	4.2	4. 3

Resource: National Bureau of Statistics. *China Statistical Yearbook 2010*. Beijing, China Statistics Press, 2011.

China has the largest population in the world. Most of the rural population does not have any social security. In the past, the state-owned enterprises provided medical, pension and other support systems to maintain the urban security and stability. However, after the radical restructuring of state-owned enterprises, many enterprises went bankrupt and many workers were laid off simultaneously (see Table 2.1). Although the increase in unemployment was not caused by the restructuring of state-owned enterprises, but the continuing increase in the number of unemployed people are related with the restructuring.

At the same time, many new labor forces entered the job market, labor and social security and employment immediately become very prominent issues. There is a log of pressure in economic, social and political fields. We must recognize the fact that certain social economic base will produce corresponding culture and ideology. This consciousness not only has the potential to surpass the base, but also imprint the base. When introducing Western market economic theory, we must distinguish the theories of general objective laws of market economy and the capitalist ideology. We must try our best to prohibit the capitalist ideology impeding the development of Chinese market.

Aware of different bias

Neo-liberalism became popular in the contemporary international community, especially after the disintegration of the former Soviet Union. However, history is always a story of twists and turns. An American scholar thinks that the collapse of the Berlin Wall and the Soviet Union does not mean the victory of liberalism. On the contrary, liberalism began to fall into decay. After 1989, the world entered the era of post-liberalism. Various political trends and social phenomena in globalization continue to change, and the pattern of Cold War history will not be re-staged again (Wallerstein, 2002). Fortunately, in the tortuous and complicated process of reform, the top leadership of the Chinese Communist Party and the Chinese government grasp the general direction of reform and keep a clear head of the liberal economic theory. All the utopian system innovation is suppressed, and the so-called deepening reform with privatization as the goal is abandoned.

To develop the socialist market economy with Chinese characteristics, the government and people should explore the law of the scientific socialist market economy for the actual situation in China. We should clearly understand the "left" or "right" erroneous ideas and abandon the blind anti-foreign narrow sense of the past. Naturally, in the current case, the speech and behavior of Pan-Marketization economy should be abandoned firstly. Otherwise, it would be very easy to get lost.

Abandon the Pan-Marketization economy

Some of the people blindly follow the free market economy. They seem to totally ignore the economic activities' new trend, commodity production and its new characteristics in contemporary capitalist society. They follow the puerile liberal economic theory that favors privatization suggested by Smith and Say. These people, who blindly advocate dissolution of the large state-owned enterprises, think small is good, and China should return to the puerile capitalism, small enterprises and private ownership as the main body. China's economic construction practice has proved yet that the planned economy is not worthless. The planned economy and market economy can exist in the market in a harmonious way. The key to the development of socialism market economy with Chinese characteristics is to combine the advantages of both market economy and planned economy. We can neither boast about the role of the market, nor overly emphasize the planned functionality.

The construction of the socialist economy must abandon the rigid contents in old traditions and keep scientific and reasonable core factors. At the same time, under the guidance of the right theory, the government should implement economic macro-control on the major projects related to the national economy and the people's livelihood to unite the goal of economy and society. The national management should combine with the market regulation. We must recognize the dual character of the free economic theory. In short, government and market should have their own managing scopes which cannot be mixed up. This is exactly the standpoint of the scientific development perspective.

Strengths of Market Economy

Historical facts show that the market economy does not exist in isolation, but appear and develop in a certain social system and some historical conditions. Therefore, we need to have the scientific concept of development to follow the objective laws of market economy; to seek the best resource allocation; and to optimize economic and social benefits.

Correctly Guide the Operation of Market Economy

How to correctly understand the market economy? What are its essential characteristics? The simple research results above show that the first research step of market economy is to analyze its existing economic system. Simply speaking, the market economy is a kind of basic approach to disperse policy decisions based on bartering. Commodity market, as a part of the market economy, is both abstract and concrete. It is the specific performance and reaction of social economic activities since the beginning of commodity production. The market's all connotations are given by the human. They would not exist without the human market. From another perspective, it is the assembly of all economic activities of human society taking the market as the goal and the starting point. In addition to the market-oriented economic activities, the humanity also has another way to contend economic activities. Such as the peasants' productive labors for their own consumptions and labors of the environmental protection workers.

Therefore, from the point of view of human society, market economy can just be a part of the human social economy, but not all of it. Admittedly, developing the market economy is an important aspect to promote the development of social economy. However, the market economy cannot replace the other parts of social economy. The development of human society needs the all-round advancement of all facets. The thought of excessive emphasis on market economy but ignorance of other aspects of social economy apparently does not comply with the all-round development of human society.

Follow the rules of market economy

Just like all other things in the world that have their own special existence laws, market economy also has its market operation rule which does not shift with people's subjective will. What is the market rule? The so-called market rule, in fact, is the performance of people's economic activities in the market and the market reflection to people's economic activities. It contains two basic points: one is the supply of the market performance and its reaction to market changes; the second is the demand of the market performance and its reaction to market changes. These two aspects of performance and reaction are reflected through the intermediary of currency. Therefore, the market rule also is the reaction of the market supply and market demand. Simply put, the price will rise when demand exceeds supply and vice versa. These two kinds of reverse change make the relation of supply and demand remain in equilibrium.

In modern times, the most popular textbook in China is Economics, written by Samuelson. The first chapter of this book expounds the famous market regulation principle, namely the invisible hand theory. In the regulation of the invisible hand, economic structure and institution get adjustment and operation automatically; resources obtain the most effective configuration; and it will never have the case of excess capacity and insufficient supply in the long term. To this extent, capitalism thoroughly gets rid of the cyclical economic crisis. This view is the extension of the Say's Law that supply automatically creates demand. From the perspective of history, Adam Smith does not uncover the inner relation of the market discipline when he finds and expresses the market rule for the first and earliest time limited to the social and economic conditions at then. Therefore, he regards the market rule as an invisible hand beyond people's understanding and control category.

However, with further development of the human society and improvement of science and technology, people not only obtain new understanding on the market and its law, but also explore some means and methods to master it, such as market research and forecasting, market supervision and control, pricing discipline and tax regulation. Commercial institutions and government can guide the market through these means and methods, and thus weaken the decisive role of the market rule on the social economy. The Russia's implementation of Sachs shock therapy and Harvard 500 Days program takes the market economy as the only mode of operation. The result is even criticized by the upright economic scholars in capitalist society. In the United States, economists and government all claim to implement wide range of administrative or social regulation. Antitrust laws, industrial and social regulations, and industrial policies are the main ways that government uses to regulate economic structure, production and project engineering (McConnell & Burl, 2001). These regulation means maintain the economic growth of the United States. They also become the important contents of economics textbook. The purpose of those plans is clear. However, blindly following behaviors only ends up in failure.

Punish illegal and undisciplined behaviors

All people in today's Chinese society know the market economy. In addition to the propaganda of news media, the commodity market around the land tells people that market economy is existent. With market economic means to solve all kinds of problems seem to have become an indispensable way. Some people also treat market economy as a panacea that can settle China's social and economic diseases. It is this incorrect understanding of market function that brings a series of problems.

On June 23, 2010, the 15th meeting of the Eleventh National People's Congress (NPC) held the second plenary session. In this meeting, Liu Jiayi, the chief auditor of the State Auditing Administration, presented that the number of case clues on major illegal issues and economic crimes that the audit office submits to the state council or directly delivers to relevant departments is up to 104, involving 473 people (Lin and Miao, 2010). And on December 26, 2011, the national industry and commerce administration conference held in Beijing disclosed that Chinese industry and commerce system handled 1.3895 million economic illegal cases of all kinds, valued 26.868 billion Yuan (Liu, 2011). We can see all the violators have a common motive that seeks personal gains, regardless of the situation they are in.

These facts have proved that the thought that all things should be linked with benefit, money and market is wrong. This incorrect understanding can not only easily make mistakes, but in theory will lead to error propagation. The banking system is one of the most significant institutions. It is worthy of further investigation. The focus of the regulation should be placed on the following fields, namely: bad loans, real estate loan risks, asset disposal behaviors of asset management company, connected transactions of trust and investment company, credit to related interest in rural credit cooperatives and the authenticity of increase in capital and share, because the occurring rate in these areas is highly frequent and extremely harmful.

At present, there are also some social programs for public good that have been shaped by the market. It seems to prove that commercialization is more in line with the world trend. The wealth gap is widening. Education and medical treatment are prone to the development of marketization. These situations are not normal in people's basic living needs. Therefore, we need to correctly understand the market economy, and to reflect from theory to practice. People cannot completely comply with the rule that development must accord to the market economy. Moreover, we cannot ignore all sorts of evil fruits brought by the Pan-Marketization. It is not sensible to give too little care to the legitimacy of the accelerated commercialization. We should look at these problems from new perspectives and cannot just let the public suffer and endure the consequences. A feasible method is to intervene with the excessive market pricing behaviors by effective policies.

The Models of World Market Economy

Free economy as a form of expression is not the most magical mode in economic system. The modern western countries have realized that the invisible hand is not the omnipotent God. The operation and management methods of market economy must accord with the actual situation of the country. Free-market economists propose the absolute exclusion of government intervention. Industrialized countries have modified the proposal. In the western countries, different market economy systems arise and the management methods are also not the same.

We might as well observe the market economy from the 17th century, the time of the embryonic stage of market economy. Different countries form different modes of market economy because the extent and methods of intervention and the recognition to the nature of the market economy are diverse. They can be summarized as of the following kinds:

Firstly, the free market economic mode of America. The market economy of the United States inherits its special cultural and liberal tradition. The character of its operation is the highly dispersed economy. The American society opposes that the government intervenes with economic activities in any form. However, previous governments in effect had been participating and regulating economic activities in diverse ways. The American free market economy is not entirely free.

Secondly, the welfare market economic mode of the Nordic. The Nordic countries form an organic system consisting of economic system, economic organization and social policies. The system is based on the private ownership and is formed in the practices of pursuing economic efficiency and social equality. It stresses the private enterprise as the major driving force of economic development, highly developed social welfare, mutually cooperative spirit, etc.

Third is the social market economic mode of Germany. Social market economy is a kind of capitalist market economy based on free competition. The guideline of this economy is that government makes proper adjustment and makes the social security as the basic safeguard. After the World War II, various economic policies formulated by all previous governments of Germany are basically based on it. Social market economy adheres to two basic principles: first, the main content of economic activity is market regulation. Market, as the foundation and bond in the economic operation, is always in the leading position; second, market activities can be interned and coordinated by the state to a certain degree. The country has a function of guidance and regulation to provide social security, providing social welfare policies of social security, justice and social progress.

Fourth is the nation-leading market economic mode of Japan. After the World War II, the emphasis of Japanese government's intervention lies in the total supply, and the bidirectional constraints between the government and enterprises. The government decreases the damage to the market and helps the enterprises as far as possible. And the country gradually forms a government-leading economic system mode in which private enterprises as the foundation are guided by the government.

Fifth is the plan-guided market economic mode of France. The planned adjustment implemented by France after the World War II is the typical "mixed economy". Its rapid recovery and development of economy is the result of organic combination of the plan and the market.

Sixth is the diversified practical economic mode of developing countries. Developing countries and transition economies are based on their own national conditions and historical and cultural traditions. These countries combine with the experience of other countries' economic development and learn lessons for the adjustment of their economic policies. The purpose is to try to adopt a path of market economy development according to the nation's conditions.

From the above analysis we can see that the pattern of the market economy is diversified. Each country after the world war, especially the Western capitalist countries, constantly adjusted their own economic policies to meet the needs of the development of the so-called economic globalization. They do not perfectly mimic the U.S. market economic mode. Any country's economic mode simply imitated by others is unlikely to achieve success.

Absorb the Cultural Nutrients of Humanity

Some European countries, especially Germany, sum up an appropriate regional and national economic development mode by the socio-economic practices, namely the social market economy.

Learn from the social market economy mode of Germany

After World War II, several socialist regimes arise in the eastern European countries. These countries' economies and cultures experience a rapid development period, and have of an increasingly far-reaching influence. Combined with the push by the organizations of the Communist Party, the socialist ideology comes up to the surface in the veteran capitalist countries one wave after another. The Christian Democratic Union of the West Germany's conservative parties also proposed a guiding principle of Christian socialist. The union considers that the capitalist economic system does not meet the national and social interests of the German people, and advocates the establishment of a new economic system. This party won the election in 1949. It signs the establishment of the first cabinet of the Federal Germany, the Adenauer government. The federal government proposes the principle of social market economy and put it into effect. The national economy of the West Germany smoothly transmits into the social market economy from the wartime system through implementation of a series of reasonable policies, such as the currency reform which has laid a good foundation for the future economic development (Qiu, 1988).

From the early 1950s to the first half of the 1960s, the Federal Germany enjoyed a rapid economic growth of development just because of implementation of the social market economy. Many Western economists call the outstanding economic achievements in this period as an economic miracle. The post-war federal government of the West Germany implements a complete set of measures that guarantee the people's minimum consumption and basic living standard. They are an important part of the social market economy. The main purpose is to increase the actual income and the real purchasing power by controlling money supply and financial expenses that alleviate the inflation rate. The real implementation of the social welfare system includes providing subsidies to unemployed workers, and providing pensions, medical insurance to the retired or incapable workers (Zhu and Lin, 1989).

The basis of the social market economy is a mixed ownership economy. On the one hand, it exerts great emphasis on the market competition. On the other hand, it also advocates the national intervention with the economy, namely the national functions of macro-control. This regulation includes not only monetary policies and fiscal policies, but also the national plans and the government's policies, such as government relief to the unemployed. The high-speed development of the state ownership is one of the major features of the social market economy. Although this form of ownership is secondarily compared with the dominant capitalism, but it plays a key role in the national economy, especially in the cases that the nation order goods or directly take over the low-profit enterprises and economic departments (the national defense industry for example), and the state-owned capitalist enterprises supply non-state-owned enterprises with cheap means of production. There exist huge conflicts between the China's social market economy and that of the Europe and Germany, but China can still learn some meaningful experiences to avoid some of the errors.

Assess the assumptions of the market economy system

Some people advocate that the liberal market economy is different from the social market economy. Free economy as a special kind of system, the internal mechanism is the market behavior of individuals, who pursues the personal maximum economic interests, reaches the optimal resources allocation under the guidance of the market price. However, the market price mechanism cannot play a role in isolation. In the process of the realization of the optimal resources allocation, it also needs some preconditions: first, each market economic actor has the rights of free choices in the precondition of no harm to the interests of others; second, the individual self-interest can be coordinated with the mutual benefits of all parties.

In addition to the assumptions above, the development of modern economy and economics also require the optimal resource allocation in market economy conforming to the following conditions: (1) Complete and symmetric economic information. Buyers and sellers in the market have completely sufficient information about the content and quality of transaction. (2) Perfectly competitive market. The market has numerous manufacturers so that each size is small. Any potential competitors can enter this market without any obstacles. Each manufacturer is the price recipient and has no ability to manipulate price. (3) Constant or decreasing returns to scale. The unit cost of the product is unchanged or decreasing along with the manufacturers' production scale expansion. (4) No externality. The productive and consumptive behaviors of businesses or individuals in the economic activities have no extra impacts on the external environment. (5) No transaction costs. (6) Rational economic man. Economic actors can always maximize their own welfare. The free economy cannot run without these assumptions, but, this cannot be fully realized in the real world. Therefore, the free economy does not exist.

From the negative situations appeared in the process of China's economic reform, people have reasons to suspect this kind of people's motivation who indoctrinates the privatization theory into China. The security of the modern developed capitalist system is based on the social security system of welfare capitalism. Obviously, it is wrong to advocate the implementation of the Pan-Marketization economic system reform. The implementation of the reform of state-owned enterprises is a way that is too radical. It breaks the old labor insurance and welfare but does not establish a feasible social security system. The historical experience of China for thousands of years shows that the emergence of many unemployed populations has always been a signal of danger, and the root of social chaos.

Avoid the Defects of Market Function

The market economy system already exists in Western countries for hundreds of years forming many mature management methods that improve the social productive forces. However, this system still has some serious flaws, especially in the early stage of its development. Provided that the macroeconomic regulation is still not standardized, systemic and sound enough, the intense impact force of market operation can easily bring damaging effects on the original economic harmonious relationship. The western market economic theory attached to the development of market economy undoubtedly has many excellent ideas. China's reform also confirmed that there is a lot to learn from the development experience of the Western industrialized countries. Nevertheless, we cannot accept the theory unreservedly, especially when the western world has been continuously introducing innovations in it.

Since the 1990s, the western economic theory, from a macro perspective, points out that the market and the market mechanism itself have some activity boundaries, such as political boundaries, allocation boundaries, social boundaries, ethical boundaries and ecological boundaries, that is, the market economic activities in these areas often fail. The construction of socialism does not work only depending on the market mechanism, and it also cannot obtain high benefits in some critical areas including the key industries adjustment of the national economy, public welfare investment projects, social security system, ecological and environmental protection. The market economy is not a panacea. Some drawbacks happened in the current Chinese economy confirm this judgment. Capitalism is led by personal interests to apply and develop the market economy. It expands the inherent flaws of market function. Some western people suffered the pain brought by this institutional shortcoming. Although the capitalist system has not come to the door of hell, the call for reforming the system defect is growing louder and louder. Thus, with the rapid development of Internet and the rapid expansion of economic globalization, people from developed countries pay more attention to the pursuit of common interests, especially in the United States, France and Germany.

For example, both German kindergarten games and American MBA courses tell how to cultivate the concept of teamwork and cooperation. International business competition also pays attention to seek the cooperation with rivals for striving to achieve a win-win solution. There will be no development of the so-called modern company if no cooperative exchanges recognized by each happen because profits are generated from exchanges. The inexperienced staff training rules in many world-famous multinational corporations prohibit the boost of individualism and selfishness. The actual operations of multinational corporations all involve teamwork items. This is in fact to advocate a win-win situation, namely reaching the goal of common interests. The French economist Albert once said: The Greater Europe has created a social market economy, and China has created a socialist market economy. Naturally, there are many differences and similarities between the two. They can become one of the magic weapons in the 21st century if they are able to integrate (Albert, 1999).

We can see that the common interests meet the common requirements of the progress of human society, and make the common aspiration of mankind come true. We need to notice here that the rational utilitarianism and wealth-pursuing activities should be encouraged, and the market economy is able to provide a channel for the realization of these rational pursuits. Market economy can effectively exercise incentive mechanism to achieve a higher economic growth rate. National wealth comes from the high-efficient production. The high productivity of social labor can increase the wealth, and it will be a significant increase in the supply of goods. However, the normal operation of the market economy needs a favorable and sound legal system to provide protection. Otherwise, the regulatory role of economic leverage on resources cannot be achieved.

In a nutshell, the implementation of the market economy in China brings high economic performance. Meanwhile, its congenital deficiency is also exposed to the world which is that the market economy can achieve the best efficiency only if the whole country is able to synchronize his actions.

Ideological Misunderstandings

The modern society has almost completely different economic characteristics from free economy. From the real life, people clearly realize that the development of the country would suffer if the law of the market economy fully takes the place of other laws and regulations. As a result, we should make an in-depth understanding of the market economy. The reasonable development of the means of production is the main way of the future social construction. It needs to further emancipate mind, to break through the Western neoliberalism, and to correctly distinguish the real cause of the social conflict and benefits friction and then to seek reasonable solutions.

Reduce the Opportunity Cost of Market Failure

Western economic theory summarizes the market economy as the abstract pair of supply and demand curves. These two curves rise and fall relative to each other under the guidance of price signals, and finally produce a balanced intersection point. This conclusion is only valid under some assumptions. As a matter of fact, the growth of socio-economic equilibrium involves a lot of factors. The price leverage is only one aspect. Therefore, not only is the Western economic theory defective, but the market mechanism itself is not perfect. The argument of Pan-Marketization, however, extensively boasts the function of the market mechanism, propagandizing the enforcement of fierce economic competition, survival of the fittest that help the country quickly reach the restructuring of the international economic institution. In some places, the actual reality after the successful enforcement is ineffective, numerous errors happen in the process.

First, survival of the fittest means fierce economic competition in the market economy. The result of strong implementation of economic competition can only exacerbate the polarization on the distribution of benefits, and increase the disparity between the rich and the poor which is clearly not consistent with China's national traditions.

Second, the coercive implementation of some global, long-term, and public-service socio-economic activities and investment do not receive the expected effectiveness. Moreover, the pursuit of maximum profits of microcosmic subjects is contradictory to the macroscopic interests. The pursuit of local and short-term interests often damages the global and long-term interests, which deviates from the direction of the important thought of the Three Represents. Third, the hysteresis quality of the market price signals can mislead the resource allocation on some production projects or cannot meet the market demand, or squander valuable resources. This put China, which has populous population and fewer resources per capita, at a disadvantage.

Fourth, the market mechanism guiding the spiritual, cultural, and political life is not only ineffective, but also misleading. Taking a radical way to implement market economy is easily prone to breed corruption because it is a by-product of pan behaviors. In short, the market economy is not an omnipotent economic form. We must be acutely aware of its congenital defects.

Government must deal with the problems generated by market failure that cannot be solved by the market itself, particularly in the public goods. In the spring of 2006, China released the people's livelihood index, a Chinese public environmental protection index for the first time. It offers the public reliable and exact information to the consequence of market failure. More than half of the public consider air pollution caused by industrial pollution as the most serious environmental problem. Environmental rights and clean water right that the public understands are quite right. The most common way people complain about environmental issues is to reflect the situation to the neighborhood committee or street office (Gu, 2006).

Obviously, the mere implementation of the market economy cannot handle the economic contradictions and problems in China. According to the report, "build the indicator system of people's livelihood index, the preliminary findings and policy recommendations", released by the NPC Financial and Economic Committee Research Group in 2011, there is not a single positive correlation between economic development indicators and overall human development level. The indicator system of people's livelihood index contains four primary indicators, including the residential living, ecological environment, social environment and public services. The system is composed of two parts, objective indicators and subjective indicators. Objective indicators use the data from governmental Statistics, accounting for 70% of the people's livelihood index; subjective indicators obtained mainly through questionnaires, accounting for 30%. A combination of the both is exactly the people's livelihood index reflecting the local people's livelihood development status (Zhao, 2011).

The assertion that market economy cannot solve China's economic contradictions does not mean that we are against the market economy. In effect, people do recognize that some positive features of the market economy inspire the wealth growth. What people are against is the argument of American-style free market economy. It is the narrow and one-sided subjective theory of market economy. Eichner, an American economist, indicated in his book "Why Economics is not yet a Science" that the indifference curve, the equal product curve, the supply curve and the marginal product curve in the Western economic theory have theoretical defects. However, they are the basic theoretical framework of microeconomics, and the basis of macroeconomics (Eichner, 1983). Put it in another way, the entire Western economic theory system is to collapse if these four parts are be verified.

In his book, Eichner also wrote: the most surprising thing is that the four theoretical structures have not yet been confirmed in practice by economists, although they are in such a prominent position (Eichner, 1983). These words not only represent his opinion, but reveal the very nature of the existing reality. Although the deficiencies of market mechanism cannot be cleared by manpower, we can proactively reduce the opportunity cost brought by these defects through correct understanding and active prevention. The economical ideological trend of Pan-Marketization has affected China's reform and has misled the economic works losing plenty of high-value opportunities to the society. This work is by no means the pure academic affair in academia that uncovers that kind of wrong-preaching and gorgeously camouflaged coat, and reduces the opportunity cost it produces, but has serious social and political significance. China should take the road of socialist market economy full of local characteristics, a development road that balances society and market economy. When developing the market economy, the country cannot ignore social construction activities of other non-market economy.

Clean Up the Fallacy of Neo-liberalism

Various contemporary market organizations exert their influences through a series of formal institutional arrangements, rules and traditions. The developed market economy in western countries is the result of institutional evolution in several hundred years. The process is full of twists and turns. It also derives a variety of economic theory schools. These different views of economic schools sum up the experience and lessons the economic institutions of capitalism had experienced and put forward development recommendations in line with different circumstances of capitalist system. For example, the neo-liberalism propagandizes the omnipotence of private ownership market economy to the utmost and attacks on government intervening in economic activities (Alan Haworth, 1994). Without a doubt, the capitalist ideology contained in this theoretical system is very clear and has a dual purpose. On the one hand, it plays a positive role with respect to the unity and stability of capitalist society. On the other hand, it exerts destructive and disintegrative effects on the socialism, the antithesis of capitalism.

However, the argument of Pan-Marketization insists on the pursuit of neoliberalism, and openly preaches the promotion of reform. We cannot deny the fact that this is a way that brings some of the capitalist system into China. Cleaning up the neoliberalism is to resist the erosion by capitalism, and to establish a socialist market economy. But for China, it is really a tough task that, within a brief period, achieves the level of the west which has developed for several hundred years. Designing a series of possible systems not only needs to participate in the design procedures; the more important is to create specific conditions for cultivating them. Reform is like the reposition of institutional arrangements. It is a great pioneering work, and has great significance without doubt.

Despite this, reform will sometimes meet with difficulties, even get into trouble. Each far-reaching and significant reform happened in the Chinese history, no matter radical or progressive, is inevitably accompanied with exceptionally tricky situation. In this case, the cost and several types of risks of reform will undoubtedly increase. The semblance of reform at this moment appears to be in a state of stagnation. However, it is very necessary and extremely useful. Reform is somewhat like mountain climbing. Climber needs a rest to stop for a breather to re-ascend. It is necessary to put on the brakes to decline the excessive speed of development. The buffer period provides a chance for people to calmly think the current situation and to resolve conflicts arisen in the process of reform. For example, it's necessary to let the rich deeply understand the sufferings of the poor, and to let them know that paying back to the society is a good merit; conversely, the poor also can fully understand the bitter side of starting a business that the rich had tasted. Naturally, the poor will not look upon rich men with hatred and are willing to challenging work to become well-off. The high-quality development is worth waiting if we can build a harmonious relationship of mutual respect between these people.

Therefore, we might call it a buffer period in the early reform process of the "Twelfth Five-Year". Those practices including reform reflection, experience summarization and policies' adjustment are to redesign the future reform process. The reform is linked closely with the future and destiny of China, so we need to keep sober all the time. Chinese people have recognized that the "Twelfth Five-Year" plan cannot be successfully conducted without caution and courage. Harmony is prior to development. The future is bright with harmonious development.

Chapter 3

Pan-Marketization Phenomena in Contemporary China

China's reform and opening up has entered a new stage of building a moderately prosperous society, developing socialism with Chinese characteristics and building an innovative country. There is no doubt that the Chinese people are writing a great new chapter in the history of humankind. However, in the process of reform and opening up, there have been many unavoidable problems. In the first decade of the new century, some contradictions hidden in Chinese economic and social institutions have gradually emerged. What is worth pondering upon is that the appearance of these contradictions results from some misleading theories and erroneous ideas. In addition, some human errors have aggravated the chaos during the economic and social transformation. It is very necessary to criticize the ideological misconceptions and to create a proper development concept to maintain and implement the 12th Five-Year Plan.

Power of the Socialist Market Economy

Under the guidance of Deng Xiaoping Theory, "Three Represents" and "A scientific outlook on development", the Chinese national economy has finished its second five-year period. The second economic census in 2009 showed that the number of legal units of secondary and tertiary industries was ￥7,099,000 RMB at the end of 2008, with an increase of 37.3% as compared to the first economic census in 2004. Meanwhile, in accordance with international practice, the state statistics bureau revised the GDP in 2008 and announced their results. The GDP after revision was ￥314,045 RMB in 2008. The added value of primary industry was 33,703, which accounted for 10.7% of GDP. The added value of secondary industry was 149,003, which accounted for 47.5% of GDP. The added value of tertiary industry was 131,340, which accounted for 41.8% of GDP (Ma, 2009). Adopting its reform and opening up policy, China has maintained a uniquely high economic growth rate for a third of a century. The Chinese people, led by the Communist Party of China and the central government, have created a miracle in the history of the world economy. After conducting a contrastive study on the comprehensive strength of China and other countries, China's Academy of Social Sciences on December 24, 2009 held a meeting to report on the 2010 world economy and international situation.

In the Report Meeting of World Economy and International Situation held on December 24, 2009, "World Economy Yellow Book", "International Situation Yellow Book", "Analysis and Prediction of 2010 World Situation" and "Annual Report on International Politics and Security, 2010" were released. The Yellow Books showed that the comprehensive national strength of the United States, Japan and Germany ranked in the top three positions, and China ranked seventh out of 11 advanced nations. Moreover, the military power of the United States, China and Russia ranked in the top 3 positions (Social Sciences Academic Press, 2009). The socialist system has played a key role in the rapid growth of China's comprehensive national strength. For example, under the guidance of a correct political line, China has maintained a long-term stable social environment, macro-controlled national resources, and has carried out sustainable construction guidelines and has fully mobilized its labor force.

China's achievement has been favorably noticed by the entire world. The Millennium Development Goals of the Millennium Summit of the United Nations in 2000 was most persuasive when evaluating a country's development. In 2008 in an interview with reporters of Xinhua News Agency, the deputy secretary general of the United Nations, Zukang Sha, who was responsible for economic and social affairs, stressed that the Chinese government and people had made painstaking efforts to achieve the Millennium Development Goals and had made great achievements. China halved the proportion of poor people ahead of schedule. China had fulfilled the goal of guaranteeing that all children finish their primary education; this goal was supposed to be realized in 2015. What's more, China also had made great achievements in reducing the mortality rate of children under 5 years age and in improving maternal health. At the same time, some authoritative international reports gave credit to China's development. The United Nation's Millennium Development Goals Report (2008) attributed the dramatic fall in poverty of East and Southeast Asia to the rapid economic development of China (Xinhua, 2008).

The Support from the Chinese People

The achievement of China's economic and social development should be attributed to the implementation of the reform and opening up policy and the socialist market economic system. Before 1978, China was a country with a low level of social productive forces and a backward economy. Chinese people were living in poverty. China's second leader generation led by Deng Xiaoping broke the previous rigid ideology and opened up a new period of reform. Deng pointed out that poverty was not socialism, and that the life and productivity in a socialist country should be better than that in a capitalist country. Therefore, reform was the only choice for China to break the status quo. Thus, exploratory reform arose from difficulties. The main challenge in that period was the shortage of materials. Moreover, there was a most pressing need for China to develop its productive forces. According to China's actual situation, Deng designed the blueprint of reform and opening up, whose core philosophy could be summed up in one of his classic sayings: "A mice catching cat is reputed not because of its color, but its capability", which means that as long as it was good for China's socialist construction, all methods were acceptable. Deng chose a strategy to concentrate all efforts on the development of social productive forces and to mobilize all people to engage in the activities of the commodity economy. Under the guidance of is chief architect, beginning in rural areas, China's reform achieved a remarkable success in a very short period. Peoples' lives improved much. What is more, by giving priority to efficiency with due consideration to fairness, social fairness was better maintained. Reform was deeply rooted in the hearts of people, and national strength was strongly developed.

Energetic Socialist Market Economy

The most important problem in human social and economic activities is the contradiction between unlimited material needs and limited natural resources. So, the primary goal of all production activities is to produce the most consumer goods with the least resources, which is also the resource allocation issue of economic theory. The planned economy China applied before reform which advocated the allocation of resources by administrative practice also had the problem of low efficiency. Absorbing the experience of western industrialized countries, China has changed the original mode of production and shifted from a planned economy to a market economy.

Optimal allocation of resources improves productivity. The most effective functions of the market economy are: to optimize the allocation of resources; to select the superior and eliminate the inferior through market competition; to promote the progress of science and technology; as well as to greatly improve economic efficiency. The high efficiency of the market economy has been proved by history. In the "Manifesto of the Communist Party," Marx and Engels pointed out that "the bourgeoisie, during its rule of scarce one hundred years, has created more massive and more colossal productive forces than have all preceding generations together". The bourgeoisie colonized other countries with guns; engaged in business; and even involved in evil people trafficking.

To facilitate trade, the bourgeoisie built large-scale railroads in order to transport goods, and introduced telegrams to exchange business information. By promoting commercial production and the exchange trade, ancient farming practices were changed. Just as described by Marx and Engels, this is what occurred: the subjection of nature's forces to man, machinery, application of chemistry to industry and agriculture, steam navigation, railways, electric telegraphs, clearing of whole continents for cultivation, canalization or rivers, whole populations conjured out of the ground (Marx and Engels, 1995). It was the material force for bourgeoisie to overcome feudal nobles and lords. From the perspective of history, the mechanism of the market promoted the survival of the fittest and efficiency in commercial products, in factors of production, in enterprises and manufactories. In addition, this function of the market mechanism has had unique advantages as compared with other mechanisms. Therefore, the market economy plays a significant and irreplaceable role in the efficient allocation of resources and in the development of social productive forces.

This has helped China to experience a new record of rapid growth of wealth, rapid development of economic globalization, large sums of foreign exchange reserves, cross-border investment, the ability to allocate resources, and rapidly increasing profit. According to the financial report published by People's Bank of China, since early 1999, China's foreign exchange reserves have kept hitting new highs in recent years. In the past two years, foreign exchange reserves almost made a new record every day. At the end of 2010, China's foreign exchange reserves were up to $2,847,338,000,000. And at the end of June 2011, reserves reached $3.1975 trillion, with an increase of 30.3% (People's Bank of China, 2011). According to the website of the Administration of Foreign Exchange, at the end of 2011, China's foreign exchange reserves were $ 3,181,148,000,000. Foreign exchange reserves of China keep ranking first in the world, which is almost thrice the amount of the second-ranked country, Japan. The huge foreign exchange reserves of China demonstrate the fact that increasingly powerful national strength not only has set a more solid financial base for China's participation in international economic competition but also has provided a strong guarantee for defending various risks. That's because of abundant exchange funds that China can carry out its macro-control policies step by step; can maintain a balance of international payments; and is able to give more support to economic and social development.

In a word, the world is paying attention to tremendous economic development of China and her playing a significant role in the world economy. Under the guidance of Deng Xiaoping Theory and "Three Represents", China will achieve greater economic and social progress at a higher level. The Chinese people will be able to complete their historical mission.

Income Gap is being Widened

The building of socialism is an unprecedented process of civilization, accompanied by many difficulties, and so is the process of China's reform. Nowadays, Chinese people clearly know that in 1978, China was suffering from the catastrophe of "the cultural revolution" and the national economy was near the brink of collapse. The Chinese Communists led by Deng Xiaoping turned back the powers of darkness and opened a new era in the history of China. However, the situation in China at that time called for limited reform and the opening up of certain aspects of the economic system. It was impossible for China to get total victory if it did not carry out a reform and opening involving all industries and areas. The reform could not be perfect, and that is why we should continually reflect on the reform process.

A comprehensive summary and self-examination of economic historical development is the prerequisite for the continuing advancement and development for any society. Review of the past and self-examination are two aspects of social thinking. People should have the courage not only to review the wrong practice in the past, but also to self-examine. Self-examination does not mean denial, but reverse thinking and analysis of a society's social status or analysis of the things that have already been established. Reflecting on China's social reality is to go beyond difficulties in order to raise questions and to think in reverse. Materialist dialectics of Marxism state that things trend upward in a circular fashion, and therefore, we need to follow the law of negation.

Reflecting on reform is to revise the errors made in the process of effecting past reforms, and to base current reforms on facts, which is also the requirement of social reality. With the development of reform, people gradually found that, because of the influence of Pan-Marketization ideas, some places overemphasized the pace of development and ignored the effective use and protection of resources and the environment on which humans rely for their existence. Unscrupulous predatory exploitation seriously destroyed the friendly relations between humans and nature. Excessive pursuit of economic interests led to loss of morality, lack of soft constraints, and declining cohesion. Some unscrupulous people forgot honor at the prospect of profits and did things in irregular ways instead of working hard. Commercial credit, business ethics and business image became fragile in the market economy. Some people misinterpreted national policies to serve their own immediate interests, as well as sectional interests, which seriously violated social equity. The Chinese people did not appreciate this behavior.

The widening gap between rich and poor rings the alarm as China is a socialist country with the prosperity of the masses as its constitutional goal. In the new century, China is trying to build a harmonious socialist society. One of the most critical issues to complete this task is to rationalize social allocation, which is not only a requirement for social stability, but it is also the essence of socialism. According to the survey data released by World Bank in 2010, 5% of the population in United State occupied 60% of the national wealth. However, in China, 1% of the population occupied 41.4% of the national wealth. China became the country with the most serious polarization in income distribution. The Gini coefficient rose from 0.28 at the beginning of reform and opening up to 0.48 in 2007. In recent years, our Gini Coefficient has reached to the international alertness line level (Talent Chanel of China Cement Website, 2010).

The Gini coefficient is an important international analysis indicator to evaluate a country's residents' income distribution. The economic implication of the Gini coefficient can be thought of as the ratio of equality over total income. The international alertness line level is 0.4. Gini coefficient ranges from 0.4 to 0.6 represent uneven income distribution, and a Gini coefficient over 0.6 represents a high degree of uneven income distribution. There is a serious disparity in income in China. Outside the rows of high-rise buildings are tile-roofed houses. We can still see the shadow of villages in the downtown area of a city. The term urban-village has vivid significance. Different industries in which people work and the various positions of urban residents lead to the income gap. Although a difference in the distribution of income is inevitable, this income difference should be controlled within a moderate range in a specific period, also considering social tolerance and other factors.

At the same time, the income gap measured as Chinese family per capita income is expanding (see Table 3.1 and Table 3.2). In 1999, the income gap of household per capita income between urban and rural residents was just only ￥3000 RMB, while in 2004, it rose to ￥6485.2 RMB. In 2004, the income gap between urban and rural areas exceeded ￥10,000 RMB. The gap reached ￥12,021.5 RMB in 2009. During the period between 1999 and 2007, the income gap between urban and rural residents has a linear upward trend, with ￥33,300 RMB as the highest, 26,500 as the lowest. Although the gap narrowed slightly in 2008, it was expanded in 2009, reaching a peak in 2007. Adding subsidies and benefits, the ratio of the gap reached 4-5, which, surprisingly, was an even higher. As farmers make up a big section of the population, they are the driving force to promote economic development and to form the basis of country prosperity. Undoubtedly, the gap between urban and rural areas has become China's most serious and urgent problem. We should carry out some practical measures to control the income differentiation and to rationalize the income distribution in China.

History shows that when the Gini coefficient is ultra-high, low-income groups will have a feeling of relative deprivation, hatred for the rich and a desire to revenge society, leading to a series of social problems. At the same time, it is difficult to achieve fair competition and an efficient allocation of resources because of the serious polarization. The authoritative inquiry above shows that China's Gini coefficient has reached the international warning line 0.4. The gap between rich and poor has become a disturbing social problem in China.

Table 3.1 Income of Urban and Rural Residents (1999-2004)
Unit: yuan/person, ratio

Gap \ Year	1999	2000	2001	2002	2003	2004
Urban per capita income	5854.0	6280.0	6859.6	7702.8	8472.2	9421.6
Rural per capita income	2210.3	2253.4	2366.4	2475.6	2622.2	2936.4
Income gap	3643.7	4026.5	4493.2	5227.2	5850.0	6485.2
Urban per capita income over rural per capita income	2.65	2.79	2.90	3.11	3.23	3.21

Notes: 1, Urban per capita income refers to the per capita disposable income of urban residents; rural per capita income refers to the per capita income of rural residents. 2, the ratio of urban per capita income over rural per capita income is based on the net income of farmers as 1.

Source: National Bureau of Statistics, *China Statistical Yearbook, 2010*, Beijing: China Statistics Press, 2010.

Table 3.2 Income of Urban and Rural residents (2005-2009)

Unit: yuan/person, ratio

Year / Gap	2005	2006	2007	2008	2009
Urban per capita income	10493.0	11759.5	13785.8	15780.8	17174.7
Rural per capita income	3254.9	3587.0	4140.4	4760.6	5153.2
Income gap	7238.1	8172.5	9645.4	11020.2	12021.5
Ratio of urban per capita income over rural per capita income	3.22	3.28	3.33	3.31	3.33

Notes: 1, Urban per capita income refers to the per capita disposable income of urban residents; rural per capita income refers to the per capita income of rural residents. 2, the ratio of urban per capita income over rural per capita income is based on the net income of farmers as 1.

Source: National Bureau of Statistics, *China Statistical Yearbook, 2010*, Beijing: China Statistics Press, 2010.

The uneven distribution of wealth in China has attracted the attention of international community. The report released by Boston Consulting Group on May 31, 2011 showed that the world economy recovered with an increase of 8% at the end of 2010. The number of families all over the world with more than one million U.S. dollars assets increased by 12.2% over 2009 levels, reaching 12,500,000. 0.9% of the families all over the world were super-rich and occupied 39% of the wealth, with an increase of 2% over 2009. Compared to other countries, the number of rich in China increased the most, accompanied by the largest gap between the rich and the poor. Before 2010, 1.1 million families in China earned more than one million dollars, while only 0.4 million families were earning at this level in Germany. However, the national per capita income of China still lagged far behind other developed countries. According to the National Bureau of Statistics, annual per capita income in China was ￥13,476

RMB, and the annual per capita income of rural residents was only ￥5,919 RMB. And according to the World Bank Statistics, China's Gini coefficient in 2010 reached 0.47, which was almost twice that of 30 years ago (BCG, 2011).

Early in 2005, some scholars pointed out that rich people in China had specific characteristics as compared with those in Europe and the United States. Their condition can be summarized by three characteristics: (1) elevated level of cash holding, which reaches as high as 71%, while the global average level is 34.6%; (2) strong affordability of risk, prefer the rapid trading of financial products such as stock; (3) tend to be directly involved in the decision-making process of investment, and firmly believe that they can get higher return than the managers in financial institutions (Cheng, 2005). Because most wealth is concentrated in the hands of a few people, this situation does not meet the goal of socialism that is common prosperity. It has become necessary to adjust the income distribution structure. From the perspective of policy, the government should levy income tax and inheritance tax on high-income groups to regulate their income and should introduce policies to encourage them to be involved in charity and public welfare. What's more, the government should improve the social security system to guarantee basic living standards of the unemployed and to promote their reemployment. The implementation of these measures is conducive to social stability and development.

Illegal behavior of making a huge fortune overnight and the relatively large income distribution gap between urban residents impedes greatly the development of society. Against the background of reform and opening up, some people have first gotten rich with the help of national policies. Meanwhile, rich people become public figures whose consuming behaviors have significant external effects. There is no doubt that over-consumption can cause bad social impacts and impede the building of a harmonious society. As some people take possession of too much wealth, the situation of other people will become more difficult.

For example, Shanxi Province is the largest source of coal in China. The spendthrift behavior of some coalmine owners has drawn widespread criticism. It was reported that in Shanxi Province, after getting rich quickly, a coalmine owner not only spent 37 million buying the most expensive villa in Beijing but also bought a Hummer vehicle for each family member who was older than 15 years. From the historical perspective, he belonged to the pioneering generation. Partly, his spendthrift behavior was caused by the fact that he earned his money too easily, which is economically termed as "extraordinary profits". In a competitive market system, earning average profit is an irreversible economic law. Usually, only the companies with high-tech innovation or super-economic coercion can obtain monopoly profits. As it is difficult for coal enterprises with aging facilities and backward technology to make high-tech innovations, super-economic coercion became the key factor for coal enterprises to earn monopoly profits. There are three factors of super-economic coercion as described below.

First, the wages of miners are too low. According to a survey, until the 1980s, the salary of miners had been at the forefront of the industry. However, since then, miners' salary has sunk drastically. In the new century, a miner earns the second-lowest income among 49 industries and the per capita household income of a considerable number of miners is lower than that of local farmers. Secondly, too little money has been invested to guarantee security. In recent years, safety accidents have occurred frequently in coal enterprises, causing heavy casualties and property losses. The key reason is that, in order to score maximum profits, the fund for production safety was arbitrarily cut. Thirdly, the government's tax policies are distorted. Until 2011, the tax policy concerning coal resources has not been substantively adjusted for 20 years.

The State Council issued the decision of "amending the resource tax regulations of the People's Republic of China in October 10, 2011, and then published the "Implementing Rules of the Provisional Regulation on Resource Tax in People's Republic of China on October 31". It was implemented officially on November 1. This policy raised the per-unit tax of ￥8 RMB/ton to ￥8.20 RMB/ton on rare coal, coking coal resource, and ￥0.3-5 RMB/ton on other coals. Although this reform adjusted the tax on coking coal in a relatively large fashion, it was less meaningful for the whole coal industry. That is because, for large-scale coal enterprises, a tax increase of ￥10-20 RMB on resources could be easily internalized. What is more, as coal enterprises had strong bargaining power, it was easy for them to pass the increasing tax to their downstream steel and coking enterprises (Fu, 2011). As a result, this reform of coal tax failed to solve the key problems in the coal industry. These facts indicate that the opening and reform policy and an unreasonable tax regime rather than individual wisdom played a key role in increasing wealth for coal bosses.

What is more important is that the three factors mentioned above are reasonable for not only coalmines but also for other industries that produce many spendthrift rich people. Essentially, the government should adopt administrative measures instead of letting market mechanisms regulate these factors. However, in fact, they are under the control of the invisible hand of market because of people's misunderstanding of theory. This situation puts workers in an extremely unfavorable position "in the first distribution of income" and makes government fail to achieve secondary allocation. As a result, the income gap between the rich and the poor will be larger and larger in China. Aiming at achieving a harmonious society, the tangible way to solve this problem is to start from these three factors, and implement administrative regulation to narrow down the income gap.

Ironically, in contrast with the rich coal bosses, many people in Shanxi Province live in poverty. In general, Shanxi Province is still a relatively poor and backward province in central China. According to the government reports of 31 provinces in 2009, the per capita disposable income of urban residents in Shanxi Province was ￥13,997 RMB, with an increase of 6.7%, ranking 23rd among 31 provinces, and last in the 6 provinces in central China. What's more, especially compared with the eastern coastal areas such as Jiangsu, Zhejiang, Guangdong and other provinces, the per capita income of urban residents in Shanxi Province has been lagging for years (Development Herald, 2010). On July 22, 2010, the Statistics Bureau of Shanxi Province released the operational report of the economy in Shanxi. In the first half of 2010, the GDP of Shanxi Province reached ￥414.34 billion RMB, with an increase of 17.5% over that in the same period of previous year, 6.4 percentage points higher than the average national level. The CPI rose moderately. Consumer prices rose 2.1%, with an increase of 3 percentages points over that of the previous year, but still 0.5 percentage points lower than the average national level (Shanxi Evening News, 2010). Although per capita disposable income and consumer prices increased with the support of wealthy mine bosses, it did not definitely mean that the income and life of low-level income groups also became better off significantly. What is the living condition of those people with per capita income below the average level (Cheng, 2005)? Are their lives significantly improved as well? Because these people are the group who really need help, we should pay special attention to them and try our best to achieve a common prosperity.

Management leakage: power of rent-seeking

The spendthrift behaviors of rich mine bosses are more serious than rumors. Many facts show that a few mine owners bribe relevant government officials to make exorbitant profits, and some officials make use of their power to collude with mine owners to get kickbacks, which brings calamity to the country and to the people. Although the central government has repeatedly issued documents to prevent coalmine accidents, they still occur often and kill many miners. According to statistics published by the relevant departments of the State Council, the number of coalmine accidents that killed more than 10 people in 2005 was 134, and fatalities had increased 17% as compared with fatalities in 2004. In addition, there were four accidents which killed more than 100 people.

They were "214 gas explosion accidents in Sunjiawan coal mine in Fuxin", "87 flooding accidents in Meizhou coal mine in Guangdong Province", "1127 dust explosion accidents in Dongfeng mine in Qitaihe", and "127 gas explosion accidents in Liuguantun coal mine in Tangshan" (Qi, 2006). The statistics released by the State Administration of Work Safety showed that industrial accidents in 2010 killed 79,552 people, with a reduction of 3648 people, 4.4% less than in 2009. Based on this calculation, 218 people were killed in accidents every day (China Economic Weekly, 2011). We can see that the number of causalities was very large. How many sinister secrets are hidden behind these security accidents? We may find the answer from the sacking of Li Jiucheng, the Coal Administration Secretary of Henan Province. The court found that, during 1999 and 2008, Li Jiucheng took advantage of his position and duties to obtain cash and stocks 53 times, adding up to ￥18,898,700 RMB, $ 10,000 dollars, £30,000 pounds, and a car worth ￥230,000 RMB.

According to the prosecutor, the corruption case of Li Jiucheng was very typical involving all the 30 bribery and corruption behaviors identified by the judiciary (Lookout, 2010). People are facing a grim social reality. On the one hand, a few coal bosses live extravagantly, drive luxury cars and amuse themselves in high-level entertainment places. On the other hand, coal mine accidents are emerging; and working conditions and the living environment of miners is worrisome. This sharp contrast between mine boss and miners hurts the heart of every person with a conscience. This is not to say that there is corruption behind every accident. But the collusion between government officials and mine owners is an indisputable fact and should not be tolerated by government. In the supervision of mine safety, the government should encourage the public to work together to report corruption activities and to punish the people who are responsible for the accidents.

In 2006, under the guidance of the new generation of collective leadership of the Communist Party of China, relevant departments took legal and administrative measures to fight against corruption in management. According to statistics released by China's Ministry of Land and Resources in January 20, 2006, in order to curb the collusion and bribery between businessman and government officials, since 2005, the government rectified and standardized the regulations of mineral resources development, and forbade government officials from taking charge of mining fields, receiving gifts, and backing illegal mining fields.

On January 14 and 15, 2012, a national conference of work safety was held in Beijing. Deputy Secretary of State Administration of Work Safety, and Minister of State Administration of Coal Mine Safety, Zhao Tiechui said, for the first time, death of coal mine accidents dropped below 2,000 in 2011; fatality rate per million tons for the first time dropped to 0.564; the number of significant serious accidents was reduced to 1, and the occurrence period was extended to 390 days for the first time, creating the best record of 23 years (Coal Information Exchange Network, 2012). As a representative of the public interest, the Chinese government has adopted practical action to regulate coal mine production. During "Eleventh Five-Year" period, under the correct leadership of the CPC Central Committee and the State Council, the administration and supervision departments of the National Coal Mine Safety Agency adhered to the principles of "safety first, prevention first and comprehensive management", and firmly established the scientific concept of safe development, resulting in a steady improvement in coal mine safety. The total amount of coal mine accidents declined year by year, reducing from 2,945 in 2006 to 1,403 in 2010, with a decrease of 52.4%, and the number of deaths reduced from 4,746 to 2,433, with a decrease of 48.7%; fatality rate per million tons was reduced from 2.04 to 0.749, with a decrease of 63.3%. The operation of gas control and waterproofing got new achievements (China Coal News, 2011). This policy fully reflected the developed thinking of "people oriented", which was conducive to the establishment of a harmonious society.

We should realize that China is a country with a large population with many complexities and the gap between different regions and industries continues to exist. Judging from the present situation, it is impossible to achieve complete equality in China. However, the reality is that the problem of disparities of wealth has become more and more serious in recent years. Some people spend money prodigally, while some people still live in poverty. And some of the reasons include malignant mine accidents, rent-seeking and corruption, all of which is very distressing. These facts have demonstrated that a few people amass huge wealth unscrupulously, while most people become relatively poor because of being deprived of development opportunities. Such differentiation and disparity absolutely is not the vision of a harmonious society. The obvious polarization in income distribution not only deviates from the aim of socialism, but also causes the hatred of rich, resulting in social disruption. Revealing the problem and dissecting contradictions does not mean the negation of reform. In accordance with the spirit of academic independence and freedom of thought, we should seek truth from facts, reveal contradictions and find out reasons. Eventually, we will be able to uphold the truth, correct errors and improve the current situation.

In short, because peoples' disapproval of the widening social wealth gap continues to grow, the government should implement new policies to encourage people to obtain wealth by challenging work. The government should also oppose predatory practices and put an end to the notorious conduct of earning money from accidents. Letting all society members share the fruits of economic development and grow social wealth, to mobilize the enthusiasm of low-income people and in order to accelerate the development of social production, the government should employ economic and administrative measures to adjust the distribution of social wealth and to create equal opportunities for more low-income persons.

The contradiction and problems of income distribution in China accompany with market-oriented reforms. Solving income distribution problem is directly related to the government. The government should take the responsibility to play a leading role so as the public services won't be over-market-oriented. As we all know, the root of widening income gap and social distortions is the notorious abnormal private ownership of natural resources. Therefore, the primary thing the government should do is to develop a more suitable property right system that delivers prosperity and opportunity for the public more equitably. At the same time, a relatively perfect competitive market can promote the full flow of production factors and is conducive to narrowing the income gap. Therefore, the government should effectively regulate tax system and tax collection system to provide more public facilities. Furthermore, under the circumstance with serious income gap in China, government should be concerned about the impact of policy factors on different income groups.

The Ambiguity of the Medical Service System

Every Chinese citizen desires to avail good medical insurance, to maintain a healthy physical and mental condition, to enjoy the good times of life, to make more contributions to the society and to the state. The people's desires also correspond to the requirements of the new era of socialism. Medical and health service, largely, is a common cause and needs fanatical support from the government. The Chinese medical and health system has played a significant role in protection of people's health, but there also exist some problems.

Difficulty and Excessive Cost of Getting Medical Care

China's social and medical services agencies cannot satisfy the public needs, especially in rural areas and mountain districts where the medical facilities are quite insufficient and the health care conditions are extremely poor. Illness caused by poverty is not rare anymore in China.

The pan-market tendency exists in hospitals in many countries, particularly in the industrialized countries, where the health care network covers the entire country and benefits all legal residents. The specific institutions that implement medical treatment are mainly public hospitals funded by the states. China also has a public hospital system, from the township to the capital city. The angels in white dedicated to public health and safety selflessly work all day long. In addition, in recent years, the Chinese government has played heroic efforts to save lives. The public hospitals, which are financially supported by the government, undertake their responsibilities by healing the wounded and rescuing the dying, consequently winning profound respect from the public. The government has strengthened the supervision of the operation of medical enterprises and has publicly announced a reduction in the prices of some drugs several times. For a rather extended period, the results of medical care have not been satisfactory. Breakthroughs in service were not made until the last couple of years. By the end of September 2011, basic medical insurance covered a population of 1.295 billion, coverage greater than 95%. There was an increase of 17 million entries in NRCMS. Medical insurance for urban residents expanded fully and the number of insured reached 216 million. Nearly 8 million retirees and workers from bankrupt enterprises and striving enterprises have been included in basic medical insurance. The latest additions to the system who have received benefits are mainly from the grassroots population (Network of China, 2010).

While we are delighted at the progress of the medical system, there still exists in public hospitals a pan-market phenomenon that should not have happened. Incidents "5.5 million sky-high medical expenses event" in Haerbin City, Heilongjiang Province and "1.2 million sky-high medical expenses event" in Shen Zhen City, Guang Dong Province are of frequent occurrence. In 2001, 49-year-old Wu Xi Ying, a migrant worker who came from Hubei Province went to the Guangji Hospital in Fenggang Town, Dongguan City as she was ill of gallstones. After 28 days treatment, she did not recover and died unfortunately on 21st March. What she left to her husband was a nine-page bill that showed that there was a balance of 450,000 in the hospital's favor. The hospital listed 320 items, among which were expenses for the infusion of 330 kg fluid in a month, fees for the transfusion of more than 14,000 milliliters blood, and other costs billed after the death of the patient. These charges raised questions. The hospital said the medical expenses incurred when the hospital adopted reasonable treatment and medication according to standard salvage therapy and there were no problems with the astronomical medical expenses (Xi'an Daily, 2011).

The Dongguan Municipal Health Bureau got involved in the investigation. Chief of Finance of the council planning Miss Dai Lihong said whether the medical costs were too high should be judged based on the doctor's advice, nursing orders and relevant treatment documents. The number of the charges was simply a result of standard medical procedure. The more critical issue was to look at the course of treatment compliance which needed to wait for third-party autopsy results. Under the intervention of Dongguan Health Bureau, the hospital and the bereaved signed an agreement on March 30th and decided to send the body to Shantou University Forensic Center for an autopsy in order to verify the "medical malpractice" doubt raised by family of the patient (Xinhua, 2011).

The above events were all related to hospital charges. The difference is that some happened in public hospitals while others were in private hospitals. But essentially, they are all evidence of pan-market oriented thinking. Unlike other money-making projects, hospitals are based on the fundamental interests of human beings. Regardless of the type, hospitals must first follow the scientific, rigorous practice of medicine. Putting money above all is taboo, while good service and contribution to society are the public wishes and aspirations which should be the ultimate purpose and primary principle of the hospitals (China News, 2011). The purpose of commercial behavior is to make money which is clearly reflected in the early commercial behavior of Europe, the birthplace of market economy.

In his famous writing Critique of Political Economies published in 1930, the founder of Communism, Karl Marx pointed out the unfortunate mental state exhibited by Money Fetishism. He ironically quoted the remark of Columbus who was once regarded as the representative of the world's commercial capital when he traveled across oceans in search of gold: "Gold is an amazing thing! Whoever possesses it is lord of all he desires. By means of gold, one can even get souls into Paradise." (Marx and Engels, 1962) Some hospitals haven't adopted a proper philosophy towards money. Profit is their prime concern and the health needs of the people are ignored. Such behaviors obviously depart from hospital working principles. Healing the sick and saving lives must be the highest moral code in medical field. In no case should hospitals deviate from the purpose of medicine.

Nowadays, people are generally complaining about unreasonably high medical expenses. The government's measures of reducing drug prices have failed to solve the problem fundamentally. According to survey data collected by Tianjin Statistical Bureau, the annual per capita medical expenses was ￥521 RMB in 2011, with a growth of 7.4% over that in the same period of the previous year (Bohai Morning Post, 2012). Although the growth rate has slightly slowed, medical expenses of families are still growing.

Some people hold the idea that the medical industry should increase profits rapidly to update medical devices to be able to cure their patients more effectively. Theoretically, this goal is not wrong. However, the reality is far from this. Many public hospitals only focus on expansion and introducing new medical equipment regardless of affordability to patients. Some hospitals charge patients much higher expenses than the medical cost. It has become a social problem that a patient does not have enough money to see a doctor or may become poor because of illness. It has affected national stability and unity. How to reduce medical expenses of residents should be solved from the perspective of institutional reform. Early in 2006, in the first news conference given that year by the Ministry of Health, the spokesperson admitted that nowadays public hospitals had lost sight of their main objective and had refused to bear their proper responsibilities.

The Ministry of Health, it was stated, would vigorously implement a new policy to establish low price hospitals (Wang, 2006). The Ministry of Health realized the fact that public hospitals were not behaving properly, and criticized the practice of regarding profit as the evaluation criterion. In addition, the measures implemented by Ministry of Health aimed at easing the heavy burden of some patients received a warm welcome from the Chinese people. In order to change the unsuitable situation of medical services, on one hand, the government should reorganize health care institutions to establish different-level hospitals and should regulate the payment mechanism; on the other hand, China should establish a joint management institution joining government and society in order to promote sports activities and to strengthen people's physique.

Deficiencies in the Medical Management System

Before reform, most of public hospitals were funded by the government with the purpose of protecting the health of the people. As institutions and state-owned enterprises offered public health services, public officials and workers of state-run factories were supplied with free drugs. However, this medical insurance system had obvious deficiencies with low efficiency and staggering waste. The reform of the medical system was implemented thoroughly, and a market mechanism was introduced. Although the intention and practice of these reforms was undoubtedly correct, the reform actions were impeded by Pan-Marketization ideology.

Unsuitable measures of health care reform as China's reform have been carried out, and the reform has faced a lot of difficulties. Owing to the significant changes in the structure of state-owned units, the coverage of public security has been narrowed. The old system was not working, while the new system is facing resistance in operation. And the inadequacies have been expanded rapidly as the market economy system has advanced.

For example, the information released by the Administration Department of State Food and Drug and Drug Safety Supervision Department, the reported number of adverse drug reactions has been growing. The number was 173,500 in 2005, with an increase of 300 times as compared to that in 1988 which was 500 (Bai, 2006). In 2010, the reported number of adverse drug reactions was 692,904, with an increase of 8.4% over that of the same period of the previous year; new and serious reports tell it as 109,991, with an increase of 16.3%, accounting for 15.9% of the total number, showing a stable growing trend (People's Daily, 2011). One obvious reason for such a big growth rate was opaque incident handling and a high false negative rate. Now, strict working norms have made astounding problems begin to emerge. At the same time, it indicates that some serious loopholes exist in the medical management system. The hospitals that announced themselves to be public hospitals contracted with some medical departments in the private sector. The doctors turned into "economic men", aiming at earning big money by curing people. This departed from not only the original intention of the country which was to set up public hospitals, but also contradicts the general direction of health care reform.

China's socialist system is established for happiness and health of people. So, no matter how a public hospital is operated in a complex reform environment, people's basic medical needs should be put in the first place. Because a public hospital is a unit set up by the government to serve the public needs and to provide basic medical insurance for the nation. The practice of contracting with private hospitals is not reform. Of course, it is an undeniable objective fact that the financial investment provided by the government is not enough to afford the operation of some hospitals. Therefore, we should review the direction of public hospital reform from two aspects.

Firstly, we should strive to solve the problem of lack of public input. The administrative department that has the right to control funds should adopt scientific methods to deploy resources through letting the treasury fully play its role. During the reform period, financial funds have kept growing. However, because of erroneous investment direction and mismanagement, funds have been very inefficiently deployed. The operation and management of public utilities for universal welfare should be planned carefully and implemented accurately. However, some medical management agencies do not fulfill their social responsibility, regardless of the taxpayers' interests. A lot of high-tech medical equipment is left unused with a surprisingly high damage rate.

Secondly, we must grasp what is the proper direction of health care reform. The highest standards of the medical industry will work to provide excellent service for patients and to improve health. However, some medical units seek privilege to manipulate information and right to receive medical activities, which has changed the nature of public hospitals. Some hospitals raise drug prices irrationally without considering patients' financial capacity. Therefore, the government should develop policies and take effective measures to promote health insurance to let people engage in economic construction without worry.

Some people in the medical field fail to refuse the temptation of sugar-coated bullets and become the blind followers of Pan-Marketization. The officers in the administrative departments of the State Pharmacy who accept bribes and misappropriate national assets are very harmful to the society. On November 29, 2011, the Westtown Procuratorate of Beijing announced findings concerning crimes in medicine and health during the past decade. According to the statistics from the prosecutor, there were 163 crimes which involved health service, with corruption and bribery accounting for 95.09% of the crimes. In the past decade, 179 hospital directors, department heads, chief physician and purchase and sale staff were involved in crimes. According to the prosecutors, there were three reasons for crimes in the field of medicine and health: the concentration of leadership; non-standardized financial systems; and weak enforcement of the law (Beijing Evening News, 2007). In any case, the people who committed these crimes could not escape legal sanctions.

"Angels in white" are performing a sacred work. Any practice of corruption is forbidden in the medical system. There is no doubt that, in order to correct the deficiencies in management and to put an end to economic crimes, the medical system should sing the praises of superior people and should encourage communication between colleagues. At the same time, prosecutors and judicial authority departments should coordinate closely to strengthen the supervision of the medical field.

Inadequate investment in public services in the 21st century, the world has entered the era of economic integration. Therefore, the income gap between countries has expanded. Overall, there was a significant improvement of investment in basic public services during the period of the "Eleventh Five-Year Plan". According to the work report of the Chinese government, investment in basic public services including education, health, social security, housing, and culture in 2010 increased by 19.9% over that in 2009. Based on several key indicators of basic public services in China, investment should be further increased. According to the data in 2008, the ratio of the investment in education, health care and social security to GDP was 13 percentage points below that of countries with average per person GDP lower than $3000, and 24 percentage points below that in countries with average per person GDP between $3000 - $6000 (China News, 2011).

According to the "Blue Book of Public Service" released by the Chinese Academy of Social Sciences on July 17, 2011, housing, social security, employment and medical care received the most concern. The survey showed that the evaluation of basic public services by the public was quite low, but still in the bearable range. Nanning invested about 37% of its GDP on basic public service, while the investment of Hohhot, Jinan, Lhasa, Shantou and Urumqi did not exceed 1% of GDP (Lianhe Morning Post, 2011). As medical and health services are directly related to the health of people, the government should increase investment in these areas.

In order to solve the problem exiting in the current medical services system, some policies are recommended. First, the government should increase the investment in medical services to provide public with better medical services and strengthen the responsibility in medical regulatory system. In the field of general medical service, the government should strengthen its responsibility of funding and allocation. Since the reform and opening up, the direct or indirect reason of the medical service problems is the declining proportion of governmental investment in total medical service expenditure. On the other hand, government should strengthen its intervention in the medical service system. Second, more draconian policies should be formulated and implemented for cracking down on the popular corrupt practices that threaten the health care reform. During these years, there have been many problems in medical services field. Prosecutors and judicial authority departments should take enough responsibility to solve the problem in the health care system and the problems of service providers, coordinate closely to strengthen the supervision of the medical field.

Third, the government should rationally design the drugs circulation mode to guarantee the security and rationality of drug circulation to maximize the benefits to the masses. Most countries in the world choose to implement separation between hospital and pharmaceutical operation. The practices of other countries prove that it is good for the development and advancement of medical technology. What's more, the separation between hospital and pharmaceutical operation can cut the economic interests between hospital, doctors and pharmaceutical operators. As a result, the doctors prescribe reasonably according to symptoms instead of aiming at selling expensive drugs to patients.

Environmental Pollution Issues

The Rio Declaration, the Climate Change Convention, the Biological Diversity Convention and other important documents adopted by the United Nations Conference on the Environment and Development in June 1992 delivered a warning that the survival of humanity is facing ecological security issues because of alarmingly increasing environmental degradation. After the mid-20th century, global ecological deterioration has been expanding mainly because of human unscientific styles of production and life. The natural environment of China is quite grim if one considers the gradually worsening of global warming. After the arrival of the 21st century, ecological security has been prominently placed in front of the countries across the globe. The concept of ecological security is the natural self-evolution of the ecosystem, which people depend on for their survival and development. More specifically, when the system, including water, soil, atmosphere, forests, grasslands, oceans, and biological systems, etc., can sustain human society and economic development, the global or local ecology is secure. During the period of the "11th Five-Year Plan", China will build a resource saving and environment friendly society as an important implementation of a people-oriented and scientific concept of development. Under the circumstances of rapid economic growth and a significant increase in the consumption level of the public, each region and department will continue to intensify environmental protection efforts, and they will have made positive progress in environmental protection due to a series of major policy measures taken by the government.

There has been a significant increase in public awareness of environmental protection. The achievements of China's environmental protection work in the "Eleventh Five-Year" period can be summed up in nine aspects: fulfill the task of reducing emissions of pollutants; make efforts in promoting economic development; comprehensively promote the preservation of rivers and lakes; explore the establishment of the prevention of air pollution and control mechanisms to manage air pollution; concentrate on the management of prominent environmental problems, such as heavy metal pollution impacting on people's livelihood; steadily promote nuclear safety and radioactive pollution; constantly improve the laws, regulations and policies regulating environmental standards; and effectively strengthen the enforcement supervision of those responsible for maintaining environmental law (Environmental Alliance of China, 2012). In short, China's environmental protection during the "11th Five-Year Plan" has experienced a huge change from theory to practice. Only through the participation of the whole society will the development of environmental protection have a lasting power.

From the point of view of economic theory, the ecological environment belongs to the public. Nobody can own ecological environment and people do no need to pay for living in the ecological environment. The producer cannot obtain normal returns from his investment, and consumers can consume with no need to cover costs. Then, in the economic activities of the Pan-Marketization, the protection and construction practices of the ecological environment will also face heavy resistance.

Three Wastes of Industry Causing Pollution

Since the reform and opening up, China has accelerated the pace of industrialization, and the same is true with regard to economic advancement. At the same time, the "three wastes" pollutants produced by industry have had an extremely profound influence on the environment. At present, China ranks first in the world as to industrial emissions. The management of environmental pollution places intense pressure on China.

Because of the historically accumulated effect of environmental pollution, the lax environmental governance, and the frequent occurrence of safety accidents, and so on, China has entered a high-incidence period of accidental environmental pollution. The degree of the Yangtze River pollution is high and has never been seen so in history. After the Songhua River pollution incident happened on November 13, 2010, the number of abrupt environmental incidents occurring in China was up to 76, happening on average every second day (Gao, 2011).

Hindered Formulation of Environmental Protection Laws and Regulations

The trial implementation of Environmental Protection Laws has proceeded for 32 years since 1979. China's environment has not only been protected, but has become worse and worse. Therefore, there have been many scholars who have said that the environmental protection law is one of the worst laws about effectiveness in contemporary Chinese society. For many years, appeals for the revision of the environmental protection law have been loudly heard, but actual progress is nil. The revised draft of the environmental protection law was submitted to the National People's Congress in early November 2011. It is a substantial step, although there is still a long way to go (Bocai Website, 2011).

In the development of humankind, the initial liberation is to conquer nature, to get rid of material oppression, and to make a broad space for social progress. The second is to love nature, to seek a harmonious way in coexistence with nature to lay a foundation for sustainable development. The ecological balance of a country and its prosperity are closely linked. The process of the first liberation is long. As well, the process of the second liberation is hard. To obtain a fresh start, we must abandon the market economy concept of Pan-Marketization; we should reflect on a productive and ecological guiding policy; we should adjust unreasonable economic structures, and cease fixing on economic growth as the only goal of production; and we should strengthen infrastructure construction in order to maintain ecological balance.

Why the industrial pollution is so terrible in China? And why the formulation and implementation of environmental protection laws and regulations are so hard? There are some reasons behind the two questions. The first reason is the current loose environment protection laws. The second is single goal of pursuing economic growth while ignoring almost everything else. Of course, environment is no exception. In this case, how do we settle the urgent problem for balancing the ecological system? Firstly, the government should be guided by the scientific concept of development to implement a comprehensive, coordinative, and sustainable development strategy. It also should develop the overall urban plan comprehensively and carry out urban construction and environment remediation progressively to satisfy residents' needs of living environment. Secondly, the government should seize the hotspot of local environment, and then manage the environment in a planned and systematic way. Thirdly, the government should improve the regulation and policy support to solve the disputes in environmental law enforcement and pollution dealing.

Reform should be People Oriented

Following the basic principles of Marxism-Leninism, Mao Zedong, as the representative of the first generation of the Communist Party's leaders of China, has led the Chinese people to successfully carry out a social revolution and has established the People's Republic of China, a country in which the people are the masters, and where the Party has laid the social-economic foundation for initial industrialization. Many major changes have happened in the strong feudalistic superstructure. These changes have been caused by the establishment of a Chinese economic foundation that has made public ownership as the mainstay, while the social superstructure has also been repeatedly adjusted according to reforms, to adapt to the evolving social-economic infrastructure. Every adjustment and reform involving these two aspects has been to resolve various existing contradictions and conflicts. The reform and opening up policy implemented by Deng Xiaoping, the representative of the second generation of the Communist Party of China's leading group, still constantly adjusts and reforms the social superstructure in order to promote the development of the social and economic infrastructure, and for guiding the Chinese people to embark upon the path of wealth.

The new generation of collective leadership with Comrade Hu Jintao as general secretary of the Communist Party of China has inherited Deng Xiaoping Theory and the important thinking of the "Three Represents". They have summed up the experience of reform and opening up during the past 28 years, and have restored and developed the Party's fine traditions. They have also emphasized the perspective of scientific development to guide the development of socialism with Chinese characteristics, aiming at building an innovative country. The ultimate purpose has been, in order to seize the opportunities and challenges brought by the integration of the global economy in the 21st century, that the nation needs to aggregate the power and wisdom of all the people to develop a creative labor market, and to constantly enhance the comprehensive strength of the country to meet the nation's historical task of revival.

Implementation of new policies in order to maintain the sustained, steady and rapid development of the emerging economy is necessary to be taken to respond to the changing and complex international situation. To this end, we must deepen the reform of matters incompatible with the economic development in accordance with national institutions. We should rationalize the relationship between management departments, and we ought to coordinate administrative command and economic operation. We should also resolve the contradictions that affect the building of a harmonious society and mobilize all positive factors, etc.

Analyze Contradictions and Discern the False from the Genuine

The elaborate analysis described above shows that the reform and development of China is indeed entering a historic new stage presently. At the same time, China is facing some recent problems that it has never encountered before. The so-called reforms reflect public opinion, that is, the public's overall assessment of the situation of developmental change is to look carefully at the work of the past and to carefully and meticulously make plans. China's economic and social system need to be further improved; the economic and social reforms also need to be further promoted. Under this set of environmental circumstances, some of the problems that have existed in the reality of economic and social life have deteriorated sharply, which has also exposed serious defects in the reform process, the success of which depends on major theoretical concepts and policy measures. Economics had done some summarization and explanation in the past.

For example, first, social conflicts caused by the widening gap between rich and poor, the unfair distribution of wealth, and the proliferation of administrative corruption has gradually increased, and has aroused a strong dissatisfaction on the part of the people when facing real-life negative phenomena. Second, a legal environment necessary for normal operation of a modern market economy has been long delayed. Third, basic education and social security and other public services provided by the government are steadily shrinking. Fourth, the extensive method of growth adapted to the traditional socialist economy is difficult to transform to an intensive growth mode (Fu, 2006). In this case, the problems of China's reform and development broke out during 2004 to 2005. This situation indicates that we must seriously reflect on the achievements and shortcomings of China's reform, as well as the challenges we are facing now and will face in the future. At this moment, every citizen and every economic actor has the responsibility for providing their own professional thinking on this.

Of course, every historical stage of every nation has had problems and contradictions because life is a contradiction and contradictions constitute life. However, the preceding simple analysis shows that China's economic and social conflicts suddenly have become visible in recent years. The most important reason for this is that the ideological trend of “Pan-Marketization" has stirred up radical economic reform measures that have induced large numbers of illegal actions in violation of the rules and regulations. Therefore, there is no doubt that Pan-Marketization will intensify economic and social contradictions. Many facts have proved that a variety of the propositions of Pan-Marketization are faux reforms packaged with market economy theory. They seem to reform thoroughly, but, they can be labeled as sham reforms. They are trying to steer China down a road which leads to true reform. The most typical economic outcomes are income, education, health care, housing, employment, etc., which are closely related to people's lives; however, these are ignored. Irregular economic activities, irrational administrative and non-scientific production operations simultaneously appear in Pan-Marketization theory.

The public has failed to obtain the expected benefits from the rapid development of the economy. Many unreasonable and illegal actions happen in economic and social life and disrupt the peaceful life of people. Recently, the number of people who have begun to talk about illegal and black-market activity is on the rise.

Adhere to Principle and Maintain the Truth

How should we penetrate those hypocritical, misleading and so-called arguments of "market economy reform"? This requires fundamental analysis, pondering over events at the source, and mercilessly criticizing those arguments which have appeared under the banner of a deceptive theory. Refuting erroneous statements does not mean to merely apply labels, but, also describing the painful lessons Chinese people have learned in the past. For example, cracking down on some person or advocating the opposite route in the Great Cultural Revolution only brought chaos and eventually caused the nation to suffer catastrophe. We need to reflect on reform and to distinguish truth and falsity in accordance with facts and reason, not only to know how to maintain an excellent situation of stability and unity, but also in order to know how to explore the new channels for pushing ahead. The radical implementation of the policies of a market economy indeed has promoted a thriving business sector. Some people accordingly insist that reform is sailing smoothly, and that there is no need to reflect on the reform process. Under the instructional policy of "Let some people get rich first", "get rid of the concept of the communal pot ", and "bravely go into business", put forward by Deng Xiaoping, some people have profited from the market economy and now live a wealthy life. However, the time belonging to the last generation has passed away and things have changed sharply.

An argument dogmatizing Deng-era theory of wealth has emerged, and insists that it is the timelessly true theory. It seems that there are many ostensible reasons to say that this criterion (the primacy of wealth) is important. In fact, it is not true. Adhering to this theory of wealth does not mean that society should ignore the erroneous money-oriented tendency today due to the influence of Pan-Marketization ideologies, and it does not mean that there is no need to study the reasons for the large gap and to look for ways to narrow the gap. The persons who support this kind of argument also tout that it adheres to Marxism with Chinese characteristics and is entirely correct. In fact, this is a kind of dogmatic Marxism, which appeared before Marx. Engels had said to some French "Marxists" in the late 1870s: "I only know that I am not a Marxist"(Marx and Engels, 1976). The French "Marxists", who did not gain recognition by Marx, used dogmatism to distort and stifle the quintessence of Marxism. Marx, in this work Das Kapital, created a Socialist Political Economics, which dialectically looked at economic contradictions, but this is certainly not the end of Socialist Political Economics. History used as a mirror can tell us the truth. Starting from actual conditions in the economy, and using the Marxist method to observe, interpret and transform the world, has really combined Marxism with China's realities, and has really implemented the Deng Xiaoping Theory and the important thought of the "Three Represents", and has set up the socialism with Chinese characteristics.

Realistically observing all these Chinese factors from a macro-level, we can perceive that all market-oriented approaches do not let things get better: the wealth gap is widening, medicines are much more expensive than people can afford, etc. This situation cannot mobilize the enthusiasm of the people. In terms of economics, it is not the optimal configuration of resources, and this situation makes it difficult to build a harmonious society. In the initial stages of reform, the country faced a distressed situation. The nation's economy was on the edge of collapse caused by the Great Cultural Revolution, and China had to endure some negative effects in the short term for long-term economic indicators to surge. In contemporary society, however, the requirement of economic and social development is that the economy should be people-oriented and that comprehensive prosperity should arise across the nation.

The fact that few development indicators soar, while some others rise slowly or even retrogress falls short of the goal of building a moderately prosperous society. Development indicators are logically inter-related. Indicators of the entire system will be disordered when the internal relations get disordered. Sustainable economic growth is the only real development. A country's leadership management, in fact, should be a well-coordinated leadership management having a variety of relationships. The formation of comprehensive national strength is also generated by the collaboration of various forces. China's total economy is still not strong enough. It needs to continually and vigorously develop productive forces. Nevertheless, increasing productivity must rely on the optimal allocation of capital, technology and labor, and a society can never have an efficient allocation of resources without coordination.

In short, a scientific and reasonable allocation is particularly important when the reform reaches a certain level. Because this relates to the fairness of society and to the long-term stability of society, it eventually determines the development of the ecological environment. Are all members of society allowed to enjoy the fruits of development based on their abilities and contributions to create a harmonious, happy and peaceful society? On the other hand, does the nation continue to allow some people to grab the wealth of society, resulting in the disparity between the rich and the poor and eventuating in reform which is sidelined and which will eventually endanger social justice, stability, and which will increase the disharmonious factors present in Chinese life today? In this regard, Hu Jintao, the General Secretary of the Chinese Communist Party, and Wen Jiabao, the Premier of the State Council, have given a clear answer at different periods and occasions.

In the planning proposals of the "12th Five-Year Plan", in order to center on energy conservation and emission reduction, to improve incentives and to improve restraint mechanisms, to accelerate the construction of resource-saving, to encourage environment-friendly production methods and consumption patterns, to enhance the capacity for sustainable development, and to raise the level of ecological civilization, the Chinese Communist Party has pointed out that we should vigorously build a harmonious society through implementing the scientific concept of development to establish a green, low-carbon development concept. Here you can clearly see that the previous simple, disharmonious, and environment-unfriendly development concept has been completely abandoned, having been replaced by the green and sustainable development concept of harmony between man and nature. Development is the mainstream of society, which is a historical necessity. The Chinese Communist Party in its landmark literature clearly indicates that we cannot develop at the expense of other people's rights of subsistence and development. This stage of development must be built on the foundation of harmony creating a dynamic and just target, and marching towards a relatively stable path of development within the limits of social tolerance and historical license. Therefore, we must continue to make efforts to promote the process of reform to improve the socialist institutions of China. This approach is the scientific and harmonious development concept that we should strongly advocate.

Eradicate the Old and Forge Ahead

Varieties of proposals, theories and ideas have emerged in the reform process. Reflecting on the process of reform, and establishing a new concept is not only a process of theoretical explorations and continuous advancement, but also the process of the full release of labor productivity. Some people refuse to criticize the argument of Pan-Marketization, and refuse to criticize it as negative nonsense in its evaluation of the market economy. They tend to attribute errors which have occurred such as high education fees, hospital charges, etc., to distorted market economic theory. These people seem to have forgotten a large number of evil consequences in the field of distribution, health care, education, and environment and in other fields, which have led to the pan-market economy. It's dangerous for policy makers to understand an economic theory only vaguely, and then to merely use it in general. The concept is correct which states that some people should get rich through labor, as a first step. However, the severe polarization of wealth, namely the ever-widening income gap between urban residents and rural residents and the Gini coefficient having almost exceeded a reasonable value of around 0.4, is not good news. The gap is so large that it will breed hatred for the rich if there are not taken certain effective measures in future.

Of course, it is undeniable that there are objective factors at work in those who practice an extreme behavior. The implementation of a market-oriented operation in private schools is not wrong. People routinely criticize individual corruption in the education sector on the internet. The problems are not so serious in aspects of compulsory education, medicine and health. The time of problem solving has been delayed because of the influence of the Pan-Marketization idea. The correct direction of proper governance is that the executive departments gather and analyze these comments, formulate a comprehensive reform of economic and management systems, narrow the urban-rural income distribution gap, and provide equitable educational opportunities. When unreasonable factors are eliminated or reduced, the Chinese economy will progress naturally. Deng Xiaoping pointed out: beneficial or harmful to the realization of the four modernizations should be the most fundamental standard of measuring all work (Deng, 1994). There would be no modern industrialized countries if market economic theory is wrong. The real reason for China's troubles today is the appearance of the Pan-Marketization theory. It has disrupted the implementation of the strategic plan of the "Four Modernizations". Criticizing the spread of Pan-Marketization economics, of course, is not to deny the theory of the market economy.

For example, the idea of self-reliant economic development and hard-working practices, which China has always pursued during the leadership period of Mao Zedong, can be re-raised as the current Chinese development strategy in the face of current entrenched power and dominating hostile forces. Reintroduction of the idea of self-reliance does not mean that we should close the nation's portals to the outside, but rather it means advocating considering self-sufficiency as the nation's major driving force. Similarly, re-advocating challenging work does not mean that all people should suffer a poor quality of life, but rather it means putting an end to the tendency of fickleness, extravagance and waste in contemporary China. More and more people are aware of the negative effects brought by Pan-Marketization ideas in these years. The pace of progress will be blocked without profound understanding of the lessons of the past reforms, and if there is no analysis and critique of the Pan-Marketization fallacy, progress will be further harmed. Undoubtedly, the progress of both thought and practice is the result of the development of human civilization. Before the overall happiness of humans arises, as well as a harmonious society, objective reality needs people to reach a consensus to maintain the sustainable economic development of human society. The world is unsafe and individual countries and nations will also be not peaceful when ignoring the common problems of mankind. A catastrophic outcome should never be allowed to emerge. Criticism of pan-market thinking is necessary to prevent harm to the future. It is to declare war on behalf of progress against backwardness, and on behalf of science against ignorance.

Chapter 4

The Development of Market Economy in China

Market economy is different from the commodity economy that existed in China 2000 years ago. Its external forms and underlying meaning are mutually incompatible with the Chinese traditional culture. In the world's recent history, market economy has strongly supported the development of the industrial countries and has created an amount of wealth within a short span of 200 years, which is much more than the total wealth created by feudal society in thousands of years. By implementing market economic system within the framework of socialism, China's strength is continuously increasing and the standard of living is constantly improving. Now, China has become the second largest economic entity in the world. However, the Pan-Marketization argument confounds right and wrong and it advocates so-called economic theories which are unsuitable to China's basic conditions. Not only does it disrupt the rational development order of China's economy and society, but it also harms the basic interests of most of the people. Studying the development history of market economy can help us clearly understand that the concept of Pan-Marketization is an indefensible flaw.

Market Economy History

The formation of market economy is based on large-scale production, marketization and modern commodity economy. It is a resource allocation method. It is not only a form of social and economic operation, but also a form of social and economic development. Under the conditions of market economy, all factors of production enter into the market, with the market mechanism as the basic means of allocating resources. Commodity producers and operators of goods produce and circulate products in accordance with the objective laws of the market economy.

The Origins and Characteristics of Market Economic Theory

In contemporary industrialized countries, the market economic theory which occupies the mainstream is closely linked with capitalism and classical political economics. In the late 18th century, one of the industrialized countries, the United Kingdom, was at the eve of the Industrial Revolution. That special historical environment produced classical political economics which has a profound impact on contemporary capitalism, with an Englishman Adam Smith as its representative. From the late 15th century to the 17th century, along with the world's great geographical discoveries, capitalist economic relations appeared and developed within the European feudal countries. As the production and development of capitalist economic relations demanded large monetary capital, the greedy and bloody primitive accumulation of capital lasted for several centuries. Mercantilism was the school of economics that represented the business interests of the bourgeoisie in the primitive period of capital accumulation, and the "pre-history" of bourgeois political economy. It had a profound effect on the formation of classical political economics.

The Formation of Classical Economics

Market economic theory was emerged in the United Kingdom. Its main early concept was put forward systematically by Adam Smith. The era of Adam Smith (1723-1790) was a time where handicrafts continued to occupy the main forms of production in the UK and the economy was in the classical liberal market economy stage. It was a second stage in the development of capitalism. The first stage was the era of primitive accumulation period of capitalism. It was the primary stage of capitalism and the heyday of mercantilism in economic theory. In 1767, Hager Reeve invented the improved textile machine in England. In

1771, Kerouac successfully invented textile machine which used horsepower at first and hydraulic power later. As we all know, the emergence of the textile machine represented the transition from manual techniques to machine production in the United Kingdom and cued the development of the capitalist production mode. In 1778, Watt invented the steam engine representing the beginning of capitalism industrial machine era. Thus, capitalism began to develop rapidly from the British island to the European continent. The bourgeoisie gradually reached a dominant position in the UK.

Before Adam Smith, the prevailing British mercantilism was an economic genre which represented the commercial interests of the bourgeoisie in the period of primitive accumulation of capital. For example, an Englishman Thomas Mun (1571-1641) the representative of late mercantilism wrote two books, namely "On the Trade between England and the British East India Company" and "England's Treasure by Foreign Trade", and proposed that international trade was an important source of wealth in the United Kingdom, and summarized the Trade Balance Theory. In addition, some academic thinking about the principles of market transactions, such as personal utilitarianism of Bentham, promoting the idea that personal behavior was motivated by self-interest and self-love also appeared in the UK. Deeply influenced by mercantilism and personal utilitarianism, Adam Smith conducted a research based on personal experience and put forward early market economic theory. Adam Smith stressed that there was some invisible hand directing the management of all economic activities and the coordination of social contradictions.

In *An Inquiry into the Nature and Causes of the Wealth of Nations*, Adam Smith had a classic formulation, which states that as every individual endeavors as much as he can both to employ his capital in the support of domestic industry, and so to direct that industry that its produce may be of the greatest value, every individual necessarily labors to render the annual revenue of the society as great as he can. Indeed, he generally neither intends to promote the public interest, nor knows how much he is promoting it. By preferring the support of domestic to that of foreign industry, he intends only his own security; and by directing that industry in such a manner as its produce may be of the greatest value, he intends only his own gain, and he is in this, as in many other cases, led by an invisible hand to promote an end which was no part of his intention. Nor is it always the worse for the society that it was no part of it. By pursuing his own interest, he frequently promotes that of the society more effectually than when he really intends to promote it. I have never known much good done by those who affected to trade for the public good.

The market economic thinking of Adam Smith can be described as a laissez-faire market economy universal theory. He advocated free competition that was against any form of state intervention. He lamented that if the management of the land was owned by the government, the society would not get a quarter of the existing production. The reason is that "the government agency and agent management was negligent, wasteful and arbitrary." In 1930s, a British economist Eric Roll, wrote a very famous book named "History of Economic Thoughts" and gave a comment about the essence of Adam Smith's liberal economic theory as below: "When Adam Smith applied the rules of the natural order in economic affairs, he became a formidable opponent of the government which interfered in industrial or commercial matters in various forms. Each individual was trying his or her best to reap the maximum benefits."

Adam Smith strongly advocated the implementation of a laissez-faire policy. Did he really expect to maximize the economic and social interests? After a profound analysis, Eric Roll pointed out: Smith regarded the national non-intervention nature laws as the basis of economic policy; he was to provide a theoretical basis for the main interests of the entrepreneurial class. In western society, it was always said that Adam Smith was on behalf of the interests of a single class. It was doubtlessly correct from either historical significance or subjective terms. Adam Smith advocated the free economy and the anti-national management, which was very much in line with the needs of the emerging bourgeois. In Western economics textbooks, he was known as the Father of Economics.

In fact, the laissez-faire theory Adam Smith advocated is untenable and childish. When establishing a scientific theory of communism, Marx had conducted an in-depth study on Adam Smith's theory. He pointed out, on one hand, Smith was exploring the internal relations of the various sectors of the economy, or the hidden structure in the bourgeois economic system; on the other hand, he pointed out the contacts in competition and in the eyes of non-scientific observers who involved in the production process of the bourgeoisie. Adam Smith saw only the appearance of things, not the true meaning. The reality is that when everyone is seeking the best interests, they will tend to damage the interests of others. Not only can the community not achieve maximum benefit, but also the society is likely to fall into chaos.

The era that Adam Smith said that the invisible hand guided all economic activities, was the era during which the western capitalist primitive accumulation period had long been over and the past years was a bloody hell for most people and a paradise for few selfish people. Looking back the events happened in history, such as the brutal British Enclosure Movement, Black slave plantation system, Western Gold Rush and the blood and sweat labor system in 18th and 19th century, the invisible hand sounds gorgeous. But this wantonly waving hand also produced endless human tragedy. History is a mirror that lights up the true colors of the laissez-faire market economy movement. Modern China must not allow the kind of beautiful Pan-market-oriented economic theory run amok.

From the views of the balance between individual and collective interests, if everyone contributes a little love, the world will become a better one. But if everyone becomes selfish, the society will certainly be disharmonious. In the ancient Chinese sage Confucius perspective, the highest purpose of political thought is that the world is shared by people. The society should select people of high moral character. All people must emphasize on integrity and cultivate harmony atmosphere.

So, people not only take care of their own parents and bring up their children, but also try hard to feed the elderly until the end of their natural life span. The middle-aged people should make contribution to the society. The young children can successfully grow up. And the old man without wife, old woman without husband, and the child lost father when young, the old people without sub, and the disable people can get support. The men have occupations, and woman can get married timely. As a result, there would not be any thief, rebellion and evil won't happen, every household do not need to close the gate. It is called the ideal society.

The people all over the world are in the pursuit of common ground, and the realization of the ideal world should not rely on selfish behaviors, but the ideological guidance of the entire world as one community. And then the society can achieve harmonious development status. As such, the people become very selfish, only care about themselves and ignore the interest of other people…then intrigues and wars happen.

As people only care about themselves and their relatives, it results in wars and tragedies. In fact, a person should take the needs of others into account, and then he can achieve personal interests without infringing the interests of others. Another Chinese ancient sage, the Mencius suggested, we should care about our own parents and as well the parents of other people, at same time we should not only take care of our children but also the children of others. If we can make it happen then we can control the world easily.

Only the person who loves others as his or her family can get endorsement and support of others. But according to Adam Smith, if the invisible hand plays a full role in suppressing the intervention of the state, the individual and society can get the maximum benefit at the same time. It does not work. If each person becomes selfish and unscrupulous, it ultimately will damage their own interests. If the interests of society as a whole are completely destroyed, how to achieve the purpose of individuals that gain the greatest benefits at the least cost?

The analysis of Adam Smith on the constitution of the value of the goods is correct. He said, “labor was the yardstick to measure the value of all commodities exchange". He regarded labor as the only source of value. And the amount of labor contained in a commodity was the yardstick to measure this value. This labor theory of value is undoubtedly correct. Marx made a thorough research on Adam Smith's doctrine and gave a fair evaluation about his historical position: Adam Smith developed political economy into overall. The scope he included had been formed to some extent. Marx’s political economy critically inherited and evolved based on the classical political economy.

As China never experienced market economy but some different forms of commodity economy, so Adam Smith's theory including the mistaken views was consciously or unconsciously accepted in the country's reform and opening up process. It should be noted that the market economy is different from the commodity economy that existed in China 2000 years ago. Commodity economy is the primary form in which only commodities entered the market for commodity exchange. Market economy is a product of production socialization: (1) all the factors of production such as capital, labor, land, information, and technology and so on enter the market; (2) it forms a nationally and globally unified and not divided market. Only this way, the price signal is not blocked, and the price reflects the scarcity of resources; (3) market becomes the center of the resources allocation so that the law of value, supply and demand law, and competition law help to allocate resources and productivity, coordinate the relationship between supply and demand. As the market economy is very complex, people are looking for personal interests. There is no government that can step in to regulate the market. China's reform has proved that the rational allocation of various complex production factors, especially the national strategic resource reserves and production, must be under government’s unified intervention and deployment.

The differentiation of classical economics

Since the end of the 18th century and the early 19th century, the industrial system of the capitalist machine was basically established. At the same time, contradictions of social class were becoming increasingly acute. The classical economics founded by Adam Smith began to differentiate. One thought was the income constitution axiology which gradually developed into political economy defending for capitalist economy, and its representative was Say Jean Baptiste (1767-1832). Say lived in the era of the French bourgeoisie trying to seize power. The French utopian socialism criticized the shortcomings and contradictions of the bourgeoisie, and encouraged the struggle of the working class. The contradiction between the proletariat and the bourgeoisie became sharper. At the same time, some French economists and political activists such as Garnier were writing books to express their points of view. Say published *Introduction to Political Economy* in 1803, which was his masterpiece that advocated liberal economic views. Marx said tartly: after Garnier, Say, Jean Baptiste published his vulgar book "Introduction to Political Economy (Marx & Engels, 1972).

Say expanded some erroneous ideas of Smith and set up political economy for the defense of the capitalist economy. Marx sharply criticized that Say was the vulgarization of Smith's theory (Marx & Engels, 1972). Say established economic views which fully advocated laissez-faire based on theory of supply and demand, and production costs, against the state interference in product price and other economic activities in any ways. A central feature of Say's theory was that the effectiveness was the determinants of value. In his view, the value of all the production elements came from the value of their products. All elements have the necessary characteristics to create value: scarcity and indirect utility.

Say put forward a so-called theory of distribution from an argument that utility determined the value, and strived to promote the view "supply creates demand". He advocated that, under conditions of economic freedom, the phenomenon of insufficient supply of one product and excess supply of another at the same time would not exist forever (Say, 1983). Because of the self-regulation of the law of value, production was always conducted in accordance with the needs of the community, the general overproduction would never happen. The internal contradictions of capitalism made the value of the commodity to become the abyss capitalists faced and Say attempted to solve this dilemma encountered by capitalist production. Therefore, this argument was regarded as "Say Theorem" in the economic circles of the capitalists and became a sacred dogma of modern western economics. Say's ideas later became one of the foundations of bourgeois vulgar political economy theory. The British economist mentioned above, Eric Roll viewed Say Theorem and its disciples that they gradually abandoned the labor theory of value, and applied another different principle of interpretation; this principle excluded the remaining concepts. In technical terms, this meant that the development of a utility value theory will inevitably result in recognizing capital was productive (Roll, 1981).

What is the core idea of Say's theory? Marx criticized Say's vulgar economic concepts from a deep level, especially the theory of distribution. Say opposed the government's intervention in production and was opposed to the products flow compelled by government (Say, 1983). Say's theory tried to prove that the market economy has inherent stability; governmental intervention in the economy should be abandoned. If Adam Smith's theory of free economy was to crusade against that feudalism impeded free economic competition; it reflected the historical trend of the development of the commodity economy in a period of rising capitalism. It has the role of promoting the progress of the development of the capitalist economy. "Say theorem" directly denied the contradictions of capitalist production and consumption and thought that supply would automatically create a demand; there was no possibility of widespread overproduction crisis, and the capitalist economy could be in balance forever.

The Evolution of Market Economy Theory

Adam Smith's free competition and laissez-faire theory was popular in the United Kingdom, the United States and other capitalist countries in the early 18th and 19th centuries. It was because the enterprises existing in such capitalist countries generally were small scale. It was difficult for an individual private enterprise to hold a monopoly in the market, so the set of theories were feasible under that historical circumstance. Owing to the widespread implementation of the Adam Smith's free-market economic theory, Western countries' social productivity was higher than ever before, achieving rapid development of science and technology, and a sharp increase in material wealth. However, by the mid-19th century, the development of capitalism had created many large enterprises whose monopoly had become increasingly evident. The problem of the market economy also became prominent. The characteristic of the market economy was that resources and wealth kept flowing from low efficiency to high efficiency.

Therefore, it caused serious bankruptcy, unemployment, and polarization. Private ownership of capitalists with small business owners as the main society had large conglomerates, which is different from Adam Smith's new capitalist society. Capitalist exploitation was more brutal than ever before. Labor workers became the talking machine. This also meant that Adam Smith's theory of free competition failed. Because of the seriously unfair society, early western capitalist society was facing surging workers movement. The confrontation between employers and employees became fiercer and fiercer and the society tended to be turbulent. In this background Marx put forward the theory of the socialist economic system and socialist revolution, aiming at promoting planned economy which advocated equal interests in the community.

What is the basis for doing it? Adam Smith demonstrated that the market economy was not a panacea, and had some limitations like any other economic systems, such as: (1) competition in the market could not always be perfect competition, and imperfect competition had a greater proportion of economic activities. (2) The phenomenon of increasing returns to higher scale may lead to monopoly. (3) There were incomplete externalities and public goods in economic activities. (4) The allocation in the market economy could not be fair. (5) Owing to the presence of irrational individual economic behavior, transaction risk caused fluctuations in the economy. About the historical role of capitalist market economic system, the founder of the theory of communism, Marx made an objective evaluation: bourgeois society is most complex and the most developed production organization in the history. At the same time, he also issued a warning to the limitations of economic system, "If the argument that bourgeois economic category contains a form which was suitable to all the other social forms was right. Then, this could only be understood in a certain sense. The final form of historical development was always built on the development of past historical forms. As historical development only self-criticizes under specific conditions, it always one-sided understands the past forms (Marx and Engels, 1962).

The development of history is a continuous process, so is the development of an economic system. It was no longer the private enterprises style economic structure in the 1870s (Hobsbawm, 1999). Now, the United States still pursues Keynesianism which advocates massive government intervention in the economy. It is very different from the market liberal economy of Adam Smith. Some people developed the government intervention theory of the Keynesian theory and formed the Post-Keynesian school. The reason is that the capitalism in the 19th century was classical naive capitalism and primitive accumulation stage, in the form of "free market capitalism." In the 20th century, especially in the second half of 20th century, the capitalist economy had fundamental changes. Government interfered more and more in the economic affairs.

Success of the Socialist Market Economy

In the first half of the 20th century, some politicians and scholars in western capitalist countries reflected on the reasons for recession and learned from the successful experience of the emerging socialist countries in the post-World War II. The brilliant success of building socialism of the former Soviet Union, Eastern European countries and China, the early planned economy and the great power of the social security system, as well as the resolute struggle of the working class and the revolutionary party in capitalist countries shocked upper representatives of the capitalist countries. In the process of trying to come up countermeasures, the upper representatives in capitalist countries were forced to learn a lot of excellent management experience of socialism in the Cold War within the socialist camp. Under the control of executive power and the premise of the capitalist exploitation system, Britain and other countries have carried out many social and political self-improvements, aiming at demoralizing and conditionally easing the domestic revolt of the working class. The major capitalist countries got rid of the dying plight after getting the excess profits from information technology. The country's economy slowly recovered. Errors within the socialist camp also provided an opportunity for capitalism to flourish.

In the 1930s and 1970s, market economy countries faced two global economic crises and suffered great losses. So, the market economy countries became painfully aware of the fact that the market mechanism had its natural defects and that the government must use macro-economic control to operate the market. After the 1980s, the morphology of the market economy transitioned from a free market economy to a modern market economy on a global scale. This is known as the control of invisible hand and visible hand. The invisible hand controlled the micro field and played the role of stimulant.

On the other hand, visible hand controlled macro-areas and played the role of coordinator. According to the trend of the global economic system reform, the capitalist countries with the United States as their representative, are trying to strengthen the governmental function, seeking effective interventions of government in economic operation. Although there are some conservative representatives in western countries who are stubborn and dogmatically insisting on the idea of Smith; their intention is not purely for economic interests. They believe that the executive intervention is detrimental to social democracy and freedom. In short, the historical changes in the economic system show that the market economy has two sides. It is not only an invisible hand which promotes the development of human beings, but also an invisible "foot" which impedes the pursuit of personal interests.

The socialist countries, with China as their representative, have developed socialist market economy with Chinese characteristics by introducing market economy theories and implementing reforms. Over a period, China made great efforts to shift from a planned economy to a new policy. Chinese government should timely develop and implement the most appropriate and comprehensive strategies according to the actual situation in China, the development of the implementation of the benefits of the best strategies and policies. In the process of establishing socialist system, China has explored some unique economic theories and economic policies, and the practice has proven that these theories and policies are effective and consistent with Chinese people's interests.

Neo-liberal Penetration in China

In "Das Kapital", Marx pointed out that the most fundamental contradiction of capitalist system was the contradiction between socialized production and private ownership of the products. The intensification of this contradiction would cause economic crisis and production stagnation, which lead to social chaos and world-wide turmoil and wars. The internal mechanism of the capitalist system only creates and exacerbates the conflict, so this system will inevitably die and be replaced by the new socialist system. History has proved Marx's brilliant thesis.

Neo-liberalism

During 1974 and 1975, the contradiction between large-scale socialized production and private ownership was re-intensified in the capitalist countries, which led to a cyclical new world economic crisis, namely the new economic crisis in the form of stagflation phenomenon in Western industrialized countries. Keynesian interventionist policies failed to rescue the economy, so the politicians and tycoons of the capitalist countries were eager to seek a solution to solve the dilemma. In 1978, the American economists, Rose and Milton published "Free to Choose", that criticized the Keynesian interventionist economic policy, and attempted to find out a solution which not only maintained the capitalist system, but also eliminated the new cyclical economic crisis. And then, many other scholars tried to find out solution from a new perspective, such as Friedman's monetarist policies, Lucas rational expectation theory and supply-side theory. This trend of thought is called Neo-liberal ideas in the West. As their representatives and believers gathered in the University of Chicago, it is also known as the Chicago School (He, 2004). These people advocated and interpreted the free economy of Smith and Say, and opposed to Keynesianism. Therefore, they were also known as the Post Keynesian Revolution. After a period, neo-liberalism spread around the world and penetrated in China, attempting to influence the reform and opening policy of China.

The neo-liberal "beautiful new world"

Neoliberal writings discussed money supply and monetary policy and utilized mathematical formulas such as monetary equation and the Cambridge equation to analyze the changes in the economy. The book "Free to Choose" published in 1979 was written by the former president of the American Economic Association, Friedman. Friedman was also an economics professor at the University of Chicago, who worshipped free economic operation and Smith's invisible hand. He said that the "hand" was his imagination. In this way, voluntary actions of millions of people can be coordinated through the price system, without the guidance center (Friedman, 1982). In the "Free to Choose", Friedman wrote, Voluntary transaction dominates the economy; the inside has the potential to promote prosperity and human freedom. It may not take full advantage of its potential in these two areas, but as far as we know, the main organization form of prosperous and free society must be voluntary trade... free trade is a necessary condition for prosperity and freedom (Friedman, 1982).

Friedman is a leader of the neo-liberal monetarist. In his view, the fundamental flaw of the socialist system is the national plan, which was contrary to the "voluntary transaction" law. He strongly advocated liberal economy and opposed to the socialist system. He won the Nobel Prize in Economics. An economics professor named Xijun Gao who was from Taiwan, China, wrote a book entitled The World of Economics, aiming at making Friedman's monetary theory easier to understand. Xijun Gao describes the Paradise Model of neo-liberalist as below: the government control is reduced to a minimum; people's incentive reaches the highest; consumers have enough information to make an informed choice. The manufacturers should be allowed to expand when in benefit, and allowed to bankrupt when in losses; there is no deficit in governmental budget, the money supply should be stably controlled; give cash when poor people apply for relief; give tax cuts when the rich create wealth; Personnel capital goods can flow freely in domestic without national intervention and limitation of other countries; In a fair competition, efficiency is more important than the fairness, freedom is more important than equality.

This Beautiful New World is wonderful and extremely harmonious, and the road to this world is the free market economy. About how to enter it, Gao further commented that Adam Smith used the concept of invisible hand to point out that everyone directed the operation of the economic activity in the pursuit of self-interest. It resulted in consequences of self-interest and win-win - price mechanism. But this invisible hand was not as wonderful as described.

Facing the Great Depression in 1930, the political sector – the visible hand - had no choice but interfere. On the one hand, it brought a change in the capitalism nature of the Western world; on the other hand, it made Keynesian theory be popular for five decades (Gao, 1987).

The results of implementing "neo-liberalist"

In the 1980s, the neo-liberal economic thoughts were quite active in the Western world, and had a major impact on the governmental decision-making in the United States and European countries. Ronald Reagan and Margaret Thatcher ever applied neo-liberal thoughts in economic policies and actual economic and social affairs. Such policies focused on two points: first, to minimize government function and advocate libertarianism; second, the economic system tended towards privatization and liberalization. However, the results of the implementing neo-liberal economic policies did not reach rulers' expectation and did not produce the paradise described by Professor Friedman. For example, in order to get rid of the "stagflation" of the economy, Margaret Thatcher government of the United Kingdom launched a privatization campaign, attempting to stimulate British economy. But during the implementation of this policy, the number of unemployed in Britain suddenly increased. Workers set off a strong strike to protest the capitalists' brutal exploitation of workers. In 1979, British Steel workers went on strike. During 1983 and 1984, coal miners set off a large wave of strikes. The social contradictions in Britain were suddenly intensified. The ruling class fell in a panic, and blamed each other. The strikes of coal miners led to a 1% decrease in gross national product of the United Kingdom and £4 billion loss in international balance of payment. The British government was forced to suspend the privatization process.

The substance of new system school

There is a genre of neo-liberalism called "new institutionalism" represented by North and Ronald Harry Coase. North systematically put forward the theory of Institutional Change in the books "Structure and Change in Economic History" and "System Innovation and United States Economic Growth". On the premise of "economic man" assumptions, North believed that all people were selfish and pursuing personal utilitarianism and free competition. It was not only the basis of the system, but also the motivation of institutional transition. North stresses that Institutional equilibrium was such a state that when the bargaining power of the actors and the contract negotiations of overall economic exchange were given, no actor can get profit from using resources in re-establishment of the contract (North, 1994). This argument was carried out in the situation of Pareto marginal optimal equilibrium which did not exist.

The Institutional Change Theory proposed by North has a clear purpose. He believed that the main clue of economic history is the history of institutional change. It is not only the process of institutional change, but also the process of political behavior. North attribute the economic growth of the Western world to the incentive mechanism provided by the capitalist system. In his view, the reason for the rise of the Western world is the development of an effective economic organization. Effective economic organizations need to build institutional facilities and determine the ownership of property to continuously lead the individual economic efforts to become social activities (North, 1988). He also specifically disclaimed that if a social ownership system clearly defined the exclusive right of everyone, then the community would be more innovative. And this process was a systematic innovation process. As the school of New System Economics speaks highly of capitalist system, it gained an acclaim from the capitalist world.

The other important thought of New System School is the "Property Rights Theory". In 1937, Ronald Harry Coase published an economic paper named "The Nature of the Firm", and first proposed the concept of "transaction costs", establishing the initial theory of Property Rights System Change. Coase described the effectiveness of property rights that was embodied in the capitalist system. It enabled people to automatically know what to do and how to get benefit in the transaction process, and ultimately achieve maximum benefits. In 1960, Coase published another paper *The Problem of Social Cost*, and in 1988 published *Notes on The Problem of Social Cost*. He systematically discussed the relationship between property rights, transaction costs and resource allocation, which is called the Coase Theorem by his followers.

Objectively speaking, the Property Rights Theory made up for the theoretical errors made by the capitalist political economist and played a role of stabilizing capitalist economic system. Coase clearly expresses his aim of studying property rights arrangement is to create a theory which can help us analyze the determinants of the production's institutional structure (Coase, 1990). Coase's statement about the changes in property rights system attempted to demonstrate that privatization can stimulate economic development. The theory of New System School has certain significance for China's economic reform. However, some Chinese academicians regard it as a treasure and deny its class nature and effectiveness, attempting to change the structure of property rights in China. This approach is absurd, and the consequences are extremely bad.

The "Shock Therapy" of the New System School

The most powerful historical evidence of New System School's political tendency is that, during 1980s and 1990s, arguments about the change of ownership were spread to the former socialist countries in Eastern Europe to provide a theoretical basis for the privatization movement there. For example, some United States scholars who had obvious ideological tendency continued spreading liberal economic ideology to the former Soviet Union and designed the so-called reform plan to improve economic efficiency, such as "Sachs Shock Therapy" and "Harvard 500 Days Program" to induce them to carry out the reform of property rights. However, the total privatization economic reform applied by the Gorbachev - Yeltsin government resulted in very serious consequence. The economy of Russia collapsed; the society fell into chaos and people's living standard declined sharply. The property rights revolution in the former socialist countries in Eastern Europe also resulted in a decline in production, the depressed market, and economic and social chaos.

After nearly 20 years of sweeping privatization reform, the original state-owned enterprises in the former Soviet Union and most Eastern Europe districts were completely destroyed. The national economy lost competitiveness in the world market and the domestic market. But Ronald Harry Coase was greatly praised by the Western countries. And in 1991, Coase won the Nobel Prize for Economics. North won the Nobel Prize for Economics in 1993. After the reform of property rights and economic privatization, Eastern Europe and the Russian have become a new market for Western transnational monopolies to find new living space. Russia's strong economy and industry has generally collapsed, which provides a realistic possibility for the United States to implement the national missile defense system (NMD) and attempt to dominate the world directly. This is the outcomes and goals of neo-liberal economy, and China will never allow them to succeed.

Disguised Ideological Tool

The historical facts show that the neo-liberalism's academic atmosphere is only in appearance; it is essentially an ideological tool. Its most praiseworthy achievement in the Western world is to destroy the economies of the former socialist countries. This paper has introduced Say's theory that "supply automatically creates demand" and the government should not interfere in the economy. Say was called as the godfather of the liberal economics by Western economists.

However, Say's theory has been refuted by some Western scholars. The German economist Friedrich List (1789-1846) had systematically criticized the "liberalism" and exposed the true face of the Say's theory. He indicated that Say did not have extensive knowledge of national policies and profound observation ability, and enough political and philosophical vision, either. Based on the insights taking from others, Say tried to find examples and facts that could support his views from history, politics, and statistics as well as industrial and commercial relations (List, 1961). List was not in favor of the socialist ideology that had been popular in Europe, but he was against Say's liberalism pseudo-science. His critique is undoubtedly correct.

Although the Keynesian school of economics saved the capitalist economy for a brief period of time. Owing to the insurmountable contradictions within capitalism, the western capitalist economies had a serious "stagflation" situation again in the 1970s. So, in addition to the monetarist school, another representative genre of the United States Post Keynesian revolution, the "supply-siders" appeared. This school thought that the error of Keynes was to deny the validity of "Say's Law", and blindly implement expansionary fiscal and monetary policies to interfere in the economy which resulted in stagflation. A representative of this school, George Gilder argues that the various changes of Say's Law are the basic rules of supply-siders ...... Say's Law is important because it focuses on the supply and the ability to stimulate capital investment (Gilder, 1985). He appealed to abandon Keynesianism and to go back to the liberal economic route advocated by classical economics. Marx pointed out that vulgar economics just used bourgeois agent's view to explain, systematize and defense (Marx, 1966). The purpose of Neo-liberal economics is to cover up the fundamental contradiction of the capitalist economy.

Features of Western Contemporary Economic Entities

From the 1870s to the 1930s, the production technology of the capitalist world improved tremendously. The industrial production grew rapidly and the scales of enterprises became larger and larger. Many joint-stock companies and monopoly organizations appeared because of the increasing concentration of capital and production. Capitalism transited from free competition stage to monopoly capitalism. The founder of the world's first socialist state, Lenin, in his famous book "Imperialism is the highest stage of capitalism", profoundly analyzed the subjectivity changes of capitalism. Lenin seized the opportunity to launch a war against imperialists, and established a new socialist country in the history of mankind. He turned Marxist theory into reality.

The strengthening capitalist monopolies and the intensified economic crisis resulted in the profound changes of capitalist economic entities and the school of economics. Especially in the 1930s, the economic crisis of the capitalist world led to a profound social crisis, which forced Western economic powers to take some regulation policies of the new social system and gradually form a mixed economic system. Take the changes in the United States since 1930 as an example- the U.S. economy gradually changed to become a capitalist-oriented mixed economy. Both individual and government had economic influence in the market. The characteristic of most industrial sectors of the United States was that a relatively small number of large-sized enterprises rather than many small-sized competitive enterprises dominated the entire sector.

Pre-existing private ownership of the free-market capitalism changed. This form of market is called "oligopoly" by Lenin. At present, monopoly companies in the western countries have become large multinational companies. These super companies are dominating the economic lifeline of the world. The operation of Multinational Corporation is not purely economic. Administrative intervention has a strong impact on the company. In Germany, the famous Volkswagen AG and Lufthansa Airlines are multinational companies with national shares. Even in Britain, state-owned enterprises still occupy a prominent position in the national economy.

How Neo-liberal economics thoughts penetrate China

When China is implementing reform, the developed Western countries are seeking to obtain high profits from global economic integration. Some multinational companies with political background invest in China, aiming at occupying the Chinese market instead of helping the China's social construction. Out of the global strategic considerations, some Western powers are trying to carry out value penetration by introducing neo-liberal economic views in China. This is not surprising. In the entire history of the 20th century, the Western economic powers used a variety of ways to promote and implement capitalist system. For example, the United States has been selling its own values to the world. However, in fact those ideologies are not suitable to China.

Through several channels, the neo-liberalism prevailing in the United States, Britain and other countries was transited into China. Some advocates of the neo-liberal thoughts praise the change of ownership in an exaggerated manner. For example, a neo-liberal economics professor arbitrarily said that the economy of every country with rapid growth is built on the base of private enterprise system. It means that most of the productive resources are owned by the private person and are free from government intervention. He even advocated anarchism that there is no corruption if there is no government control and regulation. He also arbitrarily judged, the total elimination of government is equal to the total elimination of corruption (Zhang, 2000). This so-called theory is totally inconsistent with the reality of contemporary capitalism, and cannot find any meaningful proof in the history of capitalism.

Modernized mass production is a complex cyclic process. The efficient operation of every link needs a variety of supporting conditions to guarantee. Privatization cannot solve all the problems. The privatization of each process is unable to achieve the multinational large-scale joint operations. In the social development process, certain social superstructure is always adjusted with a certain social and economic infrastructure. The situation of economic base determines the nature of superstructure; in return, the superstructure serves the economic basis. The modern mainstream economics is Anglo-American genre, which develops ideologies and theories based on the economic activities in the United States, Britain and other industrialized countries. Many theoretical explanations and case studies are studying how to make industrialized countries more prosperous and more profitable. There is no theory studying the economic activities in developing countries until 1960s. This new theory named "development economics" observes and analyzes the market situation, investment opportunities, financial market and foreign exchange of developing countries from the perspective of outsider. Obviously, this theory is to provide advice for the industrialized countries to occupy the markets of developing countries.

Neoliberalism Influences China's Reform

Since mid-1990s, China's economic reform concept has been significantly affected by "neo-liberalism" views, especially the so-called property rights revolution of new systematics. Some people on mainland China simplistically assert that the deficient performance of state-owned enterprises is because of the unclear property rights. They think that if there is a change in the property rights system of state-owned enterprises in China, it will be able to immediately improve the production efficiency of enterprises which lag in technology. A few people are trying to develop unrealistic "joint-stock reform" program, aiming at splitting the public property rights with private person. State-owned enterprise is decomposed and eroded. The property accumulated by some units for decades are turned into private property instantly. Improving the efficiency of production is a complex process. Property rights reform is just a part of the process. The key to improve social productivity is the science and technology innovation. Science and technology are primary productive forces. Changes in property rights cannot be a substitute for inventions.

The more fundamental problem is that property rights are the most central element in the economic entity. The changes in the property ownership have a significant impact on the normal operation of the economic entity. The nature of the economic entity undergoes a qualitative change after a change in property rights. For example, in a period, under the instigation of the Pan-marketization thoughts, some people advocated to trade in the market for technology in mainland China. In order to import the technology of the Western countries, some state-owned enterprises gave up property rights and turned into a joint venture. Finally, these state-owned enterprises were merged by foreign enterprises. We can see that the contemporary capitalism is not the laissez-faire capitalism which is built based on so-called clear property rights, but capitalism which advocates foreign expansion, mergers, and monopoly.

After China's state-owned enterprise turned into a wholly foreign-owned enterprise, the actual operation is not as per the expectations. As these state-owned enterprises lost market, it meant that they also lost technology and rights of ownership. Among all the radical reform practices influenced by Pan-Marketization thoughts, the measurement of "clear property rights" is out of control, resulting in the fact that the reform of old system aiming at improving state-owned enterprise effectiveness does not reach the expectation. The contemporary socialist reform should keep learning, so that the people recognize the true face of neo-liberalism. Only in this way, the economic construction can get development.

The Loss of State Owned Assets

A few economic powers always want to impose their own values to the Chinese people. Under the cover of neoliberalism, these countries admire laissez-faire economic policies and advocate that privatization of enterprise property rights is the only way to develop productive forces. It is easy for the people with philosophical knowledge to know that, although the superstructure has a dynamic role on the economic base, there is no mutual relation between the superstructure and the economic base. Neo-liberalism is just a slogan and ideology and can never become an active and effective economic policy. The neo-liberalism theory of Economics Anglo-American genre was born in the Western industrialized countries.

It is the abstract principles of economic and social activities in the United States and Britain. Most of the teachers and advocators live in the industrialized countries, or receive education in those countries. As a result, these theories aim at maintaining economic interests of those countries. People who think independently will see through neo-liberal's intention is to replace socialism "opening up thought" with capitalism liberalization and attempt to bring socialist economy into the orbit of the capitalist economy. Some people in China are interested in analyzing China's social and economic life by capitalism theologies. It does not conform to China's national conditions.

Table 4.1

Registered Unemployed and Unemployment Rate of China Urban

Unit：million people；%

Year / Item	1990	2000	2007	2008	2009
Urban registered unemployed people	3.83	5.95	8.3	8.86	9.21
Urban unemployment rate	2.5	3.1	4．0	4.2	4．3

Data Source From: The National Bureau of Statistics (2010), China Statistical Yearbook, Beijing: China Statistics Press.

China has the largest population in the world. Most of the rural population does not have any social security. In the past, the state-owned enterprises provided medical, pension and other support systems to maintain the urban security and stability. However, after the radical restructuring of state-owned enterprises, many enterprises went bankrupt and many workers were laid off simultaneously (see Table

4.1). Although the increase in unemployment was not caused by the restructuring of state-owned enterprises, the continuing increase in the number of unemployed people are related to the restructuring.

At the same time, many new labor forces entered the job market, labor and social security and employment immediately become very prominent issues. There is a lot of pressure in economic, social and political fields. We must recognize the fact that certain social economic bases will produce corresponding culture and ideology. This consciousness not only has the potential to surpass the base, but can also imprint the base. When introducing Western market economic theory, we must distinguish the theories of general objective laws of market economy and the capitalist ideology. We must try our best to prohibit the capitalist ideology impeding the development of China market.

Awareness of Different Biases

Neo-liberalism became popular in the contemporary international community, especially after the disintegration of the former Soviet Union. However, history is always full of twists and turns. An American scholar thinks that the collapse of the Berlin Wall and the Soviet Union does not mean the victory of liberalism. On the contrary, liberalism began to fall into decay. After 1989, the world has entered the era of post-liberalism. Various political trends and social phenomena in globalization continue to change, and the pattern of Cold War history will not be re-staged again (Wallerstein, 2002). Fortunately, in the tortuous and complicated process of reform, the top leadership of the Chinese Communist Party and the Chinese government grasped the general direction of reform and keep a clear head of the liberal economic theory. All the utopian system innovation was suppressed, and the so-called deepening reform with privatization as the ultimate goal was abandoned.

In order to develop the socialist market economy with Chinese characteristics, the government and people should explore the law of the scientific socialist market economy from the actual situation in China. We should clearly understand the "left" or “right” erroneous ideas and abandon the blind anti-foreign narrow sense of the past. Naturally, in the current case, the speech and behavior of Pan-Marketization economy should be abandoned firstly. Otherwise it is easy to get lost.

Some of the people blindly follow the free market economy. They seem to totally ignore the economic activities’ new trend, commodity production and its new characteristics in contemporary capitalist society. They follow the puerile liberal economic theory that favors privatization as suggested by Smith and Say. These people, who blindly advocate dissolution of the large state-owned enterprises, think small is good, and China should return to the puerile capitalism with small enterprises and private ownership as the main body. China's economic construction practice has proved yet again that the planned economy is not worthless. The planned economy and market economy can exist together in the market in a harmonious way. The key to the development of socialist market economy with Chinese characteristics is to combine the advantages of both market economy and planned economy. We should neither boast about the role of the market, nor overly emphasize the planned functionality.

The construction of the socialist economy must abandon the rigid contents of the old traditions and keep scientific and reasonable core factors. At the same time, under the guidance of the right theory, the government should implement economic macro-control on the major projects related to the national economy and the people's livelihood in order to unite the goal of economy and society. The national management should combine with the market regulation. We must recognize the dual character of the free economic theory. In short, government and market should have their own managing scopes and cannot be mixed up. This is exactly the standpoint of the scientific development perspective.

Rationally Apply the Principles of Market Economy

Historical facts show that the market economy does not exist in isolation, but appear and develop in a certain social system and in some historical conditions. Therefore, we need to have a scientific concept of development to follow the objective laws of market economy to seek the best resource allocation for optimizing economic and social benefits.

Correctly Guide the Operation of Market Economy

How to correctly understand the market economy? What are its essential characteristics? The simple research results above show that the first research step of market economy is to analyze its existing economic system. Simply speaking, the market economy is a kind of basic approach to disperse policy decisions based on bartering. Commodity market, as a part of the market economy, is both abstract and concrete. It is the specific performance and reaction of social economic activities since the beginning of commodity production. They would not exist without the human market. From another perspective, it is the assembly of all economic activities of human society taking the market as the goal and the starting point. In addition to the market-oriented economic activities, the humanity also has other ways and types of economic activities such as the peasants' productive labors for their own consumptions and labors of the environmental protection workers.

Therefore, from the point of view of human society, market economy can just be seen as a part of the human social economy, but not all of it. Admittedly, developing the market economy is an important aspect to promote the development of social economy. However, the market economy cannot replace the other parts of social economy. The development of human society needs the all-round advancement of all aspects. The thought of excessive emphasis on market economy economics but ignorance of other aspects of social economy - does not comply with the all-round development of human society.

Follow the Rules of Market Economy

Just like all other phenomena that have laws governing their existence, market economy also has its market operation rule which does not shift with people's subjective will. What is the market rule? The so-called market rule, in fact, is the performance of people's economic activities in the market and the market reflection to the people's economic activities. It contains two basic points: one is the supply of the market performance and its reaction to market changes; and the second is the demand of the market performance and its reaction to market changes. These two aspects of performance and reaction are reflected through the intermediary of currency. Therefore, the market rule deals with the reaction of the market supply and market demand. Simply put, the price will rise when demand exceeds supply and vice versa. These two kinds of reverse change make the relation of supply and demand remain in equilibrium.

In modern times, the most popular textbook in China is "Economics", written by Samuelson. The first chapter of this book expounds the famous market regulation principle, namely the "invisible hand theory". In the regulation of the invisible hand, economic structure and institution are adjusted automatically; resources are obtained in the most effective configuration; and there will never be excess capacity and insufficient supply in the long term. To this extent, capitalism thoroughly gets rid of the cyclical economic crisis. This view is the extension of the "Say's Law" that supply automatically creates demand. From the perspective of history, Adam Smith does not uncover the inner relation of the market discipline when he finds and expresses the market rule for the first and earliest time, limited to the social and economic conditions at then. Therefore, he regards the market rule as an invisible hand beyond people's understanding and control category.

However, with the further development of the human society and the improvement of science and technology, people not only obtain new understanding on the market and its law, but also explore some means and methods to master it, such as market research and forecasting; market supervision and control; and pricing discipline and tax regulation. Commercial institutions and government can guide the market through these means and methods, and thus weaken the decisive role of the market rule on the social economy. The Russia's implementation of "Sachs shock therapy " and "Harvard 500 Days Program" takes the market economy as the only mode of operation. The result is even criticized by economic scholars in capitalist society. In the United States, economists and government all claim to implement wide range of administrative or social regulation. Antitrust laws, industrial and social regulations, and industrial policies are the main ways through which government regulates economic structure, production and project engineering (McConnell & Brul, 2001). These regulations are meant to maintain the economic growth of the United States. They have also become the important contents of economics textbook. The purpose of those plans is clear. However, blind following behaviors only end up with failure.

Punish Illegal and Undisciplined Behaviors

All people in today's Chinese society know the market economy. In addition to the propaganda of news media, the commodity market around the land tells people that market economy is existent. Some people also treat market economy as a panacea that can settle China's social and economic diseases. It is this incorrect understanding of market function that brings a series of problems.

On June 23, 2010, the 15th meeting of the Eleventh National People's Congress (NPC) held the second plenary session. In this meeting, Liu Jiayi, the chief auditor of the State Auditing Administration, presented that the number of cases on major illegal issues and economic crimes that the audit office submitted to the state council or directly delivered to relevant departments is up to 104, involving 473 people (Lin 2010). And on December 26, 2011, the national industry and commerce administration conference held in Beijing disclosed that Chinese industry and commerce system handled 1.3895 million economic illegal cases of all kinds, valued at 26.868 billion yuan (Liu, 2011). We can see all the violators have a common motive that seeks personal gains, regardless of the situation they are in. These facts have proved that the thought that all things should be linked with benefit, money and market is wrong. This incorrect understanding can not only easily make mistakes, but in theory will lead to error propagation. The banking system is one of the most significant institutions. It is worthy of further investigation. The focus of the regulation should be placed on the following fields, namely: bad loans, real estate loan risks, asset disposal behaviors of asset management company, connected transactions of trust and investment company, credit to related interest in rural credit cooperatives and the authenticity of increase in capital and share, because the occurring rate in these areas is highly frequent and extremely harmful.

At present, there are also some social programs for public good that have been shaped by the market. It seems to prove that commercialization is more in line with the world trend. The wealth gap is widening. Education and medical treatment are prone to the development of marketization. These situations are not normal in people's basic living needs. Therefore, we need to correctly understand the market economy, to reflect from theory to practice. People cannot completely comply with the rule that development must accord to the market economy, and they cannot ignore all sorts of evil fruits brought by the Pan-Marketization. It is not sensible to give too little care to the legitimacy of the accelerated commercialization. We should look at these problems from new perspectives and cannot just let the public suffer and endure. A feasible method is to intervene in the excessive market pricing behaviors by effective policies.

Study the Model of World Market Economy

Free economy as a form of expression is not the most magical mode in economic system. The modern western countries through the actual reality have realized that the invisible hand is not the omnipotent God. The operation and management methods of market economy must be according to the actual situation of the country. Free-market economists propose the absolute exclusion of government intervention. Industrialized countries have modified the proposal. In the western countries, different market economy systems arise and the management methods are also not the same.

We might as well observe the market economy from the 17th century, the time of the embryonic stage of market economy. Different countries form different modes of market economy, because the extent and methods of intervention and the recognition to the nature of the market economy are diverse. They can be summarized as the following kinds:

Firstly, the free market economic mode of America: The market economy of the United States emerged from its special cultural and liberal tradition. The character of its operation is the highly dispersed economy. The American society opposes government intervention with economic activities in any form. However, previous governments in effect had been participating and regulating economic activities in diverse ways. The American free market economy is not entirely free.

Secondly, the welfare market economic mode of the Nordic: The Nordic countries form an organic system consisting of economic system, economic organization and social policies. The system is based on private ownership and is formed in the practice of pursuing economic efficiency and social equality. It stresses the private enterprise as the major driving force of economic development, highly developed social welfare, mutual cooperative spirit, etc.

Thirdly, the social market economic mode of Germany: Social market economy is in essence a kind of capitalist market economy based on free competition. The guideline of this economy is that government makes proper adjustment and makes the social security as the basic safeguard. After World War II, various economic policies formulated by all previous governments of Germany are basically based on it. Social market economy adheres to two basic principles: first, the main content of economic activity is market regulation. Market, as the foundation and bond in the economic operation, always is in the leading position; Second, market activities can be interned and coordinated by the state to a certain degree. The country has a function of guidance and regulation and to provide social security, providing social welfare policies of social security, justice and social progress.

Fourthly, the nation-leading market economic mode of Japan: After World War II, the emphasis of Japanese government's intervention lies in the total supply, and the bidirectional constraints between the government and enterprises. The government decreases the damage to the market and helps the enterprises as far as possible. And the country gradually forms a government-leading economic system mode that private enterprises as the foundation is guided by the government.

Fifthly, the plan-guided market economic mode of France: The planned adjustment implemented by France after World War II is the typical "mixed economy". Its rapid recovery and development of economy is the result of organic combination of the plan and the market.

Sixthly, the diversified practical economic mode of developing countries: Developing countries and transition economies are based on their own national conditions and historical and cultural traditions. These countries combine with the experience of other countries' economic development and learn the lessons for the adjustment of their economic policies. The purpose is to try to go a path of market economy development according to the nation's conditions.

From above analysis we can see that the pattern of the market economy is diversified. Each country after the world war, especially the Western capitalist countries, constantly adjusts their own economic policies to meet the needs of the development of the so-called economic globalization. They do not perfectly mimic the U.S. market economic mode. Any country's economic mode simply imitated by others is unlikely to achieve success.

Absorb the Cultural Nutrients of Humanity

Some European countries, especially Germany, sum up an appropriate regional and national economic development mode by the socio-economic practices, namely the social market economy.

Learn from the Social Market Economy Mode of Germany

After World War II, many socialist regimes arose in the eastern European countries. These countries' economies and cultures experienced a rapid development period, and had far-reaching influence. Because of the push by the organizations of the Communist Party, the socialist ideology came up to the surface in the veteran capitalist countries one wave after another. The Christian Democratic Union of the West Germany's conservative parties also proposed a guiding principle of Christian socialism. The union considered that the capitalist economic system did not meet the national and social interests of the German people, and advocated the establishment of a new economic system. This party won the election in 1949. It signed the establishment of the first cabinet of the Federal Germany, the Adenauer government. The federal government proposed the principle of "social market economy" and put it into effect. The national economy of the West Germany smoothly transmitted into the "social market economy" from the "wartime system" through the implementation of a series of reasonable policies, such as the currency reform, which laid a good foundation for the future economic development (Qiu, 1988).

From the early 1950s to the first half of the 1960s, the Federal Germany enjoyed a rapid economic growth of development just because of implementation of the social market economy. Many

Western economists call the outstanding economic achievements in this period as an economic miracle. The post-war federal government of the West Germany implemented a complete set of measures that guaranteed the people's minimum consumption and basic living standard. They were an important part of the social market economy. The main purpose was to increase the actual income and the real purchasing power by controlling money supply and financial expenses that alleviate the inflation rate. The real implementation of the social welfare system included providing subsidies to unemployed workers, and providing pensions, medical insurance to the retired or incapable workers (Zhu and Lin, 1989).

The basis of the social market economy is a mixed ownership economy. On the one hand, it exerts great emphasis on the market competition. On the other hand, it also advocates the national intervention with the economy, namely the national functions of macro-control. This regulation includes not only monetary policies and fiscal policies, but also the national plans and the government's policies, such as government relief to the unemployed. The high-speed development of the state ownership is one of the major features of the social market economy. Although this form of ownership is secondary as compared with the dominant capitalism, but it plays a significant role in the national economy, especially in the cases that the nation order goods or directly take over the low-profit enterprises and economic departments (the national defense industry for example), and the state-owned capitalist enterprises supply non-state-owned enterprises with cheap means of production. There exist huge conflicts between the China's social market economy and the Europe and Germany's, but China can still learn some meaningful experiences to avoid some of the errors.

Assess the Assumptions of the Market Economy System

Some people advocate that the liberal market economy is different from the social market economy. Free economy as a special kind of system, the internal mechanism is the market behavior of individuals who pursues the personal maximum economic interests, reaches the optimal resources allocation under the guidance of the market price. However, the market price mechanism cannot play a role in isolation. In the process of the realization of the optimal resources allocation, it also needs some preconditions: first, each market economic actor has the rights of free choices in the precondition of no harm to the interests of others; second, the individual self-interest can be coordinated with the mutual benefits of all parties.

In addition to the assumptions above, the development of modern economy and economics also require the optimal resource allocation in market economy conforming to the following conditions: (1) Complete and symmetric economic information. Buyers and sellers in the market have completely sufficient information about the content and quality of transaction. (2) Perfectly competitive market. The market has numerous manufacturers so that each size is small. Any potential competitors can enter this market without any obstacles. Each manufacturer is the price recipient and has no ability to manipulate price. (3) Constant or decreasing returns to scale. The unit cost of the product is unchanged or decreasing along with the manufacturers production scale expanded. (4) No externality. The productive and consumptive behaviors of businesses or individuals in the economic activities have no extra impacts on the external environment. (5) No transaction costs. (6) Rational economic man. Economic actors can always maximize their own welfare. The free economy cannot run without these assumptions which cannot be fully realized in the real world. Therefore, the free economy does not exist.

From the negative situations appeared at the process of China's economic reform, people have reasons to suspect this kind of people’s motivation who indoctrinates the privatization theory into China. The security of the modern developed capitalist system is on the basis of the social security system of welfare capitalism. Obviously, it is wrong to advocate the implementation of the Pan-Marketization economic system reform. The implementation of the reform of state-owned enterprises is way too radical. It breaks the old labor insurance and welfare but does not establish a feasible social security system. The historical experience of China for thousands of years shows that the emergence of a large number of unemployed populations has always been a signal of danger, and the root of the social chaos.

Avoid the Defects of Market Function

The market economy system already exists in Western countries for hundreds of years, forming many mature management methods that improve the social productive forces. However, this system still has some serious flaws, especially in the early stage of its development. On the condition that the macroeconomic regulatory is still not standardized, systemic and unsound, the intense impact force of market operation can easily bring damaging effects on the original economic harmonious relationship. The western market economic theory attached to the development of market economy undoubtedly has many excellent ideas. China's reform also confirmed that there is a lot to learn from the development experience of the Western industrialized countries. Nevertheless, we cannot accept the theory unreservedly, especially when the western world is continuously bringing innovations in it.

Since the 1990s, the western economic theory, from a macro perspective, points out that the market and the market mechanism itself have some activity boundaries, such as political boundaries, allocation boundaries, social boundaries, ethical boundaries and ecological boundaries; that is why the market economic activities in these areas often fail. The construction of socialism does not work only depending on the market mechanism, and also it cannot obtain high benefits in some key areas including the key industries adjustment of the national economy; public welfare investment projects; social security system; ecological and environmental protection. The market economy is not a panacea. Some drawbacks that happened in the current Chinese economy confirm this judgment. Capitalism is led by personal interests to apply and develop the market economy. It expands the inherent flaws of market function. Some western people suffered the pain brought by this institutional shortcoming. Although the capitalist system has not come to the door of hell, the call for reforming the system defects is growing louder and louder. Thus, with the rapid development of Internet and the rapid expansion of economic globalization, people from developed countries pay more attention to the pursuit of common interests, especially in the United States, France and Germany.

For example, both German kindergarten games and American MBA courses tell how to cultivate the concept of teamwork and cooperation. International business competition also pays attention to seek cooperation with rivals, striving to achieve a win-win solution. There will be no development of the so-called modern company if no cooperative exchanges happen, because profits are generated from exchanges. The inexperienced staff training rules in many world-famous multinational corporations prohibit the boost of individualism and selfishness. The actual operations of multinational corporations all have teamwork items. This is in fact to advocate a win-win situation, namely reaching the goal of common interests. The French economist Albert once said: The Greater Europe has created a social market economy, and China has created a socialist market economy.

Naturally, there are many differences and similarities between the two. They can become one of the magic weapons in the 21st century if they are able to integrate (Albert, 1999). We can see that the common interests meet the common requirements of the progress of human society, and make the common aspiration of mankind come true. We need to notice here that the rational utilitarianism and wealth-pursuing activities should be encouraged so that the market economy is able to provide a channel for the realization of these rational pursuits. Market economy can effectively exercise incentive mechanism to achieve a higher economic growth rate. National wealth comes from the high-efficient production. The high productivity of social labor can increase the wealth, and it will be a significant increase in the supply of goods. However, the normal operation of the market economy needs a favorable and sound legal system to provide protection. Otherwise, the regulatory role of economic leverage on resources cannot be achieved.

In a nutshell, the implementation of the market economy in China brings high economic performance. Meanwhile, its congenital deficiency is also exposed to the world, which is that the market economy can achieve the best efficiency only if the whole country is able to synchronize its actions.

Walk out from the Ideological Misunderstanding

The modern society has almost completely different economic characteristics from free economy. From real life, people clearly realize that the development of the country would suffer if the law of the market economy fully takes the place of other laws and regulations. As a result, we should make an in-depth understanding of the market economy. The reasonable development of the means of production is the main way of the future social construction. It needs to further emancipate the mind, to break through the Western neoliberalism, and to correctly distinguish the real cause of the social conflict and benefits friction and then to seek reasonable solutions.

Reduce the Opportunity Cost of Market Failure

Western economic theory summarizes the market economy as the abstract pair of supply and demand curves. These two curves rise and fall relative to each other under the guidance of price signals, and finally produce a balanced intersection point. This conclusion is only valid under some assumptions. As a matter of fact, the growth of socio-economic equilibrium involves a lot of factors. The price leverage is only one aspect. Therefore, not only is the Western economic theory defective, but the market mechanism itself is not perfect. The argument of Pan-Marketization, however, extensively boasts the function of the market mechanism, propagandizing the enforcement of fierce economic competition, survival of the fittest that help the country quickly reach the restructuring of the international economic institution. In some places, the actual reality after the "successful" enforcement is ineffective; numerous errors happened in the process.

First, survival of the fittest means fierce economic competition in the market economy. The result of strong implementation of economic competition can only exacerbate the polarization on the distribution of benefits, and increase the disparity between the rich and the poor, which is clearly not consistent with China's national traditions. Second, the coercive implementation of some global, long-term, and public-service socio-economic activities and investment do not receive the expected effectiveness. Moreover, the pursuit of maximum profits of microcosmic subjects is contradictory to the macroscopic interests. The pursuit of local and short-term interests often damages the global and long-term interests, which deviates from the direction of the important thought of the "Three Represents". Third, the hysteresis quality of the market price signals can mislead the resource allocation on some production projects, cannot meet the market demand, or squander valuable resources. This put China, which has populous population and fewer resources per capita, at a disadvantage. Fourth, the market mechanism guiding the spiritual and cultural and political life is not only ineffective, but also misleading. Taking a radical way to implement market economy is easily prone to breed corruption, because it is a by-product of pan behaviors. In short, the market economy is not an omnipotent economic form. We must be acutely aware of its congenital defects

Government must deal with the problems generated by market failure that cannot be solved by the market itself, particularly in the public goods. In the spring of 2006, China released the people's livelihood index, a Chinese public environmental protection index, for the first time. It offers the public reliable and exact information to the consequence of market failure. More than half of the public consider air pollution caused by industrial pollution as the most serious environmental problem; environmental rights the public understands are the quiet right and the clean water right; the most common way people complain about environmental issues is to reflect the situation to the neighborhood committee or street office (Gu, 2006).

Obviously, the mere implementation of the market economy cannot handle the economic contradictions and problems in China. According to the report, build the indicator system of people's livelihood index, the preliminary findings and policy recommendations, released by the NPC Financial and Economic Committee Research Group in 2011, there is not a single positive correlation between economic development indicators and overall human development level. The indicator system of people's livelihood index contains four primary indicators, including the residential living, ecological environment, social environment and public services. The system is composed of two parts, objective indicators and subjective indicators. Objective indicators use the data from governmental Statistics, accounting for 70% of the people's livelihood index; subjective indicators obtained mainly through questionnaires, accounting for 30%. A combination of the both is exactly the people's livelihood index reflecting the local people's livelihood development status (Zhao, 2011).

The assertion that market economy cannot save China's economic contradictions does not mean that we are against the market economy. In effect, people do recognize that some positive features of the market economy inspire the wealth growth. What people are against is the argument of American-style free market economy. It is the narrow and one-sided subjectivity theory of market economy. Eichner, an American economist, indicated in his book "Why Economics is not yet a Science" that the indifference curve, the equal product curve, the supply curve and the marginal product curve in the Western economic theory have theoretical defects. However, they are the basic theoretical framework of microeconomics, the basis of macroeconomics. Put it in another way, the entire Western economic theory system is to collapse if these four parts cannot be verified.

Eichner also wrote: the most surprising thing is that the four theoretical structures have not yet been confirmed in practice by economists, although they are in such a prominent position (Eichner, 1983). Such an opinion not only represents his opinion, but also reveals the very nature of the existing reality. Although the deficiencies of market mechanism cannot be cleared by man power, we can proactively reduce the opportunity cost brought by these defects, such as correct understanding and active prevention. The economical and ideological trend of Pan-Marketization has affected China's reform and has misled the economic works, losing plenty of high-value opportunities to the society. This work is by no means the pure academic affair in academia that uncovers that kind of wrong-preaching and gorgeously camouflaged coat, and reduces the opportunity cost it produces, but has serious social and political significance. China should take the road of socialist market economy full of local characteristics; a development road that balances society and market economy. When developing the market economy, the country cannot ignore social construction activities of other non-market economy.

Clean Up the Fallacy of Neo-liberalism

Various contemporary market organizations exert their influences through a series of formal institutional arrangements, rules and traditions. The developed market economy in western countries is the result of institutional evolution in several hundred years. The process is full of twists and turns. It also derives a variety of economic theory schools. These different views of economic schools sum up the experience and lessons the economic institutions of capitalism had experienced, and put forward development recommendations in line with different circumstances of capitalist system. For example, the neo-liberalism propagandizes the omnipotence of private ownership market economy to the utmost, attacks on government intervening in economic activities (Alan Haworth, 1994). Without a doubt, the capitalist ideology contained in this theoretical system is very clear and has a dual purpose.

On the one hand, it plays a positive role with respect to the unity and stability of capitalist society. On the other hand, it exerts destructive and disintegrative effects on the socialism, the antithesis of capitalism. However, the argument of Pan-Marketization insists on the pursuit of neoliberalism, and openly preaches the promotion of reform. We cannot deny the fact that this is a way that brings some of the capitalist system into China. Cleaning up the neoliberalism is to resist the erosion of capitalism, and to establish a socialist market economy. But for China, it is really a tough task that, within a brief period, achieves the level of the west which has developed for several hundred years. Designing a series of possible systems not only needs to participate in the design procedures, the more important is to create specific conditions for cultivating them. Reform is like the reposition of institutional arrangements. It is a great pioneering work, and has great significance without doubt.

However, reform will sometimes meet with difficulties, even get into trouble. Each far-reaching and significant reform happened in the Chinese history, no matter radical or progressive, is inevitably accompanied with exceptionally tricky situation. In this case, the cost and diverse types of risks of reform will undoubtedly increase. The semblance of reform, at this moment, appears to be in a state of stagnation. However, it is very necessary and extremely useful. Reform is somewhat like mountain climbing. Climber needs a rest to stop for a breather to re-ascend. Therefore, it is necessary to put on the brakes to decline the excessive speed of development. The buffer period provides a chance for people to calmly think the current situation and to resolve conflicts arisen in the process of reform. For example, it's necessary to let the rich deeply understand the sufferings of the poor, and to let them know that paying back to society is a good merit; conversely, the poor also can fully understand the bitter side of starting a business that the rich had tasted. Naturally, the poor will not look upon rich men with hatred; instead, they will show willingness to work hard to become well-off. The high-quality development is worth waiting if we can build a harmonious relationship of mutual respect between these people.

Therefore, we might call it a buffer period in the early reform process of the Twelfth Five-Year Plan. Those practices including reform reflection, experience summarization and policies adjustment are to redesign the future reform process. This reform is linked closely with the future and destiny of China, and we need to keep sober all the time. Chinese people have recognized that the Twelfth Five-Year plan cannot be successfully conducted without caution and courage. Harmony is prior to development. The future is bright with harmonious development.

Chapter 5

Socialist Market Economic System in China

The report of the 13th Congress of the Communist Party of China had epoch-making significance. It was a major harvest in the field of political thought and ideology forming the theory of the primary stage of socialism. The reports released by the congress showed that the development of the economic system with public ownership playing a dominant role and diverse forms of ownership developing side by side was a basic characteristic of the socialist economic system at the preliminary stage. This is decided by the quality of socialism and the national situation in preliminary stage and has been proved by practice. According to the instruction of political and ideological line and socio-economic development ideas established in the 13th Congress of the Communist Party of China, the comprehensive and balanced socio-economic development is the guiding principle of development. Simply pursing business profits and market efficiency is not the goal of development. The political reports published during the 13th and 17th Congress of the Communist Party of China regard the primary stage of socialism as China's basic national conditions forming a coherent, and consistent political consensus. It also helps lay a theoretical foundation for holding the banner of socialism with Chinese characteristics, building an innovative country, reform and opening-up policies.

Twists and Turns of Reviving China's Economy

The General Secretary of China Communist Party Central Committee, Hu Jintao pointed out in the report of the 17th Congress that after years of unremitting efforts since the founding of New China, especially since the reform and opening up, China has made remarkable achievements in the development of the productive forces and relations of production. And the economic base and the superstructure have experienced far-reaching changes. However, China is still in the primary stage of socialism and will remain so for a long time to come. The basic national conditions of China have not changed. The principal contradiction in our society is still one between the ever-growing material and cultural needs of the people and the backwardness of social production. The recognition of the basic national conditions in primary stage of socialism is not to belittle ourselves or to be divorced from reality, but to regard it as the fundamental basis of pushing forward reform and the plan for development.

Before 1978, China had a planned economy, which was due to the historical conditions of that era– learning the development mode of the Soviet Union. But in the early stage of the founding of New China, the planned economy gave full play to concentrate human, financial and material resources in a brief period and build many urgent economic projects for national economic development. With the assistance of the Communist Party of the Soviet Union led by Stalin and the assistance of Soviet people, China established 156 major projects as the infrastructure of country's economic development during the period of the "First Five-Year Plan".

However, with the continuous expansion of economy size, the planned economic system had exposed some serious flaws, especially the "Cultural Revolution". In theory, its aim was to consolidate the socialist system, but the actual behavior was exactly the opposite. Under the guidance of opportunism, China's planned economy system gradually became less efficient and failed to promote production. The entire national economy was near the brink of collapse. So, how to build socialism? There is only one answer: according to the needs of people and the national development, China should follow the objective law to determine the major policies of the socialist construction. Engels ever indicated that the socialist society is not a final or static state of being but a society that should be continually changed and reformed (Engels, 1962). So, in 1978, under the guidance of the second generation of collective leadership of Communist Party of China led by Deng Xiaoping, China began to implement the new policy of reform and opening up, aiming at establishing a socialist market economic system and building a powerful nation by learning and introducing the market economic system in industrialized countries.

The Establishment of Socialist Market Economic System

The Third Plenary Session of 11th Central Committee Chinese Communist Party developed a correct ideological and political line and a series of principles and policies launching a great economic and social reform in the history of China guiding the people to embark on a new path of socialist development. In 1984, Deng Xiaoping concluded the national development in five years and pointed out that, "Overall, this road is called the road of building socialism with Chinese characteristics". The main task in the socialist stage is to develop the productive forces as economy is the core of nation-building. For economic construction, the reform and opening up provides the experience of using market-based instruments to develop production and improve efficiency. In the famous Southern Talk of 1992, Deng Xiaoping expressed, "More planning or more marketing is not the substantial distinction between socialism and capitalism. Planned economy is not equal to socialism, capitalism also has plans; market economy is not equal to capitalism, either, because socialism also has a market". This important thesis fundamentally pointed out the direction for the formulation of socialist market economy theory and the establishment of the socialist market economic system. On June 9, 1992, in a speech for the Central Party School, Jiang Zemin affirmed the socialist market economy for the first time. After that, on October 12, the report of the 14th Party Congress formally proposed that the goal of China's economic reform is to establish a socialist market economic system.

Since the Opium War in 1840, China has been invaded and humiliated for more than a century. Chinese people adopted Marxism to conduct new democratic revolution and establish a new China. The practice told Chinese people a truth that only socialism could save China. As Deng Xiaoping summarized profoundly, Capitalism does not work in China; China must establish socialism. If China chooses capitalism instead of socialism, the confusion in China will not end, and the poverty cannot be changed (Deng Xiaoping, 1993). Departing from the socialist direction to build market economy does not accord with China's national conditions, and it is contrary to the will of the people and current era development trend. The practice of Marxism in some countries has proved that socialism is not naturally established and developed. It cannot succeed without being under the protection of the people's regime. China's socialist economic construction should be guided by right strategies and policies and being macro-controlled by the national authorities. At the same time, market should play the basic role of resource allocation. Only in this way, economic development and social construction can achieve fruitful results -fulfilling the goal of building a well-off society.

Since China's economic system was transferred from a single planning system to a socialist market economic system, the national economy has developed outstandingly. Especially in the "Eleventh Five-Year" period, China’s originally irrational economic structure was increasingly optimized and the total economic output increased steadily. In the "Eleventh Five-Year" period, the three industries have maintained a rapid development trend. From 2006 to 2010, the average annual growth of the first industry was 4.5%, the average annual increase of the second industry was 12.1% and the average annual growth of the tertiary industry was 11.9%. Viewing the industrial structure, the proportion of the primary industry decreased from 12.1% in 2005 to 10.2% in 2010, with a decrease of 1.9 percentage points. The proportion of the secondary industry decreased slightly from 47.4 % in 2005 to 46.8 % in 2010, with a decrease of 0.6 percentage points. The proportion of the tertiary industry increased from 40.5% to 43.0%, with an increase of 2.5 percentage points. Owing to the larger national investment in rural area and the urgent requirement for sustainable development, the proportion of the primary industry decreased significantly. The decrease in the proportion of the secondary industry was because of the rapid industrialization in national economy.

The employment structures have undergone significant changes, too. From 2005 to 2009, the total employment proportion of the primary industry decreased from 44.8% to 38.1% with a decrease of 6.7 percentage points. The total employment proportion of the secondary industry increased from 23.8% to 27.8%, with an increase of 4.0 percentage points. The total employment proportion of the tertiary industry increased from 31.4% to 34.1%, with an increase of 2.7 percentage points. The direct effect of modernization in economy structure was that the industries represented by information and heavy chemistry had replaced the traditional industries, becoming the pillar of economic development. With the deepening of reform, the economic sector increasingly diversified and many new service industries emerged, so the rise in the proportion of the tertiary industry has become a trend.

China's population is mainly agricultural population; the affluence of farmers is the most important symbol of country's prosperity. Transferring agricultural labor to industrial sectors and optimizing the proportion of industrial structure are important ways for helping farmers become richer. During the "Eleventh Five-Year" period, Chinese government's ability to control the market economy was constantly enhanced; the policies for urban and rural development achieved remarkable success, and the various targets of macroeconomic regulation were realized smoothly. As more and more farmers work in cities, the income of rural population was improved greatly. According to the result of the Second National Agricultural Census released by Agricultural Census Office and the National Bureau of Statistics on February 21, 2008, the employment ratio of three industries were 70.8%, 15.6%, and 13.6%; 130million rural household labors leave the township to work; men accounted for 64%, aged 40 and under accounted for 82.1%, junior middle school education background and above accounted for 80.1%,the labors who work outside their home-county accounted for 80.8%. China has a large population, and the transfer size of rural labor to urban areas is very big. Chinese government should create opportunities to solve the employment problem. As there are more than 20 million new labor forces every year, it is not an easy thing to arrange jobs for them.

The achievement of the socialist market economic system reform is not only enjoyed by domestic people, but also appreciated by the world. "China Rising" is the article subject for the world's major media. The peaceful rise of China has become a basic fact and a major trend; you cannot deny or ignore it. An article entitled *How China Manage World Economy*: *Events in China have bigger impact on global wages, profits, prices and rates* was the cover story of British "Economist" magazine on July 30, 2005. We can proudly say that China's reform and opening up not only has a profound impact on China, but also has a far-reaching impact on the entire world. This Achievement is a victory of adhering to the socialist direction and uniting reform as a "second revolution" and the "self-improvement of socialist system.

Twists and Turns of the Economic and Social Development

Although the market economic reform has achieved particularly evident progress in the volume and structure of China's economy, the national development has still not reached the desired level. An important downside is that the rapid growth of material wealth does not benefit all the people generally. Economic development gap between rural and urban regions is becoming larger and the uneven distribution of national income obviously exists there. Since the establishment of the socialist market economy with Chinese characteristics is an unprecedented pioneering work in history, the imbalance in the economic and social development is inevitable.

How to solve the contradictions in the society? Firstly, we should understand these contradictions to identify the major contradiction from the complicated social environment. The founder of the People's Republic of China, Mao Zedong ever said in his famous book "On

Contradiction", "there are many contradictions in the development process of complex things, there must be a major contradiction. Its existence and development will regulate or affect the existence and development of the other contradictions". People need to re-study Mao's opinion to correctly understand contradictions and then resolve the contradiction. If the judgment of the principal contradiction is wrong, then the loss in the actual work will be very painful. Recalling the history of the Communist Party of China in economic construction is very necessary for solving real-world conflicts.

On September 15-27, 1956, the Eighth National People's Congress of the Communist Party of China was held in Beijing and passed the famous political report given by Liu Shaoqi on behalf of the China Communist Party Central Committee. This report determined that the principal contradiction of Chinese society has changed and the focus of the work of the Communist Party should strategically shift from liberating productive forces to protecting and developing productive forces. In the preceding months, taking example of the socialist construction experience in the former Soviet Union, Chairman Mao Zedong and other leading comrades of the China Communist Party Central Committee summed up the exploratory experience of the socialist transformation in China and made a preliminarily correct strategic plan of how to develop socialist China. Accordingly, Mao Zedong wrote a glorious book titled *On the Ten Major Relationships*. As Liu Shaoqi pointed out in the report of the Second Session of the Eighth National People's Congress, the work report of the First Session of the Eighth National People's Congress is made according to Mao Zedong's principles and policies of dealing with the Ten Major Relationships.

The political reports and resolutions of the Eighth Chinese Communist Party pointed out that, after the basic completion of the socialist transformation of production private ownership, "The contradiction between the proletariat and the bourgeoisie has been basically solved, at present, the main contradiction of China is the contradiction between the people's requirement of establishing an advanced industrial country and the reality of a backward agricultural country, and the contradiction between the people's requirement for rapid economic and cultural development and the current economic and cultural situation cannot meet people's need" (Liu, 1998). This conference developed a correct line and pointed out the direction for China's socialist economic development and China Communist Party building. Deng Xiaoping summed up the task of the congress that the task of the Eighth National People's Congress is to mobilize all positive factors and all forces to build China into a great socialist industrial country (Deng, 1994). It represented that the work focus of the China Communist Party is transferred with the change of the main social contradictions.

Unfortunately, in the eleventh Supreme State Conference, Mao Zedong made an important speech clearly pointing out that the large-scale class struggle during the revolutionary period has basically ended and the theme of China's political life is to correctly handle the contradictions among Chinese people. This is a continuation and development of the correct principles in the Eighth National People's Congress, and has great theoretical and practical significance. But soon, a nationwide anti-rightist movement began. This movement affected people from every walk of Chinese society, especially the intellectuals who appeared to favor capitalism and were against collectivization. On June 19 of the same year, *On the Correct Handling of Contradictions among the People* was published in the *People's Daily*. As seriously overestimating the domestic situation, the author added some arguments which were incongruous with the spirit of the original speech, such as the emphasis on class struggle and the misjudgment of the contradiction between socialist and capitalism in China (Mao, 1999).

In October of the same year, the Third Plenary Session of the Chinese Communist Party discussed the contradiction between the proletariat and the bourgeoisie; the socialist road and the capitalist road regarding the "struggle between the two classes and the two roads struggle" as the social principal contradiction and wrongly changing the correct formulation of Eighth National People's Congress. Since 1957, the fundamental guiding ideology of China Communist Party and China's development was in taking class struggle as the key link, and later became continuing the revolution under the dictatorship of the proletariat in the Cultural Revolution. Practice test is the sole criterion of truth. Prior to 1978, the social production activities of China were interfered and repressed by class struggle, and Chinese people did not have enough to eat and wear.

China has not announced the poverty line before 1978, but we can calculate the poverty line in accordance with the standards of nutritional knowledge. The usual standard of neurology requires that calorie intake cannot be less than 2150 calories per person per day. If food in diets provides 90% of the heat for per person per day, per person per day should at least consume 540.5 grams of food, per kilogram of food generally contain 3580 kilocalories. At least 197 kilograms of grain should be consumed per person per year, which is the minimum food consumption standard of World Bank. Based on Chinese residents' need of normal physiological function, Chinese Society of Nutrition thinks that the calorie intake cannot be less than 2400 kcal per person per day. National Bureau of Statistics of China stipulates that the minimum food consumption is 220 kg per person per year (Zhu & Jiang, 1994). Therefore, taking 220 kilograms of grain per person per year as the standard to measure the poverty line in China before 1978, the extreme poverty line was 197 kg.

According to the average food consumption data of the urban and rural residents per capita per year before 1978 (units: kilograms) provided by the Chinese Ministry of Agriculture, we can draw the following data: in 1952, food consumption per person per year in China, urban: 241 kg, rural: 192 kg; 1957, urban: 196 kg, rural: 205 kg; 1960, urban: 193 kg, rural: 156 kg; 1965, urban: 211 kg, rural: 177 kg; 1970, urban: 202 kg, rural: 185 kg; 1975, urban: 210 kg, rural: 187 kg; 1977, urban: 211 kg, rural: 189 kg; 1979, urban: 211 kg, rural: 206 kg; 1981, urban: 216 kg, rural: 220 kg; 1984, urban: 240 kg, rural: 250 kg; 1986, urban: 245 kg, rural: 260 kg (Agriculture Ministry Planning

Department, 1987). The data showed that before 1978, the food consumption of Chinese urban and rural residents was below the poverty line of 220 kg, and in many years, it was even below the extreme poverty line of 197 kg. According to the estimation of World Bank, in 1978, there were 270 million people in absolute poverty in China, accounting for about 1/3 of China's population (World Bank, 1993). A monograph of the Chinese scholars pointed out that "in the commune period, almost half of the farmers were in the state of insufficient nutrition, among which those lived in a serious shortage of food accounted for almost 1/3. If encountering a bad harvest, this proportion would be close to 60%" (Xia, 1995). Because of the misjudgment of social contradictions and the implementation of wrong policies, Chinese society ever fell into severe poverty and experienced a great national catastrophe, and the national economy slide into the brink of collapse.

After the "Cultural Revolution", the biggest problem of China's society was the shortage of material goods; social instability caused by poverty was spreading over the entire society. China's most urgent task was to shift the center of the government policy to economic development and motivate social productivity development. As many people were still constrained by Two-Whatever (We will resolutely uphold whatever policy decisions Chairman Mao made, and unswervingly follow whatever instructions Chairman Mao gave) and the shadow of the "Leftist" had not disappeared, some brave Communists adhered to the principle of seeking truth from facts and tried to bring order out of chaos. A branch of China Communist Party of Xiaogang Village in Anhui Province went through great risks to carry out a land contract reform secretly, showing Communists' strong determination to insist Marxism. Later, the Anhui Provincial Committee of China Communist Party with Wan Li as a secretary supported the reform of Xiaogang Village and seized the opportunity to promote the reform experience in Anhui Province when the land contract reform got initial success. A Chinese expert who is a German named Garth Le Pere evaluated the reform as experiment against hunger without the discussion and approval of central committee (Li, 1994).

After summarizing the reform experience in Anhui, Sichuan and other provinces, in December 1978, the Communist Party of China held the Third Plenary Session of the 11th Central Committee of the Chinese Communist Party. This meeting re-established the principal contradiction in Chinese society as "the contradiction between people's growing material and cultural demands and the undeveloped social productivity", thus made a strategic decision with economic construction as the center. It inherited and went beyond the spirit of the Eighth National People's Congress. To guide Chinese people how to get rid of poverty, in 1986, the State Council established a specific group to lead the economic development in deprived areas, and then published the criteria and the number of state-level poverty-stricken counties. In 1993, the central government formulated the "8-7 National Poverty Reduction Plan", aiming at increasing poverty alleviation efforts. In October 1996, the "Decision of the CPC Central Committee and the State Council on Solving the Poverty Problems in Rural as Soon as Possible" was formally introduced. Government offered greater financial support to help the rural residents get rid of poverty. By the end of 2000, China had basically solved the food and clothing problem. This was the greatest achievement of China since the formation of the Chinese nation. The world widely expected that the 21st century would be the century of China's peaceful rise.

We should not forget the historical experiences and lessons. Recognizing the principal contradiction of the society and correctly identifying the general direction are directly related to the national development and people's life. As Mao Zedong said that all problems can be solved if we seize the principal contradiction (Mao, 1968). Failing to seize the principal contradiction may cause confusion and even disaster.

Objectives and Orientations of the Reform

The goal of China's market economy reform is the revival of Chinese nation, so we must act in accordance with the objective laws of market economy and socialist construction. It is clearly wrong if we operate radical marketization practice regardless of the principles and ideals of socialism.

Reform under the Guidance of People's Willingness

China's reform began in the crisis caused by the "Cultural revolution" and the most urgent task was to increase the production of food and industrial products to meet the people's living needs. In other words, high-speed economic development and increasing total supply of products was the most important task. The market economy mechanism pursuing maximum economic benefits was basically mature in China. At the end of the 20th century, the powerful role of the market economy was displayed in China, promoting the rapid development of the national economy. During the first few years of the 21st century, China's GDP growth rate was in the world front rank. The analysis of China's National Statistics Bureau showed that China's economy had maintained a growth of about 10% for five consecutive years since 2003. The economic growth rate during 2005 to 2007 was 10.4%, 10.7% and 11.4% respectively. Even after the Wenchuan earthquake and the global financial crisis in 2008, it was a miracle that China still maintained an economic growth rate of 9% and 8.7% in 2008 and 2009. In 2010, the economy gradually recovered, and the economic growth rate returned to a prominent position 10.3%. During the "Eleventh Five-Year" period, China's economy appeared with a steady growth with a good start and rapid recovery.

Although during China's "Eleventh Five-Year" period, the economic and social development plan was over-fulfilled, the national social conflict was also quietly changing during this period. Things are always changing and developing, and the emergence of contradictions is a normal objective phenomenon, so people need to constantly re-understand contradictions. Mao Zedong ever said before, "In a certain process or a certain stage of contradictions development, the primary contradiction and secondary contradiction may exchange position because of the increase and decrease of their strength" (Mao, 1968). What is the contradiction in Chinese society today? How to identify the principal contradiction? How many aspects does principal contradiction have? An important indicator of measuring conflicts is the change of people's willingness. The desire of the people is the most crucial factor in social development.

Adhere to the Socialist Principles of Economic Reform

Before 1949, China had never met people's need for food. Through new China's socialist construction and the practice of economic reform, China's GDP achieved a rapid growth for many years. At the end of the last century, the GDP statistics indicators showed that country production had got substantial growth, which brought huge material wealth. The food and clothing problems of Chinese people which had plagued China for thousands of years were basically solved for the first time under the condition of the socialist system. However, when a primary contradiction was basically solved, a new contradiction appeared. After getting satisfied with material needs, people may complain about working environment, education, medical fees, living condition and so on. All these complaints are related with social equity.

Equity and efficiency has been the two fundamental questions of economic research for a long time. Fairness and efficiency have dialectical unification relations of interrelation and interaction. There is no real efficiency without equity, and the true equity is not egalitarian. "Giving priority to efficiency with due consideration to fairness" has a certain positive significance economic activity. However, in the political and ethical aspect, it is difficult to rank equity and efficiency successively. About the principle of fair competition, the correct implementation method is that we should hold a positive attitude toward the practice if it is able to stimulate the upward development of all walks of life but will not lead to unbearable competition. However, once the competition exceeds a certain limit or deviate from the original intention of Chinese people, it will eventually lead to bad results. At this point, the government should not hesitate to interfere with it and the people have the power to reject it.

The field of market economic failure is the public goods production and distribution chain, which happens to be a continuation of the inherent contradictions of capitalism. History tells people that solving the contradiction between private ownership and socialized production relies on class struggle, violent revolution and the establishment of the people's regime. In the process of implementing China's economic reform, the government should play the role of resource allocation to solve the contradiction between people's growing public goods demands and the insufficient public goods supply. What's more, the government can adopt compensation mechanism to redistribute and narrow the income gap to ensure the legitimate rights and interests of different sectors of society. This is not only an expression of the superiority of the socialist system but also an important measurement to maintain social stability and security. The traditional culture of China attaches immense importance to equity and common prosperity. In the initial stage of China's reform and opening up, Deng Xiaoping explicitly pointed out, "In short, the fundamental principles of socialism we should adhere to are the dominant position of public ownership and a common prosperity. We should resolutely implement and realize these principles of socialism" (Deng, 1993). When emphasizing the efficiency of the market economy, we should not discard these unique properties of socialism against the tendency of money worship

After market-oriented reforms and sustained economic growth for decades, although the phenomenon of lacking personal goods still exists in some regions of China, it can be said extreme shortage of private goods has ended. Market economy, free competition and globalization help solve the social contradictions in initial and medium stage of reform and opening up. China, a country once with large area of poverty, has successfully achieved a well-off society. The development of the things is always complex. The traditional agricultural society is being transformed into an industrial society. As Chinese society is in the historical stage of rapid transformation, the frictions between old and the new institutions become fiercer and fiercer, and the Pan-marketization economic thought also took the opportunity to sweep across the society. This thought advocates Western economic theory blindly regardless of the real situation in China.

In recent years, some negative phenomena appeared in Chinese society, such as the widening social gap between the rich and the poor, the excessive consumption of limited resources, decreasing innovative technologies in the manufacture of industrial products, and increasing dependence on overseas markets. These phenomena which damage the interests of the citizens show the fact that if we blindly rely on the "economic man" assumptions of western economic theory, the sustainable and stable development of China's economy will be impeded. At the same time, some people are obsessed with money and unscrupulously pursuing personal interests. Media are flooding with articles preaching the supremacy of market economic benefits, and the good traditional culture of China for thousands of years has been invaded and abandoned.

In the initial stage of new China, the country's economy was in a mess. There was no industrial production. Food shortage and inflation were very serious. But after just a few years of construction, the national economy recovered rapidly and got excellent achievement. At that period, there was no ample supply of goods and people could not get generous profits from working. About what China has relied on to make a miracle, Deng Xiaoping summarized, rely on what? The answer is Marxism and socialism. People may wonder why China engages in socialism. We say that capitalism is not feasible in China; China must build socialism (Deng, 1993). Material incentive cannot substitute for the ideal of communism. Economic system reform introduced market economy, implemented free competition, took in private property rights and opened the domestic market to foreign capital. However, these practices are not to copy the economic and social model of capitalism.

The classic Marxist writer, Marx once took capitalist society as an example to profoundly analyze the causes of community poverty in the modern history. Marx believed that capitalist ownership and capital accumulation is the root cause of the poverty of the proletariat. Property ownership is the ultimate cause to determine the class, class economic status as well as the political status. The proletariat without property ownership has no choice but become employer, contributing their "surplus labor" as a condition of employment. With the increasing organic composition of capital and capital accumulation, the proletariat fell into poverty (Marx, 1975). Of course, in the development history of capitalism, the poverty of the proletariat does not occur at any time and under any circumstances. The actual situation of the workers in the contemporary major industrialized countries is very different with the situation of the workers during Marx period.

The living standard of the public is indeed higher than in other countries. However, we absolutely should not think that the capitalist system is the paradise on earth or copy the social system of capitalism blindly. As some people deny capitalism is the cause of poverty, in 1902, Lenin said, it is very necessary to recognize the poverty of the masses under capitalism, and that does not mean the absolute increase of poverty (Lenin, 1986). This indicates that in different capitalistic countries and different historical development stages of the same capitalistic country, the poverty of the people has different pattern of manifestation. The poverty in capitalistic country is relative poverty.

The private property tenure system of semi-feudal and semi-colonial society leads to China's long-term poverty and backwardness. The capitalist property tenure system leads to the poverty of proletariat in many countries of the world. Despite the external manifestation of poverty is different, it is mixed with absolute poverty and relative poverty. Therefore, the property tenure system of the exploiting class is the root cause of the poverty of the masses. To eliminate the poverty, the property tenure system of exploiting classes must be overthrown. In the celebration of the 40-year anniversary of the People's Republic of China, on behalf of the Communist Party and the government, Jiang Zemin delivered an important speech. He said, if we do not adhere to socialism, but go back to take the capitalist road as some people advocate, many people will fall back to poverty (Jiang, 1989). Only the socialist system can help China gradually fulfill people's aspiration for common prosperity.

Adhere to the Direction of Socialist Civilization

To eliminate the wrongful arguments in society, the government should effectively solve the social problems that confused people and educate the young people who regard money and benefits as everything. We should vigorously strengthen the socialist ideological and moral construction, and consolidate the guiding position of Marxism in the ideological field. What's more, the government should promote the thought of national unity and inherit the revolutionary spirit of the Red Army, to form a positive and healthy social climate. Spirit is a magic weapon to defeat the enemy. During the revolutionary war years, the army led by the Communist Party faced extreme situation of material shortage. In the famous Liaoning-Shenyang Campaign, hundreds of thousands of People's Liberation Army gathered in Jinzhou which abounded with apple. It was autumn when the Western Liaoning Battle happened, and the people had a lot of apple at home. But the soldiers of the People's Liberation Army did not eat the apples. The masses were acutely aware that it was an army which served the people wholeheartedly.

Mao Zedong said, we must advocate working hard and plain living as our political nature (Mao, 1999). Because of the noble political behavior, the Liberation Army got people's support and successfully defeated the foreign reactionaries. Today, although China has a stable and harmonious development environment, this spirit should be passed from generation to generation. There is still a long way to build a powerful modern country. On the eve of building the new China, Mao Zedong warned the party that this victory was only the first step in building a communist society and the future revolution and construction work would be more arduous. Our comrades must be taught to remain modest and prudent, not from arrogance and rashness in style; comrades must be taught to preserve the style of hard struggle (Mao, 1968). The "Two Musts" proposed in war years is also a very valuable spiritual wealth for modern people.

The best way is to inherit the spirit of "Two Musts" in the economic field. This may be done by finding out the reform orientation based on correctly understanding the economic situation in contemporary China. China's current economy is in the form of mixed economy. Owing to the impact of the planned economy and the feudal ideology lasting for thousands of years, China is still in a semi-marketization institutional status, compared with the marketization degree of economically advanced countries. Naturally, when a developing country transforms from a planned system to a market economic system, there is a period with dual systems. During this period, the old constraint system collapses and the new constraint mechanism is not perfect; thus, there will be a loophole in the market management and moral constraints. As People's profit-seeking desire has been suppressed for many years under the planned economic system, once the constraint is relaxed, it is easy to breed some predatory operations in the market and corruption in government. These phenomena are some-how related to pan-marketization thoughts. Analyzing from the historical perspective, this is Ananta-culture countercurrent. Some people get rich firstly by taking advantage of the loopholes in the market system. For example, as China adopted double-track price system in the middle and later periods of 1980s, some people purchased commodities in planned system and then sold goods in market system. As a result, the commodity price soared.

Of course, when more and more people get rich, there are some serious problems emerging in China's society, such as employment pressure, the spread of corruption, environmental degradation, ethnic separatism and other issues. Employment pressure is one of the most urgent and fundamental problem. The priority mission for the government is to create employment opportunities. There are 900 million agricultural people in mainland China. With the space of industrialization speeding up, there will be more and more farmland become non-agricultural land, so there will be more and more agricultural population going to urban cities for jobs. At the same time, many working-age population and laid-off workers because of economic structural adjustment in urban cities come upon the stage; the number of work force is even huger. Employment problem is closely related with people's lives, and has a significant impact on social stability. Faced with these problems, the governmental departments should make historical research to solve the problems. In dealing with these complex economic and social problems, we must always grasp the direction of socialism and avoid the influence the pan-marketization ideology.

Criticizing pan-marketization argument does not mean totally exclude the Western economic system and economic theory. China needs to learn and absorb the essences of different systems to master all the wisdom of human. So, China should learn the capitalist management systems and knowledge of the United States, Britain and other developed countries. Now the world has entered into an information age with computer technology and the Internet as its most distinctive features. Through the Internet, people can get a panoramic view of the world. Dialectical materialism and historical materialism tell the Chinese people that more advanced civilization can only be generated based on capitalist civilization, not based on denying or eliminating capitalist civilization. The growth of a new socialist civilization must inherit the results of all civilizations instead of completely breaking with the old civilization. This is also the far-reaching significance of the "Three Represents" thoughts.

Querying Subjectivity of Market Economy Theory

To meet the needs of China's reform and opening up, economics gradually became a famous social doctrine over the years during which a lot of good scholars and some systematic economic theories have emerged. However, some self-proclaimed "elites" ignore the independent study and academic demonstration of economics but try to please the public with claptrap. For example, they simply attribute employment problems to the necessary cost of building market economic system. However, employment problem has been argued by economists for years. Keynes wrote a book *The General Theory of Employment, Interest and Money*, creating "Keynesian" which ever became popular for a time (Ma, 2002). China is in the historical stage of transforming from an agricultural country to an industrialized country; and here the employment issue is very complicated. So, the reason of employment problems in China is diverse. If the scholars have done an in-depth socialist economy's theoretical study based on Marxism, they will not simply regard the employment problem as a necessary cost of building market economic system. The rapid economic development impelled by China's reform and opening up does not produce high quality scientific theory report. It is worth thinking about deeply for the researchers in China.

Grasp the Direction of Market Economy Reform

The practice shows that in the process of establishing China's socialist market economic system, the ambiguous theories lead to economic and social contradictions and chaos. For example, some theories have demonstrated the reasonability of economic optimization and reorganization. However, in fact, many state-owned assets flow into the private property. Some theories keep talking about the benefits of high salary for a clean government; there are many corruption cases that officials embezzle the wealth of nations. These phenomena are not the inevitable cost of establishing market economic system. The essence of those "cost" arguments is based on one idea– subjectivity theory of market economy. The logic of this theory is that because China's economic reform is to establish a socialist market economy with Chinese characteristics all problems in the process of establishing a market economic system are acceptable. In fact, the error of subjectivity theory is that it loses the two principles - socialism and Chinese characteristics.

Extreme Subjectivity Theory of Market Economy

After losing the two principles, subjectivity theory of market economy becomes an extreme argument. Market economy is the main subject of social and economic operation; it is necessary to let the market play its basic role. Subjectivity theory simply argues that the socialist economy after China's reform and opening up is a market economy, and this market economy can develop systematically under the socialist system. In other words, the subject which develops in a planned way is market economy. After economic reform achieves this goal, the combination of market economy and planned economy no longer exists in China's socialist economy. There is only socialist market economy developing in a planned way. This is the most basic and important thought and point of subjectivity theory, which seems to advocate socialist, but in practice, it only follows the law of market economy. However, without social base, laws will not be able to play a role.

The subjectivity theory of market economy even declares that for an oriental power like China the market economy has important practical significance. Because of China's large population, if we do not mobilize all social forces to develop economy but depend on the arrangement of government, the future will be gloomy for Chinese people. Market economy is particularly important to China. Market economy is to mobilize all social forces to develop economy, so it is in line with the socialist spirit. On the contrary, it is difficult for public ownership to have sufficient strength to solve the living problem of Chinese people, so it is violation of the socialism spirit.

In economics, market is a mechanism that combines the producer and consumer of commodity through exchange (Parkin & Robin, 2000). This mechanism consists of two basic aspects, namely the way of exchange and place of exchange. The contemporary Western Marketing often defines market as consumer groups who have the purchasing desire and purchasing power for the same product. Therefore, the market is both abstract and concrete; it is a specific embodiment and reaction of human social and economic activities since the emergence of commodity. All the connotations of market are conferred by human beings. Without human, market cannot exist. From the perspective of human society, market economy is only part of human social economy, rather than all the social economy.

Admittedly, vigorously developing the market economy is one aspect of socio-economic development, but it is also an important aspect. However, the market economy cannot replace the other content and pattern of social economy. The development and progress of human society needs us develop social economy comprehensively. The thought that over emphasizes market economy while ignoring other aspects of the social economy, obviously does not conform to the comprehensive development of human society.

The subjectivity theory of market economy emphasized that market economy is the main subject of social economy. In fact, it is tantamount to denying the importance of other non-market economy in socio-economic development. Subjectivity theory of market economy advocates that we should let the market play the most basic and decisive role in the process of socio-economic development. Though the people who support subjectivity theory admit the function of regulatory plan, on the other hand, they regard market discipline as the premise of controlling social economy. In fact, they think that human society and economy should unconditionally obey the so-called "objective" laws of the market.

It is undeniable that market economy is the main economic operation mode of most countries including China. The subjectivity theory of market economy has gone through several stages: the exclusion theory, negative combination theory, positive combination theory, and finally the subjectivity theory. In fact, instead of transformation and innovation, subjectivity theory only deprives market mechanism of "socialist" and "Chinese characteristics" and then puts it into China's economic system. It completely does not allow social vulnerable groups to have the right to speak. It is gratifying that some economic viewpoints have appeared in these days to correct the error of subjectivity theory and get the initial recognition of people.

In the early 1980s, China's education, health care, housing, transportation, finance and other industries were still in the planned economic system. State-owned enterprises occupied most of the total social production. And the opening up had only just begun, while foreign investment and goods were not free to enter the Chinese market. Within the framework of planned economy, along with the opening policy and the introduction of competition mechanism, some enterprises in China achieved effective economic profit and social effects. During this period, due to the constraints of the planned economy framework, the positive role of market was obvious and the negative effects were hard to appear.

Chapter 6

Educational Progress and Issues

Since ancient times China has been a state which has highly valued ceremonies. Chinese value knowledge and etiquette. Access to education and educational development after the reform and opening up, especially compulsory education and the elimination of illiteracy, have achieved fruitful results. However, at the same time, because of the wide-spread thought of industrial education, the development of education is facing many difficulties. There exist high education fees in some provinces. Besides, education quality in some provinces has seriously declined.

Educational Progress in the Process of Reform

Chinese traditional history and national culture have always emphasized on education. Education can make people knowledgeable and competent in social activities. Confucius, the founder of ancient education, said: never blame heaven and others, become learned from reflecting on trifles (Analects of Confucius). Confucius also advocated the implementation of the educational ideal "No Child Left Behind". After the foundation of New China, the leaders of the Republic have regarded education as a long-term objective in the construction of socialism. Mao Zedong, the first-generation leader of Communist Party of China, wrote the inscription: Study Hard and Make Progress Every Day. The country attaches immense importance to primary education to cultivate the talents of socialist construction starting from school age. From the beginning of the reform and opening up policy, Deng Xiaoping, the chief architect, led the implementation of the policy which resurrected the University Entrance exam, laying the foundation for the prosperity of the country.

In 2000, representatives of the Chinese government attended the Dakar meeting convened by UNESCO and signed the famous Dakar Framework for Action. After this meeting, the Chinese government invested heavily in education, and mobilized all social forces for the development of EFA (education for all). In those five years, the EFA (education for all) programs achieved new breakthroughs; compulsory education accomplished historical development. The basic strategies of nine-year compulsory education and elimination of illiteracy among young and middle-aged adults also acquired progressed significantly (simply described as the "two basics" below); and rural compulsory education got unprecedented attention and promotion. The amount of investment, teaching quality and educational conditions has been markedly improved. In the first few years of the new century, the central government has led the implementation of the "two basics" in the western regions, especially the implementation of a series of policies to provide funds to students in deprived areas. These measures have had a positive impact in practice. For example, in the case of lowering the dropout rate in rural schools and ensuring the timely enrollment of school-age children and in other aspects, these policies have promoted the development of rural compulsory education.

In the period of the "Eleventh Five-Year Plan", China's education business has made enormous progress, basically meeting its objectives. According to the National Bureau of Statistics, the gross enrollment rate of three-year pre-school education is 56.6 per cent in 2010, a substantial increase of 15.2 percentage points compared to 2005. Since 2005, compulsory education and consolidation levels have remained high. The net enrollment rate for primary schools across the country has been maintained at more than 99 per cent, which is higher than the average of 96 per cent in developed countries; the raw enrollment rate of junior middle school was 100 per cent in 2010, the three-year retention rate was 94 per cent, which were an increase of 5.1 percentage points and 1.02 percentage points compared with 2005, respectively; the raw enrollment rate of senior high school reached 82.5 per cent, an increase of 29.8 per cent compared to 2005; the gross enrollment rate of China's higher education was 26.5 per cent in 2010, 5.5 percentage points more than in 2005, and 1.5 percentage points higher than the planning objective (Statistical Bureau, 2011). In short, China has practiced the Dakar Framework for Action adopted by the international community, and not only has trained many knowledge workers devoted to the construction of the country, but has also contributed to the development of human civilization.

The Spread of Industrialization Thoughts in the Field of Education

The 21st century is an international era with high-technology, information, intelligence and talent competition. Chinese have a high expectation of the benefits of education. The construction of the country also needs many high-quality talents. The education business in China has performed remarkably well, but there is an imbalance in supply and demand, and the gap is still huge in some respects. Entering into the new century, the nation's educational system and quality are still the focus of public debate. The overall situation can be described by the sentence said by Deng Xiaoping when he summarized the efforts in the early stage of reform many years ago: "There are developments and deviations in the reform, but the biggest mistake occurs in the education area". Just as other sectors in China, the ideological trend of pan-marketization also erodes the Chinese education industry. It has a direct impact on the training of personnel, scientific and technological progress, and the development of economic production. As mentioned above, the industrialization of education is a typical representative of this spreading ideological trend.

As early as 1992, education was placed firmly in the tertiary industry category and was a fundamental industry that had overall effects on the development of national economy. This is also a common point of view in the international community. In the United States, which has the most developed system of education in the world, the higher education system is divided into two categories: public and private. Examples of public universities are the State University of New York and Rand University. Some of the most famous universities are private or church-funded, such as Harvard University and Stanford University. The same is true of the higher education system in the United Kingdom, France and other countries. Therefore, the documents of State Department are scientific and objective from the global perspective. There is no doubt about whether China's education needs marketization. China absolutely must not industrialize education, and should not go contrary to the developing trend of globalization. However, the question is how to do education how to implement compulsory education in the context of a market orientation. Bill Gates, the founder of world-renowned Microsoft, established his company in his college years, making an outstanding contribution to the information age.

The tendency for China to industrialize education is the result of the spreading of the pan-market ideological trend. This industrial behavior has abandoned the basic principles of education, and has turned compulsory education into education for profit. It seriously interferes with the deployment of the "two basics" the nation comprehensively promotes, and makes arbitrary changes visible everywhere. Some of the socially vulnerable groups of school-age children and adolescents are forced to drop out due to poverty. The quality of education also has suffered a significant decline. Despite the senior leadership of the Chinese Ministry of Education is repeatedly stressing that the highest administrative department of education has never published documents that support education industrialization; the arguments and practices of education industrialization are common in practice.

Articles on education industrialization can be seen everywhere, whether on network television or in several types of journals. The education sector, academia, the media sector, etc., have successively joined the critical trend of education industrialization. For example, during the first news conference of the 17th Party Congress held on October 16, 2007, Zhou Ji, the Education Minister of China, said in response to a reporter's question: this congress report has explicitly pointed out that we insist on based on nonprofit education, we must increase government investment in education, and we are firmly opposed to education industrialization (Xi'an Daily, 2007). An article entitled *Industrialization of Education' Should Cease* in 2010 clearly indicated that education industrialization gave birth to the arbitrary changes of education. Arbitrary educational changes not only increased the burden of students, especially poor students in rural regions, but also severely damaged the image of the schools and the teachers in the minds of students, delivering a tremendously negative impact that should not be ignored (Liu, 2010). Yan Qiuluwei, a well-known TV reporter of Phoenix Satellite TV, is also very concerned about the problems of education industrialization. She wrote an article entitled "Education Industrialization". She said many people regard education as a business, whether kindergarten or university. Education has been a tool to make money (Yan, 2011). It's easy to see from comments above that the arbitrary changes and education industrialization as a pair of twins. What should we feel about this situation now?

Compulsory education of the whole people has had a great responsibility as directed by the Dakar Framework for Action adopted at the World Education Forum in 2000. Compulsory education belongs to government investment. China has no possible means to monopolize education considering the current fundamental realities of the country. In recent years, the implementation of cost-sharing mechanisms in education in accordance with the guidance of the Ministry of Education at all levels and types and stages of education is a major education reform. We must continue to adhere to the right direction and to the principle of public welfare education at this stage. Educational development should put government investment in the significant role; should strengthen the responsibility of the government for educational development; and should make education become one of the most important works.

The spokesman of the Chinese Ministry of Education has indicated through the Xinhua Network, an extremely influential web medium in China, that the Ministry of Education unequivocally has opposed education industrialization from the date it first occurred, and holds that education industrialization would destroy China's education (Xinhua Website, 2010). Of course, we should not only pay lip service, the lynchpin of any successful reform is its implementation. Work is just like playing the piano, playing out of tune is equal to do nothing or to making noise. The final unfortunate results of education industrialization are certain to be magnified without firm execution and implementation of reform.

In the spreading ideological trend of education industrialization, the compulsory education Chinese people look forward to often could not be successfully implemented in the previous period, even though the time has been prolonged. In large and medium-sized cities, compulsory education seems to be the sole obligation of the parents. However, in the vast countryside, the promotion of compulsory education is facing huge difficulties. Financing their children's attendance at primary school is a heavy burden for some farmers, and constitutes an economic shackle. Owing to a variety of tuitions and fees, mountainous rural children drop out of school because their families cannot afford the entrance ticket to an education. Some ethnic regions in western China are lagging behind in economic development. The task of meeting compulsory education standards is merely hollow words if not coupled with implementation.

The result of a research group on the case of the transition of China's major education policy shows that there still existed a serious dropout rate in Chinese rural areas in June 2011. In a survey, sampling 17 rural junior high schools in different townships, the research group found the dropout rate to be uneven. The highest was 74.37 per cent; the average was about 43 percent, greatly more than the less than 3 per cent required by the policy of the "nine-year compulsory education" plan for rural places. Liu Bin, the former deputy director of the State Board of Education, was a participant of the appraisal meeting which appraised the research item. He pointed out that a developed city could receive education surcharges of up to more than ￥1 billion RMB to

¥2 billion RMB, but some leaders would rather take the money to set up affiliated schools than implement compulsory education free. Therefore, the gap among schools is growing (China Youth Daily, 2011). We can easily know that a high dropout rate is closely related to high education expenses. Furthermore, the appalling point is that the evil phenomenon of arbitrary charges can be seen everywhere.

On August 29, 2011, the official website of the Ministry of Education issued a notification concerning the typical cases of arbitrary charges. The Ministry of Education investigated 12 primary and secondary schools in Gansu, Anhui, Jiangxi, Hubei, Sichuan, and Henan Province. Thirteen responsible persons got a policy discipline punishment and three were removed from the principal's position. Let us take a Key University's affiliated high school for an example. The school is changed from a public school. The annual fee charged each student was ¥20,000 RMB; the school had 10 classes and each class had 60 students. So, the annual income of the school was up to tens of millions RMB (People's Daily, 2011).

This undoubtedly heightens the already heavy education burden of ordinary Chinese people. The chaos of education is a misery for society and the state. Owing to the spreading of education industrialization in recent years, absurdity and bitterness have flooded into the Chinese education system. From the social level, the unfairness in education has become the largest social injustice. From the perspective of awareness dissemination and personnel training, the chaos of education not only stimulates the desire to obtain a diploma, but also hinders a generation of high-tech talent potential from obtaining the Nobel Prize.

The arbitrary charges were more than ¥30 million RMB, while 244 people got punished in Jiangxi province in 2011. Concerning outstanding problems in compulsory education schools with regard to school choice fees, management and governance of teaching materials, Jiangxi discovered 305 events of violation charges, with ¥30.844 million RMB involved (Jiangxi News Website, 2012).The province had investigated and dealt with 108 events of arbitrary charges, with ¥4.4838 million RMB involved, while three principals dismissed

(Jiangxi News Website, 2012).Some schools can be said to have done their best to set fee items. In the past two years, the problem of arbitrary charges about which citizens began to complain became gradually serious in Guangdong province. In 2011, the investigation of ten cases of arbitrary charges, illegal service charges and collection charges accounted for a considerable proportion of total charges, including all sorts of excuses to charge sports training, bicycle storage, etc., while 576 students were charged ￥8,640 RMB for bicycle storage in Shangxu junior high school, Potou district, Zhanjiang city, Guangdong province. Mo Guanquan, the principal of the school, was dismissed from office (Shantou Daily, 2011).

From the viewpoint of the full implementation of compulsory education, the urban plan was basically implemented, but the results were not so ideal in the countryside. Education has become the biggest expense for rural areas. Therefore, there is a significant gap between the rich and the poor in education, and the disparity results in educational unfairness. Many instances have fully demonstrated that more effective measures concerning compulsory education need to be carried out to fully implement the Dakar Framework for Action launched by the United Nations.

Faced with increasing educational spending, poor residents are unable to cope with. Suicide happens occasionally among students because of the unaffordable tuition fees. Two pupils killed themselves by taking poison in October 2011, because they had no money to pay for the remedial teaching fees and could not bear the repeated dunning of the teachers (Law Evening News, 2011). This is just primary school. What happens at universities and colleges that ask for higher tuition fees? A survey of students in China shows that the average annual expenditure of an undergraduate is ￥7,000 RMB, including tuition fees, living expenses and accommodation fees. Therefore, a typical undergraduate spends at least ￥28,000 RMB in four years, equivalent to the net income of a poor country farmer for 35 years, without considering his living expenses, such as eating, clothing, medical care, and other expenditures (China Finance Newspaper, 2006).

Officials from the Ministry of Education pointed out that the total number of students in National Ordinary College was 22.85 million in 2009, 5.27 million of which were from poor families, who accounted for 23.06 per cent of the total enrollment, and 1.66 million were from extremely needy families, who accounted for 7.27 per cent of the total enrollment (China Consulting, 2010). It is well recognized that poor quality education is the root of poverty in China. Education expense is so high that not everyone can afford a good education, poor knowledge results in poor education, and poverty is the inevitable outcome, resulting in deficiency of wisdom and talent. This is a chain reaction. Therefore, educational equity is the most important prerequisite required to narrow the gap between the rich and the poor. As early as 30 years ago, there were no fees and tuitions in primary and secondary schools of the United States and many countries in Europe. Until now, the policy of “nine-year compulsory education” has not yet been fully implemented in China, although in some areas the plan has been implemented well.

The education problem in China has always been highly controversial. As early as September 2003, Katharina Thomas Tomasevski, the special investigator of the United Nations in charge of affairs on education rights, investigated for two weeks in China. She critically noted that China paled in comparison with Uganda, a poor African country, in terms of the guarantee of the right to basic education." China's expenditures on education account for only 2 per cent of the GDP (gross domestic product), much lower than 6 per cent, the minimum requirement of the United Nations." She said, "The government provides only 53 per cent of school funding, the rest is borne by the parents. The proportion the government commits is lower than all countries which implement a policy of compulsory education" (Business Week, 2004). This kind of criticism is very sharp. But we cannot consider domestic and international criticism of education industrialization as malicious attacks targeting some facet of Chinese education. The famous book "Serve the People", written by Mao Zedong, who is the first-generation leader of China, stresses that the

Chinese Communist Party is the political party that serves the people and that the Party is not afraid of receiving criticism of pointing out the shortcomings in its work. "We will act upon it if people can benefit from the method, no matter whoever comes up with it". Practice shows that acceptance of criticism and correction of errors will make things get better.

Negative Impacts on Education

China's higher education becomes more unbalanced when basic education tends to be increasingly unfair. Some colleges and universities, on the one hand, just require a low academic performance of candidates. On the other hand, its requirement of economic affordability is on the rise.

Relaxation of the enrollment standard does exist in some industrialized countries. However, that is an education mode of lenient entry but stringent exit appropriate to their national conditions. In China, there is almost no standard about some market-oriented higher educational institutions. You can easily enter some schools only if you are able to afford the "entrance fee". The quality of education cannot be guaranteed completely because of inferior teaching and low standards for graduation. We would hope that institutions of higher education could not sell degrees for pots of cash. This educational style has no possibility of cultivating talent. In addition, relaxed enrollment standards are also unable to train talented persons. It's refreshing to see that people are starting to raise doubts about these phenomena. Various criticisms gradually arise in conferences, meetings and media. How to eliminate such phenomena? The managers are responsible for advanced preparation. Just like clogging a flood, those in charge should use prior observation to predict the flood situation, and they should dredge the river as soon as possible, and they should build dams. Only issuing warnings when facing the flood, of course, is of no help.

The phenomenon of education industrialization has caused a big negative impact in that some high-ranking public servants obtain high degrees by the way of so-called “in-service education”. Administrative officials mainly rely on their own diligent efforts and prominent achievements to make greater political progress. But some officials have obtained a doctor’s degree without effort using the public’s money, more precisely, the money of taxpayers. The doctor’s degree is a serious academic and educational indicator. This approach is extremely bad. Although the certificate is true, the academic level of the diploma-holder is not real. Throughout the ancient and modern history of doctoral education and government officials, it is not difficult to find that high-level public servants take public funds to study for a PhD with in-service education. This only appears in the contemporary imperfect Chinese educational system with its disordered education management. It’s an ugly phenomenon of an anti-social civilization. This ideology, uprooted from the official standard which was prevalent in China's feudal society is a blasphemy to science and to the academy. The proliferation of this kind of doctorate education is detrimental rather than beneficial to the country. Imagine those doctoral students who have experienced rigorous doctoral program trainings. How can a Ph.D. student who lacks a rigorous doctoral program training master the scientific knowledge and methods he/she should have? A doctorate is a kind of recognition to a specific scholar who has obtained a high academic level and who has undergone rich academic experiences: a doctorate is not, rather, the recognition of a person’s work experiences.

The negative effects of these practices on the academic field, no matter in the long term or in the short term, are enormous and far-reaching. If China continues to allow the spread of this chaotic phenomenon, a doctoral education will be a joke in the world of international higher education. The lesser consequence is that the international community will not recognize China’s doctorate, while the graver consequence is that the integrity of the citizens and the image of the nation will suffer serious detriment. In China, some public servants with these superficial high-imitation diplomas, purporting to represent a master’s degree or doctor’s degree grasp plenty of chances to grab more power and more interests. This phenomenon is detrimental to the glorious image of the Communist Party.

Admittedly, the Chinese Communist Party has had a successful experience in selecting excellent cadres from practice in the revolutionary periods. Selecting potential people to go to school is an institutionalized practice. However, for the training of cadres, a strict management system must be established. We cannot walk into a stray path for seeking an invisible reputation. Public servants, because they are in important positions, should leave their posts in the learning period because earning an academic degree has always been a serious academic and educational task. We all know that one person can't have his cake and eat it too. The ideological root of this ugly social phenomenon has left a legacy from China's feudal society that in the past produced an official standard handed down for thousands of years, a standard which is completely contrary to the spirit of social public servants, as promoted by Marx, and the thinking of serving the people, as proposed by Mao Zedong.

The idea of the "official standard" has been the core of the ruling institution of the feudal landlord class since the Qin Dynasty. Since the time of the Qin Dynasty, the Emperor has had the supreme authority. Everything in the nation is dependent on the king (Suma Chien). Government officials below the emperor at all levels have their corresponding powers according to a hierarchical stratification, and these powers are tied together with the acquisition of wealth. Therefore, the Han Dynasty and the Wei-Jin Dynasties implemented the “nine-rank system”. The Sui Dynasty and the Tang Dynasty established the “imperial examination system” instead, and this system continued to function until the Qing Dynasty. These practices constituted the cultivation and construction of the institution of the “official standard". The "official standard" gradually becomes the ruling consciousness in China for thousands of years. The Scholars, written by Wu Jingzi in the late Qing Dynasty, Officialdom’s True Features, written by Li Baojia, Thick Black Theory, written by Li Zongwu, etc., all provided vivid and deep descriptions of the official standard, and included sardonic and critical words. China's current modernization has followed the foundation of history. Therefore, the decadent ideology of feudalism has inevitably corrupted the new society.

After summing up historical experience and lessons learned therefrom, Jiang Zemin, who once served as the chair of the Communist Party of China, profoundly pointed out: the so-called “official standard” is “official- oriented”. He seriously exposed the phenomenon of the “official standard” within the party, and criticized the erroneous ideas of some party members, especially the leading cadres. He said: "Some members or even leading cadres of the party consciously or unconsciously become the captives of this 'official standard' awareness. So, the phenomenon of buying and selling official positions arises; the phenomenon of false reports and fraud for honor and position arises; the phenomenon of doing everything for their official positions arises; and the phenomenon of abuse of power arises" (Jiang, 2001). Based on the construction of socialism and the interests of the people, Jiang Zemin severely criticized the decadent ideas that were endangering the party and the nation. There is no doubt that clearing up the high degree of fraud is a serious political struggle and must be implemented immediately.

Undoubtedly, the phenomenon of “false” diplomas connected to the ‘official standard’ is caused by the indulgent Chinese modern higher education system. It not only violates the normative principles of education, but also has other very bad effects, such as regarding diploma acquisition as the start, the process, and the result of education. Departing from the self-interest of individuals, the seemingly true but false master’s or doctor’s diploma acquired through non-formal channels is very useful because it can enhance the competitiveness of civil servants, or bring other personal benefits. However, when education, especially higher education, transforms into “diploma education”, far from “quality education” and “character education”, higher education is destined to become a powerful force for the retrogression of Chinese society. This is the scary point. The industrialization of education has not only flooded society with various "really fake diplomas" and "falsely true diplomas", but it also has distorted the concept of talent forged by the experience of centuries. Serious and scientific personnel training, in some places, have become a power-for-money deal. The whole society has paid a huge opportunity cost for these things.

In 2000, the World Education Forum of UNESCO adopted the Dakar Framework for Action, which established a goal that every citizen and every society should achieve six goals, making the goals of EFA (education for all) more specific. EFA is not just an educational issue but is first a development problem. Among the six EFA goals (literacy elimination, preschool education development, elementary education generalization, promotion of equal educational opportunities for men and women, life skills training, and comprehensive improvement of the quality of education), three (elementary education generalization, promotion of equal educational opportunities for men and women) have been included in the Millennium Development Goals adopted by the United Nations General Assembly. The promotion of EFA (education for all) development and the promotion of the Millennium Development Goals are inextricably linked together. Obviously, the implementation of industrial education is contrary to this program.

It is undoubtedly correct that administrative officials in charge of education should never show affection to the industrialization of education. Organs of state power must think twice before taking actions. In the process of deepening market economic system reform, all schools scrambled to expand their size no matter what their conditions and no matter what the results would be. At the end of the last century, Peking University took the first step by tearing down the south walls in order to build a row of store buildings. This has been a trend determined by actors who seek profits above all else, and promoted by great interests. In 2005, Peking University pulled down the shop buildings on the south, and re-built the school walls to correct the mistakes made in the past. However, this problem cannot be solely solved by the attitude of a single department. Actually, an erroneous ideological trend can never easily disappear in a few days.

When an erroneous ideological trend emerges like the tidewater, we should uphold the truth from the bottom up. Mao Zedong said, "More importantly, the administrative authorities should take more responsibility to guide this trend to the right direction". This means that the evaluation of management performance and the actual situation people live in is not determined by discussion or declaration, but by the reality of the social situation. Practice is the sole criterion for testing truth, and is also the sole criterion for the evaluation of management performance. Development is of overriding importance, including social equity. Education is the basic way of ensuring the criterion of social equity. There is no equity without education, and without education, the economy cannot get developed. Education problems in some places have become severe. The grievances of the public can be felt daily. At this critical moment, administrative organs should take more effective actions to correct errors in order to maintain social stability and to eliminate the risks of instability.

The coordination between government departments is very poor and the coordination mechanism is not perfect. The arbitrariness of administrative coordination between government departments is greater than the binding. To solve the problem of inconformity between national development strategy and specific policies, and the inadequate response of educational policy to national strategy, the government should speed up to establish a horizontal coordination mechanism with educational departments.

The government should construct an accountability system which emphasizes effectiveness, to protect right to education, actively promote the construction of administrative accountability system. The government should improve education regulatory regime to supervise the public school and try to achieve the transformation of educational decision making from experience-based type to modern democracy type.

Education Weakens the Position of China in the World

Higher education is an important part of national education. Its level of development is a crucial factor in measuring the overall strength of a country or region. Different from the credit system in the United States, colleges and universities in China have relaxed the guidance and management of students, lowered the demand for failing students in many courses, and implemented the so-called "cleaning test" to ensure that students will not repeat their grades, which is very different to the credit system in the United States. In the United States, the academic status of students will be evaluated through the credit system and performance points, whereas the flexible management is carried out via performance points and credit system. This is one of the differences between China and the United States, which shows the enormous difference between exam-oriented education and quality education.

The Chinese students are taking exam-oriented education from primary school to high school. It adopts a top-down education mode in which teachers give lessons and students receive knowledge in class passively. This kind of education mode lacks interaction and exchange of ideas; thus, the learning enthusiasm reduces greatly. This is a binding education model with teachers' constraints in the schools and parents' constraints at home. The students lack self-discipline and over-depend on external power, which will result in the intolerance after their entering the society. Some students even do not know how to look for suitable jobs and they let their parents arrange jobs for them. In contrast, the students are independent under the American-style education, although the parents in the United States are also more "ruthless" than the parents in China. By the age of 18, their children are left for self-reliance. Not to mention the fact that even parents in China do their best to help their children find a job. This is extremely absurd and impossible for parents and students in the United States. If China wants to surpass the United States to become the world leader, at least there is still a long way to go in education.

In the current era of knowledge economy, the issue of education relates to the improvement of the quality of the entire nation as well as the development of the country and even its existence. To a certain extent, Darwin's law of "superiority and inferiority" still applies. However, the winners of the future world are no longer the slaughterers of violent wars, but they belong to the nation whose education is more popularized and whose culture is more developed. The world will be developed in the direction of "wisdom taking". After all, peaceful development is the theme of the world today. As announced by the Board of Education recently, "The only way to sustain and improve our competitive edge in the world is to devote all our efforts to reforming our education". The 21st century is an era of knowledge expansion and the new society. The new era has given China a new historical responsibility. There are prophets who predict that future illiterates will no longer be just illiterate people, but the people who are incapable of action. Therefore, the Chinese people must develop their self-learning abilities in their studies. However, China's exam-oriented education ignores this point specifically.

Empowering the country by focusing on education is not unprecedented in the world history. For example, Russia in the time of Peter I, Japan in the Meiji Restoration, and Germany in early Bismarck achieved unparalleled growth because of their emphasis on education. A common characteristic of them all is that they attach importance to challenging work, which is unlike the China's current emphasis. Peter dressed personally to go to Western Europe to learn shipbuilding technologies; Japan sent many students to the West to learn advanced education; and Germany, a learning-oriented country, never do things without outcomes unlike China. China overemphasizes the knowledge of the books. China has always had the reputation of "not hearing the word out of the window and reading the books of saints". But in the world today, China will not be able to become the world leader only by reading sages. To become the world leader, China must have an open-minded attitude to overcome the "shortcomings" in her development. As discussed before, China's education is weakening the opportunity to be the world leader for China. It is high time for China to consider what to do about this indispensible issue.

There is no doubt that education is relevant to every family, and even to the entire nation! Education is the foundation. The problem of education is more important than all other social issues. If the vicious circle of education continues, the ultimate victim will be everyone and the future of the entire nation! If the education system does not change, the victims will be the succeeding generations in the future. If the embarrassment of education continues, who are going to build China in the future? Mr. Yi Zhongtian, as a famous educator, once said with emotion: "There is no hope for China's education, it is even worse than Chinese football". This metaphor carries a bit of ridicule and sarcasm, but this is the cry of an educator. If so, what a sad it will be for China's education! After the founding of New China, the Chinese nation is no longer a "coward" to be on the verge of death. China has confidence to believe that the future of education in China will be getting better and better (Perry, 2014).

Chapter 7

Construction of New Socialist Society and Its Ways

China is a large agricultural country. Since the implementation of the household contract responsibility system, business circles, political circles and academic circles have been exploring constantly how to make the Chinese agriculture move forward along a sustainable, rapid, and sound development way. Because of complex rural problems, currently it is still the top priority for the Chinese Communist Party to solve Three Rural Issues, which are agriculture, countryside and farmers. Starting from a brand new strategy, China identified the general guidelines for building a new socialist countryside during the Twelfth Five-year Plan period: agricultural modernization should be promoted with further development of industrialization and urbanization to improve the long-term mechanism of industry stimulating agriculture and urban areas leading rural areas; to increase the efforts of enhancing agriculture and benefiting farmers; to enhance agricultural modernization level and farmers' living standard; and to construct beautiful homeland for farmers' happy life. By completion of rural development systems and mechanisms, economic, political, cultural and social construction in rural areas should be comprehensively promoted to make rural areas become a new world of prosperity, affluence, democracy, civilization and harmony.

From the "First Rich" to "The Rich"

The traditional small-scale peasant economy is basically the largest component of Chinese society. All splendid achievements of Chinese Reform and Opening Policy resulted from the production quotas to each household in a small village. At first, a dozen farmer households took risks for feeding themselves, but they finally created a historical trend which provided experience for the overall economic reform including urban economic system. It is still enlightening for these successful experiences to solve the Three Rural Issues. Enhancing agriculture for benefiting farmers as well as accelerating construction of new socialist countryside in the Twelfth Five-year Plan period was put forward on the basis that fabulous changes have taken place in rural areas. It is a strategic plan proposed from the perspective of historically solving recent problems in new stage. However, at the same time of speeding up development of modern agriculture, broadening the channels of increasing farmers' income was listed as a top priority.

Constantly Improving Farmers' Living Standard

Chinese farmers' living standard in the 21st century was much higher than that in the early seventies of the last century; it was a great achievement of the Reform and Opening Policy. Reform in China was originated from the countryside and the reform was begun by the farmers themselves. Before 1978, Xiaogang Village in Fengyang County of Anhui Province was the famous "Three Dependence Village" around the county for "eating by return selling, money on relief and production by loan". Almost every family went out to beg for food after autumn harvest each year. On November 24, 1978, eighteen farmer households in Xiaogang Village started the "All-round Contract", which meant that the beginning of Chinese rural reform was officially unveiled. In the autumn harvest of next year, household-based contract system was proved to be effective in Xiaogang Village. The overall food production reached 66000kg. It was the first time for the villagers to deliver tax grain to the state and to pay off the loan. In 1980, grain production in Xiaogang Village reached 69500kg, while in 1997, it increased to 380000kg. Deng Xiaoping who keenly sighted and summarized the rural reform experience with the direction to start historical process of the Reform and Opening policy in China and march the second reform under the leadership of Chinese Communist Party. The adventure of production quotas to each household conduct by Xiaogang Village led to introduction of a rural property rights system reform throughout the China.

In 1982, the Chinese Communist Party issued the Central Document No.1, which pointed out clearly that the production quotas to each household, the household-based contract system and the all-round contract, all were "the socialist production responsibility system". This Central Document No.1 not only broke through traditional system frame of "the means of production in the countryside are owned by the people's commune, the production brigade and the production team, with basis on teams", affirming the "Double Contract" (the production quotas to each household contract and the household-based contract) system, but it also stated that the "Double Contract" was "different from the small-scale individual economy before the collectivization, while it was a part of socialist agricultural economy". From then on, it was the production quotas to each household conduct, an ancient and rustic method that stepped on the political stage in China. As a result, momentous changes have taken place in rural area around China as well as the economic society has taken on an entirely new look. Of course, the road of rural reform was not everything going off smoothly. In that period, it also went through a substantial number of difficulties and setbacks.

China is a country whose population is mainly farmers. To increase farmers' income is the basis of making the country rich and strong. Affected by some objective factors, the increasing rate of farmers' income became relatively small since nineties of the last century. Therefore, it has become a problem which influences the development of China and stability of society. During the "Tenth Five-year Plan" plan, China adopted a series of policies and measures to promote the economic development in rural areas putting much emphasis on solving the problem of farmers' living standard by raising farmers' per capita net income and the growth rate to a great extent. The annual growth rate of Chinese farmers' per capita net income increased from 4.2% in 2001 to 6.2% in 2005 and farmers' per capita net income raised from 2366 yuan in 2001 to 3255 yuan in 2005, with an average annual rate of 5.3%. Not only did it exceed the annual average growth rate of Ninth Five-year Plan period, but also surpassed the goal of 5% for Tenth Five-year period. Additionally, in 2011, the growth rate of farmers' per capita net income raised to 11.4%, reaching up to 6977 yuan.

During the "Eleventh Five-year Plan" period, the development of rural economy continued advancing triumphantly. Rural residents' per capita net income increased from 3255 yuan in 2005 to 5919 yuan in 2010, achieving the average annual growth rate of 8.9% which was greatly over the growth goal of 5% for the Eleventh Five Year Plan. People could "enjoy delicious food, dress comfortable clothes, settle down peacefully and respect their customs", which is a perfect realm described by Chinese ancient sages(Laozi, Spring and autumn period). Although the above changes having taken place in Chinese contemporary society had a great distance from the realm described thousands of years ago, it was the first time to happen since Pan Gu had separated the heaven and the earth. There is no doubt that the development made by people deserves heartily applauding and admiration.

Although the agricultural economy and rural society had made a great progress after the Reform and Opening-up Policy in China, the central government and people clearly knew that China was still a developing country whose agriculture was still on the difficult stage of rise. There is still a trend of widening income gap between income of the urban and rural dwellers. The most prominent contradiction is the low growth rate for farmers' income. Topic of the Central Document No.1 had been "Three Rural Issues" (agriculture, countryside and farmers) for six consecutive years, from 2004 to 2009, emphasizing the status of the "Three Rural Issues" as the top priority in Chinese socialist modernization period. On 29th January 2011, China issued *the Decision Made by The CPC Central Committee and the State Council on Speeding Up Water Conservancy Reform and Development*, which deployed the water conservancy work for the first time. So far, China has continuously issued eight Central Document NO.1 giving instruction on the work related to Three Rural Issues in the 21st century, which stimulated farmers' production and income growth effectively and raised comprehensive productivity of agriculture. They created a new phrase of socialism, new countryside construction, and brought a strong driving force to farmers' persistent income growth and secular stability in rural areas as well.

Typical Marxist writers thought highly of issues related to agriculture, countryside and farmers. Marx, Engels and Lenin used to start from the universal law of agricultural development, emphasizing the basic position and the function of agriculture in national economy development and paying attention to the analysis of industry-agriculture relation and rural-urban relationship in capitalism period. Especially, the problems related to farmers were put forward by them as the major issue of proletarian revolution and socialism construction. They studied issues of worker-peasant alliance from the need of proletarian revolution and they also emphasized that it was significant for proletarian revolution and socialist construction to build and consolidate the worker-peasant alliance in the countries which are dominated by peasant population. It was them who considered how to solve problems of farmers, countryside and agriculture from the perspective of socialism construction, which was the Three Rural Issues put forward by China now. They also made a scientific prediction of development prospect for farmers, countryside and agriculture.

Engels, who wrote the famous works named *Germany Peasant Wars* and *The Issues of Germany and French Peasants*, used to study the issues of European farmers carefully. He put forward the idea that if the proletariat take the national state in violent ways in the future, they should conduct a principle assumption for small-scale peasant economy transformation in socialistic society through demonstration and offering social assistance to it instead of the use of violence (Marx and Engels, 1995). Lenin, in the early victory of Russian October

Revolution, introspected the "mistakes" made by the ultra "leftist" idea promoted by Bolshevik in Russian rural areas from 1918 to 1920 and determinedly persuaded the comrades in central committee of the Russian Communist Party to carry out "New Economic Policy" in the Spring of 1921, which was put forward by him. That was an accurate guideline to solve the rural issues in Russia. One of the important components of the New Economic Policy was to replace surplus grain collection system with grain tax policy (Compilation and Translation Bureau of the CPC Central Committee, 2001). Why was the New Economic Policy introduced? Because the first a few years after the October Revolution, Soviet Russia was under a military attack from foreign powers so that the situation became extremely severe. The Russian Communist Party was forced to adopt the radical policy to strengthen state ownership of land and expand free collection of farmers' surplus grain.

Lenin pointed out the negative consequences brought by the radical policies that we came across a great political crisis in the interior of Soviet Russia, which I thought was the most enormous. Not only did the crisis make a considerable part of farmers dissatisfied, but it also caused workers' dissatisfaction. A substantial number of farmers stood on the opposite side at that time so that peasant uprisings are a common phenomenon in Russia. Lenin deeply understood the reasons for that: what leads to this special situation that we also think to be extremely unpleasant? It is because we have gone forward so far away on the path to boost economy that we did not ensure ourselves adequate base area. People have felt that it is not in our power to directly transfer to the pure socialistic economy form and the pure socialistic distribution. If we cannot retreat while merely completing some easy tasks, we would be in danger of extinction (Lenin, 1960).

In fact, what Lenin sparkplugged to carry out was the retreating New Economic Policy which guaranteed farmers' benefit and won victory in early years of the new nation. Stalin prematurely announced to stop retreating in the process of leading former Soviet Union socialist construction, no longer carrying out the important content of

New Economic Policy which was still feasible at that time. He did not solve the issues of countryside, agriculture and farmers in Soviet Union; instead, to a considerable extent, he brought about industrialization by depriving farmers there. Of course, there were certain historical reasons for this approach. However, after the end of World War II, former Soviet Union still did not correct its mistakes on Three Rural Issues, which was an important reason why the Soviet Union finally failed.

Before establishment of the People's Republic of China, there was backward economy; shortage of community services; and high illiteracy rate of people in Chinese rural areas. How to construct a rich and flourishing countryside? What do farmers need? Communist Party in China conducted painstaking exploration patiently. Mao Zedong indicated, now farmers are dissatisfied with the alliance set up by us and them in the past, which is based on agrarian revolution. We must benefit them in a new way nowadays and that is socialism (Mao, 1978). To develop rural economy is to construct socialism. If China breaks away from this general direction, farmers could not get rich and the agriculture would still be laggard. It is a pity that the socialist construction in Chinese countryside followed a tortuous path for a long time. After China carried out the Reform and Opening-up Policy, top decision-makers of the Communist Party in China started everything from reality, gradually deepening the guiding ideology and basic line for socialist modernization construction and development with Chinese characteristic. Deng Xiaoping, who designed and conducted Chinese rural reform, distributed the land to peasants in patches. The essence of land contract responsibility system is a way to sublet the land. In fact, the rent is public rations paid to government from peasants, which is equivalent to the grain tax. As compared with the New Economic Policy carried out by Lenin, it was a free collection system using limited tax in kind (rent) to replace all surplus grain (or public grain).

Having deeply understood the national conditions and the state of people, both Deng Xiaoping and Lenin implemented the policy of recuperation to settle down citizens and enrich the people, whose great historical significance and effects were recognized throughout the world. From the Sixteenth National Congress of the Communist Party of China to the Third, the Fourth and the Fifth Plenary Session of the 16th National Congress, CPC Central Committee had formed overall thoughts, measures, goals and demands to solve the Three Rural Issues in the new century and the new stage. The Central Document No.1 issued in February of 2006 stated the theoretical policies to construct socialist new countryside, putting forward the idea that we should insist on the policy of giving more, taking less and more flexibility to speed up building the long-term system of promoting agriculture by industry, leading countryside with towns (Staff Writer of Xinhua News Agency, 2006). This is the epitome of the basic idea and thought to solve the Three Rural Issues since the Sixteenth National Congress that the Party Central Committee comprehensively implemented the Scientific Development Concept. Reviewing the offering social service anticipated by Engels and providing new benefit for them put up by Mao Zedong, it is clear to know that the pathfinder of the world socialist theory, the founder of socialism in new China, directors of new rural construction in socialist China in the new century and leaders of the Communist Party from different nationalities and various times share the same spirit.

There is no doubt that living standard and educational level of peasants would be raised steadily by following the new generation leaders in China. The socialist rural construction could be successful and the historical goal of building a moderately prosperous society in all respects could be achieved if material civilization, spiritual civilization and political civilization in rural areas are fully developed.

Carry Forward the Institutional Improvement

The Chinese modernization construction is based on farmers, countryside and agriculture, while the Three Rural Issues are still facing numerous difficulties. Especially the slow growth rate of farmers' income so far, the substantial number of farmers and the growing gap between the rural and urban incomes; causes for these problems are some flaws in the institutions, but to solve them there is a long way to go. On 29th November 2011, the central poverty alleviation work conference convoked in Beijing decided to make rural per capita net income 2300 yuan (about 355.6 dollars) as a new standard for poverty alleviation. The new one increased 92% as compared with the standard of less than 1196 yuan. The new "poverty line" of 2300 yuan means that population of poor people in China raised from 26.88 million in 2010 to 128 million, taking up 13.4% of overall population in rural areas of China. It accounts for nearly one tenth of the national population (except Hong Kong, Macao and Taiwan), which is more than the overall population in many countries.

At the same time, according to the statistics issued by the World Bank and data released by China, GDP of China was 6.62 trillion more than that of Japan in 2016, ranking the second in the world, but the per capita GDP was almost three times less than Japan. On the other hand, though China has overtaken Japan as the second largest economy in the world, it is still a long way to catch up with America, the largest economy, whose economic scale was about 11 trillion dollars. It was three times as large as the economic scale in China. According to the data released by International Monetary Fund and other international organizations, per capita GDP of China ranked about 74th in the world in 2016 (The World Bank, 2016). China still had 150 million impoverished people according to the United Nation's standard of everyone earning 1 dollar every day. As the former prime minister Wen Jiabao had summarized when he visited Austria in April 2006, so far per capita GDP of China still ranked after hundredth in the world, but it is the largest developing country in the world. "There is a long way to go for China to realize modernization, which needs several or even dozens of generations to untiringly struggle for it (Wen, 2006). It is not allowed to have slackness or complacency at any time. Otherwise, it is impossible to achieve common prosperity for the whole country.

First, to increase farmers' income should be the priority in construction of new countryside. At the Fourth Plenary Session of the

Eleventh National People's Congress, the former prime minister Wen Jiabao clearly indicated that China should take the Three Rural Issues at the top priority. As the further development of industrialization and modernization, agricultural modernization should be promoted synchronously to consolidate and develop achievements in agriculture and rural areas. By referring the development of rural modernization to a strategic altitude, there is no doubt that it is a new explanation to realistic problems and a new level after enhancing understanding, which provides theories, instructions and decision basis to construct socialism. Wen Jiabao emphasized to guarantee supply of agricultural products, increase farmers' income in multiple channels, enhance the standard of poverty alleviation and intensify the efforts to fight poverty (Wen, 2011). Though farmers' income has raised much during the last two years, there is no change in the widening income gap between urban and rural residents so the slow growth of farmers' income is still the most prominent contradiction. There are also some shortages in social programs of rural areas. Farmers only benefit from a small proportion of modern social services. In recent years, the percentage of food expenditure per capita in living consumption has declined in rural households indicating that the problem of food has been basically solved. However, the proportion of expenditure on clothing, household facilities, services and other commodities remains low. What's more, expenditures on educational and entertaining facilities have shown a downward trend (as shown in table 7.1). It shows that farmers lead a monotonous life and the social support service is insufficient. Farmers do not benefit from the welfare brought by the Reform and Opening-up Policy.

As illustrated by *National Education Funds Execution Statistics Bulletin in 2016* in China, the per capita budget of public expense for ordinary primary school students was 2610.80 yuan in 2016, which increased 7.25% as compared with 2434.26 yuan in the last year. The per capita public expenditure for rural students was 2402.18 yuan. Though it was 6.99% more than 2245.20 yuan of the last year (*National Education Funds Execution Statistics Bulletin, 2016*), it was still below the national average level, even much lower than the average public expenditure for urban students. It was the same for the average public expenditure for ordinary junior school education in China. There is an undisguised gap between urban and rural areas.

In 2016, the Ministry of Health in China published the *Statistical Bulletin on National Health Development.* The three-year plan for the new medical reform, one of whose overall goals is to "reduce residents' medical burden", came to the final year of implementation in 2016. However, according to the statistics of bulletin in 2016, the average medical expense for outpatients each time in hospital and the per capita medical expense for inpatients increased 5.0% and 4.1% respectively in 2016, as compared with the price of the former year. The average daily medical expense for inpatients was 914.8 yuan, with a growth rate of 6.1%, which was a little higher than the increase rate of per capita medical expense for inpatients. Thus, the medical reform is full of difficulties.

Table 7.1 Consumption Expenditure of Rural Resident Households 1990 to 2009

Unit: %

Item \ Time	1990	1995	2000	2005	2008	2009
Living Expenditure	100.00	100.00	100.00	100.00	100.00	100.00
Food	58.80	58.62	49.13	45.48	43.67	40.97
Clothing	7.77	6.85	5.75	5.81	5.79	5.82
Living	17.34	13.91	15.47	14.49	18.54	20.16
Family Equipment and Service	5.29	5.23	4.52	4.36	4.75	5.13
Transportation	1.44	2.58	5.58	9.59	9.84	10.09

Equipment and Service of Culture, Education and Entertainment	5.37	7.81	11.18	11.56	8.59	8.53
Medical Treatment	3.25	3.24	5.24	6.58	6.72	7.20
Other Commodities and Service	0.74	1.76	3.14	2.13	2.09	2.11

Data Source: Edited by National Statistical Bureau. Chinese Statistical Yearbook 2010. Beijing: Chinese Statistical Press, 2010.

We can find from the statistical report issued by the Ministry of Health in China that though in total health expenditure of recent years, the proportion of civilian personal medical expenditure has been decreasing year by year, the absolute number keeps on increasing. For example, it was 26.701 billion in 1990 and it was 119.965 billion in 2015, with the compound annual growth rate of 16.44%. These intractable medical problems are caused by long-term accumulation of several reasons, which mainly are the imbalanced structure of medical resources, unequal expenditure for health, unstable drug circulation order, complex and expensive medical service as well as incomplete medical market supervision.

Structural disequilibrium of medical resources in China causes the problem of "difficult to get medical service, expensive to get medical treatment", particularly for farmers. To solve the problem that farmers cannot afford the medical expense, it takes plenty of financial capital and human resources, without expectation to solve problems at one time. Therefore, at "the Sixth Chinese Comprehensive Prosperity Forum in 2012" held on 11th December 2012, Chen Wenling, director of the Comprehensive Department of the Research Office in the State Council, put forward the policy of "sharing, development and win-win cooperation" to solve the great difference of medical and health service between urban and rural areas (Chen, 2011). To be specific, it refers to that urban and rural residents should benefit from the affluent medical resources together and carry forward integrated design in urban and rural areas. There should be qualified doctors, advanced equipment, good technology and excellent service in urban and rural areas. By transformation of medical service system and integrated medical supply for both urban and rural areas, win-win situation in both areas can be achieved.

People's health condition is also closely related to quality of the ecological environment. The bad ecological environment would spread diseases to directly influence quality of people's life. Owing to the laggard economy development in rural areas, the technology of agricultural production is low so that farmers are short of capital and ability to beautify their homeland. Thus, the quality of ecological environment in Chinese rural areas shows a downward trend year by year. In most of the countryside, there are still low-level farming and outdated traditional production which overuses pesticides, chemical fertilizers and other chemicals. There are small-scale livestock breeding everywhere and other related industries with excrements of livestock and arbitrary slaughter.

Ecological environment in the countryside is damaged severely day by day because of crop residue burning, garbage pollution, decrease of Greenland and so on. It appears that the development trend is transforming from structural damage to functional disorders. At the same time, pollutants produced by urban industries without restriction have a direct influence on the ecology in the countryside. Specifically, the worst consequence would be that the problem of soil erosion has not been solved, but the problem of land desertification is prominent, with increasing salinization of land in some areas. Though coverage of forests rises, the function is going down. The acreage of grassland is decreasing constantly and the quality is also declining. Unreasonable exploitation of water resources causes rivers cutting off, with withering lakes and oases as well as downward level of underground water. Owing to the exploitation of mineral resources, coverage of damaged land is large and it shows an upward trend. The worsening ecological environment in rural areas not only has a direct effect on farmers' physical health, but it also retains development of agricultural economy at low level. If China does not adopt more effective measures to solve this problem, it would directly influence the progress of building a common prosperous society.

The outline of "Eleventh Five-year Plan" regards construction of socialist new countryside at the top priority, and it put forward many new guidelines and strategies, which were summary and heritage of the experience to construct an economic society in the past. The economic history of New China shows that it has gone through long-term exploration of how develop new rural construction. In the last fifties, China had put forward the issue of socialist new rural construction when it drew up the Second Five-year Plan and Third Five-year Plan for the national economy. However, there were great differences between the socialism new rural construction of the Eleventh Five-year Plan and the former ones because it had distinct background of times and great historical and realistic significance, which was the foundation of modernization. It is even more important for the Twelfth Five-year Plan to inherit and carry forward these guidelines.

Therefore, the leadership and implementation should be strengthened while carrying out the policy of the Central Committee about Three Rural Works to grasp important opportunities for the development of national agriculture and rural areas. To increase farmers' income should be the central task of constructing a well-off society in rural areas, with further adjustment of agricultural structure and measures of strengthening industries to nurture agriculture and cities to promote rural development. Long-term and effective system to increase farmers' income should be established and intensified. Thus, China should improve farmers' life standard constantly and dispose urban-rural relationship properly by starting from economic reform and overcoming difficulties that hinder rural development.

Secondly, unreasonable "scissors differential" and land expropriation stole rural wealth. Before the Reform and Opening-up Policy, Chinese society was centered on the household registration system. Urban and rural population, economy and social life were separated into two detached parts artificially. There were two different institutions between urban and rural areas for the redistribution of resources in China. Because of these institutions, residents living in two different areas were provided with different economy and social benefits, which could not circulate freely. A great number of rural resources were extracted to urban areas to support the progress of industrialization. The "price scissors" of industrial and agricultural products was unreasonable for a long time. At that time, products that urban people consumed was mainly from countryside while the large part of urban residents' income flew into countryside through purchasing necessities of life. However, influenced by "ultra-Left" thought, peasants were paid little for their labor. Farmers in many rural areas worked hard for the whole year, but what they got were mainly work points that could be used in physical distribution and very little cash. What's worse, in some specific places, farmers even owned production teams a debt at the end of the year. A large amount of wealth in rural areas was gathered to cities by unreasonable "price scissors", becoming the investment capital of industrial development. The little rural development was because of lack of investment capital. The fracture morphology caused by urban-rural dual structure was distinct. After the Reform and Opening-up Policy, the urban-rural dual structure went through a deep evolution.

Especially during the recent ten years, marketization promotion has become more and more rapid. Cities rush into the era of durable goods of consumption, a large part of which are imports. We can speak that cities are running into the era of luxury. Numerous expensive luxuries from French, German and America German are pouring into China. The excessive consumption led by the rich is spreading rapidly in cities, but it does not become the reality of rural consumption. Objectively, countryside is excluded from the enjoyment of modern life. The expenditure of housing, cars, electric appliances, medical treatment, education, travelling and other urban consumption are becoming more and more enhanced. They are difficult to flow into countryside. Meanwhile, the proportion of agricultural products produced in rural areas of China accounts for in urban residents' consumption becomes smaller and smaller. The price farmers pay for currency recycling was more than that at the time of People's Commune. Farmers have become vulnerable groups and a large proportion of them are pushed into the margin of modernization progress reluctantly.

Currently, industrialization and urbanization expropriate land in low prices to transfer rural wealth. The land is the most fundamental production factor for farmers and rights of land are the most important property rights for them. To realize factor capitalization and market-oriented allocation is internal requirement to improve the market economic system. With the market economic system, elements of land allocation and commercialization of real estate asset are the essence of land contracting exchange, which should be based on the clear definition for property rights. The institution of farmland property rights is setting and categorizing a variety of functions including farmland ownership, right of use, right to earnings, disposition and so on. It is an institutional system to standardize the farmland usage relationship. As an important profitable subject in the rural land relationship, farmers' property rights of land are closely related to the institution of farmland property rights. Land ownership definition, land ownership transfer, land relationship legislation and other sessions could directly influence the equities of farmers. However, these legislations are not impeccable at present. Farmland property rights are absent, while it is unreasonably land expropriation that damages farmers' equities, leading to sharp contradiction.

There are three prominent problems of land expropriation system in China. Firstly, the application scope of land expropriation is expanded. The main reason that farmers' equities are damaged is that the land expropriation scope is too broad and a substantial number of profit-oriented projects take the advantage of public power to requisite land. Secondly, the procedure of land acquisition is short of rationality. With the current system, it is easy for governments to integrate self-interests with interests of enterprises and develop the relationship of complicity to conduct land expropriation optionally, because of the pressure of finance, the agent of profit and tax and effect of political achievement. Farmers are short of opportunities and skills to negotiate, which would lead to overlook their rights of land paid in some ways. Thirdly, the compensation for land expropriation is too low and it experiences layers of exploitation. In developed market economic countries, there would be compensation for owners of the land based on "fair market price". The standard of compensation should not only take the current market value of land into consideration but also should be concerned about the prospective earnings of land. China also implements the system of compensation for land acquisition. Though there are different compensations for different regions, compensation in cash would be given to people.

However, there are some radical marketing measures in some areas, retaining the compensation arbitrarily, which used to take place frequently. A survey was conducted in Jiangsu Province in 2004 when there was frequent land expropriation, which indicated that if the cost of land expropriation was 100%, the allocation of earnings would be 20%-30% taken by governments, 40%-50% occupied by enterprises, 25%-30% taken by village organizations and only 5%-10% for peasants (Chen, 2004). The peasants who lost their farmland are in difficulties because they cannot receive fair compensation and social security.

As early as 2005, Chinese Academy of Sciences released a research report to analyze the market-oriented phenomenon of unequal wealth transfer. The report shows that if it is calculated from 1979 when China carried out the Reform and Opening-up Policy, and averagely various buildings occupied four-million-mu farmland every year, the coverage of farmland expropriated during this 25 years is nearly 100 million mu. If there is 10 thousand yuan per mu, real estate property farmers offered to industrialization and modernization has been equivalent to ten trillion since the Reform and Opening-up Policy. After using three exclamation marks in succession, the report states the reality: it is estimated that farmers who lost their land only received one twentieth compensation. During the 20 years, the compensation for those farmers who lost their land was not more than 500 billion yuan. In the industrialization and urbanization of the 25 years, the state, with urban industry and commerce, transferred and accumulated more than nine-trillion property from low prices of rural collective land. Furthermore, the government has played a driven role for a long time. For example, governments could expropriate farmers' land at a low price, which transforms the collective land to the national land that could invite public bidding. It could sell to bid winners who need construction land and differences of prices can reach hundreds of yuan even more than thousands of yuan.

Until early 2011, *Housing Expropriation and Compensation Clauses on National Land* was introduced. It is decided that demolition in cities would compensate people at market price, but the expropriation and compensation of collective land are still vague for people. It is not difficult to imagine that transfer of the substantial number of real estate assets between urban and rural areas in industrialization and urbanization is merely an epitome of the urban-rural dual problem in China nowadays. In fact, it is a new form of breakage between the rural and urban areas, which was not mainly caused by the household registration system of administrative nature. The main reason is the radical marketization that is not in accordance with the realities in China. Plenty of farmers who lost their land have become unemployed vagrants, whose life is in trouble. Though the urban-rural dual structure is an inevitable historical phenomenon, the chaos caused by market-oriented land expropriation is a sort of profound urban-rural segmentation and an internal turbulence that could threaten social stability.

It damages most peasants' interests that their land is expropriated at a low price. Not only does the land expropriation not makes the farmers wealthy, but it also causes many farmers losing their farmland and jobs. The gap between the urban and the rural areas does not narrow, but it increases social inequalities. Consequently, to protect peasants' interests is the core of land expropriation system reform, to allow collective non-agricultural land for constructions in rural areas to enter market circulation directly. Related laws and regulations should be revised. There should be equal negotiations between developers and land owners, giving opportunity for land owners, the peasant collective economic organizations, to directly negotiate and trade with local governments so long as it complies with land use program and it is under strict land use restriction. China should allow and encourage the farmers to take part in the secondary distribution of land income by lease, stake and other ways, to obtain long-lasting and stable profit. In recent years, the issues of farmers' land properties have been thought highly of by high-level policy makers.

From 11th November to 12th November in 2011, in the Second Session Legality and Market Academic Seminar about Territorial Resources held in Beijing, "the land acquisition system reform" became the focal topic once again. Specialists taking part in the seminar reached the consensus that it was hard to continue the current pattern of land acquisition, so China need to realize the great significance of land expropriation system reform from implementing Scientific Development Concept and promoting economic development pattern. Obviously, Communist Party in China and the top leaders have set out to prepare for the reform of land expropriation system and make it as important as the household registration system reform, to carry out the equal employment institution for urban and rural employees as well as to build and improve various rural social security systems which match the economic development level. About the land issues, historical mistakes cannot be made again and laws should fully adopt to manage the land to practically protect farmers' rights of land properties.

Eliminate Wrong Argument that Impedes Equal Distribution of Wealth

With a growing gap between urban and rural incomes, the social inequality enlarges. Especially for farmers, their incomes are lagging so that they become vulnerable groups and tens of millions of people have not solved the problem of clothing and food, which is the most difficult reality that China is facing now. In all ages, the traditional ideology and cultural custom in China is to concern more about income equality than the amount of income and concern more about the stability of people's life instead of poverty of people. Income inequality is most likely to cause social instability and it is even a major factor that can directly affect national rise and fall. The ancient sage, Confucius, said if wealth is equal, there would be no poverty and the country would be in peace so that the population can enlarge. Therefore, how to move forward to "the rich" from the reform of "first rich", how to make the whole peasantry become wealthy and how to conduct more equal social wealth distribution are all important problems for China to deal with at present. When faced with the gap between the rich and the poor, the marketization theory overlooked inequity at first, but later this ideology advocated to not cherishing the "hatred of the rich" because it was harmful. Problems in China cannot be solved by depending on the rich to help the poor. After that, there was a new theory asking what the equity was. In the past, it was thought that the equal distribution is equity. Then people thought that the equal opportunities' provision was equity. Nowadays, equity comes from identification. If someone can assimilate into communities and is recognized as a member of them, there would be a sense of equity. There are still such kinds of wrong arguments existing which impede to solve the problem of farmers' income growing slowly, so it should be eliminated.

Firstly, what is equity and what is identification on earth? With scientific analysis, identification is extensive, such as national identification, ethical identification, cultural identification, social identification and so on. Apparently, the comprehension of rural-urban income gap is social identification. Social identification, which has similar mental mechanism with religious identification, linguistic identification, regional cultural identification, class identification, professional identification, sexual identification and others, is an organizational identification. The organizational cohesion caused by social attraction is not the interpersonal attraction formed by similarity, interdependence and exchange of personal characteristics between the group members, or the organizational cohesion caused by that. However, it is a form of organizational identification. This identification is a sense of "WE", which is the mental foundation to build up business community and interest community. The sense of "WE" means that individuals ascribe themselves to groups, to regard themselves as members of groups. The members of the group would stand together regardless of situation motivated by the consciousness of "WE" because the organization is "ours", not "his" or "theirs".

Stimulated by the sense of "WE", people at all levels of power could respect their subordinates outside the organizational power structure, because the organization is "ours", not "mine". Similarly, motivated by the consciousness of "WE", people at the same level of an organization especially leaders at the central level could reduce and avoid power contention and working friction, for the organization is "ours", not "mine", not "yours", neither is "yours". To form the mental mechanism of social attraction is to finish individual "self-categorization". Mentality group would come into being and then there would be an effect of "group cohesion". In the individual psychological process, there are four experience stages of social comparison, social categorization, social distinction and social orientation. Finally, people have a sense of "WE" and they could condense into community. Thus, identification has dual meanings. Firstly, from the perspective of individuals, it is to seek and acquire a sense of belonging as well as to be accepted by the group. Secondly, from the perspective of communities, it is to recognize and adopt (someone as a member of the group) an individual (membership of the group). We can see that identity is a two-way process that the identified should not only take the initiative to identify, but they also should obtain identification passively. If the identified only have subjective identification but does not attain objective identification or if the identified have been identified objectively but do not have subjective identification, the identification is unilateral, which does not have practical meaning.

We should see what the equity is, what the components of it are and what the meaning it does have. Equity is one of the important values of human morality. Though, it has strong subjectivity, it is an objective existence. So far, there are few recognized concepts and standards for all people. Equity is explained into a wide variety of meanings in the Holy Bible. Classical theorists of Marxism also have discussed the equity ever. As a matter of fact, equity refers to dealing all issues based on absolute equality, to establish the harmonious and sincere relationships among people under the condition of absolute equality. The equity is evaluation from comparison of people's relationships and the essence of equity is the reflection of co-relationship among subjects. The nature and extent of equity depend on the nature and extent of interactional social relations between subjects. Equity can be analyzed from the different perspectives of economy, politics, culture, and so on. As a judgment of morality and value, equity, a historical concept, has class foundation and economic foundation. We cannot study social equity without specific economic relationship and social relations.

Secondly, what is the equity in economic life? People always discuss about economic equity in various positions and they never give way to each other. To summarize, there are three rough aspects of the dispute: equity of rules, equity of capital, and equity of result. Rules are registration for people when taking part in economic activities (games). The equity of rules refers that whether it is equal for people to participate in economic activities or not in terms of rights. From the perspective of people's social life, equity is mainly used to judge people's process of economic life and its consequence. According to

Marxism, the equity of economic rules manifested itself as equality and freedom between workers. The equity of rules is an important and major aspect to manifest equity. Capital refers to resources of land and fund, capacity, education and other resources owned by producers and operators, whose differences and inequalities indicate the inequity of capital. Marxism held the opinion that the inequity of capital is the main source of the unfair outcome, which is also the origin to cause social problems --- poverty, crime and social chaos. The society should implement capital equity --- communism, and equity of consequences --- equal distribution of consumer goods. Clearly, equity not only refers to equal distribution of labor results, but it is also equal allocation of resources. Most importantly, it is the equity in terms of opportunities. It is the construction of socialist market economy that is constantly transforming the traditional interest structure and values of people. When people are faced with the social transformation, different economic components, forms of organization, mode of distribution and different life styles in the society, people's income gap is enlarging so that social equity has become a popular issue which people are concerned about. To study the problem of social equity has important academic value and applied value. From the perspective of academics, modern reconstruction of the relationship between subject and object, adjustment and control of the social structure, diverse options for social path and so on are all closely related to the study of social equity. Only when we study further on the issue of social equity can people have a scientific command of the above important theoretical problems. In terms of application, the issue of social equity can directly influence the formulation of basic policies in the advanced stage of socialism.

The argument of extensive marketization (those favored by the interest) or some upstarts think that the inequality of consequences is the best way to stimulate producers, which could promote the society to produce efficiently only in this way. These people who overemphasize the equity of rules think that social productivity could increase greatly and material wealth would be enriched if there are fair economic rules as well as free and equal competitive rules. It sounds contrived that when the pie is made big, the living standard of people would be naturally improved integrally. They hold the opinion that market economy is the best economic mode to guarantee freedom and equality. However, because of the government intervention, the equity of economy would always be destroyed and the initiative of producers would be suppressed. Furthermore, it is insufficient to change the result of distribution. They think that it would sacrifice efficiency to redistribute income and cause efficiency declining and inequity, which is unavailing. Naturally, equity and efficiency are the fundamental issue of economic study. "Equity gives priority to efficiency" has certain positive meanings in specific economic activities, but there should not be an order in terms of politics and ethics. Meanwhile, whether the society is fair or not is an objective existence and an integrated response to measure and calculate various socioeconomic indicators along with parameters, while it is not originated from illusory identification.

Starting from the practical and realistic thinking method and routes to work that are advocated by the Communist Party in China, we should acknowledge the fact boldly that it broadly appears the significant difference of benefit and income distribution all over the country during the radical transition to market economy. The differences are in the internal enterprise, inter-enterprise, inter-industry and inter-region, especially in rural areas. Originally, it is natural to have variance, but the distinction should be controlled within the scope identified by the social equity. If it exceeds the scope identified by social equity, it is not merely an issue of identification, but a serious social problem. It cannot be denied that the economy is more prosperous nowadays than before, but at the same time there also appear the acute contradictions that the number of laid-off workers are increasing, with enlarged gap between the rich and the poor and people who are sick dare not to treat. Children living in rural areas who cannot afford the tuition drop out of schools. This severe situation is originated from the "Competition is Everything" advocated by the marketization trend, which is the negative effect of that if there is economic efficiency, social equity can be ignored.

The real power of a state lies in its systems and management methods. If everything is exercised according to the truth, justice and peace, the state would be powerful. So, what is the power of equity? Its power bases on that the equity can satisfy the strong demand of equality of a person or a state from the bottom of their hearts. Equity helps people's lives to pursue the most authentic and most equal condition. Equity can stop the voice of complaint which is the greatest threat to the security of a country and is a national crisis. The exterior attack coming from abroad is not the most horrible thing for a national state, but it is the interior instability caused by unidentified social equity. At present, a wide variety of chaos and instabilities in China are all originated from that.

Seriously, the reason why there appears great inequality between the rich and the poor as well as huge differences in wealth distribution around China is closely related to the dead imitation of economic theories and economic systems advocated by extensive marketization. The misleading trend disregards the reality and cultural traditions of Chinese society and it imposes absurd theories on government decision-making department. Moreover, it is the reason that mentality of "hatred of the rich" does exist. However, there was no such thing as resentment among Chinese people originally. People do not hold hatred toward those like Yuan Longping who became rich because of scientific innovation, like Li Ning who became wealthy by specific skills as an athlete, and like Guo Fansheng who became rich because of his entrepreneurship and his creative labor share system in running his family firms. There are millions of people becoming rich by their own entrepreneurship and demanding work and on the contrary, people admire and respect them. People hate those very much like Mu Suixin, a malfeasant who became wealthy by leasing public rights, Lai Changxing who became rich by smuggling, and the rich who bribe and break the laws. People should be allowed to hate these pests of society because their wealth is illegal and is based on making more people poorer.

China should pay more attention to adjust the income distribution reasonably and transform the contradiction existing in the field of current income distribution, which means that innovative ways are needed. Some practices that are with Chinese rural features are thought as low-level or even ridiculous by some scholars who have studied abroad or by some public servants. However, it is more convenient of the operations. Why does this like that? This answer is most close to the reality: foreign goods are "modernity" goods that conform to the rules of internationalized market economy; the old methods stand for "traditions" that bound to some doctrines of the planned economy. Are the rules of market economy universal? Let's see those who are living in the developed market economy countries how to think about it. Robert Kurtz, a German scholar, thought that though market economy was the basic system of developed capitalist countries and the commodity competition makes many areas become wealthy, the capitalism only makes a small number of people become wealthy but most people become poor from a human point of view. The scientific and technological process that is praised widely has become a heavier and heavier burden on people.

There is a basic paradox of capitalism that commodity economy is not serving the people while people are the dependency of this system (Kurtz, 2003). While this scholar attacked countless specious specific phenomenon thinking logic and academic opinions produced by capitalism, he put forward many unique views and tremendous opinions. Under the influence of extensive marketization theory, some oddities that happened in China several years ago verified Kurts' conclusions. At present, there are some examples of socialist new countries construction in some places demonstrating that some foreign rules of extensive marketization theory in the rural situation seem to be very inopportune and the results make people uproarious. Therefore, people cannot indiscriminately look down upon some reasonable factors contained in planned economy and rebuke that old methods or planned economy has very bad influences. In fact, the socialism and collectivism that are dominated or advocated by the state are the most precious component element of socialist culture. To develop the socialist new rural construction, people should come down to the earth, working together, and make solid process.

It is a Highway of Modern Development

Nearly a century ago, a group of pioneers tried to transform the rural features. Though it produced no considerable results, it was still worthy of being respected. The Chinese Communists deeply understood the importance of rural work when leading the new democratic revolution and they explored how to change the old rural features in a difficult condition for a long time. It is the best choice to summarize the former experience and lessons to make solid progress in the process of constructing the new socialist countryside in a new century.

Explore an Appropriate Path for Countryside Development

In the early stage of the last century, some passionate and famous young intellectuals in Chinese society such as Liang Suming and others once led a new rural movement. He and some of his colleagues left Beiping and went to the rural villages in northern China. They lived in farmers' homes and successfully conducted the new rural movement experiment. Zhou Zuoren, who went to Japan twice from July to August in 1919, visited the Utopian village established by Iwai Mushanokoji at that time with great enthusiasm. Then Zhou Zuoren wrote articles and made speeches after coming back to China, becoming the most active advocate and organizer of the new rural movement in China. At that time, Mao Zedong, who was still a youth, had never seen Lu Xun, but he had made a special visit to Zhou Zuoren on April 7, 1920. He was drawing up the proposal of new rural construction, a part of which had been published on the monthly magazine named Education of Hu Nan. Mao Zedong devoted himself to changing the old rural features in China during the long-term revolution of founding the party and the state. His first classic work in Chinese revolution history is *Investigation Report on Peasant Movement in Hu Nan* that was written and published in March 1927. In this famous revolutionary literature, Mao Zedong summarized the work of peasant association which came down to "Fourteen Great Achievements". These momentous events achieved by farmers fundamentally changed the rural politics, economy, society and cultural features. Some of them still have instructional significance, such as spreading political advertisement, cultural movement, building roads, building dams, and so on.

Since the establishment of New China, what Mao Zedong, the State President, had been most concerned about was the construction of rural areas. Since 1950s, agrarian revolution and cooperation movement have been in process constantly. At the peak of the Great Leap Forward in 1958, people's communes were built in rural areas around China. Especially, it should be mentioned that the Central Committee of the Communist Party still hold the sober judgment and make right choices when many comrades in the party are at the most optimistic status. In settlements like Tibet and Sinkiang of the Zang, Uyghur nationality and other minorities, central decisions are not implemented or the implementation of the people's commune system is postponed. These policies play a key role in national solidarity and national defense consolidation.

The "Great Leap Forward" failed at the early stage of the new nation, which made the Communist Party of China realize the importance of economic laws and the difficulty of rural construction. Though China was learning the construction model from the Soviet Union at that time, Mao Zedong had realized the danger of copying foreign model from the end of 1958 to 1959. From a new and profound perspective, he gave the suggestion of reading books to the whole party. He gave the advice that party members should read the *Socialist Economic Problem in the Soviet Union* written by Stalin, to study economic rules and seek economic laws. They should reflect on the socialist economic construction in China and avoid making mistakes. Mao Zedong summarized the experience and lessons of rural constructions and he seriously criticized the conspicuous mistakes in the Great Leap Forward. He acutely pointed out that, "Nowadays 'satellites' are launched in any case. To fight for reputation, people counterfeit". What's more, he gave some examples of falsification events in some places in detail that "Greening is said to be done every year but actually not and there are less and less trees. People promised to eliminate the four pets and the village should be without four pets but the four pets are everywhere in fact" (Mao, 1999). The Central Committee of the Communist Party of China took some measures to correct some serious errors of the work, but it is a pity that the "left-leaning" route appeared in the Great Leap Forward cannot be amended thoroughly. Though Mao Zedong knew the mistakes of launching "satellites" and falsification events, he did not deeply understand the root of "left-leaning" mistakes in his mind so that his thoughts and decisions did not lead the later national economic constructions along the correct direction that he was aware of before. It is a regret that the event ended in tragedy.

The Communist Party of China is a new generation of central leadership group whose general secretary is Xi Jinping, which inherited Marxism used in the peasant movements by Mao Zedong in Hunan. It combines the national condition of China in 21st century to lead the new socialist construction. It has been more than 90 years from 1927 to now. Nowadays, in the socialist new rural construction in China, we should not only remind ourselves of the spirit of "Ten thousand years is too long, seize every minute" to have a sense of historical mission and the urgency of times to fulfill giants' last wish, but we should also follow the socialist core values and use moderate policies to move forward solidly as well as develop economy, society, culture and other programs in rural areas. From the practice of rural construction in industrial developed countries around the world, we can see that it is such an arduous task that we cannot succeed if we rush things through, which is said to be more haste, less speed. Under the unified position of the State Council, China has started the second census of agriculture, which would be the first-hand material to find out the real situation and put forward national policies in the new rural construction.

Steady Progress Should be Made in Rural Economic Development

The key to rural development in China is to mobilize the enthusiasm of farmers through extensive publicity and mobilization. Because this reform, as the second reform in China, rose from countryside, the socialist new rural construction lays a substantial foundation for the great reform. As Mao Zedong remarked on the essence of the first reform in China to surround the cities from the countryside, "It is the vast peasants to complete their historical mission". Those peasants who are awakened "will break through all bondage for them and run on the way to liberation" (Mao, 1968). During the first civil war of China, the peasant movement led by the Chinese Communist Party was impressive, the important reason of which was that the peasant association motivated the farmers to make new features appear in rural politics, economy, society and culture. In modern China, the whole state has acted in accordance with the outline of "Twelfth Five-year" Plan, and also help is offered to farmers within the framework of socialist market economy to encourage peasants to arrange and construct a beautiful rural homeland.

Firstly, there should be overall planning for rural economic development. There is a large population in China so that there are great differences between areas around the country. To achieve the goal of socialist new rural construction, China should start from reality based establishment of a moderate development strategy. The idea to "overtake" developed countries and the unpractical awareness to realize agricultural modernization like North American countries should be put away. To build a moderately prosperous society in all aspects was the striving goal for the early twenty years of this century, which was put forward in the Sixteenth Chinese Communist Party National Congress. It experienced Chinese "Tenth Five-year" Period and "Eleventh Five-year" Period from 2000 to 2010. As a result, according to *the Statistics and Survey Program of building a Moderately Prosperous Society in all Aspects,* the National Bureau of Statistics and regional statistical research departments had statistics and survey around China on the progress of moderately prosperous society construction in all aspects from 2000 to 2010. In 2010, the moderately prosperous society construction in all aspects achieved 80.1% in China, with an increase of 20.5% and an annually average growth of 2.05% as compared with the figures in 2000.

However, from the perspective of "Tenth Five-year" Period and "Eleventh Five-year" Period, the progress of Chinese moderately prosperous society construction in all aspects averagely increased 1.51% every year during the "Tenth Five-year" Period, with an annually average increase of 2.59% during the "Eleventh Five-year" Period, which was 1.08% more than that of the "Tenth Five-year" Period and the increase rate was also growing (The National Bureau of Statistics, 2011). At the same time, we should have more sober understanding when we saw our achievements. A research report released at the beginning of 2011 by the survey group on rural moderately prosperous society construction in all aspects indicated that there are several difficulties and emphasis on the construction in the coming days. They are mainly in the following areas: with a weak agricultural foundation, it is of great pressure to guarantee basic agricultural products supply; the progress of comprehensive prosperous society in western rural areas was backward, which makes it hard to achieve the goal of comprehensive prosperous society construction in countryside at time; it is even more difficult to keep the growth rate of farmers' income increasing, which has not reached the halfway point of comprehensive prosperous society construction; the rural pension security program has just begun, so the comprehensive prosperous society construction is of low level (Staff Writer, 2011). The above problems need planning and coordination for further measures toward their stepwise solution.

The new rural socialist construction is an all-round construction instead of simple economic construction advertised by the extensive marketization theory. While the construction is developed under the background of market economy, people should accurately understand and have a command of the nature of "market economy" to avoid getting into the trap of extensive marketization. There was a time that there was some deviation in rural construction. To realize the market economic benefits in some places, on one hand, people broke the laws and disciplines to charge administration fee in the requisition of farmers' land, or farmers were forced to give up their deserved reward under the socialist system because of unfair share of fees, which seriously violated people's legal rights. On the other hand, a few administrative departments blindly invested and constructed some unproductive enterprises to engage in "image projects" vigorously, or put forward impractical high targets to make the farmers accept property damage brought by the failed policy and take on the debt for bureaucracy. The cause of all these social problems is the extensive marketization theory. If we cannot clearly understand the essence of such social problems revealed by various individual cases, the practice of reform will be in absence of direction and solution, which is flatulent and impractical fantasy and an ultra-Right tendency covered by the thought of ultra-Left. This could be called as "wallow of development" or "growth trap".

Consequently, the new rural socialist construction needs planning and coordination to integrate the development of socialist market economy, the development of socialist democratic politics and the development of socialist advanced culture. Its nature is to constantly promote material civilization, political civilization, spiritual civilization and ecological civilization to make them coordinate and develop together. Only this way could China implement the idea of new rural socialist construction put forward by Hu Jintao, the former general secretary of Chinese Communist Party. A guiding and determinative policy could embody the spirit of working for people and the strategy of socialist production purposes. Lenin said, "Only with the socialism can we widely promote and dominate the social production and distribution of products in accordance with scientific theories, which is how to make all the laborers lead the most beautiful and the happiest life. It can only be realized by socialism" (Lenin, 1972). Obviously, to implement the strategic deployment of socialist new rural construction, material civilization should be the basis of the construction and spiritual civilization should be the direction, with political civilization as the safeguard for both. It is ecological civilization that people get along well with the nature. Without these four aspects, the new rural socialist construction would not be secured and it would become an empty talk. These four aspects are closely related to each other in the philosophical theory. They can not only develop ways to deeply understand realistic problems, but they can also stimulate to achieve the new requirement for new rural socialist construction that was put forward in the Seventeenth National Congress of the Chinese Communist Party. Meanwhile, it shows the greatest contribution of the Marxism-Leninism theory, to contribute great innovation to the civilization development of the entire Chinese nation.

Secondly, the new rural construction is a project of public interest. For moderate development, there should be planning and economic control to comprehensively solve the problems of the new rural socialist construction. However, under the attack of extensive marketization theory, the planned economy was completely abandoned. It cannot be denied that there is something to reserve in Chinese rural construction of the planned economy period, such as overall consciousness of the whole nation and social responsibility to take care of "households enjoying the five guarantees". They are not only beneficial to commercial activities nowadays, but also a sort of honest moral that should be regarded as the criterion in any national culture. If these excellent cultural spirits are inherited, it totally can be a dose of medicine to heal "Market Failure" that cannot be avoided under the condition of modern commercial economy. However, once the polarized market economy indulges itself, the slogan of "priority in benefit" would be understood parochially. The social responsibility has become a weak idea in the thoughts of some people so that the relevant practical economic behaviors also become weak activities in the society. As a result, there would some strange events happening in the rural construction: for profit, constantly there are many fake seeds and fertilizers in the market of agricultural commodities; there are various frauds of commercial companies in rural economic activities; to earn money, there are countless hidden jerry-built projects of residences and roads for relocated farmers.

All these are natural reactions of "extensive marketization" to some extent. At present, every person in countryside can deeply experience the painful consequences caused by cheating farmers and harming farmers after a lack of responsibility. Even in academia, some supporting agriculture but old methods used from 50s to 70s of last century has become the pronoun of backwardness. As we can often see in some sketches of TV entertainment programs, the honesty of farmers living in the countryside would not be thought as a kind of precious character instead of a stunt for urban residents' entertainment. Starting from the actual needs of countryside, new rural socialist construction can stop cases of damaging peasants' benefits. Therefore, new rural socialist construction is not only a meaningful term, but it contains profound social significance.

On 25th January 2006, during the 28th session of the political bureau of the CPC central committee, Hu Jintao, the general secretary, emphasized that they should proceed from the overall situation to profoundly understand the importance and urgency of new rural socialist construction, particularly to strengthen the self-consciousness and determination to conduct various rural work. This significant historical goal of new rural socialist construction should be actively, comprehensively and solidly achieved to make it a project of public interest and beneficial to all farmers (Hu, 2006). It is a project of public interest to develop new rural socialist construction, which is a good saying. The general secretary was concerned about people, which reflects the political nature of the Chinese Communist Party to bring benefits to the people. A political party can only stay young forever through emotional connection to people and mutual affinity with them. The socialist new rural construction cannot live without peasants because the rural population is the majority in China. If the agricultural and rural development cannot be stimulated and peasants' life standard cannot be improved distinctly, China cannot realize the goal of building a moderately prosperous society in an all-round way and the goal of national modernization. The common prosperity of the nation and long-term political stability in the country cannot be achieved as well.

Therefore, during the Twelfth Five-year Period, there was an overall basic ideology to promote agricultural and rural development: with deepened implementation of Scientific Outlook on Development, new rural socialist construction should be the strategic mission and the road of agricultural modernization with Chinese characteristics should be the basic direction. To accelerate the integration of urban-rural economic development, it should be regarded as the fundamental requirement, with the instructional ideology that "Three Rural" work is the top priority. The balancing of urban and rural development should be continued, to insist the basic principle of industry nurturing agriculture, the urban supporting the rural, taking less and giving more. There should be more input, innovative institutions, strengthened agricultural basis and growing farmers' income. To promote rural harmony is to lay a more solid foundation to realize the goal of building a moderately prosperous society in all aspects. The whole party should unify its thought and the top standard of behavior is people's benefit, which should be planned scientifically and carried forward solidly.

People should clearly recognize that compared with the requirements of building a moderately prosperous society in an all-around way, there are still some prominent contradictions and problems in the rural areas of China and rural development, which needs a longer historical period to be thoroughly solved. The implementation of project in the public interest can satisfy farmers' requirements to an extreme under the existing material conditions. Besides economic construction, cultural significance is the most profound in the construction of the new rural socialist construction. There had been market economy in the history of China. Before the liberation, there was capitalist development in Jiangnan area, and the Shanghai Bund was once a land of busy market economy, the popular mode in foreign countries. However, those had not become economic subject in Chinese society at last and the European capitalist powers did not allow China to develop market economy indeed. As a result, history made China have its own value system and cultural traditions. "To be more concerned about the unequal distribution of wealth instead of poverty" is the social humanity value that is most rich in Chinese characteristics. Meanwhile, there is eclecticism that is claimed by Zhang Qian to oppose excessive competition and others, which is different from the value of extensive marketization. However, to implement the new rural construction policy of "giving more and taking less", to practically promote industry nurturing agriculture as well as the urban supporting the rural and to build rural civilization as well as democratic management, some excellent cultural traditions should be inherited. In the specific stage and the specific occasion, it is necessary for people to have the spirit and consciousness of "modesty", but excessive publicity and stingy economic interest should be restrained. These measures would be beneficial to the implementation of important policies as well as the effective measures to help the growth of agriculture and rural economy.

Talent Cultivation Helps to Realize the Dream

To building a moderately prosperous society in an all-round way, the most difficult and most onerous part lays in the rural area, while it is the farmers themselves who should take the main responsibility. The modern construction is a complicated and comprehensive system engineering which needs scientific instruction, integration, distribution and devised strategies. Only the people who have a command of knowledge can be qualified for the job.

Definite the Significance of Material-Culture Construction

The new rural socialist construction is not only a process of material production, but also a process of cultural production. There is propounding dialectical conversion significance in the dual construction. The key of the dual transformation is to increase farmers' awareness and their ability to change the world, with a good command of scientific knowledge. Lenin profoundly indicated that it is impossible to construct a communist society in an illiterate country (Lenin, 1972). Education in the People's Republic of China started from an extremely behindhand foundation, but after 60-year untiring efforts especially more than 30-year opening and reform, momentous changes have taken place in China, which has achieved world-famous historical achievements. In 1949, 80% of Chinese population was illiterate, with the enrollment rate of primary school and junior high school at only 20% and 6% respectively and there were only 117,000 students in the schools. However, in 2008, the net enrollment rate of primary school reached 99.5%, with the gross enrollment rate of junior high school reaching 98.5%. The illiteracy rate of teenagers decreased to less than 3.58%; the number of population studying in various higher education levels around the whole country reached 29.07 million, with the gross enrollment rate of 23.3% (The website of the Central People's Government of the PRC, 2009）; the enrollment scale of secondary vocational education and higher vocational education around the country reached 11 million and the number of students in school are more than 30 million. The great achievements made in the education field during the 60 years around the People's Republic of China cannot be despised and neglected by people.

The superficial form of Chinese new rural construction is to introduce market economic activities into the vast region, to transform the traditional small-scale peasant economy system. However, it is not only a simple promotion of economic form and organizational system, but also an introduction of cultural organizational system. Therefore, market economy activities involve many elements such as politics, society, history, culture, mentality and so on; market economy is a kind of contract culture system. Its history can be traced back to about 3000BC ago. The earliest and the most integrated contractual culture existing in the world is *Code of Hammurabi,* which was made before 18th century BC in the Mesopotamia, one of the birthplaces of human ancient civilization. It was the law of slave society carved on the black basalt pillars using a kind of trapezoidal words that has disappeared, which was also called "Code of the Stone Pillar". In 1901, a team of French archaeologists found it in the ruins of the ancient Susa city in Iran. On the stone pillar, there are regulations and records of some basic and important activities in the market economy existing today, such as contract, creditor's rights, pledge, partnership, employment, and so on. With the development of market economy, those activities have become much more complex than that thousands of years ago and they are becoming more and more complex with the each passing day. How to develop the socialist new rural construction without culture and knowledge?

Rural education is a great and challenging task in the process of socialist new rural construction because education involves the whole situation, and people cannot only care about education. To jump out of the traditional stereotype of "only Three Rural Issues", people should think about rural education using brand innovative ideas and rural education development should be put into the broad pattern of national economy and the background of national culture. To promote rural progress with education should be the progress of the whole society. Division between the urban and the rural should be broken down and there should be new ideologies for the urban and rural education development. The administrative department for education should increase and extend various projects and educational business department for rural services and it should try to solve the problems. Parents in peasant households should not be worried about their children's education and devote themselves into farm work to make more contribution to the country at the first line of production. The government sector takes the responsibility of making agriculture rapidly develop into a modernized system, so there should be thoughtful and overall plans to use public education resources. Some special situation in the field of education should be solved timely to protect the rights and interests of farmers.

Treat the Rural Education with Institutionalized and Internationalized Vision

In the socialist new rural construction, regional governments made many projects to provide excellent infrastructure for countryside, to build beautiful houses for farmers, and to improve farmers' life as well as the environment of production, which is necessary for overall development. However, it is the most important to build up the education and cultivate talents in an effective way. Though the government arranges construction of new rural areas, repairs the roads, builds houses for farmers, and so on, there would be problems of degradation one day for these good infrastructures. If it is short of talents in rural area and the development ability of farmers cannot be improved, the degradation problem of infrastructure cannot be solved depending on farmers. The new rural structure will become an old rural structure one day. Thus, the most central part of socialist new rural construction is to equip the farmers with knowledge, skills and better ability to develop. Then all of them can improve their living standard no matter they are in the countryside or in the cities. As a result, countryside will maintain the new normal construction and cities will also keep active.

Firstly, to change the unequal education and training management. Only high-tech commodities in the market economy are highly value-added and the high technology comes from education. Modern education is not only the engine of social advancement, but also the most important and basic channel for individuals to attain personal great progress. Since the contract system was implemented in the countryside of China, small-scale labor and exchange of peasant households have become main rural economic behaviors. The commercial relation of microcosmic bodies in market economy is mainly an independent horizontal connection to constantly carry on the exchange of material, information as well as energy and optimize resource allocation. This is distinctly different from the vertical command economic connection under the natural economy, planned economy, and power economy. The horizontal connection of various social economic subjects proceeds normally depending on the contractual relationship, moral restraint and legal norm to maintain. Therefore, the modern market economy is also reputation economy and legalized economy. The process of enterprises acquiring profit is the process of culture export and culture spreading to the society; the process of resource allocation in enterprises is the process of culture import, social goods and culture inclusion. However, many farmers do not have adequate scientific knowledge, even they are uneducated, which not only weakens farmers' competitiveness, but also makes them as vulnerable groups. Owing to the thought of extensive marketization in the outside world, farmers who are short of the ability to work based on affluent knowledge are always thought to be different by some business owners with snobbish attitude in commercial activities whose essence is to attain profit. Therefore, the rights and interests of people without knowledge are often neglected or offended by those who have knowledge.

Although China has started to implement the policy of Tuition & Fee Waiver in the central and western rural areas, which is good for farmers to acquire more education. The problem at present is that educational level is high in the urban while low in the rural areas, the best in central cities and the worst in remote places. It is hard to cultivate the high-level, comprehensive talents needed by the new rural construction with low quality rural education. It is the main problem to change and improve the inferior-quality rural education after government sponsors to help teenagers at right ages receive nine years of compulsory education. Though government cancels the miscellaneous fees, rural children still cannot catch up with the children in cities in the competition of education. Nowadays, children living in rural areas are not willing to study in the school in their hometown, instead people prefer spending money to send children to the schools in town, but it is always difficult to achieve their goals. Peasant-workers who are working in cities prefer spending money on good schools for their children to provide them with modern education, but they always face the situation that though they pay the tuition fee, their children cannot get the good education. Some schools built for peasant-workers are with inferior quality of education so that those workers are not willing to send their children to study there.

The reason for the inequality is that the distribution of educational resources has great differences between the urban and the rural schools. Local administration sections do not conduct equal and reasonable teaching resources allocation and funds distribution. As for this way of educational management, we currently do not evaluate whether it reaches the standard of Scientific Outlook on Development, but we should firstly require some people at management levels to examine their conscience: do they equally treat the skill education of farmer as well as the education for farmers' children from the bottom of their heart and do they discriminate farmers in their minds implicitly? At present, the competition of entrance examinations and the competition in the market still do not benefit farmers at all because of the low quality of rural education. In fact, it is an overwhelming reality that it cannot be achieved. Though the situation cannot be changed right off, parents in rural household desire their children to get the good education. Children in the countryside are determined to participate in the social competition and realize the grand ambition to serve the country through getting education of a better quality.

However, farmers' children are naturally in inferiority in the unequal competition of education. In the modern society where gap and contradiction are existing forever, people are anxiously looking forward to equality of opportunities. If there is no equality of opportunities, it is like that the largest part of athletes who take part in the match are driven away from the starting line so that there is no development opportunities for the young people in some ways. This is the reason why measures of education that involve farmers in some places are the best game but no one plays. Therefore, in the socialist new rural construction, administrative divisions make more educational resources supply as an important supporting measure through policy and institutional adjustment, to promote the quality of rural education, which is not confined to cancel school sundry fees. The quality of education is related to farmers' survival and development issues in the urbanization, industrialization, marketization and global competition.

The basis of Chinese society is agriculture. Farmers make the most contribution to the nation and the key of modernization construction is rural issues. "Three Rural Issues" are so important that whether the rural education is in good condition and whether the service of educational management is done well or not attract the attention of people. As farmers are specially the main force of new rural construction, it is reasonable for them to be eager to receive good education. Especially when farmers pay the same currency as people in other industries in the trade do, so, they have more rights to ask for equivalent service. However, due to the structural errors in educational management, farmers originally spend money on the services, but there are only bad attitude and inferior quality services. Farmers who are the most enduring and regardless of conditions are worried and afraid. No matter from the perspective of agriculture or the basis of national economy or the view that people should take care of the disadvantaged, the education administrative department should raise the standard of services. When the administration managers are doing charitable deeds for people, they should think more about it in a deep way to strengthen management and doing things completely, which is the most practical job for good rural education practice after confirming the Twelfth Five-year Policy.

Secondly, it is to construct strong teams of agricultural experts working in the international trade. It is universal for market economy activities that its some activities promote the development of economy. For example, it helps farmers construct the export base of green agricultural products. The large-scale exported featured products assist farmers to earn foreign currency, which makes fellow villagers become wealthy. Some activities destroy the economic construction. For example, it is difficult to eliminate though the fake and inferior products that damage the agriculture and peasants were repeatedly hit; to use agricultural products export as bait, farmers pay money to cultivate the so-called rare animals and exotic plants, but as a result, the export company gains farmers' tens of millions of hard-earned money by treating. There was a mingling of good and bad, with good and evil people mixed up. These features of market economy in the 21st century is completely different from that before 20 years, which is the integration of world economy never contacted by farmers living in their rural hometown. If the commodities want to distinguish the true and false of international market economy behavior, people who are with high cultural level are needed. They should deeply understand the evolution history of market economy and the international trend, which not only seems to be the domestic commodity exchange, but also deep communication of international culture and economy.

Market economy is a form of developed commodity economy, whose characteristic difference from natural economy and power economy is that it has deep internal accumulation of economy and the culture. In the 21st century, this economy and culture surpass the national boundaries increasingly. Why does the market economy develop well in capitalist society and why does it become the basis of globalization at present? This is related to historical reasons and logic. The earliest production pattern for people is natural economy whose corresponding economic form is commodity economy, and it was produced at the end of primitive society. Commodity economy developed slowly after the slave society and the feudal society. However, until the second half of the 18th century, the world's first industrial revolution started when the steam engine came out in England. In the European society, the big machine production took the place of manual labor; the long-distance trade in ocean took the place of close trade on the land; the national integrated market and world market took the place of intersected local market; the perfect production factor market system took the place of single commodity markets; the corporate enterprise took the place of family manual mills or workshops. Then commodity economy gradually entered the mature stage and the developed stage, which was the market economy.

It is the history that shows the market economy formation was related to the generation of Renaissance, industrial revolution, sea commerce, big machine production and so on. In the early stage, it is the free competition of market economy, and the profit-oriented market economy caused the gap between the rich and the poor. To chase high profits, countries that conducted market economy such as England, France, Netherlands, Spain, Portugal and so on started the expansion to foreign countries, and they did not hesitate to start the war of aggression. The conquering country monopolized the world's market without mercy, like the economy, politics, culture and so on, which were all ruled by them. Along the way of profits – competition – monopoly – competition again – oligopoly, the free competition of market economy would transform to oligopoly, while whose extreme form is related to capitalism and imperialism. A country-wide market economy has become integration of the world economy at present. On the one hand, economic globalization is that the international capital needs to attain profit maximization at the worldwide level. As a result, the western countries dominated by the United State became richer, while the vast developing countries in the third world relatively became poorer. On the other hand, it is that developing countries directly learned the latest results in economic science and technology, which gives them an opportunity of leapfrog development to surpass the developed countries.

The historical process of market economy and its significance of economic culture play a key role in the socialist new rural construction.

The most crucial step is to cultivate numerous farmers to become the specialists who have knowledge and ability in international trade. Since China has joined the WTO, the "Three Rural Issues" have not been limited to China, because in the face of a substantial number of agricultural productions that are from America and Canada, Chinese traditional agricultural economy is fighting to win or die. As we all know, the most difficult negotiation in China's application to be a member of the WTO was agricultural negotiation and after being a member of the WTO, China feels stressed about the agriculture. From national perspective, the government has tried the best to strive for fair trade for Chinese agriculture, countryside and farmers on the negotiation table of the WTO, to make lawful and profitable conditions for farmers. For example, in the Cancun ministerial conference held by World Trade Organization in 2003, China who attended at that time faced the unequal trade of agricultural productions in the world. When faced with serious challenges, Chinese government delegation insisted that they should not only protect Chinese profits and the profits of developing countries, but also promote progress and development in the negotiation. After that, China played a constructive role with other developing members in "Twenty Countries Group" in the negotiation held in Doha and then it became the important and hard core in the most complicated and difficult agricultural negotiation of the WTO.

On 15th December 2011, the eighth ministerial conference of the World Trade Organization raised the curtain in Geneva. This ministerial conference had further memorial significance for China: the year of 2011 was the 10th anniversary for China to join the WTO. For the ten years, China had completely kept the promises made while joining the WTO. The liberalization and facilitation of trade and investment were improved significantly. China also brings many benefits to consumers in each member state and to the economy of world at the same time when it has gained self-development. The main reason why the Doha meeting was hindered was that developed countries and developing countries had a great divergence on the problem of agricultural productions subsidies. China insisted on its national standpoint of agricultural profits when actively promoting the Doha negotiation. There is no doubt that the international files that were signed by government delegation on the negotiation table should be fulfilled by qualified farming products produced in Chinese land. Finally, it was put into practice and realized by new type peasants. Therefore, what the new countryside needs is not the native figures any more, but a talented team of millions of international agricultural specialists. To organize and train the team, there should be ways completely different from that before. New thoughts, new textbooks, new instructors and new training centers are needed.

Besides emphasis on education in school to cultivate a talented team of international agricultural specialists, people should also pay attention to the farmers who are now working at the forefront of production. For farmers who have missed the chance of international academic education, a measure the administrative department should adopt to remedy is to offer them more training on international trade, productive skills of green agricultural products and so on. Although famers in the export bases of many places have received training, the problem at present is that there is something wrong in the range, the depth and the methods of training, which directly influences the cultivation effects. For example, the investment of cultivation is limited. An average of several hundred yuan or less for a farmer is inadequate to support complicated training of international business. Many trainings to farmers do not consider what kind of practical technology farmers need, which causes to make it hard for the farmers to learn the useful skills. Certainly, the deep-seated root is the problem of the training system. If the supplies of skills training are disjointed with demands, the effect of training will not be good. The best method is that the government is responsible to invite social training to bid, which will benefit farmers indeed. Farmers can take part in the market competition in a better way through training to get some true skills.

Cultivate Talents of Independent Innovation

Chinese agriculture is badly in the need of academic talents and international talents. It is not to say too much to its degree of urgency. A significant measure to see whether these talents have achieved the standard is to use high-tech agricultural products to enter the international market, to extend occupied positions, to get the right of speech, initiative and to further become a heavyweight member gradually, with more and more participation in making the global trade rules. The Chinese agricultural talents should try their best to protect the profits of vast developing countries, make achievement for equal situation in the international trade and make some contribution to the construction of the world's new economic order. At present, the most fundamental work to cultivate agricultural talents is to eliminate the tendency of education industrialization existing with a firm hand and correct the work that has been dissimilated by the extensive marketization thought, to make the inappropriate practices like the across mice that are hit by each person. Owing to the industrialization of education, China becomes the so-called marketization in fact. On the one hand, it makes some people use various vested advantages to send their children to study abroad, or to study while working and get a true but false Doctor or Master degree. On the other hand, many farmers' children or laid-off workers' children lose the educational opportunities because they cannot afford the tuition. There are constantly typical examples of dropping out of school and even people committing suicide because they cannot afford the tuition fee in China. Eliminating the industrialization of education lays the basis of independent innovation talents' cultivation in rural areas.

Firstly, to eliminate the bad influence of education industrialization. It is necessary to separate layers for rural education according to compulsory education, higher education, vocational education and so on to analyze problems in different perspectives and adopt the corresponding solutions. The overall ideology of accelerating the reform and development of education is that: "with the demands of priority in development, people oriented, reform and innovation, equality promotion, quality improvement to promote the scientific development of educational business and improve the level of educational modernization" (Anonymity, 2011) People should develop various types and levels of education to construct the study-type society of everybody learning and learning for whole life; the educational equality should be strongly promoted to rapidly shrink the gap of education; quality education should be wholly enforced to promote students' comprehensive development of morality, intelligence, physique and aesthetics; the reform of educational system should be deepened to develop the system with emphasis on the government input and multiply channels to collect educational fund.

The Chinese educational fund can be suitable investment from national finance, at the same time it can also be distributed by market because China solved the educational problems with the help of market forces, which can be dated back to 1992. In that year, Deng Xiaoping who gave the South Inspection Speech put forward the incisive comments that plan economy and market economy are both the methods to promote the development of economy, which made the discussion to name "socialism" or "capitalism" clear. Every industry in China started to search opportunities of development with the help of market and the education has been pushed to the front of market. In that year, the State Council issued *Some Provisions on Speeding up Development of Tertiary Industries* which listed education in the tertiary industry clearly and emphasized that education should insist the development rules that "the people who invest will benefit" in the form of industrial system. It is the beginning to solve educational resources distribution with the help of market in China.

We can realize that there is no mistake to make education in the tertiary industry and distribute the educational resources with the help of market forces when carefully thinking about the historical practice related to it. The key problem is that: when education listed into tertiary industry, it cannot define the compulsory education and non-compulsory education. Therefore, influenced by the extensive thought that market economy is universal, the reasonable connotation of distributing limited resources was distorted and alienated. As a result, educational layers were fuzzed up day by day and every field of education are full of the thought of market. The second is that in the process of economy market scheme being introduced to part of the educational field and schools expanding their autonomous rights, due to short of relevant restrictions and specifications, there are many unscrupulous corrupt behaviors to pursue economic interests, which cause distortion for the subject of education and behavior of schools. In fact, this is the the process of political games and public choices for people who have money and the power to select, which was quite unfair. Now it should be corrected completely.

Secondly, education works for farmers. Chinese educational conditions in rural area are still behindhand. Though China has invested much money in rural education during the “Twelfth Five-year” Period, it still cannot completely solve the laggard educational situation in the rural areas. Therefore, while cultivating new rural talents, people should exclude the distraction of extensive marketization thought because the market economy is profit-oriented but not demand-oriented. It excludes the compulsory education in its logic. If you do not believe you can see that because of the huge profit, Chinese food service is always flourishing from the northern to the southern, which causes excess supply; on the contrary, though there are demands for Chinese general education, it is hard to develop due to the low profit. and it needs to ask for external donation. Elimination of industrialization in education is to stop the educational prejudice, which is also found in the conditions for teaching the rural active labor force and the not in labor force.

The way of showing care in the field of education should be emphasized, and if it is used improperly, it will function in the opposite way to what one wishes for. For example, in 2009, in the Nanchuan District of Chongqing Province, Daonan Middle School set up “rural class” especially for stay-at-home children in rural areas, which parents are averse to and think to be educational prejudice. Some specialists of educational psychology thought that Daonan Middle School who set up "rural class" was full of kindness, but they put forward the word of "rural" on purpose, which was equal to sticking identity tag with children. To take care stay-at-home children in rural areas, people should pay attention to children's demands of spirits, mentality and emotion firstly; the second is to get their parents' identity because though the act of the sages who complied with the nature were not spoiled, and who we were successful did not privilege （Laozi, Spring and autumn period）. A team of cadres is the key to whether the government work is performed well. The government should build a mechanism of supervision which is convenient, useful, and binding, to make difference through supervision. It is important to learn and form the overall force of supervision. Comprehensively and thoroughly learning and reading is good for stabilization of the team of town and village cadres, to increase the motivation to work, to ensure the administrative authority further, to instantly improve the ways of management and enhance working efficiency. According to the requirements of implementing scientific outlook on development and the right performance concept, government should study and formulate the assessment methods that conform to the characteristics and demands of county party committee secretary, to form a good mechanism and a correct orientation of selecting and employing people.

Thirdly, to educate rural cadres positively. The key method to educate the cadres is to guide them with classic examples. The most critical issues of education are two: the first is legality and democratic politics education and the second is to share the joys and sorrows with people. Not only do the two contents conform to the reality of China, but also is an experience summary of the socialist revolution practice from a classic Marxist writer. The only one socialist construction practice Marx and Engels experienced in their life is participation in the revolution of "The Paris Commune" in France. It was from the Paris commune, the economic, political and military struggle organized by the first political organization of the proletariat that Marx and

Engels found the disadvantages that would probably appear in the future and that should be against the socialist states, which is the danger of social public servants turning into social maters. Engels highly summarized the measures of precaution, he said, "to prevent the states and state organs from turning into the social maters-----it is inevitable phenomenon in all states at present-----the commune adopts two correct methods" (Marx and Engels, 1972) One is democratic election and the other one is uniform salary for officers and soldiers. It is a good theory as well as worthy for us to learn hard and implement completely if it conforms to the will of the people and is convenient for the people.

Marxism theory is to tell the people that it is impossible to fully rationally design and instruct human behavior because people's knowledge and ability are limited. However, even though human knowledge is limited, it can also play a role in finding the right lane and avoiding the rapids. To better determine a right lane and avoid dangerous shoals, at least when the lane bump against the wall everywhere and is not feasible, there could be a spare lane, which needs to establish an ethos to encourage people to develop their cognitive ability and involve in discussions. To explore genuine knowledge in discussions so that the possibility of knowledge can be broadened as much as possible. In terms of the social and economic reality in contemporary China, we should think seriously about whether the market economy is the only way to solve the social and economic problems in China. Before the massive and radical promotion of market economy, China has made remarkable and amazing achievements in social and economic development in the world. Absolutely, it is necessary to carefully summarize the experience and lessons of achieving these achievements. The new generation of leadership group of the Communist Party of China has found many problems in the social reform and opening of China. The general secretary, Hu Jintao, put forward a political idea of "people-oriented" to manage the state affairs with a keen sense of times, and he made a comprehensive exposition of its meaning. The new governance theory has been a high-level summary of practice since the establishment of the Communist Party in China. The idea of this theory is the ideology that the Communist Party of China has consistently advocated and strived for practice for decades. To implement the thought of the new generation leadership group is to emphasize the service for farmers, the largest population in China, and to emphasize the benefit for people around China so that the direct goal of a moderately prosperous society can be achieved.

Nowadays, the Communist Party of China shoulders the historical mission. From the benefit of country and nation, development steps centered on GDP is judiciously suspended. The "Three Rural Work" is regarded as an important agenda, and socialist new rural construction is making solid progress, which is inevitably result of the self-improvement and self-development of the Communist Party of China in the turning point of history. From the perspective of the history of CPC, several generations of leadership group all thought highly of the rural problems. The new rural construction theory is full of innovation due to the summary of practice in many years. The process of modernization in rural areas is closely related to the goal of moderately prosperous society construction, which needs to mobilize the nation to practice the theory in an effective way. It is important for rural grass-roots organizations to emphasize their attribution to people and analyze the realistic problems in rural areas. There should be extensive publicity for theoretical work, rather than decreasing the rural economic investment with the excuse of pursuing profit.

Courtyard Economy and Chia Tai Model

Depending on the limited adjustment of production relations in the early stage of Reform and Opening Policy, China has effectively changed the situation of relatively low income for farmers. Agricultural production has developed rapidly and significant changes have taken place in social status of rural areas. However, because of the constantly deepening Reform and Opening Policy, farmers are gradually losing the limited benefits obtained at the early stage of Reform and Opening Policy. With an increasing agricultural production, peasants' income doesn't grow and rural construction falls behind urban construction. The "Three Rural Issue" hinders the comprehensive development of Chinese economy and society. From the reality of Chinese rural society, the following proposal put forward to solve the problem of "Three Rural Issue" is a combination of the courtyard economy and the Chia Tai model.

Courtyard and courtyard economy

The courtyard mentioned here refers to the courtyards behind or in front of the farmers' residence, and the idle land and sporadic water areas around it, including three dimensions of the court, the yard and the garden. The court refers to inside and outside of the house and the vertical space. The yard refers to the courtyard space and open space around the house. The park refers to the small area of self-sustaining land, mountains, natural water and other available space resources near the house site. Courtyard economy is an ecological farming, which refers to in the self-sustaining land, contracted land and water surface of their own residential courtyard and house sites, farmers make full use of the garden facilities, resources, labor force and other advantages with local conditions to engage in various courtyard production and operations, such as plantation, cultivation and processing of agricultural products, according to the basic principle of ecological economy and basic methods of engineering system. From planning to layout and from material, energy input to output, this business operation tends to be scientific, reasonable, efficient, low consumption, high quality and high yield. It is a form of production with good economic, ecological and social benefits. It opportunely uses the food chain (net) and symbiosis relationship. It also organically integrates the green plant production, livestock (poultry) cultivation with reproduction of microorganism, which makes the materials recycle at various levels and utilizes energy efficiently to establish a reasonable layout and beautiful environment for production and life. There could be high economic benefits and ecological benefits in the process.

To summarize, the courtyard economy is the peasant economy based on the garden ecological agriculture. With the production unit of individual peasant household, scientific integration of plantation, cultivation and processing industry, this model fully uses natural resources at various levels, such as land, air, light, heat, animal and plant wastes, to obtain the greatest benefits with the least investment, which is beneficial to ecological balance. It makes the courtyard in a cyclical benign cycle. In this way, it can not only change the "dirty, messy and poor" sanitary appearance in rural courtyard, but it also improves the output and quality of agricultural products and increases farmers' income, which leads the farmers out of the poverty and helps them become rich. Additionally, it will promote the construction of a moderately prosperous society in all-round ways.

In the vast rural areas of China, there are many advantages to develop the courtyard economy because every family has a courtyard. Some courtyards are relatively big, where people can engage in plantation in it without occupying the land for crop. Meanwhile, these big courtyards can also be used for some projects that cannot be managed in big fields, with the intensive and flexible characteristics. The courtyard economy is made up of household units where farmers can work in their leisure time. Besides, their operations are those projects that they are good at or are interested in, which stimulates the farmers to learn new techniques positively, and then a variety of highly technical industries develop. Farmers can engage in various production projects according to the local conditions.

The scale of those production projects is not big without many fixed assets, which equips the business operation with flexibility and strain capacity. Peasants can timely adjust their operation projects according to the demand of the market so that there would be less market risk. Here is the example of courtyard economy development practice in Kuancheng Manchu Autonomous county of Hebei province, to explain the development and result of courtyard economy. The experience of the county is enlightening.

In recent years, Kuancheng Manchu Autonomous county has positively organized and instructed farmers to fully use the effective space of the courtyard economy. With market orientation, it vigorously developed the "three-in-one" characteristic plantation industry, including cultivation of pigs, rabbits, chickens, snails, edible fungi and plantation of vegetables, toona sinensis seedlings as well as grape seedlings. They have increased farmers' income, resettled a place for a larger number of surplus labor, and achieved good economic, ecological and social benefits. The county realized its realities of affluent mountain areas, to develop scale cultivation and characteristic plantation emphatically. By 2010, it had built two high-quality agricultural products bases of pigs and Chinese chestnuts and 42 leading enterprises, among which are two of provincial level and twenty-two of municipal level. It helps farmers increase annual per capita income by 3000 yuan. Most farmers overcome the poverty depending on developing the courtyard economy.

Firstly, it can accelerate industrial adjustment. The practice of Kuancheng Manchu Autonomous county indicates that developing courtyard economy in vast rural areas apparently has economic and social benefits, which can accelerate the industrial structure adjustment. There are several aspects as follows:

On the one hand, there is large space of employment for majority of surplus labor in rural areas by developing courtyard economy. The reform and opening in China emancipates the productive forces, and there has been plenty of surplus labor emerged in the countryside. Broadening the labor export can find a way to release part of the remaining labor force. The rest should develop based on agriculture and the reality of rural areas, to the depth and breadth of production. Developing the courtyard economy enables the farmers to stay at home and finds them with the way to overcome poverty and become rich. What's more, there would be allocation for rural surplus labor, which is of great significance for maintaining social stability in rural areas.

On the other hand, developing the courtyard economy stimulates agricultural structure adjustment and strengthens the disaster resistance ability of agriculture. Per capita cultivated land in Kuangcheng County is 0.88 Mu. In the normal year, the average net income for every household is less than 600 yuan for a family consisting of three people if it is plantation of corn and other field crops and calculated by 400kg corn per mu. During these years, the county continuously suffered droughts that had never occurred in hundreds of years. If following the traditional cultivation concept and merely depending on the field output, most farmers will be unable to maintain a normal life. However, the county government took the development of the courtyard economy as a breakthrough point, which actively promoted the rapid adjustment of the agricultural structure and effectively strengthened the disaster resistance ability of agriculture. Maojuzi village of the Tangdaohe town suffered a severe drought in 1999, which led to total crop failure, but through development of the characteristic cultivation industry in courtyards, the per capita net income of the village reached 2630 yuan, which was 915 yuan higher than the per capita net income of 1715 yuan of the county in a normal year.

Lastly, developing the courtyard economy protects the ecological environment and improves farmers' health level as well as the quality of life. Animal wastes of pigs, chickens and rabbits that are cultivated in the courtyard are rich in organic elements and trace elements. Using organic fertilizers not only reduces farmers' expenditure on chemical fertilizer, but it also cultivates the fertility of soil and improves the structure of soil pellet, with an enhancement of drought resistance and water conservation. The courtyard raises many herbivorous animals, which not only motivates farmers to comprehensively utilize straw, but it also quickly transforms farmers' ideas to actively plant trees and grasses in farmland of more than 25-degree slope under the guidance of the government. In addition, the development of "three-in-one" pig cultivation and other courtyard industries lead all animal manure, sewage and other debris into the biogas digester, cleaning up the rural health corners and improving the living environment for farmers. The comprehensive utilization of methane saves a lot of firewood. The vegetation coverage rate in this county increases year by year, and the ecological environment is apparently improved.

Secondly, it has special advantages in production. The biggest problem for the development of agriculture in China is that there is not enough land for so many people. Therefore, using courtyard to engage in agricultural production is originated from ancient times. In fact, though the courtyard is small, hundreds of square meters inside the walls are a small world. If taken seriously, there would be great achievements in agriculture. Compared with vast agricultural economy, the development of courtyard has following advantages.

One is that the courtyard economy needs small investment but it has large output and fast transfer. In Kuancheng Manchu Autonomous County, a peasant household built a "three-in-one" methane tank of six cubic meters, which can breed three-way cross lean pigs in three batches, with the total number of 30. It not only helps farmers save energy expenditure of 600 yuan on using biogas, but it also saves expenditures on fertilizers and pesticides of about 600 to 800 yuan every year, with annual net income reaching 4680 yuan. A farmer bought 8 rabbits of two groups that can be reproduced to at least 150 in one year. It takes five months for rabbits to grow from birth to slaughter. If all production fees removed, such cost of rabbit pups, breeding expenses, epidemic prevention fees as well as water and electricity fees, the annual profit can achieve about 3750 to 4500 yuan. In the field of edible fungus, broilers, birds, chickens and other yard cultivation or characteristic yard plantation, only investment of about 3000 to 5000 yuan is needed at one time. The annual net income is more than 3500 yuan. Because of its characteristics of small investment and small scale, courtyard plantation and cultivation based on households is easy to transform to cultivate other varieties according to market demand, without the risk of loss for oversupply. On the contrary, plantation and cultivation in each household courtyard gathers parts into a whole, which can be a certain scale if getting together, to quickly occupy the market. In the Stone Pillar Village of this county, a family used a 6 square meters space house to raise snails, buying 2000 at one time. The snail reproduced to 20000 in less than 4 months, earning net profit about 10000 yuan. The other 5 household breeding snails raise more than 10000 snails in each of them and the average profit every year is more than 5000 yuan.

The other is to make full use of resources. The development of the courtyard can maximize the use of the three-dimensional space occupied by the courtyard and create considerable economic benefits. The courtyard economy can combine the economic construction with the environmental construction organically. The biogas production can not only achieve high economic benefits, but also beautify the living environment so that the economic, ecological and social benefits are highly unified. The largest advantage of the garden economy compared to the field is the small area, the fertile soil, the sufficient moisture, the stable microclimate environment and the convenient management, which is most suitable to develop high quality, intensive and meticulous farming and efficient characteristic agriculture.

Finally, it is to fully use the existing agricultural scientific achievements and give priority to the benefit. The courtyard is a micro-agriculture, and the existing agricultural scientific and technological achievements that can be applied should be initiatively tested in this small world. Science and technology is the first productive force. It is impossible for such a small environment to obtain large output without science and technology. The courtyard economy is a way to see big from small ones with reasonable arrangement, characteristic operation as well as intensive and meticulous farming (Su, 2004). The benefit of an efficient courtyard ecosystem can be seen year by year.

All in all, most of Chinese population is in rural areas or small towns. Every family has different courtyards, which can be utilized. There is enormous potential for courtyard economy development and these small courtyards can be a big agriculture industry when getting together. Full use of these existing resources has a significant effect on the development of the rural economy.

Chia Tai Model and Rural Economy Development in China

Chia Tai Group, a well-known multinational company, was established in 1921 by ethnic Chinese industrialist brothers Xie Yichu and Xie Shaofei. It is called Charoen Pokphand Group outside China. The company began with crop seed selling and it gradually grew stronger, which finally developed a comprehensive modern agriculture and animal husbandry industry chain made up of the improvement of seeds, crops plantation, feed industry, breeding industry, agricultural and pastoral products processing, food selling, import and export trade etc. It has become the model of modern agriculture and animal husbandry industrialization in the world. In the past 30 years, with the second-generation leadership of the family, the Chia Tai Group constantly reforms the business philosophy of agriculture and animal husbandry. At the same time of developing competitive industries and dominant industries, it is actively involved with other industries, such as telecommunication, petrol chemical industry, real estate, medical treatment, retailing, finance, mechanical engineering, mass media and so on. It has achieved great achievements and has become one of the largest and the most influential enterprises and groups.

The famous Chia Tai model is a business operation of combination of companies with peasant households. To open up the Chinese market, the Chia Tai feed company of Thailand provides production materials like technique services and chicken feed for peasant households, to motivate peasant households to develop chicken cultivation industry, which helps the company to keep its footing and gain further development in China. This is earlier practice of "combination of companies with peasant households" in China that is called "Chia Tai Model". This is also an initiative form of industrialization development for agriculture in China, which currently is developing in many areas of China. Based on that, there are many industrialized organization operation forms growing. These operations are involved in cultivation industry, processing transportation industry, commercial industry and other rural industries and they obtain significant economic benefits and social benefits. However, people found that with primary agriculture industrialization, though there is feasibility of cooperation among commerce, workers and peasants and they are willing to establish stable cooperation relationships, they inevitably pursue maximizing self-interest because their own interest is independent. Especially for those commercial trade departments and enterprises that used to depend on "price scissors", they regard farming industry as an object of interest. If there is industrialization for agriculture, it should be market-oriented. An equal interest constraint mechanism should be established to achieve real risk sharing and equal interest distribution in the integration of commerce, workers and peasants.

For example, Shanghai Dajiang Co. LTD with relevant enterprises is a coherent operation department which is dominated by three production departments of breed, livestock and meat. It is a multi-component and competitive enterprise with abundant economic strength and Chinese and foreign investment, which is run by the combination of factories and integrated with "three large blocks" of rural collective economic organization. The total amount of fixed assets investment of "Dajiang" and its relevant enterprises has reached one hundred million and large-scale drum feed mills have been built up. The original supported rural professional households and rural chicken farms were rebuilt as 21 large-scale modernized chicken farms. Tens of thousands of pigs and chickens raising households are integrated with hundreds of national, collective farms to develop large-scale feed and chicken series of production and marketing and conduct production and marketing integrated operation. The annual output of full price grain drum feed is 600 hundred tons, with more than two-hundred-million baby broilers of parent generation and one-million baby chickens of parent generation. The annual output of commercial chicks is one hundred million, with forty-million breeding broilers, sixty-thousand processing chickens and twenty-thousand frozen broiler outlet. The annual export earnings are more than 50 million US dollars, ranking among the best in the national husbandry.

Courtyard Economy + Chia Tai Model

In the long term, the reason why farming industry is a vulnerable industry is that agriculture engages in making primary productions, which causes hidden unemployment, the surplus labor force. Through intensive and effective plantation and cultivation, the agriculture industrialization operation emphasizes the development of agricultural products processing industry and transportation selling industry, to absorb considerable labor force. The employment creates value and the value would keep expanding. Meanwhile, agricultural products processing industry and other labor-intensive industries in urban areas transfer to rural areas which provides many opportunities for rural areas to develop the second and the third industry. Rural enterprises should regard the stressed development of agricultural products processing industry and transportation selling industry as the strategic direction. They should be properly integrated and combined with construction of small towns, to develop into many strong economic growth points and transfer more labor force. With the same condition, the less labor force agriculture takes, the higher the agricultural labor productivity, which is the general rule of agricultural development (Niu, 1997).

Modern science and technology are widely used in the process of integrated systems reproduction, which makes the growth rate of agriculture exceed the growth rate of industry. The condition of agriculture is greatly improved, making vast space and realistic prospect for the transformation of agriculture from vulnerable industry to strong industry. The pioneers have achieved superior performance. With the eloquent testimony, agriculture can transform to strong industry with high return in investment especially those more and more profitable industries like cultivation industry and agricultural products processing industry. The theoretical foundation provided by the industry development theory for agricultural industrialization is that the agricultural industrialization is an important way to promote agriculture from low level to elevated level. The law of industrial development requires agriculture modernization to stand at the height of modern economy to develop agriculture.

An important goal of agricultural reform and development in China is to develop moderate scale management. To develop scale management is to realize scale economy, which means the economic trend with lowered average cost and raising profits because of the expanding production or management scale. The international famous economic theory indicates that scale economy is decided by the degree of concentration, whose production factors are mainly technical progress. The improvement of agricultural production techniques and production tools inevitably causes the expanding of agricultural scale. Agricultural industrialization is very important to realize agricultural scale management. Through socialization, professionalization and integration, it is not only good to expand the management scale but also to develop the advantages of related industrial groups.

In terms of theories, there are two ways to fully use the scale economy. One is to expand the management scale, which means that by establishing reasonable land transfer mechanism moderate scale management could be promoted. The other is to depend on the combination of various economic objects in the group. In the combination, it is not necessary to be an economic entity but to connect many peasants together by various organizational forms. Inside it, though the scale of a peasant is small, he would avoid many barriers to enter the market and thus greatly improve the productivity because he participates in the division and cooperation of the organization and the system. As a result, the whole industrial system would gain serial effect and scale advantages, with good economic performance (Wang and Xu, 1996).

The historical experience of China and other countries indicates that it is most efficient for agriculture, especially plantation industry to conduct household management, which is also a basic institution in the farming industry of China. Though the accelerating progress of rural industrialization and urbanization provides required conditions for expanding the scale of agricultural production management, however, in a long term, the reality of small-scale agricultural management cannot be changed. Therefore, it is of great realistic significance to develop courtyard economy in China. Firstly, it is suitable for the local characteristics of large population with little land, more mountains than plains and unbalanced resources. Especially in the areas with lack of resources and advanced economy, to develop courtyard economy can solve the problem of resources shortage and open new channels to increase income for farmers at the same time of developing field economy. Secondly, natural environment and other external conditions could have few influences on developing plantation industry, cultivation industry and other industries in the courtyards, which could avoid great damage from natural disasters. It is feasible for farmers who are vulnerable to risks. Thirdly, in those under developed areas, the industrial base is weak, without the ability to conduct large-scale agricultural public investment. Agriculture face lack of capital and there are little capital and equipment needed for the projects of courtyard economy. To develop courtyard economy is to unleash the creativity of farmers, to instruct farmers to solve the difficulties at the early stage of development. Fourthly, to develop courtyard economy could motivate peasants to automatically adjust the agricultural industrial structure and change the situation of single production projects and low efficiency.

To combine the courtyard economy and the organization form of "companies + bases + peasants" can strengthen the resource development, grow output and increase the value. The main characteristic of this type of economy is the integrated production system of commerce, workers and peasants by combination of enterprises, agricultural products base and peasants.

Chapter 8

Establish an Innovative Industrial Institution

Why currently western capitalist countries are stronger than China in economy, technology and national power? An important reason is that they own modernized industrial enterprises. Though industry started late in China, it has demonstrated fierce competition advantagc by fully adjusting economic layout and learning advanced experience from other countries of China. Especially in the future process of information driving industrialization, China cannot purely copy the approach advocated by general marketization, while it should continue to use reform policies to stimulate industrial enterprises to increase productivity. Feeding agriculture with advanced equipment and technology, the competitive advantage of "International Factory" could be strengthened and market share of products in the international market could be enlarged.

Increase the Ability of Technological Innovation

From 1840 to 1949, China has suffered many insults from capitalist powers and people were in deep misery. The reason is that economy was lagging backward in the old China and the social system was corrupted. The backwards will be beaten, which would lead to national death. The only way to construct a powerful country is to reform the system that is no more suitable for historical development and vigorously develop social productivity.

Hard Start and Rapid Growth

Modern industry in China was originated from the Qing Dynasty Westernization Movement in around 1860. However, half a century before this, there was Industrial Reform in the Great Britain. Social productivity grew exponentially in a rapid way and strong gunboats for overseas expansion were made. When the British bourgeoisie were in the process of carrying out barbaric capital accumulation, the large muzzle on the ship were pointed to China, a country with rich natural resources. In the 1840 Sino-British Opium War, government of Qing dynasty, which had long been regarded as a big country in the East, suffered a fiasco. Intimidated by the imperial government of the British Isles, which was well armed in a projectile land, China was forced to sign a series of unequal treaties with humiliation. Since then, China had stepped into the fading historical stage of Colonial and semi-colonial.

The treaties, betraying the rights of bereavement, greatly aroused the indignation of Chinese people so that some officials and citizens were determined to imitate the British industry and manufacture guns and cannons to snow national shame. The dominant idea of Westernization Movement is to save the country with industry and strengthen the national military. This ideal policy experienced improvement and failure of the time, with continuing reform and failure of the Reform Movement in 1898, all of which had not been finished. After that, only through the struggle and victory of the Anti-Japanese War and the reform victory of dispelling the reactionaries to liberate China, which were led by the Chinese Communist Party, the initial ideal was eventually condensed into some valuable historical experience. This is the incisive summary of Mao Zedong's "The Second Plenary Session of the Seventh Central Committee of the Communist Party of China" that after the victory of revolution, China should quickly restore and develop the productivity and deal with the foreign imperialism to make China transform from an agricultural country to an industrial country. The theoretical concept that emerged on the eve of the establishment of New China is still right and inspiring today. If a backward country wants to avoid being insulted by the enormous power in the world and grow stronger and if it wants to ensure the prosperity and well-being of its people, it should learn and innovate. Only by constantly arming itself with advanced science and knowledge, innovating traditional industries timely and establishing a new type of modern industrial system, it can stand on its own in the worldwide nations.

Firstly, the innovation ability of science and technology was improved. In the first five years of a new century, around the goal of "innovation" and "industrialization", China made strategic deployment on two lays which were "industrial technology promotion" and "constant improvement of sustainable innovation ability of science and technology". China implemented some science and technology programs such as the 863 Program, Program for Tacking Key Problems, 973 Program, Spark Program, Torch Program, the construction of national agricultural technology park, the basic condition platform construction for national science and technology and the program of agricultural technology achievements transforming into capital and so on. Additionally, places and enterprises implemented more concrete and multiple reforms. Therefore, it prominently enhanced the innovation ability of Chinese science and technology. The information industry is strategic height of economy and technology nowadays. Through scientific and technological innovation, China made great progress at some advanced technology fields such as micro-electronic communication equipment, high performance computer, excellent materials and devices as well as automatic control, developing into high-tech products and guiding industries with Chinese intellectual independent property and cultivating many new economic growth points. Take the special project of integrated circuit as an example. The industrial output of integrated circuit design increased to nearly 10 billion yuan in 2004 from 5 billion yuan in 1999. Up to 2017, the sales revenue of Chinese integrated circuit industry has reached to 535.52 billion yuan, totally about 80.529 billion dollars. It took 23.67% in the global revenues of integrated circuit, which was 340.189 billion dollars, and took 19.7% in sales revenue of global semiconductor industry. According to forest of CCID Consulting, integrated circuit industry of China will achieve a compound growth rate of approximately 20.2% in sales in the next three years. By 2020, Chinese IC industry sales revenue will reach 930 billion yuan (Tian and Dai, 2012) and the development of integrated circuit would strongly support the national information technology and industrial development.

Because every scientific and technological program are implemented successfully, a series of innovative achievements form a great productivity, which transform the basic industries lasting for thousands of years. To speed up the construction of an innovative country, implementing innovation-driven and rural revitalization strategies, the development of agriculture and rural areas entering a new era of "transitions, structural optimization, and power shifts" is being promoted. The state increases the investment in agricultural science and technology. About production efficiency and the establishment of a long-term mechanism for increasing farmers' income, technological progress and scientific innovation played a huge role in stimulation. Statistics from the Joint Management Office of National Agricultural Science and Technology Park displayed that, until the end of 2017, 246 established parks have been built with a core area of 5.79 million mu and a demonstration area of 200 million mu. The total number of agricultural enterprises introduced and cultivated in the parks reached more than 8,700, including 1,555 high-teach enterprises, which basically covered all provinces, autonomous regions, municipalities directly under the Central Government, cities with separate plans and the Xinjiang Production and Construction Corps in China. A total of 40,900 new varieties were introduced and cultivated. It also promoted 14,600 new varieties, introduced and promoted 22,000 modern technologies of diverse types of agriculture, examined and approved 642 new varieties of plants, livestock and aquatic products at the provincial level and above, as well as obtained over 4,000 patent authorizations. It has gradually formed a development pattern of the park with distinctive features, typical patterns, and significant scientific and technological demonstration effects. According to the statistics, in 2015, the total output value achieved by the park where trained 3.74 million farmers, reached 1.2 trillion yuan. What's more, it motivated 1.7 million local farmers to be employed. The total labor productivity rate was RMB 142,500 per person, which was 60.1% higher than the national rate of RMB 89,000/person. Various indicators of innovation were obviously better than national average. Such changes increased the quality of Chinese economic growth, improved people's quality of life, and played a major supporting role in promoting sustained economic growth and overall social progress in the state. New technological development bore fruitful results.

Secondly, Chinese economic power was enhanced. After new China was founded, facing to the economic blockade from western capitalist countries, the first-generation leadership of the Republic of China, led by Mao Zedong, collectively opened a development road that gave priority to self-reliance and took the foreign aid as auxiliary. The Chinese were united and constantly strove to become stronger, then breaking through the blockade and insisting on the socialist road. A new country was found strongly. Since 1949, Chinese industries had developed greatly and grown rapidly. Up to 1978, an elementary industrial system had formed. When entering new period, under the essential conditions that western capitalist countries still stick to exploitation and enslave the national policies of developing countries, people in China use a way that is in line with the nation conditions to seize the opportunities and get great achievements in the "Eleventh Five-year" period that enhances economic strength. In 2004, the reserve balance of Chinese foreign exchange was 609.9 billion dollars, which exceeded Japanese congeneric amount, becoming the country whose reserve balance of foreign exchange increased most rapidly around the world in that year. And this situation still went on in the later few years. According to the report from the ITAR-TASS on January 13, 2012, the reserve balance of Chinese foreign exchange reached 3.18 trillion dollars till the end of 2011, which became the highest one in the history again, and it was the first time to exceed 3 trillion dollars. China continued to keep as a leader of world, and the following was Japan and Russia. On April 19, 2018, at the press conference of the State Council Information office, Wang Chunying, Director of the International Revenue and Expenditure and spokesman of the National Administration of Foreign Exchange, pointed out that by the end of March 2018, the balance of China's foreign exchange reserve was 3142.8 billion U.S. dollars, increasing 2.9 billion U.S. dollars (Lu, 2018) compared to the end of 2017. Though China made a progress, it still did not reach to the standard of developed industrial countries in the world.

The current developed industrial countries in the west have been in the capitalist development stage for more than 200 years, which had accumulated material wealth and developed science and technology. In the two world wars that took place in the last century, especially taking America as an example, not only did it not have destructive damage industrial and agricultural basis because the homeland was far away, but it also got a windfall in the war as a victorious nation. These were primary reasons why western industrial countries are stronger than developing countries in economy, capital, science, technology, national power and so on. However, due to many contradictions accumulated inside and outside of western capitalist states so that it caused a series of profound outbreak of economic crisis. With two continuous financial crisis and economic recession since 2008, many people in Europe and America started to realize that the consequence, regulated by market, always trended to the profit but not to the equity nowadays when the global economy are related and the monetary lever is everywhere. The social inequity which is stronger and stronger not only impedes the normal development of social and economic, but also always causes more imbalances that "the rich are getting richer and richer, the poor are getting poorer and poorer" (Tao, 2012). Of course, facing to the transitory retreat of the tendency of capitalist, we cannot be optimistic blindly and well-satisfied.

The transitory setbacks of western pattern do not improve our level of development and quality of development because we are still not wealthy and faced with the structural fragility. We should not be killed by praise because we are still taking a heavy burden and embark on a long road (Tian and Dai, 2012). At present, America still acts as the policeman of world, not changing the policy of expansionism, and westernization and differentiation never stop in China. From 1940s to the mid-term of 2040s, which are amounted to 105 years, China suffered aggression from almost all social-imperialist states around the world. Mao Zedong once analyzed this period of history in depth in 60s last century and pointed out that, one of the reasons was that the social system is corrupt and the other was that the backward economic and technology." Having founded the People's Republic of China, the first difficulty was solved overall. To deal with the second difficulty, China should realize the goal of four modernization to catch up with and exceed the western countries and to be faced with more difficulties. Although it is hard, Chinese will screw up their courage and push forward. If Chinese people do not strive for thoroughly changing the situation that Chinese economy and technology are far behind social-imperialist states in the following decades, it will not be avoided to take a beating (Mao, 1999). Therefore, during the "Thirteenth Five-year" period, China should go on to make science and technology as the first productive forces, making more efforts to solve it than the first difficulty, strengthening the army and the country with science and technology, constructing the socialist state and maintaining world peace.

Initiate Innovative Ways to Industrialization

Every state around the world is proceeding the industrialized construction and wants to occupy the economic commanding elevation. Though it was late for China to start the industrial construction, which needs to learn advanced experience from other countries, it is not to imitate simply, especially not to copy the doing that seeks nothing but profits, which is advocated by over marketization. China should insist on its socialist political advantages, implementing the development strategy of "people-oriented", which is the only correct road to guarantee the country to come up later.

Firstly, industrial construction should walk our own road. Going by challenging work in half a century after construction of the state, China constructed its own industrial system. Chinese industrial development does not walk on the same road as capitalist countries walk on, which avoids the pain that once appeared in human society. The development of textile industry is a classic example. The textile industry is not only the starting industry of the modern industry owned by human society, but also the bearing production operation form of market economy system during its initial establishment of Britain. More than two hundred years ago, it was also the beginning of market economy when the textile industry starting in Britain. The capitalism that sprung up at that time used cruel ways of "Enclosure Movement" and "Sheep Eating" to construct this industry, which also made market economy form gradually in laboring people's bloodstain. In socialist China, the textile industry takes another course to grow up and gets great development by reconstruction. At the annual meeting about social responsibility of China textile and apparel industry in June 28th, 2011, Du Yuzhou, the president of China Textile Industry Association disclosed that in the "Eleventh Five-year" period, the export of Chinese textile and apparel increased eighty percent where the trade surplus nearly increased 9.2%. Its five-year trade surplus occupied 7.2% percent of nationwide. It was the first time that contribution rate of value growth exceeded that of the quantitative growth in Chinese textile and apparel, which reached 5.7%. The proportion of China's textile and apparel in total import of America increased to about one quarter in 2010 from about 2.5 percent in 2005.

During the "Twelfth Five-year" period, Chinese textile industry made the main line as rapidly transforming the economic development ways and made the primary task as stimulating industrial transformation. During this period, the average rate of value growth was about 9% and its major economic indicators were in an appropriate level in the national industrial system. The Chinese textile industry showed a stable development trend of steady growth in growing economy of scale, with steadily increasing strength (Yan, 2011). Not only does China have the biggest scale, the most intact structure of textile industrial system in the world, but also it has constructed stable basis of fiber material. The China Textile Industry Federation pointed out that, the "13th Fifth-year Plan" period was the decisive stage for China to fully build a well-off society and the final stage for it to transform from a big textile country to a powerful textile country. During this time, innovation and development should be the fundamental driving force for Chinese textile industry to transform and upgrade. Coordinated development and green development are important part in the construction of strong textile country. Open development and shred development are the basic guarantee and goal of it (Yan, 2016).

It was a Chinese industrial epitome of the progress achieved by textile industry during the "Eleventh Five-year" period and the "Twelfth Five-year" period. These achievements were attributed to the implementation of the national Reform and Opening-up policy, which were achieved in the frame of socialist market economy with Chinese characteristics. The fact turned out again that market economy, as a production pattern used by human, had great plasticity. It could come from or be applied to different states, different social systems. In other words, it had different specific pattern. The reason is that every state has different productivity levels, political systems, cultural background, orientation of social value, residents' national quality and cultural quality.

If China constructs market economy it should coordinate with the nature of socialist country to avoid "Sheep Eating" as well as copying capitalism. Why China adopts the system of market economy is for the well-being of overwhelming majority of the people. Even for capitalist states, they adopt different market economic systems. For example, as the representative of America states, it implements monopolistic market economy or the consumer sovereignty market economy. Sweden, as another representative, implements welfare-type economic pattern of Nordic countries. What German implements is social market economic pattern. What Japan implements is the market pattern of "officers, enterprises and people coordinate". What South Korea and Singapore implements is the marketing economic pattern led by the government.

Besides, the market economic patterns in many developing countries also have characteristic of their national culture. However, the looming over marketization disregarded the diversity of market economy, insisting on a radical pursuit of a single model. It described some practices in the US market economic model as a golden rule. In fact, some people do not have a complete understanding of the American market economy model, and they are only using partial to make conclusion so that it is so narrow, which is far from the realistic situation. In fact, as an independent form of economic operation, market economy is not a social economy system, also not the basis of political system. It not only could be combined with the private economy, but it also could be combined with the national economy. However, after the diversity of the market was derogated by those generalized market theorists or market economy subject theorists, privatization or privatization are promoted as the core of the market. This approach was precisely a betrayal to the market economy in diversity characteristics. In their view, only privatization is the market economy so that they are desirable to see China realize privatization within one day to realize their main ideas of market economy. To critique of pan-marketing arguments, the most essential point is that, there should not be totally privatization, Americanization overall, but to establish a socialist market economy system with public ownership as the main body and a variety of non-public ownership economies in active development.

Secondly, to constantly innovate the industrial development model. In the history of human-being, there are various for a new system to replace the old system with difficult development and there would be different periods for that. However, the old system would not die out on its own, which would not stop killing the new system anyone day. Various battles between the old system and the new system would continue. China's rise in peace has won acclaim in the world and it has a profound impact on the economics and politics worldwide, which naturally invites hatred from hostile forces. It is known that China's export trade has been hardly blocked by some industrialized countries, with trade barriers violating the rules of WTO. Although domestic companies were faced with the challenges bravely and repeatedly frustrated the interception of trade protection, it is not so satisfactory. By analyzing these process, we can see that domestic companies had not made sufficient preparations before the challenges, without successful transition. To adjust the industrial structure timely would be one of the important tasks in the future.

The export of Chinese industrial products has not been smooth all the time and there have been hardships, all of which demonstrates that the concept and existence of "national industry" is not backward. Since the 1980s, color TVs of China has sold to Europe, but the European Commission adopted a trade protectionism and imposed anti-dumping duties on Chinese products from 1998 with unnecessary charges. The root cause of trade frictions between Europe and China is that the Europe refuses to recognize the market economy system in China, treating Chinese color TV companies unfairly. In 2006, the anti-dumping duty that the European Council imposed on seven Chinese color TV enterprises was as high as 44.6%. Influenced by the European anti-dumping, color TV from China has been basically driven out of European market. After that, Chinese enterprises made concessions as well as significant efforts, and sacrificed greatly. In 2012, Europe conduct anti-dumping once again, but this time it was for Chinese ceramics industry. On February 16, 2012, the website of Import and Export Chamber of Commerce in China Arts and Crafts Light Industry issued *the Notification European Commission Conducting Anti-Dumping Investigation on Chinese Ceramic Tableware,* which displayed that the European Commission had issued a notice of initiating an anti-dumping investigation against Chinese ceramic kitchen.

According to the China Ceramic Association, the case involved more than 2, 000 ceramic enterprises. If it was calculated as the trade amount of 2011 between the Europe and China, the amount of money involved was as much as 700 million dollars (Li, 2012). East American time on March 22, 2018, the Trump government issued the *"301 Investigation"* to confront the trade war with China, which made the *"China-America Trade War"* on the verge. During this period, the EU announced on April 20 that the anti-dumping duties levied on China's steel cables should be postponed for five years (Tian and Dai, 2012). The punitive tariffs imposed on Chinese products by the European Commission on many occasions are discriminatory, lack of legal basis, violating the principle of fair trade. Some Chinese enterprises, such as large footwear companies, have jointly reacted to defend the European anti-dumping. These cases illustrate that commercial war without smoke in the international market is extremely fierce.

To meet the challenges, China should carry out large-scale economy structure reform and resolve various complicated problems to establish a market economy system that conforms to Chinese national situation, which is a heavy burden indeed. China should learn the existing market economy models from various advanced industrialized countries in the world, following international practice. However, it should not copy the so-called American "free market model" that is advocated by market economic players. Therefore, it is imperative to implement some appropriate measures for market economy reform to make a socialist market economy with Chinese characteristics and oppose the practice of subjective market economy. This economic form could be defined as social-market economy. The implied content is based on overall balanced development of social economy. It aims at satisfying the material needs of Chinese people to the maximum extent and should not merely based on the market economy, which is a socialist market economy with Chinese characteristics.

At the same time, we should note that China has vast territory and many ethnic groups. The level of economic, social and cultural development in various regions varies greatly. Thus, in the process of developing market economy, various market economy models should made based on the local economic and cultural characteristics, instead of copying a model in a consistent manner. The Wenzhou model, South Jiangsu model and South Horizontal Street model, where economic forms have emerged different social characteristics in the reform, fully demonstrated that the pattern of China's market economy development is geographically diverse. To adapt to the social-market economy, the economic system should also be liberalized appropriately. State-owned, publicly-owned, collectively owned, self-owned, joint ventures and the labor cooperation proposed by some people should be treated equally in the development of Chinese socialist society and the development of market economy. It is a way that conforms to the national situation to socialist market economy in China.

The New Socialist Rural Construction and Social Work

The "Thirteenth Five-Year Plan" outline proposes that "promote coordinated urban and rural development, adhere to industry supporting the agriculture and the urban supporting the rural, improve the integrated institutional mechanisms for urban and rural development and distribute equal basic public services." During the "Eleventh Five-year Plan" China's agricultural economy has developed steadily under a more open environment, while the agriculture will be faced with a new turning point in the coming few years. Therefore, it is even more necessary for industry to support the agriculture and the whole society to support agriculture. The year 2011 is the tenth year for China to join the WTO and the agriculture was under intense pressure from competition. Government of China puts most effort among all WTO members on adjusting agriculture. From 2001 to 2015, the overall tariff level of China dropped from 15.3% to 9.8%, which was the lowest among developing countries. The average agricultural product tax was shifted from 18.8% to 15.1% and the average industrial product tax was adjusted from 14.7% to 8.9%. Since joining the WTO, China has earnestly fulfilled its promised tariff reduction obligations and has received widely acclaim from the international community (Wu, 2016). The agricultural economy is experiencing a wave of competition to join the WTO. At the same time, Chinese government is making a fair competition environment for peasants and agriculture. For example, during the WTO Doha agricultural negotiations, the Chinese government delegation argued energetically and firmly defended the interests of Chinese peasants, eliminating agricultural subsidies that violated the rules of WTO in developed countries.

Agriculture in China is still dominated by small-scale peasant economy. especially the intensification degree in western China is very low. In some ethic minority autonomous areas, there is still primitive “slash and burn” culture and the original “grazing cattle, sheep and grass” nomadic industry, and the fierce competition caused by joining the WTO hit greatly the agriculture in these areas. The price of agricultural products has been decreasing and the export has become more difficult. Joining the WTO has make the agriculture and other industries suffer shocks and put pressure on the peasants directly and indirectly. In the later five to ten years, the impact of China’s accession to WTO on agriculture and other industries will continues to show, especially the agriculture would be faced with greater competition. Naturally, agriculture and other fields have also gained new opportunities that there are great chances for the production and export of green food because there is a large area of natural environment due to its low-level development in the western region. Though some weak agricultural production and self-owned brands are still in development bottlenecks, the speed of development has accelerated under the stimulus of exports. Rural farmers have thus broadened their horizons and agriculture has gained more space for development. At the same time, fierce competition among worldwide multinational enterprises has forced them bring the latest technology to China, which, to a certain extent, stimulate the agricultural development in China. Under the circumstance of coexistence of challenges and opportunities, how to make agricultural enterprises especially agriculture industry in western region enter the market in competition is a strategic task in the "13th Five-Year Plan" period. In response to the challenges in a more open environment rural areas and peasants need assistance from the outside. Without the promotion of industry to the agriculture, the intensification and standardization of agriculture, the optimization of agricultural product structure and the extension of agricultural production chains, such series of agricultural modernization processes could not be completed.

Since the transition period of China joining the WTO will come to an end, the competitive pressure on agriculture are basically the same as totally opening-up market. Therefore, the biggest challenge agriculture faced with is innovation. Only by developing self-owned brands and innovative products with independent intellectual property rights can agriculture maintain its unique advantage. Thus, government should transform its role as soon as possible to a service-oriented government. Administrative departments should mobilize the strength of the entire society to support agriculture, increasing the input to agriculture and the rural, stimulating the adjustment of agriculture industry structure, raising the core competition and supporting peasants in changing their concepts so that production can response to market changes. For example, financial service to agriculture is not satisfying compared to the opening degree of the industry and other services. The main reason is the slow recovery of agricultural investment and the higher risk rate.

Revive the Main Force of State-Owned Enterprises

Although Chinese industrial enterprises have achieved outstanding results, the international competition environment in the new century has become more severe. It is not only more necessary to rely on science and technology to break through the attempts of foreign multinationals to monopolize the market, but also to make the economic system more effective.

State-owned Enterprises in Reform

Industrialization is a critical condition for the powerful national economy. The industry of a country must be self-contained to gain a firm foothold in the world market competition. The formation of an industrial system must have the core strength of a team. In socialist China, this team is state-owned enterprises. Before the reform, state-owned enterprises in China was operated completely in accordance with the planned economic system, the production capacity owned by the company has not been brought into play. Since the state implemented the reform of state-owned enterprises based on the establishment of a modern enterprise system, the situation has undergone momentous changes.

On November 22nd, 2011, the official Blue Book issued by the authority of the director of Institute of Industrial Economics of the Chinese Academy of Social Sciences Jin Bei and the China Industrial and Enterprise Competitiveness Research Center of the Chinese Academy of Social Sciences - "China Enterprise Competitiveness Report (2011)" was officially launched. The Blue Book Report pointed out that after more than 30 years of reform and opening up, especially after China turned to the market economy in 1992, China's competition can be summarized by "cheap competition". After more than 30 years of "cheap-style competition", Chinese industrial development has achieved remarkable achievements and pushed China to the second largest economy in the world. At the same time, it also paid a great price. Unbalanced, uncoordinated, the problem of being unsustainable is very prominent (Chen, 2011). The production capacity of Chinese state-owned enterprises has been significantly improved, and the number of listed transactions has increased year by year. The '2009 Annual Conference of Chinese Enterprise Competitiveness' sponsored by the Institute of Industrial Economics of the Chinese Academy of

Social Sciences released the ranking of the listed companies in China in 2009. Among them, Sinopec, PetroChina, CNOOC, China Mobile and China Unicom, and other large state-owned enterprises were selected as '2009 Top 10 Most Competitive Overseas Listed Companies in China'; Kweichow Moutai, China Shipbuilding, Vanke, and China Railway entered the '2009 Chinese most competitive Top 20 listed companies' (Xia, 2009). The Top 100 Listed Companies of Chinese State-Owned Enterprises in 2011 was also freshly issued. Although new listed companies have joined every year, the overall pattern of the listed companies' competitiveness has not changed. The state-owned company, Petro China, continued to maintain its No. 1 ranking. Sinopec Corp. rose from No. 3 in 2009 to No. 2 in 2011, followed by ICBC, China Construction Bank, Bank of China, and China Mobile. There were also many state-owned enterprises with strong development momentum and the status of the company has been continuously improved. For example, the Agricultural Bank of China, China Railway Group, China Railway 2nd Bureau, and Tongfang's shares have all improved significantly (Xia, 2011). The competitiveness of state-owned enterprises in listing transactions was significantly higher than that of non-state listed companies.

The industrial development in state-owned enterprises is even more gratifying. In 1992, the average total profit of Chinese listed companies was 59.698 million yuan, the average total profit of all industrial enterprises was 158,000 yuan, and the average total profit of listed companies was 379 times than all industrial enterprises. In 2004, the average total profit of listed companies was 190.96 million yuan, and the average total profit of all industrial enterprises was 5.17 million yuan. The average total profit of listed companies fell to 37 times of the average total profit of all industrial enterprises. At the same time when the economic benefits create new highs, the output of major products of the central enterprises also set a record high. According to production statistics from January to December in 2005, two coal enterprises cumulatively produced 252.826 million tons of raw coal, which increased 25.4%; coal sales were 270.349 million tons, increasing 16%. Seven power generation companies completed 1056.49 billion kilowatt-hours of power generation, an increase of 20.5%. The two power grid companies completed sales of 1,841,100 million kwh, an increase of 13.4%. The total domestic and foreign crude oil output of the three petroleum and petrochemical enterprises was 1971.11 million tons, an increase of 4.1%; the total natural gas output was 52.88 billion cubic meters, an increase of 20.5%. This is the year that new progress had been made in the restructuring of the central enterprises.

The central government owned enterprises completed a fixed asset investment of 1,045.38 billion yuan, an increase of 21.1% (Qi, 2006). In recent years, the reform of state-owned enterprises, zombie enterprises accelerated elimination, the state-owned enterprises continued to decline in the asset-liability ratio, accounting for 60% of the revenue of the central enterprises in recent years, of which the contribution of profits up to 87.3%. By June 2017, the profits of the central SOEs totaled 935.21 billion yuan, a year-on-year increase of 18.5%, and that of local state-owned enterprises was 472.02 billion yuan, a year-on-year increase of 37.5%. It is worth mentioning that the data from the Ministry of Finance showed that in June 2017, the monthly profit of central SOEs was 212.86 billion yuan. In the first half of 2017, 99 of the 102 central SOEs were profitable, of which 48 companies had profits exceeding 10% (Mo, 2017). These data showed that Chinese enterprises had a robust growth momentum. The director of the Institute of Industrial Economics of the Chinese Academy of Social Sciences and the president of the China Business Newspaper, Jin Bei, pointed out at the '2011 (ninth) Annual Conference on the Competitiveness of Chinese Enterprises' that the future industry still had a huge demand market for an extended period. Take steel as an example, according to a report released by the UN Environment Agency, Americans currently own 11 to 12 tons of steel, while China only has 1.5 tons. If we want to reach the average American steel stock in 20 years, we will need to consume about 14 billion tons of steel (Jin,

2011). The potential of industrial development of Chinese companies is enormous.

Chinese state-owned enterprises, especially large and medium-sized state-owned enterprises, have not only become the mainstay of the national economy in the construction of national socialism, but also play a role that other non-social organizations can play. They not only balance the regional layout of Chinese productivity, provide the production (business) product for the society and provide the income for the worker, but also undertake plenty of social functions, for example nurseries, primary and secondary school and employee education, safeguard social order, public welfare service and so on. Although these non-economic tasks consumed the power of state-owned enterprises, they met the needs of the public to a certain extent and maintained social stability.

However, during the process of reform of state-owned enterprises in the 1990s, many localities did not seem to consider the functions of state-owned enterprises in non-production and management, but judged according to a criterion of economic profit. Based on the so-called socialization of non-production and business functions, the original social functions of state-owned enterprises were quickly abolished. The goal is to let the state-owned enterprises move lightly to get greater profits. At the same time, however, due to the severe shortage of national social service system resources, some social functions that were originally undertaken by state-owned enterprises were paralyzed, resulting in many resentments and difficulties that have arisen in the lives of employees, and even buried some social unrest seeds in some places. Obviously, taking the market economy as standard is narrow, is at the expense of a comprehensive and balanced development of the social economy. Therefore, it is also unacceptable.

Face the New Challenges

Chinese state-owned enterprises, especially large and medium-sized state-owned enterprises, have played a huge role in the development of

China's social economy. According to the data released by the Ministry of Finance of the People's Republic of China on January 23, 2018, in 2017, the economic and economic performance of state-owned enterprises was sound, stable, and progressing. The income and profits of state-owned enterprises continued to grow rapidly, and the profit growth was higher than the income of 9.9 percentage points. According to statistics, the total revenue of state-owned enterprises last year was 5,124.99 billion yuan, a year-on-year increase of 13.6%. Among them, central government enterprises totaled 308.168 billion yuan, a year-on-year increase of 12.5%, and local state-owned enterprises reached 21383.63 billion yuan, a year-on-year increase of 15.2%. The total profit of state-owned enterprises was 298.96 billion yuan, a year-on-year increase of 23.5%. Among them, the central enterprises amounted to 1,775.72 billion yuan, an increase of 16% year-on-year; local state-owned enterprises were 1,122.87 billion yuan, an increase of 37.6% year-on-year. The main indicators of economic efficiency of state-owned enterprises can maintain a steady and rapid growth, mainly due to the adjustment of the corporate structure, especially the large-scale development of independent innovation, making the actual benefits increase rapidly. However, a series of actions by the Trump administration in 2018 caused confusion in international trade and caused a serious and destructive impact on the normal international trade order. The overall situation in the domestic and international economic environment may become more complicated in the future. Therefore, the development of state-owned enterprises will face new challenges.

Firstly, actively participate in international market competition. To gain the initiative and effectiveness in the competition of the world's industrial economy, it must have its own industrial system. According to a survey in 2006, 28% of China’s industrial output value, 21% of employment opportunities, and 53% of trade were already in the hands of foreigners. More than a third of consumers across the country were directed at the products of non-Chinese companies (Bai,

2006). This situation is very worrying, and to change this situation must have the initiative of industrial development.

The industrial economy's initiative, in the final analysis, is linked to the ownership of industrial core technologies. Modern industry relies on high-tech support, especially information technology that represents the trend of the times and guides the direction of industrial development. Western industrialized countries have an advantage in the field of information technology, especially in the most critical software information technology, and it is the United States that has exclusive power. To achieve industrialization driven by informationization, China must break the monopoly in the world of the American multinational corporations represented by Microsoft, rather than following other people. If the American company has a core chip, then the Chinese company also engage in a core chip of its own, such an approach is not in line with the principle of economics because it does not have the impact power that owned by original innovation technology and products developed independently. The advancement of society and the development of science are like running against the tide. No innovation, no openness, no learning is conservative, and it is to rest on its laurels.

Comrade Jiang Zemin once discussed the significance of opening to the outside world from the perspective of historical comparison. He said: "From 1661 to 1976, it was known as the Kangqian Shengshi in history. During this period, China's economic level was the world's leading. In the last years of Qianlong, China's economic output ranked first in the world, and the population accounted for one third of the world, foreign trade was surplus for a long time." It can be said that since the prosperity of the Tang and Song dynasties in China, this is another peak period in our national history. At the same time, however, the great industrial revolution took place in the western world, which still has influence currently. The rapid development of science and technology has led to a significant increase in social productivity. 'But the rulers of the Qing Dynasty at that time did not see the substantial changes in this world, blindly proud of itself and rejected to learn advanced science and technology.

Finally, in a brief period of more than one hundred years, it lags far behind Western countries and was easily defeated in the face of the mighty guns of the Western powers, the lessons of this history are deeply ingrained (Jiang, 2001). To accomplish its historical mission, socialism must and eventually compete with capitalism in all aspects. Therefore, Chinese should expand the sight of science and technology development to areas where competitors have not yet entered, such as cable-free optical transmission, exploration and application development of space resources, and non-destructive strategic attack power tools research. In other words, China must have its own unique things. Only in this way can the country's science and technology become stronger and the national pride can flourish. To this end, it is necessary to take a firm focus on building a technology-innovation system centered on enterprises as a strategic focus, and guide a group of science and technology-based companies to grow into highly profitable companies with outstanding innovation performance.

Secondly, grow the power of industrial companies. To study China's economic development issues, we must proceed from China's national conditions. To solve China's economic development, we must develop high-tech with Chinese original characteristics. We should not follow other people's steps. At the same time, we must adhere to the development of applicable technologies that are in line with China's national conditions and national strength, instead of opportunistically tempting to introduce it to the immediate low cost. Chinese people are fully able to rely on their intelligence, diligence, and bravery to learn, explore and innovate, and embark on a road to construction that suits China's national conditions. However, under the trend of the pan-market economy, some localities in China have introduced a tendency of over-introduction. It imitated the foreign economic system indiscriminately, and its ideas and practices are too naive. Regardless of the actual situation in China, the introduction, introduction, and reintroduction of economic and technological developments are inconsistently with the principles of economics and must be abandoned.

At present, due to the deepening development of the scientific and technological revolution, international economic crisis and the emergence of new economic formations, the market economy in the western capitalist countries has undergone some novel changes. The increased degree of nationalization or socialization and the growing government control forecasts (a plan, in my view) are contemporary trends worth attention. China has not experienced the capitalist industrial revolution and developed commodity economy stage, but it has experienced another form of economy, the planned economy, in the process of human beings' social development. Therefore, China's market economy is a reverse transformation from the planned economic system to the market economy. It is because of this that in the process of aggressive marketization, there have been many economic phenomena against the rules of market economy, which also demonstrates that at this stage, the overall radical promotion of marketization is immature. Meanwhile, it is worth attention that when some western countries increase the control of the government, China makes its own state-owned economy privatized by catching the big and ignoring the small ones, this is indeed puzzling and what exactly is this?

Direction of State-owned Enterprise Reform

The performance of state-owned enterprises is obtained from reform. The reform of state-owned enterprises has always been the key to the reform of China's economic system. The reform process of state-owned enterprises is very tortuous. Due to the historical and cultural reasons, state-owned enterprises have experienced setbacks that exceeded expectations in their reform, with significant impact from "labor pain". Some large state-owned enterprises that had been booming have turned their profits and taxes into sharp declines, leading to large losses.

Business failures and asset losses of some central enterprises have been very serious, making a considerable amount of non-performing assets.

In recent years, the loss of overseas assets of central enterprises has become the strongest enemy of the preservation and appreciation of state-owned assets. According to statistics from State-owned Assets Supervision and Administration Commission of the State Council, by the end of 2009, a total number of 108 central enterprises had invested in 5901 overseas units. The overseas assets central enterprises have exceeded 4 trillion yuan and the profits accounted for 37.7% of the total profit in that year. Even some corporate profits from overseas projects accounted for over 50% in the corporate profits. After huge loss in overseas of China Aviation Oil, CITIC Pacific's, the project volume of China Railway Construction's for the Saudi Light Rail Project increased by more than the amount of contract work, which led to a loss of 4.153 (Deng, 2010) billion yuan. At present, the overseas loss of state-owned enterprises is already huge and there would be some omissions in statistics work. Therefore, the final total amount will certainly be even worse and it may merely be the tip of the iceberg. Of course, there are many reasons for the loss of overseas assets for the central enterprises, like the negative effects of imperfect corporate management system accumulated over the years, the non-standard decision-making procedures and the imperfect control system. The loss of state-owned enterprises has become a crucial factor that restricts the further development of enterprises.

Firstly, pay attention to the social function of state-owned enterprises. It is inevitable phenomenon during the turning point of history for some of the failures of state-owned enterprises in the reform era overall and it is also an inevitable manifestation of structural defects of the state-owned enterprises. Nowadays, China's industrial structure and economic structure are basically at a preliminary level. The concrete manifestation of this is that the industrial sectors that could drive the strongest economic growth so far are still labor-intensive and export-oriented sectors that are organized by foreign capital. State-owned enterprises participate in the cruel international economic competition with relatively backward facilities. Losses are unavoidable. However, some of the losses in the reform of state-owned enterprises are related to improper reform ways.

State-owned enterprises in China are not purely economic organizations and they are not companies and companies that have traditionally seen themselves growing through the process of natural economic competition, but are economic and social organizations established within the context of the specific national conditions in China. That is, state-owned enterprises not only take the responsibility of Economic production, but also have some tasks on the shoulder that social organizations are responsible with. However, the theory of extensive marketization never proceeds from reality, which stresses too much on the role of market, even exaggerating the role of market mechanisms and advocating rapid dismantling of the non-production and management functions from state-owned enterprises. From the perspective of professional division of labor theory, this is correct. However, the aggressive marketization behavior led to sudden advances, without any accompanying policies. This severely affects the welfare of employees and results in some unstable factors in the society.

Because the state-owned enterprises that have integrated functions of production, management, society, welfare, education and entertainment, are quickly brought to the forefront of the market, where the so-called “three enterprises” that only have production/operation functions (foreign companies, private companies, and Chinese-foreign joint ventures) compete. As a result, corporate competition makes state-owned companies fail to adapt to the fierce pure market competition. Many state-owned enterprises have closed within a brief period. Many "working class" who was originally in the aura of "national masters" have become laid-off workers. The economic difficulties and social status settlement have caused them confusion and resentment. So, some contradictions in the Chinese society are sharpened and they have great potential for destructive power. For some time, some domestic cities and towns have emerged from group incidents such as laid-off workers' petition and demonstrations. The intensified contradictions have become socially unstable factors. With an in-depth analysis of those unstable factors, undoubtedly the use of radical policies and methods to promote the catalytic role of market economic reforms could be seen. The implementation of those policies with a certain degree of radicality reflects the institutional uncertainty in the system of the state administrative agencies and the lack of long-term awareness and overall considerations of governance besides the negative impact of extensive marketization misconceptions. There are some serious unstable factors that have emerged in the society, which are the enormous costs of strategic deviations. The "Twelfth Five-Year Plan" outlines the need to improve policies such as tax deductions and exemptions, job subsidies, training subsidies, social insurance subsidies, and skill appraisal subsidies, to promote the employment of college graduates, rural transfer labor, and employment difficulties in urban areas. In the future reforms, for those extensive marketization economy theories that are packaged with rhetoric, governments at all levels should have a sense of prevention. If you credibly believe in rootless rhetoric, believe in the role of superstitious invisible hand, without necessary planning measures, there should be economic affairs hard to deal with.

Secondly, constantly increase the intellectual property products of the company. Chinese economy is in rapid development and there is a significant increase in exports, which have made China a "world factory" for certain products. However, with fundamental analysis, most of China's export products are low value-added light industrial products such as clothes, shoes and toys. The proportion of high value-added electromechanical products is very small. This is because China's industrial productivity is still mainly from the comparative advantage of the large-scale labor force, but the group companies that make up the "world factory" are based on many specialized small-middle size enterprises, whose core technology of the products is introduced or basically belongs to the scope of introduction. Nowadays, the wind of economic integration prevails in the world, with capital flows freely crossing national borders, and international trade between raw materials and intermediate products appears in large numbers. Thus, through the introduction of technology, processing trade and so on, some Chinese companies do save relative investment and gain leaps in development opportunities. At the same time, however, industry and technology, high-end industries, as the country's industrial core equipment, are in decline and controlled by foreign capital, where there are comparative disadvantages. From this point, although those small and medium-sized enterprises have developed rapidly, with their own characteristics, which have achieved outstanding results and their products have entered the international market, over-introduction and excessive dependence on foreign technologies have become hidden dangers in product upgrading and constant industrial development.

By careful study, the reason why domestic companies over rely on the introduction of technology is that idea of the corporate business strategy is eroded by the trend of extensive marketization. The national boundaries of capital are erased by the extensive market argument, which encourages people to buy high-tech with money or get out of the domestic market to get high-tech. If there is requirement for original innovation or patents, companies need to invest a great amount of money and many things. It takes a long way and is very risky. At the same time, a batch of Chinese-foreign joint ventures and wholly foreign-owned enterprises have been continuously established on the land of China. Not only do they all submit taxes to the State Ministry of Finance in China, but also the senior management personnel of the enterprises are foreigners. Thus, some plausible arguments have become popular in corporate world of China, also prevalent in society, which tells that the economic, political, and nationality boundaries have become blurred and unimportant. Enterprises do not need great investment, who can also get high technology directly through marriage and sell products overseas. Is it like that? Not! The famous American Rand Corporation once pointed out in a report that technology independence of a country is the foundation of economic independence and the independence of technology and economy is the basis of national independence. As a backward, socialist country that is catching up, the trend of "capital without borders" has emerged, with some practices that voluntarily renounce technological independence and economic independence. On the contrary, it is the most powerful authority in capitalist countries, instead, proposes technological independence and economic independence. This is ironic!

In the world nowadays, international competition in science and technology has moved to original stage of innovation. The original innovation capability, key technological innovation, and system integration innovation capability have become the core of science and technology competition between countries and have become the basic conditions to determine the international industrial division of labor and the global economic structure. It has become a strategic choice for more and more countries to rely on scientific and technological innovation to enhance the overall national strength of country and core competitiveness. What strategy should China take? According to the national development plan made, innovation and development are the central link. "From present to the 2020, scientific and technological development in China should be based on increasing competitiveness of the country. To accomplish this core task, market alone does not work.

Of course, as for the current socio-economic development in China, it is unrealistic to advocate government intervention under completely planned economic condition. The social ecology in the era of planned economy has largely disappeared. Lessons from the intervention of German society under the market economic condition should be learned. Under the condition of social-market economy, government behaviors transform form mainly planning policy and administrative policy to economy policy and legal policy as main policies, from mainly direct control to mainly indirect control; government intervention should be placed under the restriction of international competition and domestic competition, which would create an economic environment with equal, open and fair competition and legal order for the main body of economic activities; government intervention is subject to institutional constraints instead of being subject to arbitrary official value judgments and interference, which is that should be legal basis for the government intervention in economic activities. What's more, government intervention itself should be constrained by legal supervision and legal restrictions. In short, government guidance and support are the guarantee of technological innovation and the strong backup for enhancing social productivity. Through government intervention, a group of competitive companies with independent intellectual property rights would be led, supported and brought up, and motivated to be the top international markets.

Thirdly, state-owned enterprise reform cannot be too radical. To support the development of state-owned enterprises does not mean competition, nor does it mean industry monopoly in the portfolio companies. At present, there is a problem in the economic development of China, that is, there are industrial monopoly or sector monopoly in certain economic fields. The telecommunications monopoly that had emerged is a typical case. From the surface, it seems that it is caused by the planned economy. After careful analysis, it has a causal connection with the once popular extensive marketization trend of thought. Due to some radical practices in the process of marketization without adequate demonstration, the reform was not implemented with relevant policies matched, resulting in a monopoly. This kind of monopoly is not only a bottleneck for economic development, but also a very bad barrier. The high profits derived from such monopoly do not reach the government, but fall into the hands of employees in the industry. This is the "insider control" phenomenon of management theory in the modern market economy.

The fact that wages and bonus for the staff in the telecommunication sector are much higher than those of other industries proves it. From the perspective of the realistic situation of the country, under the current social condition in China, some departments should be controlled by the government, such as medical care, education and so on, which are closely related to the interests of the broad masses of people. There are other departments like post and telecommunications, municipal construction and others. The management of market economy is invalid for the public products produced by them. Therefore, they are also controlled by the state in the United States and there are trends indicating that the state-controlled economic component in the United States continues to grow. In the American-style free market economy model, some non-market economic factors are also very important. Why should we make the market economy as the main development strategy in China?

Meanwhile, the facts have made the Chinese people clearly realize that the market economy cannot run with an invisible hand fully and spontaneously. According to the market economy theory summarized and proposed so far, many conditions for the operation of market economy are ideal assumptions. In fact, these assumptions do not exist sometimes, and therefore, they are unreliable. Market mechanism shows great limitations. It includes political, social, economic and ecological boundaries. For example, when a market economy is transnational, it might not work for the national interest. Which cannot achieve an equal distribution and deal with the social benefits. The market economy cannot protect environmental resources and it cannot improve the moral standards of the entire society as well. What's more, in some places over the years, the rushing implementation of the aggressive marketization process has caused some serious problems. In some places, due to vicious commercial competition, criminal cases have frequently appeared. When some hospitals treating patients as the rules of interests in the market economy, whoever has the money could be rescued first, all of which are the consequences of radical marketization. To fully implement the scientific development concept is to return things to their original appearance.

Expand International Market

China's economy has always played one of the most prominent and dynamic roles in the world economy stage in the recent quarter-century.

China has a large-scale of population, taking 1/5 of the world population. During this period, according to the guidelines of the Reform and Opening-up policy and relying on the people's efforts, the achievements of the China has drawn worldwide attention. On December 18, 2008, marking the 30th anniversary of the Third Plenary Session of the 11th CPC Central Committee, Hu Jintao, the former General Secretary of the CPC Central Committee, president of China and chairman of the Central Military Commission, pointed out that from 1978 to 2007, China's domestic gross productivity increased from 264.5 billion to 24.95 trillion, with an actual growth rate of 9.8%, which was more than three times as the average annual growth rate of the world economy in the same period. China's total economic output has risen to the forth in the world (Tian and Dai, 2012). By 2010, the total value of China's GDP was 5.879 trillion US dollars, surpassing Japan and becoming the second largest economy in the world. At 15 o'clock on January 18, 2018, the National Bureau of Statistics released the 2017 Economic Results Report of China. The annual domestic gross product was 82.7122 trillion yuan, which exceeded the threshold of 80 trillion yuan for the first time. Calculated at comparable prices, it was an increase of 6.9% over the previous year. From a separate quarter perspective, the first quarter increased by 6.9% year-on-year, the second quarter by 6.9%, the third quarter by 6.8%, and the fourth quarter by 6.8%. The growth rate of 6.9% in 2017 was the first increase since the Chinese economy continued to slow down for six years from 2011 (Zhang and Lu, 2018). Though China is still a developing country, it has played an irreplaceable role in stimulating world economy growth compared with other countries and it has become the second world economic engine coming behind the United States.

China should Calmly Respond to the International Economic Competition

On October 13, 2015, according to the series of reports on the achievements of economic and social development in the "Twelfth

Fifth-year Plan" period released by the National Bureau of Statistics, Chinese GDP grew at an average annual rate of 8.0% in five years, from high-speed growth to medium-speed and high-speed growth; economic aggregate ranked the second in the world and the per capita GDP steadily increased. In 2014, Chinese per capita GDP was 46,629 yuan. After deducting price factor, it increased by 33.6% over 2010, with an actual average annual growth of 7.5%; foreign exchange reserve ranked first in the world. At the end of 2011, Chinese foreign exchange reserve exceeded 3 trillion dollars and reached 3.843 trillion dollars at the end of 2014, with an increase of 35.0% compared with 2010 and an average annual growth of 7.8%. It has ranked the first in the world for nine consecutive years. This achievement was another fruitful season for Chinese accession to the WTO. On December 11th, 2002, there was claim at the top Homepage of WTO official website saying that China becoming the 143th member in the WTO. Although the news was brief, it had far-reaching significance. Since Chinese accession to the WTO, the external merchandise exports of the country increased year after year, and the trade surplus continued to rise (see Table 8.1 and Table 8.2). The year 2002 was the first year for Chinese accession to the WTO. Compared with the previous year, commodity exports increased by 22.4%. In the third year, 2004, Chinese exports increased by 35.4% over the previous year, and it also became the third largest trading country in the world. As mentioned earlier, the total import and export of goods reached US$2972.8 billion dollars by 2010, an increase of 34.7% over the previous year. At the same time, it also made China the world's largest trading nation. No country in the world with trading power could achieve such a growth rate. During the entire economic development process, due to Chinese unique advantages, the development of foreign trade had a certain impact on the economies of all countries in the world. However, although China made great progress in the process of global economic integration, the situation to be faced by the future is still grave because the world is still not peaceful.

Table 8.1 Total Imports and Exports of Chinese Goods from 2000 to 2004

Unit: Billion US Dollars

Age / Project	2000	2001	2002	2003	2004
Total Export	2492.0	2661.0	3256.0	4382.3	5933.2
Total Imports	2250.9	2435.5	2951.7	4127.6	5612.3
Import and Export Surplus	241.1	225.5	304.3	254.7	320.9

Table 8.2 Total Imports and Exports of Chinese Goods 2005-2009

Unit: Billion US Dollars

Age / Project	2005	2006	2007	2008	2009
Total Export	7619.5	9689.4	12177.8	14306.9	12016.1
Total Imports	6599.5	7914.6	9559.5	11325.6	10059.2
Import and Export Surplus	1020.0	1774.8	2618.3	2981.3	1956.9

With the division of the Soviet Union in the 1990s and the end of the old Cold War era that had lasted for half a century worldwide, the world was not as safe as this. In fact, a new stage of Cold War begun. The difference between the two was that the old Cold War was dominated by ideological conflicts and its manifestation was that the two superpowers, the United States and the Soviet Union, competed for global hegemony. The New Cold War is based on geopolitically -

based national conflicts of interests. Its manifestation is that Western countries, led by the United States, rely on capital, technology and the trend of globalization to find excuses for capital invading and plundering the resource to many developing countries and in the world. The resulting situation is that, in the world, developed countries are getting more developed and the backward countries are lagging behind. Within a specific nation-state, rich people are getting richer and the poor were getting poorer. In the face of such a global socio-economic and political pattern, it is not only an economic task to develop the international market, but also a political task to safeguard justice and fairness.

Firstly, insight into the international economic and social situation. Economic globalization is now the most fashionable thing in the world, but it should be recognized that it is a double-edged sword. With the back-up of the economic, scientific, and technological strengths. The United States is currently in the position of "one strongest dominator" in the international community. Therefore, some people in the United States remain the thought of "wild invading colonies" that has been called as historical garbage, who would like to implement a unilateralist policy that is conducive to their country's self-interest with the trend and environment of global economic integration, drawing excess monopoly profits, or nakedly weakening small countries with super-economically enforced means. To allow the U.S. to do what it wants in the economic globalization makes the U.S. who leads Western countries more powerful and prosperous, leaving the clear majority of developing countries in a more relative impoverished position. An American author wrote a book that illustrated the power, role, and inferred results of globalization through vivid metaphors. Globalization has brought about global social problems while promoting the revolution of new industrial technologies. Except for a few developing countries and regions (such as some countries and regions in the East Asia), most developing countries are passive participants in economic globalization, and are unconsciously involved. They are in "marginalized" status in economic globalization. They are faced with more challenges and risks (Yang, 2010). This phenomenon is the best kind of globalization.

Cuban leader Castro also talked about the risks that globalization would brought to developing countries. He took a politician's perspective from a historical, economic, social, and cultural value point of view to fully explain the origin of globalization, its development process and features, which have profoundly exposed the conspirators of globalization advocate and the brutal plunder hidden behind globalization. Castro is one of the few truly Marxists in the traditional sense of the world. He is a determined communist soldier who firmly opposes international power politics and is a national hero worthy of admiration. Castro's concepts and analysis were very profound and they were very rich in the strategic perspective of international historical materialism. He pointed out in a speech that globalization had been confined to the neo-liberalization. Its tendency is not to globalize development but to globalize poverty. It is not respect but the violation of the sovereignty of our countries. It advocates finding ways to live in unfair market competition instead of arguing for solidarity among people of all countries. He went on to analyze the historical background of the so-called globalization and pointed out that it was the liberalization of current neo-imperialism. He further stated that world trade was still under the guidance of neo-liberalization. This globalization is for the rich countries to rule, which is a factor that deepens inequalities and perpetuates them. It is a stage for fierce competition among developed countries to control the current and future markets. He reminded developing countries to be particularly vigilant to the United States because when the U.S. ruling authorities are asking for trade liberalization, they activated the "Super 301" clause to sanction the other countries. This clause is a provocative and discriminatory foreign trade bill set by the United States domestically and is a hegemonic law that threatens other countries. The U.S. uses this clause with ulterior motives to repeatedly take the advantage of human rights issues and to accuse the governments of other countries, with the aim of promoting unilateralist international policies. Castro's understanding of globalization and its arguments are worth thinking.

What should be emphasized is that historical trains are not driven by a small number of exploiting class elements. The objective laws of global economic integration itself would not be transferred by human factors. In the latter half of the 20th century, western industrialized countries adopted foreign economic expansion and they more and more relied on the multinational corporations to transfer funds and technology in a big way. That is, the transfer from its parent company in its homeland to a subsidiary company of an overseas country to carry out production. Although the profits extracted by multinational corporations from overseas are extremely rich, the benefit that the international division of labor brings to economically underdeveloped countries is to promote the integration of the world economy, which has also been recognized by the world and has been summarized as many correct economic theory perspectives. The positive result is that weak countries therefore have modern industries and absorb modern science and technology where people are gradually awakened and in turn form a powerful force against capital intrusion and exploitation. The process of globalization is no longer subject to manipulation of capital powers, but is dominated by the force of peaceful progress and common development. The negation of negation and spiral rise are the historical dialectics.

Peace and development are the two trends in the world today and they are the leading forces of globalization. However, to take a seat in economic globalization, it is not natural. It is impossible for China to enjoy this success. Instead, China should continue to fight and win victory. Reform in China take the initiative to open to the outside world. Thus, we should abandon our illusions and increase our vigilance to prevent our eyes from being confused by the glory of globalization and turning ourselves into a lamb to be killed by others. It is impossible to sacrifice the interest of Chinese nation to cater to the globalization process advocated by the big powers and its needs. It is not necessary to take the so-called globalization as a precondition and move in line with international standards with everything. It should not focus on only one superpower in the world economic activities. In other words, the development of economic exchanges with various industrialized countries should become an important strategic decision for China to participate in the international division of labor. China should vigorously develop economic interactions and exchanges with European countries such as France and Germany and develop trade relations with Canada, Denmark, Spain and other countries. China should diversify its international contacts and should not cling to only one country's position. This will not only reduce the danger of international interactions, but also obtain greater benefits that meet national needs from the international division of labor.

Secondly, clarify the tasks for future development. Since China's accession to the WTO, China has achieved some gratifying results by adhering to the diversified strategic guidance. At the same time, there has also emerged a biased error that warrants vigilance in China. Some local enterprises and companies revel in selling their short-term products to the international market, since that they boasted that they have become worldwide factories. They are satisfied with the relatively easy production methods of processing materials. As a result, they abandon to build their own independent technology and production system, which finally become a vassal of multinational corporations essentially. Such enterprises become more and more, developing into a situation where domestic business are dominated by foreign companies, and the initiative is lacked. It makes that dependence of country on foreign investment and the world market deepens. China should clearly understand that Chinese production technology is not the first-rate in the world. Even if it has made great progress, there are many competitors so there is indeed no reason for self-enchantment.

For example, Chinese shipbuilding industry has grown rapidly in recent years and has been ranked ahead of time in the international rankings. According to the information of the International Shipbuilding Network, there is such a growth curve in China's shipbuilding completion volume: It exceeded 10 million tons in 2005 and exceeded 20 million tons in two years. From 2007 to 2009, the annual growth rate was 10 million tons. Annual increase was 20 million tons in 2010. During the "Eleventh Fifth-Year Plan" period, Chinese shipbuilding capacity increased at a rapid average annual rate of 43%. Following the completion of shipbuilding in 2008, new orders received, and hand-held orders exceeding Japan, these three indicators surpassed South Korea in 2010, becoming the world's largest shipbuilding country (Zhang, 2018). The Chinese shipbuilding industry, which entered the industry winter since 2011, began to enter the cold period in 2012. In the following years, the overall trend was still irreversible.

In 2017, for the global shipbuilding industry, it was a rebound. However, Chinese shipping performance did not pick up and the loss in 2017 was 2.3 billion yuan. According to the latest data released by the China Association of Shipbuilding Industry in the first quarter of 2018, the national shipbuilding volume was 8.53 million dwt in from January to March this year, with a year-on-year decrease of 45.9%; The number of orders for new ships was 15.53 million dwt, an increase of 180% over the same period of last year; at the end of March, the number of hand-held ship orders was 93.69 million dwt, an increase of 5.7% year-on-year and an increase of 7.4% over the end of 2017. From January to March, 80 key monitoring companies in the shipbuilding industry realized core business income of 50.8 billion yuan, a year-on-year decrease of 18.6%; total profit was 210 million yuan, a year-on-year decrease of 16%. Shao Fei, an international dry bulk market analyst at Shanghai International Shipping Research Center, believes that in 2018, the entire market is still in a relatively extended period of recovery. The market is gradually picking up. The Chinese shipbuilding industry is faced with a leap-forward development opportunity (Liu ,2012), but it is also faced with serious challenges.

Shipbuilding industry is a capital-intensive and technology-intensive industry. As a basic unit company or enterprise in the domestic shipbuilding industry or its associated industries, although though there are some high-tech support, some companies have not been able to completely get rid of the extensive operation mode. Relying on high input and high consumption to support high growth, this is not only inconsistent with the current world economic development trend, but also difficult to maintain a long-term competitive advantage. In addition, the advantages of the shipbuilding industry in the high-tech field are also reflected in hardware manufacturing, and software technology is lack. At the same time, the extent and depth of current international cooperation are insufficient, which to a certain extent also affects the international competitiveness of the entire industry.

For example, the company will carry out preparation for the construction of luxury cruise liners, developing into high-end product areas and stimulating "premium shipbuilding" and "green ship repair". If the efforts of Chinese industry to enhance its international competitiveness are effective, it may change China's low position in the international division of labor and it would lead to the transformation of Chinese industries, that is, technology import and technology retrofit would transform and upgrade to technology innovation.

New Stage of Economic and Trade Development

Although China has become a WTO member, its development also faces fierce competition, such as the trade negotiations between China and the United States and the trade negotiations between China and the EU. In some international trade activities, some non-tariff trade barriers make Chinese economy to be faced with increasing technology and competition pressures in the continuous rapid growth. By 2011, it was the tenth year for China's accession to the WTO. In the past ten years, the average tariff has dropped from 15.3% to 9.8%. More than 100 service departments have developed and cleaned more than 3,000 laws and regulations. Exports have increased 4.9 times and imports have increased by 4.7 times. The foreign investment has grown from less than 1 billion U.S. dollars to US$60 billion dollars. Chinese top

500 companies in the world have increased from 11 to 54. Chinese listed companies rose to 113 in the Fortune list of Top 500 Companies in 2017, with 20 Chinese companies ranking among the 100 companies of 2017 Top 500 Global 500 list (Chi ,2011). All these data are nothing more than to convey to us such a message that China is gradually integrated into the world family with a more open attitude. Openness, competition, and risk are intertwined. Chinese economic activities are bound to grow and expand under the new rules.

Chinese companies will face greater risks and challenges in the coming years. In the current international industrial structure, many Chinese enterprises do mainly engage in low-end processing trade. As a result, they are in a low-end position in the international industrial chain. Most of the profits of many companies are earned by large multinational companies in developed countries. Because the market economy status that entered China has not been recognized by major developed countries, the international pressure on China to further open its markets has increased. Chinese service industries, such as telecommunications and finance, will also be completely open to the outside world. However, in these areas, Chinese weaknesses are clearly present. Therefore, the Chinese government is so cautious about the opening of the financial industry. Foreign companies are still faced with certain market thresholds and restrictions in these areas. According to Chinese Central Bank data, by the end of 2016, foreign banks had established 39 corporate bodies (with 315 branches) in China, 121 branches directly under parent banks and 166 representative offices. The total number of business institutions reached 1031, with distribution in 70 cities. In the same period, the total assets of foreign banks in China were 2.93 trillion yuan, compared with the total assets of 232.25 trillion yuan of Chinese national banking industry.

The scale of foreign bank assets only accounted for 1.26%. Compared with ten years ago, market share shrank by nearly a half (Zhao, 2017). As a WTO member, China cannot avoid these "weak" industries. At the same time, as a rising trading power, China has gradually entered a period of high international trade friction as the total trade volume growing rapidly year after year. The European Union and North America constantly used “special protection, anti-dumping, and technical barriers” to challenge China. The pressure on Chinese industry has increased, and the challenges it faced have become more severe. Under this circumstance, China can only open to a new world by fully and proactively opening up to the outside world on the premise of further enhancing its domestic industrial competitiveness.

However, as China participates in the process of economic globalization, many economic activities are in line with international standards. This does not mean that China should be fully Westernized. Even if we identify with globalization, we should not lose sight of the competitiveness and exclusivity of globalization, and we should not make this double-edged sword hurt China. Globalization should be viewed as a process in which countries continue to learn from each other, a process of learning from each other's experiences and lessons of economic development. It is neither "Americanization" nor economic change dominated or controlled by the United States. It is a natural product in the development of social large-scale production to a certain stage. One of the reasons that the Chinese market economic reforms in previous years showed a radical trend in some respects was that the extend marketization copied the United States’ set of standards, used them to measure the development of Chinese market and proposed some departure-from-reality and false-air reform plan. Affected by this, for a time, suppliers deliberately imitate European and American ways to provide products, and consumers desperately consumed luxury goods. Some people were pursuing the purchase of villas, compared to having a family car.

With a large population in China, there is simply no way to achieve the needs of each villa for each family. If there is one car per family, then there are more than 300 million cars running on the 9.6 million square kilometers of land in China. No matter what else, the exhausting gas will make China the most unsuitable place for human habitation. In addition, if more than a billion people could reach the current level of per capita energy consumption in the United States, it is natural that they cannot be afforded and supplied. In fact, all people are living in the limits of natural resource supply. In a few years, the world's population cannot reach the standard of living in the Europe, the United States and Japan today. China has its own social and economic development standards and there is no need to act according to US standards.

Some local governments in China have devoted themselves to the promotion of marketization over the past few years. Some of them have neglected the principle of doing what they are capable of. This kind of overheated phenomenon has occurred many times in the history of economic construction. During the Great Leap Forward era, there was the magnification and the output of grain per acre were put on satellites. The result was a very profound and typical tragic lesson. Mao Zedong profoundly summed up this mistake and repeatedly criticized and self-criticized that everything big and high-profile should not be talked about. It was very dangerous to talk like that. He remarked earnestly that economic construction should be true in every item. The honest person who dared to tell the truth, in the final analysis, is beneficial to the cause of people and would not suffer from his own loss. Therefore, he emphasized that there should be a drive, and should not be fake said (Mao, 1999). Building Chinese socialism in the 21st century, in terms of strategy, it is necessary to have "catch-up" idea in the development, and to use ideology of appropriate development. Blindly catching up is also inconsistent with the reality in China.

Therefore, it is necessary to abandon the thought of "chasing" development and establish the idea of "sustainable development" to "appropriate development." A key point in this regard is to moderately reduce the practice of simply pursuing GDP, start from the realistic national condition and cannot emphasize the thought of catching up with "developed countries" and realizing the four modernizations on any occasion. There should be psychologically prepared for a merely well-off society. The industry is nurturing the agriculture and it is also necessary to establish a strategy for appropriate development, not using "high-tech" and "knowledge economy" for all. For example, in addition to large-scale projects such as West-to-East Gas Transmission, West-to-East Electricity Transmission and the Qinghai-Tibet railway, the western development strategy should be prioritized to address the inadequacy of low-level agricultural development of science and technology in western regions so that farmers can enjoy the benefits of modern machinery, to increase the per capita speed of making wealth for farmers and to allow farmers to truly live a well-off life.

Build up New Multinational Corporations

After the Second World War, the economic exploitation to developing countries from Western industrialized countries mainly rely on the transnational corporations. Various well-known large multinational companies in the West have advantages in capital, technology, and management. Developing countries cannot establish economic entities to compete with them because of various historical and cultural reasons. Even some domestic economic organizations in developing countries have strong feudal management or belong to the tribal chiefs. Therefore, Western multinational companies had few competitors in these countries and occupy a definite dominant position. They tend to be very handy. High profits, monopoly profits, often roll into the finance of finance the company. This kind of economic deprivation is a war without smoke, which is a part of the new Cold War series.

Regardless of whether people are subjectively willing to admit or not, this existing objective reality cannot be changed. At the same time, the force of opposing war and anticipating peace in the world are increasingly powerful. Maintaining peace and seeking development are the current mainstream in the world. Therefore, China is faced with both challenges and opportunities. We should clearly understand that we cannot avoid the new cold war and we should fully utilize the potential energy of peace development. As the great ancestor of China, Zu Yu, said that we should enlighten it, correct it, assist it and protect it.

Then Chinese will be able to own enough political, economic, social, natural and international resources, seize the opportunity to get great development, and gain the initiative in the new cold war.

Firstly, the national holding contains the strong by the weak. Material is the first nature and the spirit is the second nature. This is the basic principle of Marxism. The capital for Western capitalist countries to be arrogant is the strength of industrialization and dinosaur-like giant multinational corporation. This is the material force that has accumulated over the past several hundred years. The weakness of socialist China is economic underdevelopment. Therefore, Chinese should make use of administrative methods to mobilize the national economy and social forces, establish transnational corporations with their own cultural characteristics, resist and oppose the economic attacks from overseas multinational corporations. China has accumulated wealth for more than half a century since its founding and thousands of years of outstanding cultural heritage has accumulated. The spirit of self-reliance in Chinese culture is invaluable, a magical force that unites people's hearts and stimulates their drive. In the early years after the founding of the People's Republic of China, state-owned enterprises relying on the "iron man spirit" and upholding the "Daqing Red Flag", there were numerous economic miracles created within a brief period of time, which were the most persuasive examples. It is the only correct and effective strategic decision for the country to thrive to carry forward the Chinese culture, absorb the essence of other ethnic cultures and fully mobilize the entrepreneurial enthusiasm of the Chinese working people. Everything copying the Western model of management to adapt to globalization, substantial westernization and merely see the economic profits to turn down spiritual ideals, in fact, is a a way to insult broad and profound Chinese culture and to destroy Chinese dignity.

It is not an easy task to establish state-controlled transnational corporations. Such companies in China are generally in a weak position in terms of capital, technology, management, etc. They cannot compete with the powerful companies in the west, but they can rely on the comprehensive influence of socialist countries to repair some defects and concentrate on their own strength. At the same time, using the methods of avoiding reality and breaking down each one, they will gain a more favorable position for themselves in business warfare, so that it would cost as little as possible in dealings with multinational companies that captures profits and squeezes profits and acquiring more useful trading articles for themselves. This would make them lose as little as possible in tricky situations. Backed by a strong motherland, this is a fundamental prerequisite for China's economic entities to take the strong by weakness in the unfair world market commodity transactions.

Secondly, adjust the structure to small strokes. China should seize the opportunity of the new international industrial transfer, step up efforts to adjust industrial layout, make full use of the advantages of socialism, foster new industries and strengthen national economic forces. By industrial restructuring, China has merged and combined several automobile companies, and has introduced technology from well-known foreign automobile companies, which has rapidly increased the output and the quality of domestic automobile. From 2001 to 2011, car sales in China increased from 2.34 million to 18 million greatly. For three consecutive years, it has been ranked as the largest producer and consumer of automobiles in the world, with an average annual increase of more than 24% and it has created a miracle in the international history of automobile development. The proportion of auto sales in China taking in the global auto sales also raised from 4.27% in 2001 to around 25% in 2011. The total number of vehicle ownership for civil use was only 18.02 million in 2001 in China, but by the end of November 2011, the number of domestic civilian ownership of vehicles had reached 104 million (Zhang, 2011). In the global recession of the auto industry, Chinese rapidly growing auto market has become a new target for the multinational auto companies, making multinational auto companies pay more attention to researches and development activities aimed at meeting the specific requirements of the Chinese market. China has become a new battlefield of the deer.

At present, the structural adjustment of the domestic auto industry in China continues. The joint stock structure of the large-scale giant multinational auto companies are undergoing significant changes, namely, the number of shares controlled by China is increasing. The proportion of auto parts made in China is increasing and there are new auto offline listings with state-owned intellectual property rights. These share change and expanding auto multinational companies implementing a standardized modern enterprise system in management with close trade relations with world-renowned transnational companies, their operations are continuously completing the trade that is most beneficial to the merchandise of country. The gradually established companies follow the laws of the market, but they have not yet caught up in the extensive marketization trap. These state-controlled multinational corporations import certain equipment and make full use of the potential energy they have, from reducing the probability of information asymmetry, preparing multiple sets of negotiation programs, and deploying the most appropriate exchange of goods, etc. With the same technical performance of the equipment negotiation with different countries and different companies could help to obtain the best trade results through bargaining and other trading strategies. This is exactly like a well-trained team competing against one another single person, and the status is superior. Countless cases of foreign trade show that the excessively scattered economic activities that occurred in the Chinese market and the excessively busy international trade behaviors of the operators will inevitably lead to the competition among various enterprises for price reduction in export and price increase in import. The winner is the foreign company. Various large companies established by state holdings could gather collective wisdom and strength to complete the arduous task of modernization.

The last point to be emphasized is that the activities of state-controlled multinational corporations are not only commercial behavior, but also an organic way to promote and present the Chinese culture in the international community. State-owned companies are at the forefront of foreign exchanges and international trade activities. Naturally, all kinds of commodity transactions should focus on the will and desire of the country, making it as the priority. They should adhere to the fair-trade values of the Chinese nation that have been formed since ancient times with the value of quality first, quality service. Through business cooperation based on integrity, it should establish the economic link between enterprises in the world. Values in western culture that is in accordance with the main culture in China should be absorbed and digested and the rules and conventions of international economic exchanges should be followed. Even if commercial sales are profitable, it could enrich their own cultural connotations, which will make other countries in the world appreciate and accept Chinese culture more. For the unreasonable interference from those arrogant multinational corporations, the countermeasures should be no confrontation, no concession with less talk and more efforts, to expand exports and make occupying the international business market as the main goal. It is necessary to research on and develop new products with original features and distinctive features on the commercial battlefield where there is no smoke, to meet and thwart the economic attacks from overseas multinationals, which would help to defend national interests and protect the market that has been successfully occupied.

The socialist system is chosen by Chinese history also the socialist market economy. From a macro perspective, the socialist system also maintains and promotes the great development of national productivity. Thousands of examples about this point have been discussed so no more details are given here. Therefore, the implementation of socialist system in China can better liberate the productive forces than the implementation of the capitalist system and it enables the distinctive modern industries to develop in a quicker way. From a microscopic perspective, there should be a complete set of mechanisms that can stimulate the vitality of the micro-subjects in the socialist industrial construction, to improve the micro-economic operation efficiency. These are the important contents in the way to build socialism with

Chinese characteristics after exploration. The practice of more than 30 years of Reform and Opening-up has proved that along this way, Chinese people have achieved fruitful industrial construction achievements and more will be made in the future.

Chapter 9

From Critiques of Pan-Marketization to Supply Side Reform

Supply-side Reform, a new concept guiding the economic and social development in China, was first proposed by General Secretary Xi Jinping at the 11th meeting of the Financial Leadership Group of the CPC Central Committee. He stressed that while increasing aggregate demand moderately, we should strengthen the Supply-side structural reform, improve the quality and efficiency of the supply system, and increase the momentum of sustained economic growth (Chen & Liu 2015). Therefore, the emphasis of the future economic social development in China will tend to Supply side from Demand side.

We have often used Keynesian demand management to achieve the stable economic growth for a long time. We used to think that the lack of domestic demand was the main reason for the slow economic growth. If we stimulate demand, we could boost the economic growth (Zhao 2016). However, the experience recently proved that the aggregate demand for consumption had expanded continuously, but the macro-economy had decreased ceaselessly. Hence, the strategy of only depending the active currency policies to drive the requirement can hardly achieve the sustained economic growth, and reformation and innovation are the tangible way for the development. The strategy of Supply side proposed by General Secretary Xi Jinping at the meeting of the Financial Leadership Group of the Central Committee on November 10th, 2015 has pointed out the correct direction for the economic change in China.

Supply-side Reform and the Resistance of Pan-Marketization

As early as the 1970s, Supply-side Reform had been advocated by the theory of supply economics. The theory holds that the key to improving supply is to provide appropriate incentives to improve the working enthusiasm of individuals and entrepreneurs by reducing government regulation and lowering taxes (He 2016). It must be clearly pointed out that there is a certain difference between "Supply-side Reform" and "Supply Economics" in China. The supply-side reform that we advocate is based on understanding the law of market, people can exert their subjective initiative in market economy, and the government can strengthen the management function in a market economy to adapt to the operation of market economy. We should reform from the Supply side and adjust the supply-demand relationship of the market to balance rather than simply reduce government regulation.

With such a formula of "supply side + structural + reform = economic and social development" to understand the meaning of the policy of "Supply-side Structural Reform" mentioned by China, the meaning is that based on improving the quality of supply, promote structural adjustment through reform, correct the distortion of factor allocation, expand the effective supply, improve the adaptability and flexibility of supply structure to changes in demand, improve the productivity of total factor, meet the needs of the broad masses of the people better, and promote the sustainable and healthy economic and social development (Wang 2016). Since the reform and opening, in terms of the development of national economy, China has carried out economic management mainly based on the Keynesian principle "invisible hand" and little stressed the government's management function or avoided doing it because we have been afraid to go on the path of "planned economy". Under the guidance of this thinking, there was once a period when we overemphasized marketization, exaggerated the role of the market to conduct a comprehensive deployment of resources, and then gradually moved to a wrong way and made a trend of "Pan-Marketization" thoughts.

Pan-Marketization refers that the market trade principles are applied in all fields of social life, and people use the market mechanism to adjust all economic activities, the one-sided emphasize the function of the market mechanism, deny all the control of the government in the economic operation, and then push "market-oriented operation" to all fields of social life, and make Chinese society a large market where people do anything by means of trading. It needs to be pointed out that such kind of trend of thoughts or phenomenon of "Pan-Marketization" will undoubtedly produce some resistance to the Supply-side Reform, so it must be criticized and corrected. To resist and criticize the trend of thoughts or phenomenon of "Pan-Marketization" is not to deny that the market plays a decisive role in the allocation of production factors. Letting the market play a decisive role in resource allocation refers that on the premise of respecting the rule of market operation mechanism, through the operation of the market mechanism, put the limited resources in social and economic development where it is most needed to obtain the biggest economic and social benefits. Therefore, the concept of Pan-Marketization is essentially different from the one that the market plays a decisive role in resource allocation (Tian & Dai 2012).

The Supply-side Reform in the Background of Pan-Marketization

Due to the influence of the trend of "Pan-Marketization" thoughts, China has a lot of difficulties in Supply-side Reform. It must be clearly recognized that the "Supply-side Reform" is not to go "the old way of planned economy" but to emphasize to adjust the economic and social development by market operation mechanism. The market economy theory is not wrong, but making the boundary of marketization and the authority of the government clear is the important measure to realize the balance between the government and the market. It is undeniable that under the influence of the trend of "Pan-Marketization" thoughts, there was once a period when the supply problems of education, medical treatment and other public areas in China have become very serious.

The mismatch between demand and supply led to market chaos

At present, the biggest obstacle to China's sustained economic growth is that "mismatch between supply and demand", "insufficient supply" and "insufficient demand" appeared at the same time (Jiang 2016). There was once a period when under the influence of the trend of "Pan-Marketization" thoughts, the development of Chinese real estate industry completely was dominated by the market, almost completely ignored the role of the government, and finally resulted in high house prices and the dislocation between supply and demand, which made the surprising inventory of real estate in China, and even produced the appearance of "Ghost Towns" in some places. The fundamental reason of this phenomenon is that on the one hand, the effective demand for commercial housing is insufficient, while on the other hand, the effective supply of affordable housing is seriously insufficient. You may know by a handful the whole sack. The real problem of China's economy lies in its failure to meet the needs of people (Feng 2016).

The problem of China's industrial structure is very prominent, that is the traditional industrial capacity get surplus, and the service industry and the effective supply of the high-end technical products is in shortage. The low matching of supply and demand makes our economy develop very slowly. Because the market mechanism was dominant for a long time and gradually spread to various fields, it became a kind of solidification mode for all kinds of power and money transactions between enterprises and departments. Various hidden transaction costs are increasing, and the shortage of funds impeded the innovative ability of enterprises. People need high-quality medical care, which is only provided in VIP wards; People need good education, which is possibly only available in private schools; People need safe living environment and complete infrastructure, which are only in the high-end community. But the VIP wards and the high-end communities are limited after all. This kind of examples of insufficient effective supply is not uncommon in China. The aggregate demand of our society, especially the high-quality demand, is constantly expanding, but our macro-economy has failed to break through the bottleneck. Therefore, another effective way to solve the problem of "mismatch between supply and demand" is to increase the supply of high-quality goods and services.

Reducing of the supply from the public sector harmed the social welfare

In the increasingly fierce competition in the international situation, influenced by the trend of "Pan-Marketization" thoughts, the increase of GDP was once often as a top priority in China. Consequently, all acts among enterprises put profits on the premise, and even the public services in the social life are also in "Marketization". The basic livelihood of the people in the service of basic education, basic medical treatment, basic social security, is not only a kind of welfare spending but more importantly a kind of human capital investment, which benefits not only a person but also the whole society (Sha 2010).

Some local governments, however, lack a deep understanding of the welfare of public sectors such as basic livelihood services that provides a "pure welfare consumption", which was regarded as a burden by government. To get rid of the burden, they must push the public service area to market. Consequently, we can know that due to the free competition of the market, it is inevitable that these basic services and facilities which should be free will be labeled as price tags or their costs will be implicitly tied to complements. These will lead directly to a reduction in the consumption of such services and facilities, or a decline in the quality of basic services. But the essential connotation of public service is that the government should do those things involved the whole society or industry aspects that companies are not willing to do or cannot do. These things mainly include the transaction public goods and the positive externalities. Putting public service to the market not only harms the welfare of the citizens but also causes a serious shortage of the supply of public services, which is a short board of the government functions in China's current economic management (Lin & Su 2016).

State-owned enterprises are affected by "Pan-Marketization", and effective supply is decreasing gradually, which mainly embodied in two aspects. First, due to a lack of understanding of the market economy, some domestic scholars have a blind faith in and blindly follow the economic efficiency of free market, blindly advocate to go back to the primitive accumulation state that regards small businesses and small private ownership as main body through the dissolution of large state-owned enterprises (Zhou 2015). However, the practice has proved that, in the prevailing trend of Pan-Marketization thoughts and the acceleration of the deepening of the reform of the state-owned system, many state-owned enterprises have gone bankrupt, and the state-owned economy has been weakened (Tian, Dai & Qi 2012). Of course, if we blindly increase the number of state-owned enterprises, it will inevitably result in low quality of products and loss of social welfare (Nabin, Sgro, Nguyen & Chao 2016: 200~209). However, if we do not correct or stop the excessive cutting of state-owned share and leave it unchecked, there will be a crisis that the ruling foundation of our national political power will be severely eroded and even subverted. The practice of socialist construction for a long time also made it clear that in the fields of the leading system of Communist Party of China and the democratic country, government agencies, ideological theory, judicature, military affairs, ethnic and religious affairs, further reform cannot completely "take market as orientation", and any trends of privatization cannot exist in these departments.

Second, in recent years, corruption cases have occurred frequently in state-owned enterprises. State-owned enterprises are the enterprises that are invested or operated by the government, which have certain administrative property and the property of public welfare. The ideological trend of Pan-Marketization thoughts has made the state-owned enterprises change original intention, make "trade of equivalence between power and money" on the premise of the maximization of interests, and put the rights and interests towards small interest groups, which made the over expansion of so-called rights and interests of the people with vested interests and endangered people's fundamental interests.

Unbalanced Regional economic development and labor supply

The prevailing trend of "Pan-Marketization" thoughts caused a lot of competition between local governments that only regarded the region's GDP growth as their political achievements, which made the marketization mode exist in many fields where it should not exist. This kind of economic development, which is oriented by the maximization of interests, is highlighted by the widening of the gap between regions and industries. The economic transformation of some places was so abrupt and rapid that without the guarantee of other alternative measures, many town enterprise workers and rural farmers lost much social welfare that they had before, including the labor insurance and retirement benefits of urban workers, the labor benefits in the commune period of rural citizens. Some local companies have even introduced measures of “seniority but-outs”, which resulted in tens of millions of laid-off workers. Thus, the employment problem, which was extremely sharp and prominent, has become worse, which consequently led to potential and destructive laid-off workers. Besides, because of the collapse of enterprises in cities and the reduction of employment opportunities, the chance for surplus labor in rural areas to work in cities has also decreased, which has become another serious fact.

In addition, if all enterprise pursues the market-oriented principle, they will reduce the supply of basic services and infrastructure such as social security supplies of the migrant workers and pay for the high-intensity work of migrant workers with a low salary. These unfair treatments will reduce the work supply of migrant workers labor, and then will make labor-intensive industries in the city lack labor. In short, the real reasons for the "shortage of migrant workers" are the rising cost of factors such as land and labor and the low income, the excessive costs of living and the lack of rights and interests of migrant workers (Su, Zhao & Wan 2013).

When labor supply is lacked, no matter searching for more suitable labor or employing urban labor with high remuneration, the enterprise will pay a greater price, which will increase the cost of enterprise and affect the reform of the economic system. Facts have proven that flowing labor can bring advanced culture and technology to their hometowns and affect the local farmers, which made the local government reduce the spending of institutional change of rural construction and the cost of technology diffusion (Li & Hu 2013). Thus, the reduction of the mobility of rural labor will increase the cost of government, successively affect the government's welfare supply, and finally affect the supply of rural migrant workers, which forms a vicious circle and is not beneficial to the sustainable development of economy.

Important Fields of Supply-side Reform

China brought many problems to the society while developing economy. For example, the housing price in China is rising in the process of socialization, which has exceeded the range that ordinary people can afford and seriously affected social stability and harmony. The real estate market in China is totally dominated by the laws of the market economy, and the government fails to play the role of balancing the price and completely rejects the concept of "people-oriented". But some durable consumer goods, such as housing, are necessities of life and lack of elasticity of demand. So, the higher the price is, the greater the loss of welfare is, the lower the happiness is. The excessive marketization of real estate brought a lot of catastrophic consequences to the society, such as the polarization between the rich and the poor, urban congestion, environmental degradation, the risk of social unrest and the decline in housing quality, which need us to rethink profoundly.

The housing price has fully exposed the structural problems of China's Supply side. Price disrespect will lead to supply, especially effective supply, shortage or oversupply with low efficiency or even inefficiency. We must strengthen government supervision, strengthen market price regulation and anti-monopoly law enforcement, and use the principle of price lever to improve the effective supply.

Luxury industry

With the improvement of people's living standard, the consumption of luxury goods in China has gradually increased. It is mainly reflected in China's middle-and-high-income people's preference for brand-name products and high-quality products, which also indicates the direction of China's future industrial development and new opportunities for investment. In the past, investment opportunities in China were often in areas where exports grew faster. Now that domestic sales in China are expanding, investment opportunities may also change. In the past, "Made in China" was popular. In the future, we should look for investment opportunities where the industrial foothold is in "Made for China". With the increase of urban residents' income and the increase of consumption rate, we can anticipate the consumption growth, especially that the growth of luxury consumption will be very rapid.

At present, the problem of China's luxury industry is that the luxury products are not needed for the society, which resulted in the surplus of low-end supply and the shortage of high-end supply and made the enterprises stay in the stage of low-cost competition (Zhang 2015). The luxury industry in China urgently need create its own brand and go to the international luxury market.

Under the influence of "Pan-Marketization", the share of state-owned enterprises in the luxury industry has been greatly reduced in recent years. However, the money needed to invest in the luxury industry is huge while investors have lost their national capital and the risks they will face are correspondingly increased. Therefore, to avoid risk and for rational economic men's consideration, the enterprise will reduce or even give up investment. Therefore, there is a serious shortage of luxury supply of China in the international market, and many high imitation products in the domestic market have seriously affected the international reputation of China. At the same time, due to the price chaos and price climbs caused by the excessive marketization, the public enter the erroneous area that "The more expensive, the better product is; the more expensive, the more honor you have." If we do not regulate the market operation of this kind of industry full of profit, it will inevitably lead to serious social stratification and continuous widening of the gap between the rich and the poor, which will eventually affect the long-term stability of society.

In addition, due to the lack of objective standards for a series of high-end services and products such as luxury goods and the complete dependence of consumers' subjective judgments, producers are in a passive position (2016). However, the Supply-side Reform mainly aimed at the producers and to reform from the Supply side and to improve the effectiveness of the supply. Therefore, the government should play the role of "regulator" well, formulate relevant quality standards, and improve the transparency and openness of trade in the luxury industry.

Electronic information industry

The 21st century is an era of informatization. No information technology, no voice. China's electronic information industry has developed rapidly and now is the second largest one in the world. In the business model of "Internet Plus", the electronic information industry has become a new point of economic growth in China.

In 2015, the total annual sales revenue of the electronic information industry reached 15.4 trillion yuan with the year-on-year growth of 10.4%. Thereinto, the electronic information manufacturing industry realized the primary business revenue of 11.1 trillion yuan with the year-on-year growth of 7.6%; Software and information technology services realized the software business revenue of 4.3 trillion yuan with the year-on-year growth of 16.6%. The total profit of the electronic information manufacturing industry above designated size reached 560.2 billion yuan with the year-on-year growth of 7.2%, and the rate of average sales profit of the industry was 5%. In the software and information technology services industry, the revenue of information technology services reached 2212.3 billion yuan with the year-on-year growth of 18.4%, and the growth rate increased by 1.7% faster than the previous year. These data strongly have indicated the rapid development of China's electronic information industry and the great contribution of the industry to the growth of China's GDP.

However, relative to the European and American countries, China's electronic information industry with a late start, a low starting point, unreasonable industrial structures, and small and scattered scales has not yet formed the large-scale industrial clusters that are able to compete with foreign industrial clusters. The development of China's electronic information industry in software industry and information service industry is relatively backward.

In recent years, there have been frequent incidents of security problems in electronic products. However, the public has not paid too much attention to these cases, the real reasons behind the accidents are often ignored by people, and only the parties got everyone's sympathy. This kind of phenomenon is putting the cart before the horse. The real reasons behind the accidents are ignored, but these are the most important. After the accidents, some administrative agencies such as the industrial and commercial administration should conduct a comprehensive inspection of the product quality immediately and release announcements to appease the public. But these most essential procedures did not show up. The marketizing transaction between enterprises and such institutions has worked.

Secondly, when the electronic information industry has been pan-marketized, enterprises have focused on how to deal with the government rather than product development and technological innovation. The result must be a similar tragedy. If the trend of Pan-Marketization thoughts continues to spread, there is no doubt that China's electronic information industry will have disastrous consequences. In the current situation, China's electronic information industry lacks vitality, the government's crackdown on illegal enterprises is not enough, and the enterprises copy each other. This market environment makes some enterprises unenterprising, which leads to the lack of core technology and high-end technology and the shortage of the supply of innovative products. If high-end technology can only be imported from abroad, our production will surely be disciplined by others, which will seriously hinder the economic development, so the Supply-side Reform is very urgent and necessary.

Towards the field of technological invention where the industrial developed countries do all they can, we should devote a certain amount of energy to follow up and keep up the distance. Towards the fields of science that are of great significance to the national development and security, we should seek breakthrough of innovative technology, focus on research, and continuously expand international market share in line with the principles adapted to the state power.

The medical industry

There is no doubt that the medical industry was once "poisoned" by the trend of "Pan-Marketization" thoughts. Although China has made a lot of efforts in health reform since the reform and opening, the phenomenon that people cannot afford to or dare not see a doctor still exists. The most important reason is that the medical industry has gone into the wrong region of “Pan-Marketization and push the responsibility that should be borne by the government to the market. As a result, drug prices continue to rise and medical costs are rising. For the poor people who are not safeguarded by the social security system, seeing a doctor is a huge expense.

In addition, the oddities such as doctors' "operating security costs" and the "priority" of medical services have been in vogue in hospitals for a long time. This "Pan-Marketization" of the basic livelihood of the people service went against market economic laws, ignored the fundamental interests of the people, increased the burden of the people, affected the normal life of the people, went against the original intention of socialist construction, and corroded the foundation of social stability.

On April 12, 2016, the incident that Wei Zexi, a student of Xidian University, failed to get timely and correct medical treatment and died due to the fanaticism to Baidu's recommended medical treatments undoubtedly struck a wake-up call to the social public, especially the government. This is a typical tragedy caused by the consequence of the "Pan-Marketization" of medical industry. Baidu made rankings relying on the amount of delivery cost from medical referrers, which was an economic behavior of Pan-Marketization that was money-oriented. According to the relevant statements, behind Baidu's "bidding rank" has stood the private medical capital full of assets, among which the Putian System has occupied the majority. Obviously, once the medical industry and other public services are eroded by the trend of "Pan-Marketization" thoughts, the consequence will be extremely serious, and if it does not get timely correction, more "Wei Zexi incidents" will certainly occur in the future, and our social life order will be overthrown fundamentally (Wang).

The essence of the Supply-side Reform in the new situation is to play the role of the government and to make the government become the main driving force for the Supply-side Reform (Chen 2016). The medical industry is the "Sukhavati" in our heart, and once it was contaminated by the atmosphere of "Pan-Marketization", it will be difficult to embody the superiority of socialism in China fully. Therefore, we must reform from the Supply side, increase the intensity of the investment in health and epidemic prevention, and slow down the speed and reduce the scope of the spread of diseases, which are moves beneficial to the people and China.

Push Forward the Process of Supply-side Reform

Supply-side Reform must adhere to the core of "people-oriented" and achieve sustainable development. The past "demand management model" has struggled to meet the needs of a massive economic growth. Therefore, with the further development of China's economy and society, the focus of the reform must shift from the Demand side to the Supply side. As Say's Law says, only creating demand through supply can achieve the long-term stable growth of the economy. If the Supply side blindly adapts to the demand passively, and the supply lags, eventually the effective supply will be inevitably insufficient. The core of "Supply-side Reform" is to determine a prior development mode and a supply mode. Optimize the allocation of resources and improve total factor productivity. The Central Economic Work Conference held in December 2015 made clear the five tasks of "getting rid of production capacity, getting rid of inventory, deleveraging, reducing costs and making up shortboards". Thus, Supply-side Reform was put on the agenda.

Strengthen independent innovation and increase effective supply

General Secretary Xi Jinping has pointed out that innovation has always been an important force for promoting the development of a country and a nation. China is a great developing country, which is vigorously promoting the transformation of economic development mode and economic restructuring. We must implement well the strategy of innovation-driven development. Implementing the strategy of innovation-driven development is to promote the comprehensive innovation of which the core is scientific and technological innovation, to adhere to demand-oriented and the direction of industrialization, to adhere to enterprises' dominant role in innovation, to play a decisive role of market in the allocation of resources and a superior role of the socialist system, to enhance the contribution of scientific and technological progress to economic growth, to form the new source of growth momentum, and to promote the economic sustainable and healthy development.

Under the influence of the trend of Pan-Marketization thoughts, some enterprises had blind faith in market economic theory that can contribute to the balance between supply and demand, simply followed in the footsteps of demand, supplied their products blindly according to consumers' demand, and even counterfeited for the interests, but not independently innovated from their products. This passive approach will inevitably lead to the law of supply and ultimately affect the survival of the enterprises. Therefore, the government should actively play its role, make up for the defect of market failure, provide an environment with good systems for independent innovation, crack down on a series of illegal behaviors that are unbeneficial to innovation, such as infringing patents.

Independent innovation is the foundation of national economic and social development, the foundation of holding China's destiny in our own hands, and an indispensable lifeline for the survival and development of our Chinese nation. Without independent innovation, it will be difficult for the development of a country to break through the limitation of the barriers of intellectual property and to fundamentally solve the major strategic problems that its own development and national security face. This is especially true for enterprises.

The theory of marketing is that the market can be shaped and created, and its fundamental motive is innovation. The core of Supply-side Reform lies not in the supply itself, but in the way and content of supply, which is to create demand through innovation to achieve the breakthrough of productivity and efficiency (Luo & Liang 2016). Improving supply is not simply an increase in the supply of goods; If increasing the supply of goods or labor can still not solve the demand, it will inevitably lead to another round of overcapacity.

After the basic needs are met, people are bound to pursue a higher-quality life. Low-end products and outdated products will inevitably be eliminated, and increasing the supply of high-quality products has become urgent. Our ultimate objective is to actively carry out independent innovation, to increase the added value of products, to increase effective supply, to expand effective demand fundamentally, and to match supply and demand generally. Through "Supply-side Reform", we will accelerate the cultivation of the power of "new economy", develop "incremental economy", enhance China's total factor productivity, improve the core competitiveness of industries, and finally promote the development of Chinese economic transition.

Solve the problem of overcapacity and optimize the industrial structure

"Zombie Enterprises", a loose social concept, refers to those enterprises who are hopeless to resume production, unable to participate in the normal market competition, but can get rid of bankruptcy through debt financing or the subsidies from the government (Dong & Ding 2016). The ultimate objective of Supply-side Reform is to improve the economic growth, to achieve long-term economic benefits, and to adhere to sustainable development. A series of "Zombie" enterprises, such as traditional industries, severely influenced the allocation of resources factors, and the excess capacity caused by the mismatch between production and demand is the structural problems in China's economic growth, which need us to look for a solution on the Supply side.

We cannot overly depend on the market, and the government should play the role of "decider" well, establish an effective exit mechanism for excess capacity, timely eliminate "Zombie" enterprises, speed up the pace of reform, carry out domestic excess capacity in time, and make resources flowing again. For enterprises that can continue to develop, they can continue to play their roles through the technological transformation of traditional industries and the reorganization of asset (Ma 2016). At the same time, we should go into overdrive to develop tertiary industries, including information industry, financial industry, tourism and other service industries. We should accelerate the transformation of traditional industries and fundamentally optimize the industrial structure to solve the problem of "mismatch between supply and demand".

Increase investment in education to increase the supply of skilled talents

Education is a very important area for a welfare society. As a non-profit organization, education departments should make welfare for the whole society based on the principle of fairness, justice and openness. However, the current problems that China has faced are the ceaseless disappearance of demographic dividend, the decrease of labor supply, and the rising of labor costs, which restricted the upgrade of industrial structure and aggravated the plight of Supply-side Reform. Therefore, increasing the effective supply of labor force is the urgent problem to be solved. The most effective way to solve this problem is to improve the quality of labor supply through education.

However, influenced by the trend of "Pan-Marketization" thoughts, many colleges and universities went against the original intention of the establishment of schools, made students' life and study commercialization and marketization, seriously affected the supply of high-quality teaching, and affected the students' learning outcomes, which is undoubtedly a great loss to the society and indirectly caused the short supply of high-quality talents. To compete for the resource of students and maintain their own interests, schools no longer shared information or cooperated with each other, which also influenced the management of the educational supply in colleges and universities.

Education is the main distribution channel of human capital, the most crucial factor of production. Therefore, we should go into overdrive on the Supply-side Reform of high-quality education. The essence of Supply-side Structural Reform in economic activities is how to deal with the relationship between the government and the market. So is the essence of education (Zhang 2016). For the problem of education chaos, there are three main points of Supply-side Reform:

First, increase the support for educational research. The government should increase investment to encourage students to make independent innovations and patent researches. In various professional fields, set up funds to support the development of modern technologies and the cultivation of professional talents to increase the supply of high-tech talents to the society.

Second, reform and innovate the teaching modes of schools, take the educational experience from abroad as reference, introduce social capital, provide personalized and diversified educational service, and improve the lifelong educational system (Tie 2016). Cultivate high-quality and international talents and increase the supply of high-quality talents to the society.

Third, intensify the efforts to crack down on all kinds of education chaos, distinguish the limit between the government and the market, and prohibit the emergence of the mode of marketization in students' study and life.

Encourage rural migrant workers to increase the supply of labor

In recent years, the shortage of labor supply of migrant workers has brought about the problem of "shortage of migrant workers", which has seriously impeded the rapid growth of China's economy and society. The fundamental way to solve this problem is to quicken the mobility of migrant workers and make them volunteer to work in cities.

The first is to get out of the erroneous thinking of profit-oriented caused by the trend of "Pan-Marketization" thoughts. In this regard, the government should properly intervene in the market of migrant workers. For example: stipulate the wage standard of migrant workers; provide social security for the migrant workers who have worked for more than a certain number of years. Only when the happiness index of migrant workers increases and life is guaranteed, they will voluntarily stay in the local areas to work.

Second, the government should go into overdrive to popularize legal knowledge for migrant workers, provide reeducation for them, improve the quality of the labor force of migrant workers, and reduce the costs of enterprises' management to migrant workers, thereby increase the effective labor supply of migrant workers to enterprises.

Third, we must pay attention to the integration of the second-generation of migrant workers. Because of the embarrassing status of the second-generation migrant workers, they cannot enjoy the local high-quality education or take the entrance examination in the local area, which also affected the supply of labor force to a considerable extent.

Local governments and China manage and guide, formulate and implement all kinds of measures to benefit migrant workers through the policies and laws and regulations and have created a good institutional platform for the integration of migrant workers into the city. But the participation of migrant workers who are the main participators is not high, the sense of urban substitution is not strong, and it's easy to cause a series of problems such as the lag, rigidity and systemic bias of policies and low efficiency, which increased governments' financial burden (Wang & Lang 2016). Therefore, another effective way to solve the problem of " shortage of migrant workers " is to accelerate the integration of migrant workers into cities.

Increase the supply of social welfare

State-owned enterprises are related to the economic lifeblood of the country, which reflects the state's ability to control the economy. To ensure the sustained, healthy and rapid development of the national economy, they play a key role. State-owned enterprises are closely related to the governance of the public sector, including health, electricity, national defense. Therefore, the reform of state-owned enterprises can improve the management quality of the public sector. Good public-sector management can ensure the quality of service of the public sector, promote long-term economic growth, and reduce the incidence of poverty. Under specific circumstances, the governance of state-owned enterprises is related to extending the responsibilities of the board of directors, including the management of the company's affairs. It is an effective way to deepen the reform of state-owned enterprises by strengthening the decision-making power of the board of directors in finance and lending and transferring some of the government's responsibilities to the company's board of directors.

Once upon a time, seriously affected by the trend of "Pan-Marketization" thoughts, some state-owned enterprises ignored the principle of social equity and take interests as the prerequisite of everything, and the corruption of senior executives in which was prominent. All kinds of corruption cases of state-owned enterprises took place ceaselessly, which profoundly revealed the structural problems of state-owned enterprises. We should promote the reform of state-owned enterprises and promote the transposition between the revenue and the stock of state-owned assets (Jia 2015), making state-owned enterprises well play the role of maintaining social stability, increasing the welfare supply of the people, and paying attention to the national economy and people's livelihood.

The structural problems of state-owned enterprises, especially solely state-owned enterprises, are mainly lack of necessary supervision. There are mainly two reasons: the ownership system of state-owned enterprises and the marketization operation of the supervision department. Therefore, it is an effective way to vigorously promote the equity reform, and only the diversification and decentralization of equity can activate the market (Zhang 2016).

Conclusion

To strengthen the management of the Supply side, we should regard the political economy of socialism with Chinese characteristics as a guide, adhere to the people-centered principle, provide more high-quality products to meet the needs of the masses of the people, improve people's well-being, promote people's all-round development, and gradually achieve common prosperity (Zhang 2016).

Of course, while strengthening the Supply-side Reform, we should not give up the management of Demand side easily. For industries with insufficient demand, we should improve the Supply side and increase the effective supply while continuing to stimulate demand through government funds and other means. The long-term growth and sustainable development of the economy can be achieved only through combining the management of the Demand side with the management of the Supply side (Li 2014).

We must consider the root cause of the trend of "Pan-Marketization" thoughts while criticizing it. In the fields which were eroded by Pan-Marketization, we should find the defects and reform the Supply side (Tian & Wang 2015). First, for government officials, we should give them enough benefits to avoid power rent-seeking; For colleges and universities, we should give them enough construction funds to avoid some profit-seeking behaviors; For health care, we should strengthen the legislation and improve the social security systems such as medical reform, and the government should give enough financial support. When the excess profits that need to be made by market transaction are borne by the government, the areas that should not have been touched by the marketization model are naturally isolated. Only in the society, all walks of life perform their own functions, the operation goes standardly, and the effective supply can be provided, can finally realize the common prosperity.

Bibliography

Aaker, D. (1995). Building Strong Brands. 9th ed. New York: Free Press.

Abell, D. F. (1978). Strategic Windows. Journal of Marketing, 42 (3), 21-26.

Abernathy, W. and Clark, K. B. (1985). Mapping the Winds of Creative Destruction. Research Policy, 14, 3-22.

Agriculture Ministry Planning Department of the People's Republic of China (1987). China Agricultural Economic Statistics (1949-1986), Agriculture Press.

Ahmed, S. and d'Astous, A. (2008). Antecedents, Moderators and Dimensions of Country-of-origin Evaluations. International Marketing Review, 25(1), 75-106.

Ahmed, S. and d'Astous, A. (1996), Country of Origin and Brand Effects: a Multi-dimensional and Multi-attribute Study, Journal of International Consumer Marketing, 9(2), 93-115.

Albers-Miller, N. and Stafford, M. (2007). International Services Advertising: An Examination of Variation in Appeal Use for Experiential and Utilitarian Services. Journal of Child Health Care, 11 (4), 323-340.

Albers-Miller, N. D. (1996). Designing Cross-Cultural Advertising Research: A Closer Look at Paired Comparisons. International Marketing Review, 13(5), 59-76.

Albers-Miller, N. D. and Gelb, B. D. (1996). Business Advertising Appeals as a Mirror of Cultural Dimensions: A Study of Eleven Countries. Journal of Advertising, 25(4), 57-71.

Alden, D.L., Steenkamp, J.E.M. and Batra, R. (1999). Brand Positioning Through Advertising in Asia, North America and Europe: The Role of Global Consumer Culture. Journal of Marketing, 63(1), 75-87.

Alexandre, Gohin, and Herve Guyomard (2000). Measuring Market Power for Food Retail Activities: French Evidence. Journal of Agricultural Economics, 51,181-195.

Alfred S. Eichner (1983), Why Economics Is Not Yet a Science, New York: Sharpe Inc.

Alpert, M. I. and Peterson, R. A. (1972). On the Interpretation of Canonical Analysis. Journal of Marketing Research. 9 (May), 187.

Ambler, T. and Witzel, M. (2003). Doing Business in China. 2nd. Ed. London: Routledge.

Anand, J. and Delios.A. (1996). Competing Globally: How Japanese MNCs Have Matched Goals and Strategies in India and China. Columbia Journal of World Business, Fall, 50-62.

Anderson, C. (2009). The Long Tail: Why the Future of Business is Selling Less of More. Taipei: Commonwealth Publishing Co., Ltd.

Anderson, Chris. (2004). The Long Tail. Wired Magazine, 12(10). Available online: http://www.wired.com/wired/archive/12.10/tail.html. Accessed on January 2011.

Andrew, A. (1986). The Effect of Verbal and Visual Components of Advertisements on Brand Attitudes and Attitude toward the Advertisement. Journal of Consumer Research, 13 (1), 12-24.

Anselmsson, J., Johansson, U. and Persson, N. (2008). The Battle of Brands in the Swedish Market for Consumer-Packaged Food: A Cross-Category Examination of Brand Preference and Liking. Journal of Brand Management, 16, 63-79.

Arens, W. F. and Bovee, C. L. (1994). Contemporary Advertising, 5th ed., Boston: Richard D. Irwin.

Arnold, M.J. and Reynolds, K.E. (2003). Hedonic Shopping Motivations. Journal of Retailing, 79, 77-95.

Arnould, E., Price, L. and Zinkhan, G. (2004). Consumer. 2nd ed.. NY, New York: McGraw Hill.

Atsmon, Y. et al. (2009). 2009 Annual Chinese Consumer Study.McKinsey Insights China.

Atsmon, Y., Dixit, V., Magni, M. and St-Maurice, I. (2010). China's New Pragmatic Consumers. McKinsey Quarterly. Available online: https://www.mckinseyquarterly.com/. Accessed on December 5, 2017.

Atuahene-Gima, K., Slater, S. F. and Olson, E. M. (2005). The Contingent Value of Responsive and Proactive Market Orientations for New Product Program Performance. Journal of Product Innovation Management, 22, 464-482.

Ayers, D., Dahlstrom, R. and Skinner, S. J. (1997). An Exploratory Investigation of Organizational Antecedents to New Product Success. Journal of Marketing Research, 34 (1), 107-116.

Babin, B.J., Darden, W.R. and Griffin, M. (1994). Work and/or Fun: Measuring Hedonic and Utilitarian Shopping Value. Journal of Consumer Research, 20, 644-656.

Bai, Junhong, and Li, Jing. (2011). Regional Innovation Efficiency in China: the Role of Local Government. Innovation: Management, Policy, and Practice, 13 (2), 142 - 153.

Bai, Ting and Chen, Gang (2012). Business Anthropology and Cultural Tourism Commodity Market Analysis, in Tian, Guang and Luo, Kanglong, Economic Anthropology. Yinchuan: Ningxia People's Publishing House.

Bai, Zhouwei (2006). News Comment. Beijing Evening News, 2006-3-23.

Bainbridge, W.S. (2007). The Scientific Research Potential of Virtual Worlds. Science, 317,472,

Baker, J., Parasuraman, A., Grewal, D. and Voss, G.B. (2002). The Influence of Multiple Store Environment Cues on Perceived Merchandise Aalue and Patronage Intentions. Journal of Marketing, 66, 120-141.

Balabanis, G. and Diamantopoulos, A. (2004). Domestic Country Bias, Country-of-originEffects, and Consumer Ethnocentrism: A

Multidimensional Approach. Journal of the Academy of Marketing Science, 32(1), 80-95.

Ballard, D.S. and Weigel, D.J. (1999). Communication Process in Marital Commitment: An Integrative Approach," In J. M. Adams and W. H. Jones (ed), Handbook of Interpersonal Commitment and Relationship Stability, 407- 424. New York Kluwer Academic/ Plenum Publishers.

Bandura, A. (1997). Self-efficacy: The Exercise of Control, New York: Freeman.

Barbara, B. and Gloria, M. (2007). Social Conventions in Collaborative Virtual Environments. German National Research Center for Information Technology.

Barney, J. and Hansen, M. (1994). Trustworthiness as a Source of Competitive Advantage. Strategic Management Journal, 15(special issue), 175-190.

Barney, J.B. (1986). Strategic Factor Markets: Expectations, Luck, and Business Strategy. Management Science, 9 (10), 1231-1241.

Bateson, J. E. G. (1985). Perceived Control and the Service Encounter in the Service Encounter by J. A. Czepiel, M. R. Solomon and C. F. Surprenant. (Eds.). MA, Lexington: Lexington Books.

Batra, R. et al. (2000). Effects of Brand Local and Nonlocal Origins on Consumer Attitudes in Developing Countries. Journal of Consumer Psychology, 9(2), 83-95.

Batson, A. (2010, January 21). A Second Look at China's GDP Rank. The Wall Street Journal. Available online: from http://online.wsj.com/article/. Accessed on November 26, 2010.

Battacharrya, R., Devinney, T. and Pilluta, M. (1998). A Formal Model of Trust Based on Outcomes. Academy of Management Review, 23(3), 459-472.

Bawa, A. (2004). Consumer ethnocentrism: CETSCALE Validation and Measurement of Extent. Vikalpa: The Journal for Decision Makers, 29(3), 43-57.

Beamish, P.W., Inkpen, A.C. (1998). Japanese Firms and the Decline of Japanese Expatriate. Journal of World Business, 33 (1), 35-50.

Beijing Education: Higher Education. (3).

Beijing Evening News (2007). Over 90 percent of crimes in medical field were corruption, November 30, 2007.

Belk Russell, and Janeen Costa. (1995). International Tourism: An Assessment and Overview. Journal of Macromarketing, 15(2), 33-49.

Bennett, J. and Beith, M. (2007). Alternate Universe. Newsweekly, Available online: http://www.newsweek.com/id/32824. Accessed on 15 Nov 2009.

Bennis, W., D. Berlew, E. Schein, and F. I. Steel. (1973), Interpersonal Dynamics. 3rd ed. Chicago: Dorsey Press.

Bernard F. (1974). Risk Aversion and the Consumer Choice of Health Insurance Option. The Review of Economics and Statistics, 56(2), 209-214.

Bessant, J. and Tidd, J. (2007), Innovation and Entrepreneurship. NJ: JohnWiley and Sons.

Bilkey, W.J. and Nes, E. (1982). Country-of-origin effects on product evaluations, Journal of International Business Studies, Spring/Summer, 89-99.

Birdwhistell, R.L. (1970). Kinesics and Context; Essays on Body Motion Communication, 338. University of Pennsylvania publications in conduct and communication. Philadelphia: University of Pennsylvania Press.

Bitner, M. J. (1990). Evaluating Service Encounters: The Effects of Physical Surroundings and Employee Responses. Journal of Marketing, 54, 69-82.

Blaxter, L. (2006). How to research. 3rd ed. Maidenhead: New York Open University Press.

Boer, H. and During, W. E. (2001). Innovation, What Innovation? A Comparison Between Product, Process and Organizational Innovation, International Journal of Technology Management, 22 (1-3), 83-107.

Bohai Morning Post (2012). The annual per capita medical expenses of resident in Tianjin was ￥521 RMB in 2011, with an growth of

7.4% than that in the same period of previous year, January 19, 2012.

Bonner, J.M. and Walker, O. C. Jr. (2004). Selecting Influential Business-to-Business Customers in New Product Development: Relational Embeddedness and Knowledge Heterogeneity Considerations. Journal of Product Innovation Management, 21 (3), 155-169.

Bookman, A. (2008). Innovative Models of Aging in Place: Transforming our Communities for an Aging Population. Community, Work and Family, 4 (November), 430-431.

Boulding, K. (1956). General Systems Theory: The Skelton of Science, Management Science, 2, 197-208.

Boutie, P. (1994). Who will save the brands? Communication World, 7, 24-29.

Bowersox, D. et al. (1995). World Class Logistics: The Challenge of Managing Continuous Change. Council of Logistics Management.

Bowersox, D. J., Stank, T. P. and Daugherty, P.J. (1999). Lean Launch: Managing Product Introduction Risk Through Response-Based Logistics. Journal of Product Innovation Management, 16 (5), 557-568.

Bray, D. and Konsynski, B. (2008). Virtual Worlds: Mutli-Disciplinary Research Opportunities. The Database for Advanced Information Systems, 38(4). Available online: http://ssrn.com/abstract=1016485. Accessed on March 7, 2017.

Brennan, D.P. and Lundsten, L. (2000). Impact of large discount stores on small US towns: reasons for shopping and retail strategies. International Journal of Retail and Distribution, 28, 155-161.

Brett, A., Martin, B. and Wong, S. (2003). Conclusion Explicitness in Advertising: The Moderating Role of Need for Cognition (NFC) and Argument Quality (AQ) on Persuasion. Journal of Advertising, 32 (4), 57-66.

Briley, D. A. and Aaker, J. L. (2006). When does Culture Matter? Effects of Personal Knowledge on the Correction of

Culture-based Judgments. Journal of Marketing Research, 43, 395-408.

Browne, M. W. and Cudeck, R. (1993). Alternative ways of assessing model fit. in Testing Structural Equation Models by K. A. Bollen and J. S. Long. (Eds.), CA, Thousand Oaks: Sage. 136–162.

Bureau of Statistics (2011). The 11th Five-Year Plan: Income and Expenditure of Urban Residents Keep Rising, the Quality of Life is Significantly Improved, http://www.stats.gov.cn

Bureau of Statistics (2011). The 11th Five-Year Plan: Income and Expenditure of Urban Residents Keep Rising, the Quality of Life is Significantly Improved, http://www.stats.gov.cn

Buttery, E. A. and T.K.P. Leung. (1998). The Difference between Chinese and Western Negotiations. European Journal of Marketing, 32(3/4), 374-389.

Buttle, F. and Coates, M. (1984). Shopping Motives. Services Industries Journal, 4, 71-81.

Calantone, R. J. and Di Benedetto, C. A. (1988). An Integrative Model of the New Product Development Process. Journal of Product Innovation Management, 5 (3), 201-215.

Calantone, R. J. and Montoya-Weiss, M. (1994). Product Launch and Follow-On in Managing New Technology Development by Souder, W. E. and Sherman, J. D. (Eds.). New York: McGraw-Hill. 217-248.

Calantone, R. J., Di Benedetto, C. A. and Stank, T. P. (2005). Managing the Supply Chain Implications of Launch in The PDMA Handbook of New Product Development by Kahn, K. B., Castellion,G., and Griffin, A. (Eds.). 2nd ed. Hoboken, NJ: John Wiley and Sons. 466-478.

Calantone, R. J., Schmidt, J. B. and Song, M. (1996). Controllable Antecedents of New Product Success: A Cross-National Comparison. Marketing Science, 15, 341-358.

Calantone, R.J. and Cooper, R. G. (1979). A Discriminant Model for Identifying Scenarios of Industrial New Product Failure. Journal of the Academy of Marketing Science, 7, 163-183.

Calantone, R.J. and Di Benedetto, C. A. (2011). The Effects of Launch Execution and Timing on New Product Performance: An Empirical Study in the U.S. Journal of the Academy of Marketing Science, forthcoming.

Carlson, P. (1993). Media Selection for Information Acquisition and Dissemination: A Study of Manageria Preference, unpublished doctoral dissertation, University of Minnesota.

Carrier, J. G. (Ed., 2005). A Handbook of Economic Anthropology. Northampton, MA: Edward Elgar.

Castranova, E, (2001). Virtual Worlds: A First-Hand Account of Market and Society on the Cyberian Frontier. CESifo, Working Paper, 618.

Castries, Henride. (2009). Aging and Long – Term Care: Key Challenges in Long – term Care Coverage for Public and Private Systems. Geneva papers, 34,24 – 34.

Castronova, E. (2003). On Virtual Economies. The International Journal of Computer Game Research, 3(2). Available online: http://www.gamestudies.org/0302/castronova/. Accessed on June 16, 2009.

Cavusgil, S.T., Kiyak, T. and Yeniyurt, S. (2004). Complementary Approaches to Preliminary Foreign Market Assessment: Country Clustering and Country Ranking, Industrial Marketing Management, 33 (7), 607-617.

Cervino, J., Sanchez, J. and Cubillo, J. (2005). Made an Effect, Competitive Marketing Strategy and Brand Performance: An Empirical Analysis for Spanish Brands. Journal of American Academy of Business, 6(2), 237-244.

Chan K. (1995). Information Content of Television Advertising in China. International Journal of Advertising, 14 (4), 365-373.

Chan, K. and Cheng H. (2002). One Country, Two Systems: Cultural Values Reflected in Chinese and Hong Kong Television Commercials. Gazette: The International Journal for Communication Studies, 64(4), 383-398.

Chaney, I. and Gamble, J. (2008). Retail Store Ownership Influences on Chinese Consumers. International Business Review, 17, 170-183.

Chang, K. and Chang, F. (2005). Information Content of Television Advertising in China: An Update. Asian Journal of Communication, 15(1), 1-15.

Chatterjee, S. and Chaudhuri, A. (2005). Are trusted brands important? Marketing Management Journal, 15(1), 1-16.

Chattopadhyay, A. (1998). When does Comparative Advertising Influence Brand Attitude? The Role of Delay and Market Position. Psychology and Marketing, 15(5), 461-75.

Chen G.W. and Sun Gui Ju. (2006). The Food Safety KAP Investigation of Nanjing Consumers. Journal of China's Public Pealth, 22, 604-608.

Chen Ming (2004). The Property Right is the Institutional Cause of Agricultural Land Fraud, China: Farmers' Daily.

Chen Wenling (2011). Eight Guidelines to Narrow the Gap between the Urban and Rural Medical Treatment, China: Xinhua News Agency. http://news.cntv.cn/20111213/108472.shtml

Chen, B. (2016). How the Government Promote Supply-side Reform . People's

Chen, E. & Liu, Z. (2015). What's the Meaning of Xi Jinping's Mention of "Supply-side

Chen, Qingde (2000). Reflection on Modernization in the View of Economic Anthropology. Strategy and Management, 2000 (1): 72-85.

Chen, Qingde (2010). Application and transformation of formal analysis in economic anthropology. Journal of Guangxi University for Nationalities, 2010 (4): 47-54.

Chen, Y.F., Brenda, S. (1995). Differences Between International and Domestic Japanese Retailers. The Service Industries Journal, 15 (4), 118-134.

Chen, Yingying(2011). Report on Chinese Enterprises Competitiveness. The Phoenix. 2011-11-23.

Chen, Zhi and Yang, Lake (2008). Soft Power for Cities. Guangzhou: Guangdong People's Publishing House, 2008.

Cheng, H. and Schweitzer, J. C. (1996). Cultural Values Reflected in Chinese and U.S.Televisions Commercials. Journal of Advertising Research, 36(3), 27-45.

Cheng, Jingwei (2005). Rich people in China are becoming richer, http://finance.people.com.cn, Accessed in December 14, 2017.

Cheng, Lu (2005). Who will care about the poor people in Shanxi Province? Worker Daily, December 4.

Chesney, T. Chuah, S. andHoffmann, R. (2007). Virtual World Experimentation: An Exploratory Study. Available online http://ssrn.com/abstract=1068225. Accessed on March 25, 2017.

Cheung,Wah-Leung and Prendergast, G. P. (2006). Exploring the Materialism and Conformity Motivations of Chinese Pirated Product Buyers. Journal of International Consumer Marketing, 18(3), 7-31.

Chi, Yuzhou (2011). In Memory of China's Accession to WTO for Ten Years: Will the Future Belong to China. Panorama. Net, 2011-12-15.

Chibnik, Michael (2005). Experimental Economics in Anthropology: A Critical Assessment, American Ethnologist, 32 (2):198-209.

China Advertising Yearbook. (2006). The Development of China's Advertising Industry. Beijing: Xinhua Publishing House.

China Association of Advertising. (2009). China Advertising Year Book, Beijing, Xinhua News Agency Press.

China Coal News (2011). Analytical Report of Mine Waste Disaster Accident during Eleventh Five-Year, http://www.cwestc.com, Accessed in October 12, 2017.

China Economic Weekly (2011). 97% coal mine accidents are caused by artificial factors, June 28, 2011.

China Finance Newspaper (2006). The training cost of an undergraduate is about a farmer's whole savings of poor country in 35 years, April 14, 2006.

China National Tourist Office. (2010). China Tourism Statistics 2009. Available online: http://www.cnto.org/chinastats_2009ArrivalsByPurpose.asp. Accessed on Aug. 2017.

China News (2011). Whopping medical expenses expose eagerness of Guangji Hospital in Dongguan to seek money, May 13, 2011.

China Online Marketing. (2011). Available online: http://www.china-online-marketing.com/. Accessed on August 7, 2017.

China Statistic Yearbook. (2009). Available online: http://www.stats.gov.cn/tjsj/ndsj/2009/indexeh.htm. Accessed on June 19, 2017.

China Youth Daily (2011). Sampling survey on rural junior high schools: average dropout rates up to 43, December 23, 2011.

Choi, S. and Mattila A. S. (2006). The Role of Disclosure in Variable Hotel Pricing: ACross-Cultural Comparison of Ccustomers' Fairness Perceptions. Cornell Hotel and Restaurant Administration Quarterly, 47 (1), 27-35.

Churchill, G. A., Jr. (1979). A Paradigm for Developing Better Measures of Marketing Constructs. Journal of Marketing Research, 16, 64-73.

Clemons, E.K. (2009). The Complex Problem of Monetizing Virtual Electronic Social Networks. Decision Support Systems, 48(1), 46-56.

Cleveland, M. and Laroche, M. (2007), Acculturation to the Global Consumer Culture: Scale Development and Research Paradigm. Journal of Business Research (Special Edition: The Impact of Culture on Marketing Strategy), 60(3), 249 - 259.

Cleveland, M., Laroche, M. and Papadopoulos, N. (2009), Cosmopolitanism, Consumer Ethnocentrism, and Materialism: An Eight - country Study of Antecedents and Outcomes," Journal of International Marketing, 17, 116-146.

Coal Information Exchange Network (2012). Coal mine safety production in China achieve four 'fist times', http://www.meitanwang.com, Accessed in January 17, 2012.

Coase (1990), Firm, the Market and the Law, Joint Publishing, pp. 233.

Competition and Product Quality. International Review of Economics & Finance. 43(2):220-209.

Confucius（551-479 BC. Jishi in the analects of Confucius.

Cooper, J. R. (1998). A Multidimensional Approach to the Adoption of Innovation. Management Decision, 36 (8), 493-502.

Cooper, R. G. (1979a). Identifying Industrial New Product Success: Project NewProd. Industrial Marketing Management, 8(2), 124-135.

Cooper, R. G. (1979b). The Dimensions of Industrial New Product Success and Failure. Journal of Marketing, 43 (2), 93-103.

Cooper, R. G. (1983). The Impact of New Product Strategies. Industrial Marketing Management, 12, 243-256.

Cooper, R. G. and Kleinschmidt, E. J. (1987). New Products: What Separates Winners From Losers? Journal of Product Innovation Management, 4 (3), 169-184.

Cooper, R. G. and Kleinschmidt, E. J. (1993). Major New Products: What Distinguishes the Winners in the Chemical Industry? Journal of Product Innovation Management, 10(2), 240-251.

Cox, A.D., Cox, D. and Anderson, R.D. (2005). Reassessing the pleasures of store shopping. Journal of Business Research, 58, 250-259.

Crawford, C. M. (1992). The Hidden Costs of Accelerated Product Development. Journal of Product Innovation Management, 9(3), 188-199.

Crawford, C. M. and Di Benedetto, C. A. (2008). New Products Management. 9th ed.. IL, Burr Ridge: Irwin/McGraw-Hill.

Cui, G. (1997). The Different Faces of the Chinese Consumer. China Business Review, 24, 34-38.

Cui, G. and Liu, Q (2001). Executive Insights: Emerging Market Segments in a Transition Economy: A Study of Urban

Consumers in China. Journal of International Marketing, 9(1), 84-106.

Cui, G. and Liu, Q. (2000). Regional Market Segments of China: Opportunities and Barriers in a Big Emerging Market. Journal of Consumer Marketing, 17(1), 55-72.

Culter, B. D. and Rajshekhar, G. J. (1992). A Cross-cultural Analysis of the Visual Components of Print Advertising: The United States and the European Community. Journal of Advertising Research, 32, 71-80.

Daft, R. L. (1978). A Dual-core Model of Organizational Innovation. Academy of Management Journal, 21 (2), 193-210.

Daft, R.L. and Lengel, R.H. (1986). Organizational Information Requirements, Media Richness and Structural. Design Management Science, 32(5), 554–571.

Dai, Ming, Yin, Yijin and Dai Xieer (2012). Innovation Theory 1912-2012: Commemorate the Theory of Economic Development First Edition of 100 Anniversary. Economics Trends, 2012 (4): 143-150.

Dai, Ming, Yin, Yijin and Dai Xieer (2012). Innovation Theory 1912-2012: Commemorate the Theory of Economic Development First Edition of 100 Anniversary. Economics Trends, 2012 (4): 143-150.

Dalton, G. (1971). Traditional Tribal and Peasant Economics: An Introductory Survey of Economic Anthropology. Addison: Wesley Publishing Company, Inc.

Dalton, G. (1971). Traditional Tribal and Peasant Economics: An Introductory Survey of Economic Anthropology. Addison: Wesley Publishing Company, Inc.

Damanpour, F. (1987). The Adoption of Technological, Administrative, and Ancillary Innovations: Impact of Organizational Factors. Journal of Management, 13 (4), 675-688.

Damanpour, F. (1991). Organizational Innovation: A Meta-analysis of Effects of Determinants and Moderators. Academy of Management Journal, 34 (3), 555-590.

David B. (2004). China's E-Marketing Learns to Drive. Available online: http://banners.noticiasdot.com/termometro/boletines/docs/consultoras/emarketer/2004/0404/emarketer_300404-2.pdf. Accessed on May 14, 2017.

Davis, F.D., Bagozzi, R.P. and Warshaw, P.R (1989). User Acceptance of Computer Technology: A Comparison of Two Theoretical Models. Management Science, 35(8), 982-1003.

Davis, J.P., Steur K. and Pagula Yan, R.A. (2005). Survey Method for Assessing Perceptions of a Game: The Consumer Playtest in Game Design. Game Studies. 5(1). Available online: http://www.gamestudies.org. Assessed on July 6, 20017.

Dawar, N. and Parker, P. (1994). Marketing Universals: Consumers' use of Brand Name, Price, Physical Appearance, and Retailer Reputation as Signals of Product Quality. Journal of Marketing, 58, 81-95.

Dawson, D., Bloch, P.H. and Ridgway, N.M. (1990). Shopping Motives, Emotional States, and Retail Outcomes. Journal of Retailing, 66, 408-427.

De Houwer, J. (2008). Conditioning as a Source of Liking: There is Nothing Simple About It. Ed Wanke (Ed.). Social Psychology of Consumer Behavior. New York: Psychological Press.

De Mooij, M. (2004). Consumer Behavior and Culture, London, UK: SAGE.

DeBruyne, M., Moenaert, R., Griffin, A., Hart, S., Hultink, E. J. and Robben, H. S. J. (2002). The Impact of New Product Launch Strategies on Competitive Reaction in Industrial Markets. Journal of Product Innovation Management, 19(2), 159-170.

Degen, R. J. (2012). Opportunity for Luxury Brands in China. The IUP Journal of Brand Management, 6(3/4), 75-85.

DeJesus, J. and Tian, R.G., (2004). Cultural Awareness and Consumer Behavior: A Case Study of American Perception of Mexican Food. High Plains Applied Anthropologist, 24 (1), 11-21.

Delgado-Ballester, E., Munera-Alemain, J. and Yague-Gullien, M. (2003). Development and Validation of a Brand Trust Scale. International Journal of Market Research, 45 (1), 35-53.

Deli-Grey, S., Haefner, J. and Rosenbloom, A. (2012). The Role of Global Brand Familiarity, Trust and Liking in Predicting Global Brand Purchase Intent: a Hungarian–American Comparison. International Journal of Business and Emerging Markets, 4(1), 4-27.

Deng Xiaoping (1993). Reform is the only way to Develop the Productive Forces in China, in Deng Xiaoping Collection, Vol. 3, Beijing: People's Publishing House, pp. 138-139.

Deng Xiaoping (1994). Remarks In the fourth Chinese literature and art workers representative meeting, Beijing: People's Press, pp. 2009.

Deng, Xiaoping (1993). Reform is the only way to Develop the Productive Forces in China, in Deng Xiaoping Collection, Vol. 3, Beijing: People's Publishing House, pp. 138-139.

Deng, Y. andLi Tianzhu. (2010). The Origin of Shanzhai Phenomenon and aStudy on Its Openly Innovative Features. Enterprise Economy, 1, 21-23.

Deng, Yao (2010). The Four-trillion Assets of the Central Enterprises are accused of Losing Serious. Jinan Daily, 2010-12-09.

Dens, N. and De Pelsmacker, P. (2010). Consumer Response to Different Advertising Appeals for New Products: The Moderating Influence of Branding Strategy and Product Category Involvement. Journal of Brand Management, 18, 50-65.

Denzin, N. and Lincoln, Y. (1994). Handbook of Qualitative Research. CA, Thousand Oaks: Sage.

DeSarbo, W.S., Di Benedetto, C. A., Song, M. and Sinha, I. (2005). Revisiting the Miles and Snow Strategic Framework: Uncovering Relationships Between Strategic Types, Capabilities, Environmental Uncertainty, and Firm Performance. Strategic Management Journal, 26(1), 47-74.

Deshpande, R., Farley, J. U. and Webster, F. E. Jr. (1993). Corporate Culture, Customer Orientation, and Innovativeness in Japanese Firms: A Quadrad Analysis. Journal of Marketing, 52 (1), 23-36.

Di Benedetto, C. A. (1999). Identifying the Key Success Factors in New Product Launch. Journal of Product Innovation Management, 16(5), 530-544.

Di Benedetto, C. A., Calantone, R. J. and Zhang, C. (2003). International Technology Transfer: Model and Exploratory Study in the People's Republic of China. International Marketing Review, 20 (4), 446-462.

Di Benedetto, C. A., DeSarbo, W. S. and Song, M. (2008). Strategic Capabilities and Radical Innovation: An Empirical Study in Three Countries. IEEE Transactions on Engineering Management, 55 (3), 420-433.

Dillman, D.A. (1978). Mail and Telephone Surveys: The Total Design Method. NY, New York: Wiley.

Ding, J. (2007). Concerns over the Labor Shortage of China Caused by Fertility. Semimonthly Selected Readings, 24, 9.

Dodgson, M. and Xue, L. (2009). Editorial: Innovation in China. Innovation: Management Policy and Practice, 11 (1), 2-5.

Donabedian, B. (2006). Optimization and Its Alternative in Media Choice: A Model of Reliance on Social Influence Processes. The Information Society, 22(2), 121–135.

Dong, H. & Ding, Y. (2016). Research on the Policy of "Supply-side Reform" in Electronic

Doorne, S., Ateljevic, I. and Bai, Z. (2003). Representing Identities Through Tourism: Encounters of Ethnic Minorities in Dali, Yunnan Province, People's Republic of China. International Journal of Tourism Research, 5, 1-11.

Douglas, S.P. and Craig, C. S. (1983). Examining Performance of U.S. Multinationals in Foreign Markets. Journal of International Business Studies,14 (1), 51-62.

Duan, M. (2009). Analysis on the Impacts of Population Aging on Employment on the Basis of Economics. The Economic Forum, 4,20.

Dyer, J. H. (1996). How Chrysler Created an American Keiretsu. Harvard Business Review, 74(8), 42-60.

Dzever, Sam and Quester, Pascale. (1999). Country-of-origin Effects on Purchasing Agents' Product Perceptions: An Australian Perspective, Industrial Marketing Management, 28,165-175.

E. J. Hobsbawm (1999), Empire Age: 1975-1914, Jiangsu: People's Publishing House.

Eckhardt, G. M. and Bengtsson, A. (2010). A Brief history of Branding in China. Journal of Macromarketing, 30(3), 210 – 221.

Eckhardt, G. M. and Houston, M. J. (2002). Cultural Paradoxes Reflected in Brand Meaning: McDonald's in Shanghai, China. Journal of International Marketing, 10(2), 68-82.

Edson, E. and Stern, B. (2003). Sympathy and Empathy: Emotional Responses to Advertising Dramas. Journal of Consumer Research, 29 (4), 566-578.

Elliot, R. and Percy, L. (2007). Strategic Brand Management. Oxford: Oxford University Press.

Elliott, G. and Cameron, R. (1994), Consumer Perception of Product Quality and the Country of Origin Effect. Journal of International Marketing, 2 (2), 49-62.

Emery, C. R. and Tian, K. R. (2010). China Compared with the US: Cultural Differences and the Impacts on Advertising Appeals. International Journal of China Marketing, 1(1), 45-56.

Emery, C. R. and Tian, R. G. (2002a). A Review of Empirical Research on Advertising in China from 1992-2001. Research Manuscript 2002-3, Lander University, Greenwood, SC.

Emery, C. R. and Tian, R. G. (2002b). Cross-cultural Issues in Internet Marketing. Journal of American Academy of Business, 12 (2), 217-225.

Emery, C. R. and Tian, R. G. (2003). The Effect of Cultural Differences on the Effectiveness of Advertising Appeals: A

Comparison between China and the U.S. Journal of Transformation in Business and Economics, 2(3). 48-59.

Engardio, P. and Dexter Roberts. (2004).The China Price.BusinessWeek, 3911 (December 6), 102.

Engel, J., Kollat, D. and Blackwell, R. (1973). Consumer Behavior. 2nd ed. New York: Holt, Rinehart and Winston.

Eric, Roll (1981), History of Economic Thoughts, Hong Kong: The Commercial Press.

Fan, Xiaoqing (2009). The Economic Anthropology Research in China. Journal of Huaihua University, 28 (12): 21-24.

Fan, J.X. and Xiao, J.J. (1998). Consumer Decision-making Styles of Young-adult Chinese. Journal of Consumer Affairs, 32(2), 275-94.

Fan, Xiaoqing (2009). Economic Anthropology in China. Journal of Huaihua College, 28 (12) :21-24.

Feng, Zhong Ze, and Li, Qing Jiang. (2008). The Agricultural Production Quality Safety Cognition of Consumer and the Analysis of Influencing Factors, Journal of China's Rural Economy, 1, 25-27.

Feng, H. (2016). The Practical Significance of Supply-side Problems to Economic Structural

Feng, Kui (2007). The Value of Cluster Marketing: Based on Shengzhou Neckties Industry. Commercial Research, 57, 99-101.

Feng, Zuyi (1995). Preface//Yang Tingshuo, Interphase Operational Principles. Guiyang, Guizhou: Guizhou People Publishing House 1-5.

Fernandez, D. R., Carlson, D. S., Stepina, L. P. and Nicholson, J. D. (1997). Hofstede's Country Classification 25 Years Later. The Journal of Social Psychology, 17, 21-18.

Ferry, D.L.K., Sawyer, C.Tand Sawyer, J.E. (2001). Measuring Facts of Media Richness. Journal of Computer Information Systems, 41, 69–78.

Financial & Economic Publishing House.

Financial Times (2011). Increase investment, adjust structure and deepen reform to achieve equalization of basic public services, March 8, 2011.

Fisher, R. (2005). Gender Differences in Responses to Emotional Advertising: The Effect of the Presence of Others. Advances in Consumer Research, 31 (4), 850-858.

Fisk, George. (1973). Criteria for a Theory of Responsible Consumption. Journal of Marketing, 37(April): 24-31.

Fisk, George. (1982). Editor's Working Definition of Macromarketing. Journal of Macromarketing, Spring, 3-4.

Flint-Goor, A. and Liebermann Y. (1996). Message Strategy by Product-class Type: A. Matching Model. Journal of Research in Marketing, 13, 237- 249.

Franzen, G. and Moriarty, S. (2009). The Science and Art of Branding. Armonk: M.E. Sharpe.

Fraser, D. and Raynor, M. (1996). The Power of Parity. Forecast, May/June, 8-12.

Friedman, M. (1982), Free to Choose, Beijing: The Commercial Press.

Friedrich List (1961), The National System of Political Economy, Hong Kong: The Commercial Press.

Friedrich List (1961). The National System of Political Economy, The Commercial Press, pp. 208.

Fryxell, G.E. et al. (2004). Successful Localization Programs in China: An Important Element in Strategy Implementation. Journal of World Business, 39, 268-282.

Fteschrin, M. and Lattermann, C. (2008). User Acceptance of Virtual World. Journal of Electronic Commerce, 9 (3), 231-242.

Fu, Chunrong (2006). Wu Jinglian uncovers four defects on China's reform and calls for careful plans for the future, China Business Times, February 12.

Fu, Deling (2011). The influence of resource tax reform on coal mines, Futures Daily, November 23.

Fu, Guoqun and Xueying Tong. (2003). How Do Brand Price and Place of Origin Influence Consumers' Choices to Purchase. Journal of Management Sciences in China, 06(06), 79-84.

Gadiesh, O., Leung, P. and Vestring, T. (2007). The Battle for China's Good Enough Market. Harvard Business Review, 85, 81-89.

Gang, Chen. (2011). Sustainable Development of Eco-Cultural Tourism in Remote Regions: Lessons Learned from Southwest China. International Journal of Business Anthropology, 2 (1), 121-35.

Gao, Junling (2011). Comments on the difficulties and countermeasures of China's environmental protection work, Science Communication (06), pp. 15.

Gao, Q. (2010). China Internet Population Hits 420 Million. China Daily, July 15, 2010.

Gao, Wang. (2005). The Model Estimation of the Random Coefficients of Conjoint Analysis. Quantitative and Technical Economics, 32, (07), 96-107.

Gao, Xijun (1987), The World of Economics, Taiwan: The World Books Press.

Garner, J. (2005). The Rise of the Chinese Consumer: Theory and Evidence. West Sussex, UK: John Wiley and Sons Ltd.

Gassenheimer, J. B. and Calantone, R. J. (1994). Managing Economic Dependence and Relational Activities Within a Competitive Channel Environment. Journal of Business Research, 29(3), 189-197.

Gassenheimer, J. B., Calantone, R. J. and Scully, J. I. (1994). Supplier Involvement and Dealer Satisfaction: Implications for Enhancing Channel Relationships. Journal of Business and Industrial Marketing, 10(2), 7-19.

Gatignon, H. and Xuereb, J.-M. (1997). Strategic Orientation of the Firm and New Product Performance. Journal of Marketing Research, 34 (1), 77-90.

George Gilder (1985), Wealth and Poverty, Shanghai: Translation Publishing House.

Geuens, M. and De Pelsmacker, P. (1997). Product Category Involvement and the Reaction of Polish and Belgian Consumers to Different Types of Advertising Appeals. European Advances in Consumer Research, 3, 33-41.

Ghauri, P. and Cateroa, P. (2010). International Marketing. 3rd Ed..London: McGraw Hill.

Gierl, H. and Praxmarer, S. (2007). The Effects of a Value-oriented Advertising Strategy on Brand Attitude. Der Markt, 46 (4), 148-156.

Goldhaber, M. H. (1997). The Attention Economy and the Net. First Monday. (2)4. Available online: http://firstmonday.org/htbin/cgiwrap/bin/ojs/index.php/fm/article/view/519/440. Accessed in September 2017.

Governance. 14(2):238-251.

Green P, Rao V. (1971). Conjoint Measurement for Quantifying Judgmental Data. Journal of Marketing Research, 08, (03), 355-363.

Green, P. and Srinivasan, V. (1978). Conjoint Analysis in Consumer Research: Issues and Outlook. Journal of Consumer Research, 5, (2), 103-123.

Green, P. Srinivasan, V. (1990) Conjoint Analysis in Marketing: New Developments with Implications for Research and Practice. Journal of Marketing, 54, (04), 3-19.

Green, P, Wind Y. (1975). New Way to Measure Consumers' Judgments. Harvard Business Review, 53, (04), 107-120.

Griffin, A. (1992). Evaluating QFD's Use in U.S. Firms as a Process for Developing Products. Journal of Product Innovation Management, 9(3), 171-182.

Griffin, A. (1995). Modeling and Measuring Product Development Cycle Time Across Industries. Marketing Science Institute Report. MA, Cambridge: Marketing Science Institute. 95-117.

Griffin, A. and Hauser, J. R. (1992). Patterns of Communication Among Marketing, Engineering, and Manufacturing: A

Comparison Between Two New Product Teams. Management Science, 38 (3), 360-373.

Griffin, A. and Hauser, J. R. (1993). The Voice of the Customer. Marketing Science, 12 (1), 1-27.

Griffin, A. and Page, A. L. (1993). An Interim Report on Measuring Product Development Success and Failure. Journal of Product Innovation Management, 10(4), 291-308.

Gu, Ruizhen (2006), "The First Domestic People's Livelihood Index Issues; over half of People Tell Their Feelings", Shanxi Daily, 29th January 2006.

Guangdong Statistical Yearbook. (2009). Available online: http://www.gdstats.gov.cn/tjnj/table/10/e104.htm. Accessed on Mar 23, 2017.

Gudeman, S. (2001). The Anthropology of Economy. Malden, MA: Blackwell.

Guest Commentator. (2015). Fully Play the Positive Role of Price Reform in Supply-side

Guiltinan, J. P. (1999). Launch Strategy, Launch Tactics, and Demand Outcomes. Journal of Product Innovation Management, 16 (5), 509-529.

Guo, Y. and Barnes, S. (2007). Why People Buy Virtual Items in Virtual Worlds with Real Money. The Data Base for Advancces in Information Systems, 38(4), 69-76.

Gupta, A.K. and Wilemon, D. L. (1986). The Credibility-Cooperation Connection at the Rand D-Marketing Interface. Journal of Product Innovation Management, 5(1), 20-31.

Gupta, A.K., Raj. S. P. and Wilemon, D. L. (1986). A Model for Studying RandD-Marketing Interface in the Product Innovation Process. Journal of Marketing, 50(2), 7-17.

Gustin, S. (2010). Now the No. 2 Economy, What's Ahead for China? Available online: http://www.dailyfinance.com/story/China-number-two-whats-ahead/19595235/. Accessed on Aug. 2017.

Hair, Jr., Joseph, F. Anderson, R. E., Tatham, R. L. and Black, W. C. (1998). Multivariate Data Analysis. 5th ed. NJ, Upper Saddle River: Prentice Hall.

Hall, E. T. (1976), Beyond Culture. New York: Anchor Press-Doubleday.

Halperin, R. H. (1988). Economies across Cultures: Towards a Comparative Science of the Economy. New York: St. Martin’s Press.

Han, Deqiang (2006). Why do We Say Mainstream Economist Mislead the Reform? Comment on Wu Jinglian’s remarks, First Financial Daily, January 4, 2006.

Hann, Chris and Hart, Keith (2011). Economic Anthropology. Cambridge, UK: Polity Press.

Haworth, Alan (1994), Anti-libertarianism: Markets, Philosophy, and Myth, Hove: Psychology Press.

Haytko, L.H. and Baker, J. (2004). It’s all at the Mall: Exploring Adolescent Girls’ experiences. Journal of Retailing, 80, 67-83.

Haywood, K. Michael. (1990). Revising and Implementing the Marketing Concept as it Applies to Tourism. Tourism Management, 1990, 195-205.

He, Bing Meng (2004), Neo-liberalism Reviews, Beijing: Social Sciences Academic Press.

He, J. (2016). The Research and Analysis of "Supply-side Reform" to Boost China's Economic Transformation. New Economy. (1).

He, Jun, Ji Yue Qing, and Wu Hao Jie. (2005). Consumer Behavior Mode of Fresh Food——Comparison of Supermarket and Free Market of Agricultural Products. Journal of China Agricultural University (Social sciences edition), 3, 67-71.

He, Xin (2010). He Xin View on China's Economy. Beijing: The East Press.

Heath, R. and Feldwick, P. (2007). Fifty Years Using the Wrong Model of Advertising. International Journal of Market Research, 50 (1), 29-59.

Heckler, S. and Childers, T. (1992). The Role of Expectancy and Memory in for Verbal and Visual Information: What is Incongruency? Journal of Consumer Research, 18, 475-92.

Heim, K. (1997). Foreign Ventures in China Urged to Localize Faster. In AsianWall Street Journal. 12 Dec 1997.

Hemp, P. (2006). Avatar-based Marketing. Harvard Business Review, 84(6), 48-57.

Henderson, David R. (1997). What Are Price Wars Good For? Absolutely Nothing. Fortune, 135 (9), 156.

Henley, J. and Nyaw M.K. (1986). Introducing Market Forces into Managerial Decision-Making in Chinese Industrial Enterprises. Journal of Management Studies, 23(6), 635-656.

Herbig, Paul. (1998). Handbook of cross-cultural marketing. New York: The International Business Press.

Herzberg, F. (1966). Work and the Nature of Man. OH, Cleveland: World Publishing.

Hill, T. (1989). Manufacturing Strategy. IL, Homewood: Irwin Publishing.

Hird, H. Richard (2005). Working with Economics: A Canadian Framework , Seventh Edition, pp. 83, Pearson Prentice Hall, Toronto, Canada.

Hobsbawm, Eric (1999). The Age of Revolution 1789-1848, Jiangsu: Jiangsu People's Publishing House.

Hofstede, G. (1984). The Cultural Relativity of the Quality of Life Concept. Academy of Management Review, 9(3), 381-393.

Hofstede, G. (1991). Cultures and Organizations: Software of the Mind. London: McGraw-Hill Book Company.

Hofstede, G. (2001). Culture's Consequence: Comparing Values, Behaviors, Institutions and Organization Across Nations. London: Sage Publications.

Holden, S. and Vanhuele, M. (1999). Know the Name, Forget the Exposure: Brand Familiarity Versus Memory of Exposure Context. Psychology and Marketing, 16 (6), 479-496.

Holsapple, C.W., Pakath R. and Sasidharan, S.A. (2005). Website Interface Design Framework for the Cognitively Impaired: A Study in the Context of Alzheimer's Disease. Journal of Electronic Commerce Research, 6(4), 291-303.

Hong, J. W., Muderrisoglu, A. and Zinkhan, G. M. (1987). Cultural Differences and Advertising Expression: A Comparative Content Analysis of Japanese and U.S. Magazine Advertising. Journal of Advertising, 16 (1), 55-62, 68.

Horn, Sierk A. and Cross, Adam R. (2009). Japanese Management at a Crossroads? The Changing Role of China in the Transformation of Corporate Japan. Asia Pacific Business Review, 15(3), 285-308.

Hornborg, A. (2005). Resisting the black hole of neo-classical formalism in economic anthropology. In S. Löfving (ed.), Peopled Economies: Conversations with Stephen Gudeman. Uppsala: Interface: 63-80.

Hornikx, J.M.A. and O'Keefe, D.J. (2009). Adapting Consumer Advertising Appeals to Cultural Values: A Meta-analytic Review of Effects on Persuasiveness and Ad Liking in Beck, C.S. (ed.), Communication Yearbook 33, New York : Lawrence Erlbaum. 38-71.

Hou, Jiang (2006). Reviews on News, Bejing Evening News, 12th July 2006.

Hovgaard, A. and Hansen, E. (2004). Innovativeness in the Forest Products Industry. Forest Products Journal, 54 (1), 26-33.

Hsinchun, C., Sven T. and Fu, T.J. (2008). Cyber Extremism in Web 2.0: An Exploratory Study of International Jihadist Groups. IEEE International Conference on Intelligence and Security Informatics.

Hu, Ding Huan, Yu Hai Feng, and T. Reardon. (2003). The Fresh Food Management of Chinese Supermarket and the Purchase Behavior. Journal of China's Rural Economy, 8, 13-14.

Hu, Hongbao (2006). History of Chinese Anthropology. Beijing: Renmin University of China Press.

Hu, Jintao (2006). Adhere to the Path of Innovation with Chinese Characteristics, Strive for the Development of Socialism with Chinese Characteristics and the Construction of Innovative Country. Information for Deciders Magazine. Vol. 4 & 5, pp. 48-55.

Huang, Zu Hui, Zhou Jie Hong, and Jin Shao sh. (2004). Wet Market Transform to Supermarket and the Purchase Behavior Analysis of Agriculture Product. Journal of Zhejiang Academic Journal, 5, 88.

Huddleston, P., Whipple, J., Mattick, R.N. and Lee, S.J. (2009). Customer Satisfaction in Food Retailing: Comparing Specialty and Conventional Grocery Stores. International Journal of Retail and Distribution Management, 37(1), 63-80.

Hui, A. Y., et al. (2001). An Investigation of Decision-making Styles of Consumers in China. The Journal of Consumer Affairs, 35, 226-345.

Hui, M. and Zhou, L. (2002). Linking Product Evaluations and Purchase Intention for Country-of-origin Effects. Journal of Global Marketing, 15(3/4), 95-101.

Hultink, E. J. and Robben, H. S. J. (1995). Measuring New Product Success: The Difference That Time Perspective Makes. Journal of Product Innovation Management, 12(5), 392-405.

Hultink, E. J. and Robben, H. S. J. (1999). Launch Strategy and New Product Performance: An Empirical Examination in the Netherlands. Journal of Product Innovation Management, 16(6), 545-556.

Hultink, E. J., Griffin, A., Hart, S. and Robben, H. S. J. (1997). Industrial New Product Launch Strategies and Product Development Performance. Journal of Product Innovation Management, 14, 243-257.

Hultink, E. J., Hart, S., Robben, H. S. J. and Griffin, A. (2000). Launch Decisions and New Product Success: An Empirical Comparison of Consumer and Industrial Products. Journal of Product Innovation Management, 17(1), 5-23.

Hussain, A. and Rivers, P.A. (2009). Confronting the Challenges of Long – term Health Care Crisis in the United States. Journal of Health Finance, Winter, 73.

Immanuel Wallerstein (2002). The End of Liberalism, Social Sciences Academic Press.

Immanuel Wallerstein, Terence K. Hopkins and Giovanni Arrighi (2002), The End of Liberalism, Beijing: Social Sciences Academic Press.

Itagaki, H. (2009). Competitiveness, Localization and Japanese Companies in China: Realities and Alternate Approaches. Asia Pacific Business Review, 15(3), 451-462.

J. B. Say (1983), Introduction to Political Economics, The Commercial Press, pp. 142.

Jaeger, P. T. and Thompson, K. M. (2003). E-government Around the World: Lessons, Challenges, and Future Directions. Government Information Quarterly, 20, 389–394.

Jamison, David J. (1999). Masks Without Meanings: Notes on the Processes, Consumption, and Exchange in the context of First World-Third World Tourism" Journal of Macromarketing, 19 (June), 8-19.

Janiszewski, C. (1993). Preattentive mere exposure effects. Journal of Consumer Research, 20 (3), 376-92.

Jassawalla, A. R. and Sashittal, H. C. (1998). An Examination of Collaboration in High-Technology New Product Development Processes. Journal of Product Innovation Management, 15(3), 237-254.

Jaworski, B.J. and Kohli, A. K. (1993). Market Orientation: Antecedents and Consequences. Journal of Marketing, 57 (3), 53-71.

Jefferson, G. H., Rawski, T. G. and Zheng, Y. (1992). Growth, Efficiency, and Convergence in China's State and Collective Industry. Economic Development and Cultural Change, 40 (1), 239-266.

Jia, K. (2015). Supply-side Reform in the Period of 13th Five-year Plan . Journal

Jiang, C. (2016). The Economic Significance of Long-term Care Insurance from the Perspective of Supply-side Reform. China Market. (3).

Jiang, Zemin (1989). Speech in the Celebration of the 40-year Anniversary of the People's Republic of China, People's Daily, October 1st, 1989.

Jiang, Zemin (2001). Strengthen to Train Young and Middle-aged Leaders Who Meet the Requirements of the New Century. Beijing, China: People's Publishing House.

Jiangxi News (2012). The arbitrary charges were more than ￥30 million RMB, and 244 people got punished in Jiangxi province, http://jiangxi.jxnews.com.cn, Accessed in February 9, 2012

Jin, Hao (2011). The "Enterprise Competitiveness Study" Report is Released by Jin Hao. Sina Finance, 2011-11-22.

Johansson, J. and Ronkainen, I. (2003). Global Brands? Does Familiarity Breed Contempt? in. Jain, S. (Ed.). Handbook of Research in International Marketing. Cheltenham: Edward Elgar Publishing.

Johansson, J. K., Ronkainnen, I. A. and Czinkota, M.R. (1994), Negative Country-of-origin Effects: The Case of Russia, Journal of International Business Studies, 25, 157-76.

Johansson, J.K. (1989). Determinants and Effects of the Use of 'Made in' Labels. International Marketing Review, 6(1), 47-58.

John, J. Watson and Katrina Wright. (2000), Consumer Ethnocentrism and Attitudes toward Domestic and Foreign Products, European Journal of Marketing, 34 (9/10), 1149-1166.

Johnson, W. H. A. and Weiss, J. W. (2008). A Stage Model of Education and Innovation Type in China, the Paradox of the Dragon. Journal of Technology Management in China, 3 (1), 66-81.

Jordan, Ann T. (2003). Business Anthropology, IL, Prospect Heights: Waveland Press.

Kahai, S.S. and Cooper, R.B. (2003). Exploring the Core Concepts of Media Richness Theory: The Impact of Cue Multiplicity and Feedback Immediacy on Decision Quality. Journal of Management Information Systems, 20(1), 263–300.

Kaigler-Walker, K., Gilbert, Z. and Hu, H. (2010). Domains of Chinese Women's Perception of Appearance and Use of Fashion Products: Conceptualization and Scale Development. Journal of Global Business, 4(1), 27-35.

Kajima, K. (1978), Direct Foreign Investment a Japanese Model of Multinational Business Operations, London: Croom Helm.

Kalwani, M. U. and Narayandas, N. (1995). Long-Term Manufacturer-Supplier Relationships: Do They Pay Off for Supplier Firms? Journal of Marketing, 59(1), 1-16.

Kano, N., N. Seraku, F. Takahashi, and S. Tsuji. (1984). Attractive Quality and Must-Be Quality. Hinshitsu, 14(2).

Kaocong Tian, Jixue Wei, and Yanrong Zhou. (2003). the Application of Conjoint Analysis in the Management of Hospitals. Chinese Journal of Hospital Statistics, 08, (03), 98-103.

Katherine, L. N. R. T. Rust, and V. A. Zeithaml. (2001). What Drives Customer Equity? Marketing Management, 10 (1): 20-25.

Katz, D. (1960). The Functional Approach to the Study of Attitudes. Public Opinion Quarterly, 24, 163-204.

Ke, Huixin and Paul. Frostier. (1994). The Conjoint Analysis in Marketing Research. The Mathematical Statistics and Management, 4, (6), 23-25.

Keller, K. (1998). Strategic Brand Management. NJ, Upper Saddle River: Prentice Hall.

Kent, R. and Allen, C. (1994). Competitive Consumer Interference Effects for Consumer Memory in Advertising: The Role of Brand Familiarity. Journal of Marketing, 58, 97-105.

Kiecker, P. and Hartman, C. L. (1993). Purchase Pal Use: Why Others Choose to Shop with Others in Marketing Theory and Application by R. Varadarajan and B. Jaworski. (Eds.). IL, Chicago: American Marketing Association. 378-384.

Killick, E. (2008). Creating Community: Land Titling, Education, and Settlement Formation Among the Asheninka of Peruvian Anmazonia. The Journal of Latin American and Caribbean Anthropology, 13, 22-47.

Kim, K.H., Park, J.Y. Kim, D.Y., Moon, H.I. and Chun, H.C. (2002). E-lifestyle and Motives to Use Online Games. Irish Marketing Review, 15(2), 71-77.

Kim, W. C. and Mauborgne, R. (1999). Creating New Market Space: A Systematic Approach to Value Innovation Can Help Companies Break Free from the Competitive Pack. Harvard Business Review, (January-February), 83-93.

Kleinschmidt, E. J. and Cooper, R. G. (1991). The Impact of Product Innovativeness on Performance. Journal of Product Innovation Management, 8(4), 240-251.

Knight, G. A. and Calantone, R. J. (2000), A Flexible Model of Consumer Country-of Origin Perceptions - a Cross-Cultural Investigation. International Marketing Review, 17 (2): 127-145.

Knight, K. E. (1967). A Descriptive Model of the Intra-firm Innovation Process, The Journal of Business, 40 (4), 478-496.

Kobayashi-Hillary, M. (2007). Building a Future with Brics: The Next Decade for Offshoring. NY, New York: Springer.

Kohli, A. K. and Jaworski, B.J. (1990). Market Orientation: The Construct, Research Propositions, and Managerial Implications. Journal of Marketing, 54 (2), 1-18.

Kopp, R. (1999). The Rice-paper Ceiling in Japanese Companies: Why It Exists and Persists in Japanese multinationals abroad: individual and organizational learning. S.L. Beechler and A. Bird (ed.). New York: Oxford University Press. 107-128.

Kotler, P. (2010), China Marketing, Marketing China: A Relatively New but Fast Growing Field of Study. International Journal of China Marketing,1(1).

Kotler, Philip. (2003). Marketing Management. Shanghai: Shanghai People's Publishing House.

Kozhevnikov, M. (2007). Cognitive Styles in the Context of Modern Psychology: Toward an Integrated Framework of Cognitive Style. Psychological bulletin, 133 (3), 464-481.

Kuang, Ningdan (2011). Surprising, Stamping Transcript Cost a Thousand Yuan, Information Times.

Kumar, N., Stern, L. W. and Anderson, J.C. (1993). Conducting Interorganizational Research Using Key Informants. Academy of Management Journal, 36, 1633-1651.

Kumar, R. and Best, M. L. (2006). Impact and Sustainability of E-Government Services in Developing Countries: Lessons Learned from Tamil Nadu, India, The Information Society, 22 (1), 1-12.

Kune, J. B. (2009). Population Aging and the Affluent Society: The Case of the Netherlands. Pensions, 14, (4), 231-241.

Kurlantzick, Joshua (2002). Making it in China. U.S. News and World Report, 10/07/2002, 44.

Kurtz, Robert (2003). Capitalism Black Book-Final of the Economy Market, Beijing, China: Social Science Literature Publishing House.

Kvale, S, (1996). Interviews: An Introduction to Qualitative Research Interviewing. CA, Thousand Oaks: Sage.

La Barbera, P., Weingard, P. and Yorkston, E. (1998). Matching the Message to the Mind: Advertising Imagery and Consumer Processing Styles. Journal of Advertising Research, 38 (5), 29-41.

Lan, Wen Qiao. (2006). Regional Marketing of Enterprise Cluster: Incentive and Road. Journal of Beijing Institute of Finance and Commerce Management, 22(2), 39-41.

Langerak, F., Hultink,E. J. and Robben, H. S. J. (2004). The Impact of Market Orientation, Product Advantage, and Launch Proficiency on New Product Performance and Organizational Performance. Journal of Product Innovation Management, 21(2), 79-94.

Larry, L. Carter, Jr, (2002). Consumer Attitudes Toward Cross-border Brand Alliances: Adding a Consideration of Country of Origin

Fit, unpublished thesis,Virginia Polytechnic Institute and State University.

Lavidge, R. and Steiner, G. (1961) A Model for Ppredictive Measurement of Advertising Effectiveness, Journal of Marketing, 61, 59–62.

Law Evening News (2011). Teacher buys car and house using remedial teaching fees, while student commits suicide because of no ability to afford tuition fees, December 7, 2011.

Lee, Dong-Jin, M. Joseph Sirgy, Val Larsen, and Newell D. Wright. (2002). Developing a Subjective Measure of Consumer Well Being. Journal of Macromarketing, 22 (2), 158-169.

Lee, J. and Lee, W. (2007). Country of Origin and Brand Familiarity in Consumer Product Evaluation: The Strategic Brand Alliance Perspective. American Academy of Advertising and Lee, J. S., et al. (2004). Changing Roles and Values of Female Consumers in China. Business Horizons, May/June, 17-22.

Lee, Y. and O'Connor, G. C. (2003). The Impact of Communication Strategy on Launching New Products: The Moderating Role of Product Innovativeness. Journal of Product Innovation Management, 20(1), 4-21.

Leimster, J.M., Pascal, S. and Helmut, K. (2004). Success Factors of Virtual Communities from the Perspective of Members and Operators: An Empirical Study. 37th Hawai International Conference on System Sciences.

Leng, Xionghui. (2010). The Promotion Strategy of Marketing Communication Effects-Based on Involvement. China Business, 2, 32-33.

Lenin, V. I. (1960). The Fifth Anniversary of Russian Revolution and Future of the World Revolution, Lenin Anthology. Volume 4: 694-695. Beijing, China: People's Publishing House.

Lenin, V. I. (1972). A Speech Delivered at the First Congress of the National Economic Council, Lenin Anthology. Volume 3: 571. Beijing, China: People's Publishing House.

Lenin, V. I. (1986). Lenin Collected Works Vol. 6: Comments on Plekhanov's Second Draft, People's Publishing House, pp. 212.

Lew, Alan A. (1987). The History, Policies and Social Impact of International Tourism in the People's Republic of China. Asian Profile, 15(2),117-128.

Lewicki, R.J. and Bunker, B.B. (1995). Trust in Relationships: A Model of Trust Development and Decline in Conflict, Cooperation and Justice by B.B. Bunker and J.Z. Rubin. (Eds.). San Francisco: Jossey-Bass. 133-173.

Li, D. and Gallup, A. (1995). In Search of the Chinese Consumer. The China Business Review, September-October 19-22.

Li, F. and Wang, Y. (2006). Chinese Retailing Industry in the Form of Physical Stores in The Development of the Retailing Industry in China (1981-2005) by F. Li and G.Wang. (Eds.). Beijing: Social Science Literature Publishing House. 149-168.

Li, F., Zhou, N., Nicholls, J.A.F., Zhuang, G. and Kranendonk, C. (2004). Interlinear or Inscription? A Comparative Study of Chinese and American Mall Shoppers' behavior. Journal of Consumer Marketing, 21, 51-61.

Li, H, Daugherty T. and Biocca, F. (2003). The Role of Virtual Experience in Consumer Learning. Journal of Consumer Psychology, 13(4), 395-408.

Li, H. and Zhang, Y. (2007). The Role of Manager's Political Networking and Functional Experience in New Venture Performance: Evidence from China's Transition Economy. Strategic Management Journal, 28, 791-804.

Li, Q. (2010). (a, b, c, d). The Forthcoming of the Grey Tide - Pondering over the Population Aging in China. Information on Scientific and Technical Resources ,10, 233.

Li, X. & Hu, H. (2013). Analysis of Externality of Rural Labor Force Flow in Central and

Li, Xiaolin (1994). Expectations of History - China's Poverty Alleviation and Development, People's Liberation Army Literature and Art Publishing House, pp. 94.

Li, Y. (2014). To Realize the Chinese Dream Requires Innovation in the Economic System—

Li, Yinlian (2012). European Anti-Dumping Policy Again. The Supporting Ceramics Exports was "Tortured". China Operation News. 2012-02-18.

Li, Zhengrong (2003). Ethnic People's Economic Interest Is Relative Independence. Journal of Gansu College of Political Science and Law for Adult Education, 2003 (3): 123-125.

Li, Zhongbin (2004). New Development of Ethnic Economics. Beijing: National Publishing House.

Liang, K. and L. Jacobs. (1995). China's advertising agencies: Problems and relations. International Journal of Advertising, 13(3), 205-212.

Liang, Xiaofei (2012). The arbitrary charges were more than ￥4.48 million RMB, and 41 people got punished in Jiangxi province, http://news.china.com, Accessed in February 11, 2012.

Lilien, G. L. and Yoon, E. (1990). The Timing of Competitive Market Entry: An Exploratory Study of New Industrial Practices. Management Science, 36(5), 1633-1651.

Lillis, M. and Tian, R. (2010). Cultural Issues in Business World: An Anthropological Perspective, Journal of Social Science, 6 (1), 99-112.

Lin, C. and Kao, D. (2004). The Impacts of Country-of-origin on Brand Equity. Journal of American Academy of Business, Cambridge, 5, 37-40.

Lin, M.Y. and Chang, L.H. (2003). Determinants of Habitual Behavior for National and Leading Brands in China. Journal of Products and Brand Management, 12, 94-104.

Lin, Miao (2010). The audit reports present four big attractions this year, People's Court Daily.

Lin, W. & Su, J. (2016). The Nature and Implementation of Supply-side Reform.

Linden Lab. (2010). Second Life Security Bulletin. Accessed 12 June 2010.

Liu, Changzhong (2011), "China Trade and Industry Bureau Investigates and Treats More Than 1.38 Million Illegal Cases from January to November", China News Net, 26th December 2011.

Liu, Changzhong (2011). China Trade and Industry Bureau investigates and treats more than 1.38 million illegal cases from January to November, China News Net.

Liu, Guoguang (2011). Reason and Policy of the Difficulties of Common Prosperity, Chinese Social Sciences Weekly, July15, 2011.

Liu, Guoguang (2011). Reason and Policy of the Difficulties of Common Prosperity, Social Science in China.

Liu, Hen Jiang, and Ji, Xiang Chen. (2005 a). Dynamism and Competitive Advantage: The Development Logic of Industrial Clusters. Chinese Soft Science, 2005(2), 125-130.

Liu, Hong (2010). The Chinese Economists' Glory and Dream in 1980s. Nanning, Guangxi: Guangxi Normal University Press.

Liu, Jie (2012). Under the Crisis, Shipping Industry in China are Forced into High-end Development. China Union Business Daily, 2012-02-17.

Liu, K. (2007). Unfolding the Post-Transition Era: The Landscape and Mindscape of China's Retail Industry after 2004. Asia Pacific Journal of Marketing and Logistics, 19, 398-412.

Liu, Lanjian, and Si, Chunlin. (2010). Lower Market Destroys: The Case about Shanzhai Handset. Technical Economy and Management Research, 3, 46-49.

Liu, Shaoqi (1998). Political Report of China Communist Party Central Committee in the Eighth National People's Congress, People's Publishing House, pp. 17.

Liu, W. (2008). KFC in China: Secret Recipe for Success. Singapore: Wiley and Sons.

Liu, Yingtuan (2010). Industrialization of education should cease, Hunan Education, March, pp.62.

Lookout (2010). All the 30 kinds of corruption and bribery behaviors were used, September 19, 2010.

Lovelock, C. H. (1983). Classifying Services to Gain Strategic Marketing Insights. Journal of Marketing, 47, 8-24.

Low, G. and Lamb, C. (2000). The Measurement and Dimensionality of Brand Associations. Journal of Product and Brand Management, 9(6), 350-68.

Lowry, P.B, Robert, T.L. Romano, N.C., Cheney, P.D. and Hightower, R.T. (2006). The Impact of Group Size and Social Presence on Small-Group Communication. Small Group Research, 37(3), 631-661.

Lu, Taihong (2005). Consumer Behavior. Beijing: Higher Education Press.

Lu, Xing (2018). The Administration of Foreign Exchange: by the End of March 2018, the Balance of Foreign Exchange Reserve in Chins is 3142.8 billion U.S. Dollars. Foreign Exchange Network, 2018-04-19.

Luce, Turkey (1964). Simultaneous Conjoint Measurement: A New Type of Fundamental Measurement. Journal of Mathematical Psychology, 1, (09), 1-27.

Luo, Gangyi (2009). An Analysis of Advantages and Strategies of Shanzhai Marketing. China Business. 10, 90-91.

Luo, H. & Liang, S. (2016). Discussion on the Optimization of China's Supply-side Structural

Luo, Y. (2003). Industrial Dynamics and Managerial Networking in an Emerging Market: The Case of China. Strategic Management Journal, 24 (13), 1315-1327.

Lury, C. (1996). Consumer Culture. NK, Brunswick: Rutgers University Press.

Lv, You Ping (2005). Competitiveness of Clusters of Zhejiang Based on Cooperative Marketing. Business Economics and Management, 8, 47-56.

Lyn, P. (2008). Second Life: The Seventh Face of the Library. Electronic Library and Information Systems, 42(1), 232- 242.

Ma, C. (2016). Authoritative Experts Interpret the Connotation and Path of "Supply-side

Ma, Jiantang (2009). The second national economic census has been basically finished and achieved important results http://www.stats.gov.cn/zgjjpc/jjpc2/, Accessed in December 2017.

Ma, Qingguo (2007), Theory and Implementation of Regional Soft Power. Beijing: China Social Sciences Press.

Ma, Tao (2002), Study on the History of Economic Thoughts, Fudan University Press.

Ma, Yaopeng (2010). System and the Path: The History and Reality of Socialist Economic Reform. Beijing: People's Publishing House.

MacCallum, R.C., Browne, M.W. and Sugawara, H., M. (1996). Power Analysis and Determination of Sample Size for Covariance Structure Modeling. Psychological Methods, 1 (2), 130-49.

MacKenzie, S. and Lutz, R. (1982). Monitoring Advertising Effectiveness: A Structural Equation Analysis of the Mediating Role of Attitude Toward the Ad. Working Paper No. 117, Centre for Marketing Studies, UCLA, Los Angeles, CA.

Maestas, N. and Zissimopoulos, J. (2010). How Longer Work Lives Ease the Crunch of Population Aging? Journal of Economic Prospective, 24 (1): 139- 160.

Maheswaran, D. (1994), Promoting Country-of-origin as a Stereotype: Effects of Consumer Expertise and Attribute Strength on Product Evaluations, Journal of Consumer Research, 21, 354-65.

Mai, L.W. and Zhao, H. (2004). The Characteristics of Supermarket Shoppers in Beijing. International Journal of Retail and Distribution Management, 32, 56-62.

Maidique, M. and Zirger, B. J. (1984). A Study of Success and Failure in Product Innovation: The Case of the U.S. Electronics Industry. IEEE Transactions on Engineering Management, EM-31 (4), 192-203.

Malhotra, N.K. (1996). Marketing Research: An Applied Orientation. 2nd ed.. NJ, Upper Saddle River: Prentice-Hall.

Man, Zhijie (1996). Economics before Adam Smith, Peking University Press.

Mantel, S. and Kardes, F. (1999). The Role of Direction of Comparison, Attribute-based Processing, and Attitude-based Processing in Consumer Preference. Journal of Consumer Research, 25 (March), 335–52.

Mao, Zedong (1968). The Investigation Report on the Peasant Movement in Hunan, Mao Zedong Anthology: 13-15. Beijing, China: People's Publishing House.

Mao, Zedong (1978). A Debate on Agricultural Cooperation and Current Class Struggle, Mao Zedong Anthology. Volume 5: 196. Beijing, China: People's Publishing House.

Mao, Zedong (1999a). The Boundary between China and Nepal should Keep Peace and Friendship Forever, in Mao Zedong Collection, Vol. 8, Beijing: People's Press, pp. 162.

Mao, Zedong (1999b). Strengthen the Guidance to Technological Innovation and Technological Revolutionary Movement, in Mao Zedong Collection, Vol. 8, Beijing: People's Press, pp. 152.

Mao, Zedong (1999c). Speech Delivered at an Enlarged Working Conference of the Party Central Committee, in Mao Zedong Collection, Vol. 8, Beijing: People's Press, pp. 301.

Mao, Zedong (1999d). Speech Delivered at an Enlarged Working Conference of the Party Central Committee, in Mao Zedong Collection, Vol. 8, Beijing: People's Press, pp. 291-293.

Mariampolski, H. (2001). Qualitative Market Research. CA, Thousand Oaks: Sage.

Markus, M.L. (1994). Electronic Mail as the Medium of Managerial Choice. Organization Science, 5(4), 502-527.

Martin, I. M. and Eroglu, S. (1993). Measuring a Multi-Dimensional Construct: Country Image, Journal of Business Research, 28 (3), 191-210

Marx and Engels (1995). Marx and Engels Collection, Vol. 4, Beijing: People's Press, pp.171.

Marx K. and Engels F. (1962). Marx and Engels Collected Works Vol. 37: To Otto von Boenigk, People's Publishing House.

Marx, K. and Engels, F (1973), The Theory of Surplus Value Chapter 10: The Cost Price Theory of Ricardo and Adam Smith (Critical Part), Vol. 26, No. 2, People's Publishing House.

Marx, K. (1966), Capital, Vol. 3, People's Publishing House.

Marx, K. (1975). Capital Vol. 1, People's Publishing House.

Marx, K. and Engels, F. (1962), Criticism on Political Economics, Vol. 13, People's Publishing House.

Marx, K. and Engels, F. (1972), Theory of Surplus Value, Chapter 3: Adam Smith, Vol. 26, No.1, People's Publishing House.

Marx, K. and Engels, F. (1972). Preamble of the Civil War in France, Marx and Engels Anthology. Volume 2: 335. Beijing, China: People's Publishing House.

Marx, K. and Engels, F. (1976). Das Kapital: The Letters to Conrad. Schmidt, Beijing: People's Press.

Marx, K. and Engels, F. (1995). Peasant Issue in the France and Germany, selections of Marx and Engels Anthology Volume. 4, Beijing, China: People's Publishing House.

Marx, Karl and Frederick Engels (1962), "Criticism on Political Economics", in Karl Marx and Frederick Engels, Vol. 13, Beijing: People's Publishing House.

Marx, Karl and Frederick Engels (1972), "Theory of Surplus Value", in Karl Marx and Frederick Engels, Vol. 26, No. 3, Beijing: People's Publishing House.

Mayhew, A. (1980). Atomistic and Cultural Analyses in Economic Anthropology: An Old Argument Repeated// Adams, J.(Ed.) Institutional Economics: Contributions to the Development of Holistic Economics. Boston: Martinus Nijhoff: 72-81.

McAllister, D. (1995). Affect- and Cognition-based Trust as Foundations for Interpersonal Cooperation in Organizations. Academy of Management Review, 38(1), 24-59.

McConnell, Campbell R. and Brue, Stanley L. (2001). Economics: Principles, Problem, and Policies, Fifth Edition, Chapter Thirty,

Government and Market Failure: Public Goods, Externalities, and Information Problems, New York: Irwin McGraw-Hill, Inc.

McConnell, Campbell R., Brue, Stanley L. and Flynn, Sean Masaki (2011), Economics: Principles, Problems, and Policies, New York: McGraw-Hill Higher Education.

McGoldrick, P.J. and Ho, S.L. (1992). International Position: Japanese Department Stores in Hong Kong. European Journal of Marketing, 26(9), 61-73.

Menon, A., Bharadwaj, S.G. and Howell, R. (1996). The Quality and Effectiveness of Marketing Strategy: Effects of Functional and Dysfunctional Conflict in Interorganizational Relationships. Journal of the Academy of Marketing Science, 24, 299-313.

Messinger, P.R., Stroulia, E., Lyons, K., Bone, M., Niud, R.H., Smirnova, K. and Perelgute, S. (2009). Virtual Worlds-Past, Present and Future: New Direction in Social Computing. Decision Support Systems, 47(3), 204-228.

Michael J. Barone, Anthony D. Miyazaki, and Kimberly A. Taylor. (2000). The Influence of Cause-related Marketing on Consumer Choice: Does One Good Turn Deserve Another? Journal of the Academy of Marketing Science, 28(2), 248-262.

Michael, Parkin, & Bade, Robin, Part 2, How Markets Work, Economics: Canada in the Global Environment, Fourth Edition, Addison Wesley Longman, 2000, Toronto, Canada. p.130.

Michel Albert (1999), Capitalism Against Capitalism. London: Whurr Publishers.

Migrant Workers. Journal of Guangdong Institute of Public Administration. (2).

Millson, M. R., Raj, S.P. and Wilemon, D. (1992). A Survey of Major Approaches for Accelerating New Product Development. Journal of Product Innovation Management, 9(1), 53-69.

Ministry of Education (2006). Education Industrialization Will Ruin China's Education, Xiamen Daily, 18th February 2006.

Ministry of Education (2007). Insist Non-profit Education, Oppose to Education Industrialization, Xi'an Evening News, 17th October 2007.

Ministry of Education (2010). Education industrialization will destroy Chinese education, www.xinhuanet.com, Accessed in December 17, 2010.

Ministry of International Trade and Industry Website. (1997). Highlights of the 6th Basic Survey of Overseas Business activities of Japanese companies (Definite Report). Available online: http://www.miti.go.jp/intro-e/a225101e.html. Accessed on March 1, 2008.

Mintu, A.T., Calantone, R. J. and Gassenheimer, J. B. (1994). Towards Improving Cross-Cultural Research: Extending Churchill's Research Paradigm. Journal of International Consumer Marketing, 7(2), 5-23.

Mo, Kaiwei (2017). It is Unreliable for the S & P to Downgrade China's Banking Industry Ranking. Finance. Net, 2017-09-25.

Monga, A. B. and John, D. R. (2007). Cultural Differences in Brand Extension Evaluation: The Influence of Analytic Versus Holistic Thinking. Journal of Consumer Research, 33, 529-536.

Montoya-Weiss, M. M. and Calantone, R. J. (1994). Determinants of New Product Performance: A Review and Meta-Analysis. Journal of Product Innovation Management, 11(5), 397-418.

Moore, D., Harris, W. and Chen, H. (1995). Affect Intensity: An Individual Difference Response to Advertising Appeals. Journal of Consumer Research, 22 (2), 154– 64.

Moorman, C. and Slotegraaf, R. J. (1999). The Contingency Value of Complementary Capabilities in Product Development. Journal of Marketing Research, 36 (2), 239-257.

Morgan, R.M. and Hunt, S.D. (1994). The Commitment-Trust Theory of Relationship Marketing. Journal of Marketing, 58 (3), 20-38.

Morrison, Allistar. (1989). Tourism and Hospitality Marketing. NY, Albany: Delmar.

Mortensen, L. and Nicholas, G. (2010). Riding the Tourism Train? Navigating Intellectual Property Heritage and Community Based Approaches to Cultural Tourism. Anthropology News, 51, 11-12.

Mu, J. Peng, G. and MacLachlan, D.L. (2009). Effect of Risk Management on NPD Performance. Technovation, 29 (3), 170–180.

Mu, Ming. and Wang, Juan (2007). Regional Clusters of SMEs Tourism Marketing and Its Applicability. Learning and Practice, 2, 46-47.

Mu, R. and Fan, Y. (2011). Framework for Building National Innovation Capacity in China. Journal of Chinese Economic and Business Studies, 9(4), 317-327.

Myers, M. B., Calantone, R. J., Page, T. J., Jr. and Taylor, C. R. (2000). An Application of Multiple-Group Causal Models in Assessing Cross-Cultural Measurement Equivalence. Journal of International Marketing, 8 (4), 108-121.

Nabin. MH., Sgro, PM., Nguyen. X. & Chao. CC. (2016). State-owned Enterprises,

Narver, J. C., Slater, S. F. and MacLachlan, D. L. (2004). Responsive and Proactive Market Orientation and New-Product Success. Journal of Product Innovation Management, 21(5), 334-347.

Narver, J.C. and Slater, S.F. (1990). The Effect of a Market Orientation on Business Profitability. Journal of Marketing, 54 (4), 80-93.

Nash，J. (1981). Ethnographic Aspects of the Word Capitalist System. Annual Review of Anthropology，1981（10）：393—423.

Nash，J. (1981). Ethnographic Aspects of the Word Capitalist System. Annual Review of Anthropology，1981（10）：393—423.

Nass, C. and Moon, Y. (2000). Machines and Mindlessness: Social Responses to Computers. Journal of Social Issues, 56(1), 81-103.

Nation Bureau of Statistics of the People's Republic of China. (2015). The Statistics Bulletin

National Bureau of Statistics (2015). New Normal, New Strategy, New Development---Getting Outstanding Achievements in China's Economic and Social Development during the "Twelfth

Five-year Plan" Period. National Bureau of Statistics of the People's Republic of China, 2015-10-13.

National People's Congress (2006). The 11th Five-Year Plan for National Economic and Social Development of the People's Republic of China, Xinhua Net, 16th March 2006.

National People's Congress (2011). The 12th Five-Year Plan for National Economic and Social Development of the People's Republic of China, Xinhua News Agency, 16th March 2011.

Nelson, M. R. and Paek, H. J. (2005). Cross-cultural Differences in Sexual Advertising Content in a Transnational Women's magazine. Sex Roles, 53, 371-384.

Nelson, P. (1970). Information and Consumer Behavior, Journal of Political Economy, 78, 311-329.

Netemeyer, R., Durvasula, S. and Lichtenstein, D. (1991). A Cross-national Assessment of the Reliability and Validity of the CETSCALE. Journal of Marketing Research, 28, 320-327.

Network of China (2010). NDRC: The coverage of basic medical insurance has exceeded 95%, china.com.cn, Accessed in December 29, 2010.

Nguyen, T. D. (2009). Place Development: Attributes and Business Customer Satisfaction in Tien Giabg Province Vietnam. Journal of Macromarketing, 29 December, 384-391.

Ni, Shixiong (2001). Theory of Contemporary International Relations. Shanghai: Fudan University Press.

Niu, Ruofeng (1997). The Theoretical Framework of Agriculture and Industry Integrated Management, Rural Economy in China. Volume 5.

North, Douglass C. (1988), The Rise of The Western World, Beijing: Xueyuan Press.

North, Douglass C. (1994), Institution, Institutional Change and Economic Performance, Shanghai: Joint Publishing Press.

Norton, J., Parry, M. E. and Song, M. (1994). Integrating Rand and Marketing: A Comparison of Practices in the Japanese and

American Chemical Industries. IEEE Transactions on Engineering Management, 41(1), 5-20.
Nye, Joseph S. Jr. (1990). Soft Power. Foreign Policy, No. 80, Twentieth Anniversary (Autumn, 1990), pp. 153-171.The Changing Nature of World Power, Political Science Quarterly, Vol. 105(2):177-192.
Oates, B.J. (2006). Researching Information Systems and Computing. CA, Thousand Oaks: Sage.
Okada, Erica Mina (2005). Justification Effects on Consumer Choice of Hedonic and Utilitarian Goods. Journal of Marketing Research, 42(1). 43-53.
Okechuku, C. (1994). The Importance of Product Country of Origin: A Conjoint Analysis of the USA, Canada, Germany, and the Netherlands. European Journal of Marketing, 28(4), 5-19.
Oliver, R.L. (1997). Satisfaction: A Behavioral Perspective on the Consumer. New York: McGraw Hill.
Olshansky, S.J. (2009). Future Trends in Human Longevity: Implications for Investments, Pension and the Global Economy. Pensions, 14, (3), 149-163.
Olson, E. M., Walker, O.C., Jr. and Ruekert, R. W. (1995). Organizing for Effective New Product Development: The Moderating Role of Product Innovativeness. Journal of Marketing, 59 (1), 48-62.
Ondrejka, C.R. (2006). Escaping the Gilded Cage: User Created Content and Building the Metaverse. in The State of Play: Law, Games, and Virtual Worlds by Balkin J.M. and Noveck, B.S. (Eds.). New York: New York University Press.
Ortiz，S.（Ed. 1983). Economic Anthropology：Topics and Theories. Lanham，MD：University Press of America and Society for Economic Anthropology.
Ou, W.M., Abratt, R. and Dion, P. (2006). The Influence of Retailer Reputation on Store Patronage. Journal of Retailing and Consumer Services, 13, 221-230.

Özsomer, A. and Altares, S. (2008), Global Brand Purchase Likelihood: A Critical Synthesis and Integrated Conceptual Framework. Journal of International Marketing, 16(4), 1-28.

Padsakoff, P. and Organ, D. (1986). Self-Reports in Organizational Research: Problem and Prospects, Journal of Management, 12 (4), 531-544.

Page, R. and Aaron, B. (2005). Age-Related Differences in Responses to Emotional Advertisements. Journal of Consumer Research, 32, 343-354.

Paliwoda, Stanley J. and John K. Ryans (2008). International Business vs. International Marketing. UK, Cheltenham: Edward Elgar Publishing.

Panitz, B. (2000). A Promising Future. Restaurant USA: The Magazine of the National Restaurant Association, 20(2), 13-18.

Papadopoulos, N. and Heslop, L. A. (1990). A Comparative Image Analysis of Domestic Versus Imported Products, International Journal of Research in Marketing, 7, 283-294.

Papadopoulos, N. and Heslop, L. A. (1993). Product and Country Images: Impact and Role in International, Marketing. New York: Haworth Press.

Pappu, R., Quester, P. and Cooksey, R. (2006). Country Image and Consumer-based Brand Equity: Relationships and Implications for International Marketing. Journal of International Business Studies, 38, 726-745.

Parasuraman, A., L. L. Berry, and V. A. Zeithaml. (1991). Understanding Customer Expectations of Service. Sloan Management Review, 52(3), 39-48.

Parasuraman, A., V. A. Zeithaml, and L. L. Berry. (1985). A Conceptual Model of Service Quality and Its Implications for Future Research. Journal of Marketing, Fall, 41-50.

Parry, M. E. and Song, M. (1994), Identifying New Product Success in China. Journal of Product Innovation Management, 11(1), 15-30.

Peltier, J. and Schibrowsky, J. (1994). Need for Cognition, Advertisement Viewing Time and Memory for Advertising Stimuli. Advertising Consumer Research, 21(1), 244-50.

Peng, M. W. (2009). Global Business. OH, Mason: South-Western Cengage Learning.

people tell their feelings, Shanxi Daily.

People's Bank of China, Financial Statistics Report of the First Half of 2011, http://www.pbc.gov.cn, Accessed in July 2017.

People's Daily (2011), Investigation on the arbitrary charges on Ministry of Education: the interest sharer of competent department, September 16, 2011.

People's Daily (2011). The report of adverse drug reaction was published in 2010: two types of drugs face relatively significant risk, April 26, 2011.

Percy, L. and Rossiter, J. (2006). A Model of Brand Awareness and Brand Attitude

Perry, Elizabeth (2014). Growing Pains: Challenges for a Rising China. Daedalus, 143(2):5-13.

Peter, R., Mark, B. Aukje, T. and Marcia, L. (2008). Face to Face with White Rabbit-Sharing Ideas in Second Life. New Zealand: Victoria University of Wellington

Petty, R.E., J.T. Cacipoop, and D. Schumann (1983). Central and Peripheral Routes to Advertising Effectiveness: The Moderating Role of Involvement. Journal of Consumer Research. 10, 135-146.

Pharr, J. (2005). Synthesizing Country-of-origin Research from the Last Decade: Is the Concept Still Salient in an Era of Global Brands? Journal of Marketing: Theory and Practice, 13 (4), 34-45

Phau, I. and Suntornnond, V. (2006). Dimensions of Consumer Knowledge and its Impacts on Country of Origin Effects among Australia Consumers: A Case of Fast-consuming Product. Journal of Consumer Marketing, 23 (1), 34-42.

Phillips, L. (1981). Assessing Measurement Error in Key Informant Reports: A Methodological Note on Organizational Analysis in Marketing. Journal of Marketing Research, 18, 395-415.

Pillsbury, R. (1998). No Foreign Food: The American Diet in Time and Place. CO, Boulder: Westview Press.

Podoshen, J.S., Li, L. and Zhang, J. (2011). Materialism and Conspicuous Consumption in China: A Cross Cultural Examination. International Journal of Consumer Studies, 35, 17-25.

Podsakoff, P.M. and Organ, D. (1986). Self-Reports in Organizational Research: Problems and Prospects. Journal of Management, 12, 531-543.

Pollay, R. W. (1983). Measuring the Cultural Values Manifest in Advertising. in Current Issues and Research, in Advertising by J. H. Leigh and C. R. Martin, Jr. (Eds.). Ann Arbor: Graduate School of Business, Division of Research, University of Michigan. 72-92.

Pollay, R. W. and Gallagher, K. (1990). Advertising and Cultural Values: Reflections in the Distorted Mirror. International Journal of Advertising, 9, 359-372.

Pooler, J. (2003). Why We Shop: Emotional Rewards and Retail Strategies. CT, Westport: Praeger.

Porter, M. E. (1980), Competitive Strategy. New York: Free Press.

Porter, M. E. (1986). Competition in Global Industries. Boston: Harvard Business School Press.

Porter, Michael E. (1990). Competitive Advantage of Nations. Beijing: CITIC Publishing House.

Powers, P.J. (2000). Reports on Foreign Supermarkets Woes are Misleading. China Business Review, 27, 54.

Price: Theory & Practice. (1).

Pucik, V. (1999). When Performance Does Not Matter: Human Resource Management in Japanese Owned U.S. Affiliates in Japanese Multinationals Abroad: Individual and Organizational

Learning by S.L. Beechler and A. Bird. (Eds.). New York: Oxford University Press. 169–188.

Purcell, P. J. (2007). Pension Sponsorship and Participation. Journal of Pension Planning and Compliance, 24(4), 45-46.

Purcell, P. J. (2009). Older Workers: Employment and Retirement Trends. Journal of Deferred Compensation, 5, 98- 99.

Puto, C. P. and Wells, W. D. (1984). Informational and Transformational Advertising: The Differential Effects of Time. Advances in Consumer Research. 11, 638-643.

Qi, Changfu (2006). Li Yizhong disclosed that there were 5 forms of corruption hidden behind safety accident, http://www.xinhuanet.com, Accessed in February 10, 2006.

Qi, F. (2005). Building a New Pension Mode with Chinese Characteristics. Economic Issues Inquiry, 2,59.

Qi, Zhongxi (2006). In 2005, the Operation Performance of the Central Enterprises Hit a Higher Record. Xinhua Net, 2006-01-26.

Qiu, Yuanlun (1988), The Steady Development of the Federal Republic of German Economy, Hunan: Hunan People's Publishing House.

Ramya, Neelamegham and Dipark, Jain. (1999). Consumer Choice Process for Experience Goods: An Econometric Model and Analysis.Journal of Marketing Research, 36(3), 373-386.

Rao, Akshay R., Mark E. Bergen, and Scott Davis. (2000). How to Fight a Price War. Harvard Business Review, 78 (2), 107-117.

Rappa, M. (2009). Business Models on the Web. Available online: http://digitalenterprise.org/models/models.pdf. Accessed on April 10, 2017.

Ratchford, B. (1987). New Insights about the FCB Grid. Journal of Advertising Research, 27 (4), 24-38.

Reeves, B. and Nass, C.I. (1996). The Media Equation: How People Treat Computers, Television and New Media Real People and Places. CA, Stanford: CSLI Publications.

Ren, L., Xue, G. and Krabbendam, K. (2010). Sustainable Competitive Advantage and Marketing Innovation within Firms: A Pragmatic

Approach for Chinese Firms. Management Research Review, 33 (1), 79-89.

Resnik A. and Stern B. (1977). An Analysis of Information Content in Television Advertising. Journal of Marketing, 41 (1), 50-53.

Ritzer, George. (2000), The McDonaldization of Society. CA, Thousand Oaks, Pine Forge Press.

Ritzer, George. (2007), The Globalization of Nothing 2. CA, Thousand Oaks, Pine Forge Press.

Roberts, J.and Cayla, J. (2009). Global Branding. in The SAGE Handbook of International Marketing by Kotabe, M. and Helsen, K. (Eds.).CA, Thousand Oaks: Sage.346-360.

Robertson, R. (1987). Globalization and Societal Modernization: A Note on Japan and Japanese Religion. Sociological Analysis, 47, 35-42.

Rodrigues, C. (2001). International Management: A Cultural Approach. Cincinnati, OH: South-Western College Publishing.

Rojas, D S. and Turner, E. (2011). Spam and Pop Tarts? Joint Response to Anthropology and Tourism. Anthropology News, V 52b # 4.

Romaniuk, J.and Bogomolova, S. (2005). Variation in Brand Trust Scores. Journal of Targeting, Measurement and Analysis for Marketing, 13(4), 363-373.

Ronald. H. Coase (1990), Firm, Market and Law, Shanghai: Joint Publishing Press.

Rosenbloom, A. and Haefner, J. (2009). Country-of-origin Effects and Global Brand Trust: A First Look. Journal of Global Marketing, 22(4), 267-278.

Rosenbloom, A., Marcheva, A. and Haefner, J. (2011). Global Brand Perceptions of Bulgarian Consumers: Some Contemporary Insights in Mechanisms for Managing the Development of Socio-economic Systems by Martyakova, E. (Eds.). Donetsk, Ukraine: DVNZ Don NTU, 269-276.

Roth, M. and Romeo, J. (1992). Matching Product Category and Country Image Perceptions: A Framework for Managing

Country of Origin Effects. Journal of International Business Studies, 23(3), 477-497.

Rothwell, R. (1972). Factors for Success in Industrial Innovation from SAPPHO. A Comparative Study of Success and Failure in Industrial Innovation. Brighton, Sussex: S.P.R.U.

Rotter, J. (1971). Generalized Expectancies for Interpersonal Trust. American Psychologist, 35, 1-7.

Rowley, J., Baregheh, A. and Sambrook, S. (2011). Towards an Innovation-type Mapping Tool. Management Decision, 49 (1), 73-86.

Rowley, T., Behrens, D. and Karckhardt, D. (2000). Redundant Governance Structures: An Analysis of Structural and Relational Embeddedness in the Steel and Semiconductor Industries. Strategic Management Journal, 21(3), 369-386.

Ruan, Shitao. (2009). Advantages and Disadvantages of "Shanzhai-Star" Being Spokesperson. Advertiser Market Watch, 9, 139.

Rubera, G. and Kirca, A. H. (2012). Firm Innovativeness and its Performance Outcomes: A Meta-Analytic Review and Theoretical Integration. Journal of Marketing, 76(3), 130-147.

Ruekert, R. W. and Walker, O.C. (1987b). Marketing's Interaction with Other Functional Units: A Conceptual Framework and Empirical Evidence. Journal of Marketing, 51 (1), 1-19.

Ruekert, R.W. and Walker, O. C. (1987a). Interactions Between Marketing and Rand Departments in Implementing Different Business Strategies. Strategic Management Journal, 8, 233-248.

Ruiz, S. and Sicilia, M. (2004). The Impact of Cognitive and/or Affective Processing Styles on Consumer Response to Advertising Appeals. Journal of Business Research, 57 (6): 657-664.

Rust, R.T., Lemon, K.N. and Zeithaml, V.A. (2004). Return on Marketing: Using Customer Equity to focus marketing strategy. Journal of Marketing, 68(1), 109-127.

Ruyter, K. and Scholl, N. (1998). Positioning Qualitative Market Research: Reflections from Theory and Practice. Qualitative Market Research, 1, 7-14.

Salter, D., Evans, N. and Forney, D. (1997). Test-retest of the Myers—Briggs Type Indicator: An Examination of Dominant Function. Educational Psychology Measurement, 57 (4), 590-597.

Samiee, S. and Jeong, I. (1994). Cross-cultural Research in Advertising: Assessment Methodologies. Journal of the Academy of Marketing Science, 22, 205-217.

Samiee, S., Shimp, T. and Sharma, S. (2005). Brand OriginRecognition Accuracy: Its Antecedents and Consumers' cognitive Limitations. Journal of International Business Studies, 36 (4), 379-397.

Sarrico. CS. & Rosa. MJ. (2016). Supply Chain Quality Management in Education.

Say，Jean Baptiste (1983), Introduction to Political Economics, Hong Kong: The Commercial Press.

Schaefer, A.D., Hermans, C.M. and Parker, R. S. (2004). A Cross-cultural Exploration of Materialism in Adolescents. International Journal of Consumer Studies, 28, 399-411.

Schermerhorn, J. R., Jr. and Nyaw, M.K. (1991). Managerial Leadership in Chinese Industrial Enterprises in Organization and Management in China 1979-1990 by Shenkar, O. (Eds.). London: M. E. Sharpe, 9-21.

Schwartz, H. M. and S. M. Davis. (1981). Matching Corporate Culture and Business Strategy. Organizational Dynamics, 59, 91-98.

Sekaran, U. (1983). Methodological and Theoretical Issues and Advancements in Cross-Cultural Research. Journal of International Business Studies, 14 (4), 61-73.

Senguder, T. (2000). Effects of Values and Culture on International Consumer Satisfaction. Journal of American Academy of Business, Cambridge, 12 (1), 96-103.

Senguder, Turan. (2007). Cross-National Customer Satisfaction Judgment in Turkey and the United States. in Perspectives in

Consumer Behavior: An Anthropological Approach by S. Demirdjian, T. Senguder, and R. Tian (Eds.). Fort Worth, TX: Fellows Press of America. 63-75.

Sha, Z. (2010). Analysis on the De-Marketization of Basic Livelihood Services.

Shantou Daily (2011). Changes on 'remedial teaching fee' and 'gratitude card fee, July 20, 2011.

Shanxi Evening News (2010). In the first half of 2010, the per capita disposable income of urban residents in Shanxi Province increase 10 percent than that in the same period of previous year, July 23, 2010.

Sharma, S., Shimp, T. and Shin, J. (1995). Consumer Ethnocentrism: ATest of Antecedents and Moderators. Journal of the Academy of Marketing Science, 23(1), 26-37.

Shavitt, S. and Zhang, J. (2004). Advertising and culture. Encyclopedia of Applied psychology, 47-51.

Sheng, S. and Yan, M. (2011). China vs. the United States: Market Connections and Trade Relations. International Journal of China Marketing, 2(1), 45-56.

Sheng, Y. S. and Mullen, M. R. (2011). A Hybrid Model for Export Market Opportunity Analysis. International Marketing Review, 28(2), 163-182.

Sherman, J. D., Souder, W. E. and Jenssen, S. A. (2000). Differential Effects of the Primary Forms of Cross-Functional Integration on Product Development Cycle Time. Journal of Product Innovation Management, 17(4), 257-267.

Shi, Lin (2002). Economic Anthropology. Beijing: Central Minzu University Press.

Shi, Zhengyi (1993). An Introduction to Ethnic Economics, Beijing: Minzu Publishing House.

Shimp, T. A. and Sharma, S. (1987). Consumer Ethnocentrism: Construction and Validation of the CETSCALE. Journal of Marketing Research, 24, 280-289.

Silverstein, B. (2009). Ethnic Food Brands: A Guide to the World on a Shelf. Available online: http://www.brandchannel.com/features_effect.asp?pf_id=477. Accessed in Aug 2017.

Simonazzi, A. (2009). Care Regimes and National Employment Models. Cambridge Journal of Economics, 33, 211 – 232.

Simpson. SNY. (2014). Boards and governance of state-owned enterprises. Corporate

Sin, L. Y. M.and Ho, S. C. (2001). An Assessment of Theoretical and Methodological Development in Consumer Research on Greater China: 1979–1997. Asia Pacific Journal of Marketing and Logistics, 13(1), 3–42.

Skrbis, Z., Kendall, G. and Woodward, I. (2004). Locating Cosmopolitanism: Between Humanist Ideal and Grounded Social Category. Theory and Society, 21, 115–129.

Slater, Charles C. (1979) Macro-Marketing Distributive Processes From a Societal Perspective Boulder Colorado: Graduate School of Business Administration.

Slater, Charles C. and Jenkins, Dorothy (1979) Systems Approach To Comparative Macromarketing in Macro-Marketing: New Steps In The Learning Curve by George Fisk and Robert Nason (Eds.). Boulder Colorado: Graduate School of Business.

Social Sciences Academic Press (2010), Annual Report on International Politics and Security, Published in December 2010.

Sojka, J. and Giese, J. (1997). Thinking and/or Feeling: An Examination of Interaction between Processing Styles. Advertising Consumer Research. 24, 438-442.

Solomon, Michael R. (2004). Consumer Behavior: Buying, Having and Being. 6th ed. NJ, Upper Saddle River: Prentice Hall.

Song, M. and Montoya-Weiss, M. M. (1998). Critical Development Activities for Really New Versus Incremental Products. Journal of Product Innovation Management, 15(2), 124-135.

Song, M. and Parry, M. E. (1994). The Dimensions of Industrial New Product Success and Failure in State Enterprises in the People's

Republic of China. Journal of Product Innovation Management, 11(2), 105-118.
Song, M. and Parry, M. E. (1996). What Separates Japanese New Product Winners from Losers. Journal of Product Innovation Management, 13 (3), 1-14.
Song, M. and Parry, M. E. (1997a). The Determinants of Japanese New Product Successes. Journal of Marketing Research, 34 (1), 64-76.
Song, M. and Parry, M. E. (1997b). A Cross-National Comparative Study of New Product Development Processes: Japan and the United States. Journal of Marketing, 61 (2), 1-18.
Song, M., Montoya-Weiss, M. M. and Schmidt, J. B. (1997). Antecedents and Consequences of Cross-Functional Cooperation: A Comparison of Rand, Manufacturing, and Marketing Perspectives. Journal of Product Innovation Management, 14(1), 35-47.
Song, Yan and Yin Lu. (2010). Research on "Shanzhai" Pattern Based on "Segment Zero"-A Case of the Development of "Shanzhai" Mobile Telephone. Brand Management. 6,39-46.
Spiggle, S. (1994). Analysis and Interpretation of Qualitative Data in Consumer Research. Journal of Consumer Behavior, 21, 491-503.
Spreng, R.A., Mackenzie, S. B. and Olshasky, R. W. (1996). A Reexamination for the Determinants of Consumer Satisfaction. Journal of Marketing, 60 (3), 15-32.
Stammler, F. (2008). Reindeer Nomads Meet the Market: Culture, Property and Globalization at the "End of the Land". Halle Studies in the Anthropology of Eurasia. LIT Verlag Press.
Statistical Bureau (2011). The development and achievement of education business are prominent, March 10, 2011.
Statistical Bureau (2011). The Statistical Monitoring Report on the Progress of Moderately Prosperous Society Construction in all Aspects.

Steenkamp, J-E., Batra, R. and Alden, D. (2003). How Perceived Brand Globalness Creates Brand Value. Journal of International Business Studies, 34 (1), 53-65.

Steiger, J. H. (1989). EzPATH: Causal Modeling. IL, Evanston: SYSTAT.

Stewart, D. and Love, W. (1968). A General Canonical Correlation Index. Psychological Bulletin, 70, 160-163.

St-Maurice I., Sussmuth-Dyckerhoff, C. and Tsai H. (2008). What's New with the Chinese Consumer. The McKinsey Quarterly, 45, October: 1-8.

Stuart, B. and Brand, J.M. (2008). Value in Virtual Worlds: An Axiological Approach. Journal of Electronic Commerce Research, 9(3): 195-206.

Su, H., Zhao, M. & Wang, S. (2013). Labor Mobility, Industrial Transfer and Coordinated

Su, J. (2016). View the Supply-side Reform from the Perspective of Upgrading of High-end

Sun, S. (2007). On Cross-cultural Pragmatic Failure in English Advertisements Translated from Chinese, Sino-US English Teaching, 4(6), 60-65.

Sundar, S.S. and Nass, C.I. (2000). Source Orientation in Human-Computer Interaction: Programmer, Networker, Or Independent Social Actor"? Communication Research, 27(6): 683-703.

Sunderland, P. and R. M. Denny. (2007). Doing Anthropology in Consumer Research. CA, Walnut Creek: Left Coast Press.

Swike, E., Thompson, S. and Vasquez, C. (2008). Piracy in China. Business Horizons, 51(6), 493-500.

Swink, M. (2002). Product Development – Faster, On-Time. Research-Technology Management 45 (4), 50-58.

Syring, D. (2009). La Vida Matizada: Time Sense, Everyday Rhythms, and Globalized Ideas of Work. Anthropology and Humanism, 34, 119-34.

Tai, S. H. (2008). Relationship between the Personal Values and Shopping Orientation of Chinese Consumers. Asia Pacific Journal of Marketing, 20(4), 381-395.

Tai, S.H.C. (2005). Shopping Style of Working Chinese Females. Journal of Retailing and Consumer Services, 12, 191-203.

Talamasca, A. (2008). Second Life Addiction: Do You Have a Problem? Available online http://www.secondlifeinsider.com/2006/10/13/sl-addiction-do-you-have-aproblem. Accessed on 12 Jun 2017.

Tang, E.P., Chan, R.Y.K. and Tai, S.H.C. (2001). Emotional Influence of Environmental Cues on Chinese Consumers in a Leisure Service Setting. Journal of International Consumer Marketing, 14, 67-87.

Tang, Weijie (2008). China's Thirty-year Average Annual Economic Growth Rate is More Than Three Times Than that of the Same Period in the World. China News, 2008-12-18.

Taniguchi, T. (2005). A Cold Peace: The Changing Security Equation in Northeast Asia. Orbis, 49 (3), 445–457.

Tao, Duanfang (2012). The Western Capitalism Encountered Crisis. International Herald Report, 2012-02-15.

Tao, Yonghou. (2010). Formation Mechanism of Shanzhai Model and Its Implications to Organizational Innovation. China Soft Science, 11,123-143.

Tauber, E. M. (1972). Why do People Shop? Journal of Marketing, 36, 46-49.

Taylor, B. (1999). Japanese Management Style in China? Production Practices in Japanese Manufacturing Plants. New Technology, Work and Employment, 14(2), 129-142.

Temporal, P. (2010). Advanced Brand Management: Managing Brands in a Changing World. 2nd ed. Singapore: John Wiley and Sons.

The National Bureau of Statistics (2010). Record of National Economic Performance in 2009, Office of News of the State Council, China Network, 21st January 2010.

The National Bureau of Statistics, PRC. (2011). Statistical Yearbook of China in 2011. Beijing: China Statistics Press.

The World & Chongqing. (11).

Thoelke, J. M., Hultink, E. J. and Robben, H. S. J. (2001). Launching New Product Features: A Multiple Case Examination. Journal of Product Innovation Management, 18(1), 3-14.

Thomas, Reardon and Julio A. Berdegue. (2002). The Rapid Rise of Supermarket in Latin America: Challenges and Opportunities for De-elopement. Development Policy Review, 371-388.

Thomlinson, John. (1991). Cultural imperialism: a critical introduction. MD, Baltimore: Johns Hopkins University Press.

Thompson, C.J. (1997). Interpreting Consumers: A Hermeneutical Framework for Deriving Marketing Insights from the Texts of Consumers' Consumption Stories. Journal of Marketing Research, 34, 438-455.

Tian, G. & Dai, Q. (2012). Critique of Pan-Marketization. Beijing: China

Tian, G. & Wang, Y. (2015). China and the World: towards a Higher Form of Integration (In

Tian, Guang (2013). Paradigm of Economic Anthropology in China: Academic Thought of Yang Tingshuo's Interphase Operational Model. Journal of China Mizu University, Vo. 2013 (5):11-16.

Tian, Guang (2013). Paradigm of Economic Anthropology in China: Academic Thought of Yang Tingshuo's Interphase Operational Model. Journal of China Mizu University, Vo. 2013 (5):11-16.

Tian, Guang (2014). Economic Anthropology with Chinese Characteristics: Yang Tingshuo Xiangji Operational Theoretical Model. Anthropologist Vol. 17 (2): 311-318.

Tian, Guang and Dai, Qinqin (2012). Pan-market Critiques. Beijing: China Financial and Economic Publishing House.

Tian, Guang and Luo, Kanglong (2013). Economic Anthropology. Yinchuan: Ningxia People's Publishing House.

Tian, Guang, Dai, Qinqin, and Qi, Xiaoguang (2012). Strategic Thinking on National Operations: Based on Critique Thinking of

Pan-marketization, Journal of Shijiazhuang University of Economics, 2012 (2) :92-95.

Tian, Guang, Han, Guoliang et al. (1987). Choice and Development: Economic Revitalization of the Western Ethnic Regions in China, Beijing: Current Affairs Press, 1987.

Tian, Guang, Luo, Kanglong (2013). Economic Anthropology. Yinchuan, Ningxia: Ningxia People's Publishing House.

Tian, K. and Borges, L. (2011). Cross-Cultural Issues in Marketing Communications: An Anthropological Perspective of International Business. International Journal of China Marketing, 2(1), 110-126.

Tian, R. G. (2000). The Implications of Rights to Culture in Trans-National Marketing: An Anthropological Perspective. High Plains Applied Anthropologist, 20(2), 135-145.

Tian, R. G. and Camilla Wang (2002). China National Economies, in Worldmark Encyclopedia of National Economies by Pendergast Sara and Tom Pendergast. (Eds.) MI, Farmington Hills: Gale Group.

Tian, Robert G. (2002 a). Marketing in the 21st Century: Cross-cultural Issues, The Journal of the Association of Marketing Educators, 5(3), 70-77.

Tian, Robert G. (2002 b) Anthropological Approaches to Marketing: The New Practices in the 21st Century. Practicing Anthropology, 24(1), Spring 39-40.

Tie, Z. (2016). How to Implement the "Supply-side Reform" of Universities.

Tomás, J. and G. Arias. (1998). A Relationship Marketing Approach to Guanxi. European Journal of Marketing. 32(1/2), 145-156.

Tomlinson, J. (2007). Cultural Globalization in The Blackwell Companion to Globalization by G. Ritzer (Eds). MA, Madden, MA: Blackwell Publishing. 352-366.

Towner, S. J. (1994). Four Ways to Accelerate New Product Development. Long Range Planning, 27(2), 57-65.

Travel China Guide (2011). Bai Nationality. Available online: http://www.travelchinaguide.com/intro/nationality/bai/. Accessed in March 2011.

Trend Hunter World (2010). Asian Fast Food Booms: China Restaurant Industry Remains a Huge Growth Opportunity. Available online: http://www.trendhunter.com/trends/yumbrands. Accessed in August 2017.

Trott, P. (2005). Innovation Management and New Product Development. Harlow: Prentice-Hall.

Troy, L. C., Hirunyawipada, T. and Paswan, A. K. (2008). Cross-Functional Integration and New Product Success: An Empirical Investigation of the Findings. Journal of Marketing. 72(6), 132-145.

Tsang, A.S.L, Zhuang, G., Li, F. and Zhou, N. (2003). A Comparison of Shopping Behavior in Xi'an and Hong Kong Malls: Utilitarian Versus Non-utilitarian Shoppers. Journal of International Consumer Marketing, 16, 29-46.

Tse, D.K., Belk, R.W, and Zhou, N. (1989). Becoming a Consumer Society: A Longitudinal and Cross-cultural Content Analysis of Print Ads from Hong Kong, The People's Republic China, and Taiwan. Journal of Consumer Research, 15, 452-472.

Tushman, M.L. and Anderson, P. (1986). Technological Discontinuities and Organizational Environments. Administrative Science Quarterly, 31, 439-465.

Uncles, M. and He, T. (n.d.). A Window on Consumer Behavior Research in China. Available online: http://smib.vuw.ac.nz:8081/WWW/ANZMAC2006/documents/Uncles_Mark.pdf. Accessed on 12/6/2010.

Uncles, M.D. and Kwok, S. (2009). Patterns of Store Patronage in Urban China. Journal of Business Research, 62, 68-81.

Upadhyay, Y. and Singh, S. (2006). Preference for Domestic Goods: A Study of Consumer Ethnocentrism. The Journal of Business Perspective, 10(3), 59-68.

Urban, G. L. and Hauser, J. R. (1993) Design and Marketing of New Products. 2nd ed.., NJ, Englewood Cliffs: Prentice-Hall.

US-China Business Council. (2002). Gansu province. China Business Review, 29, 17-23.

Vedrashko, I. (2006). Advertising in Computer Games. MA, Cambridge: Massachusetts Institute of Technology.

Vic, K. (2007). Watch out Second Life: China Launches Virtual Universe with Seven Million Souls. Available online: http://www.guardian.co.uk/world/2007/jun/02/china.web2.0. Accessed on 2 June 2007.

Walle, Alf H. (2010) The Equitable Cultural Tourism Handbook. NC, Charlotte: Information Age Publications.

Wang, C.L., Siu, N.Y.M. and Hui, A.S.Y. (2004). Consumer Decision-making Style on Domestic and Important Brand Clothing. European Journal of Marketing, 38, 239-252.

Wang, G., Li, F. and Liu, X. (2008). The Development of the Retailing Industry in China: 1981-2005. Journal of Marketing Channel, 15, 145-166.

Wang, G., Li, F. and Lu, Q. (2006). An Empirical Study of Customer Satisfaction of Chained Hyper-markets in China: Based on Nationwide Survey Data of 20 Chained Hyper-markets. Management World, 6, 101-110.

Wang, Huning (1993). National Culture as the Soft Power, Journal of Fudan University (Social Science Edition), 1993 (3) :91-96.

Wang, J. (2006). On China's Population Aging. The Financial Field, 1, 238.

Wang, J. (2008). Brand New China: Advertising, Media, and Commercial Culture. MA, Cambridge: Harvard University Press

Wang, J. (2016). Supply-side Structural Reform Leads the New Normal. People's Daily. 2016 (1).

Wang, Ji Chi (2001). Corporate Cluster and Regional Development. Peking: Peking University Press, 239.

Wang, Lili and Sheng Dong. (2007). More Perspectives on "Shanzhai" Phenomenon. Advertising Grand Integrated. 9th Version, 136.

Wang, Nanti and Hou Zhenwu (2011). Cultural Awareness, Cultural Self-Sonfidence, and Cultural Self-Reliance. Mao Zedong and Deng Xiaoping Theory and Research, 2011 (08) :16 -17-75.

Wang, Q. & Lang, X. (2016). The Supporting Mode and Comparison of Urban Integration of

Wang, Qiang and Liu, Lijuan (2004). Education industrialization: a debate between angel and demon, Business Week, http://finance.sina.com.cn, Accessed in November 11, 2017.

Wang, S.G. (2009). Foreign Retailers in Post-WTO China: Stories of Success and Setbacks. Asia Pacific Business Review, 15(1), 59-77.

Wang, Xuejiang (2006). The spokesman of Ministry of Health admitted that the public hospitals have lost sight of their main objective, Xinhua Daily Telegraph, January 12.

Wang, Yan and Xu, Yong (1996). The Theoretical Basis of Agriculture Industrialization, Agricultural Economy Problem. Volume 12.

Wang, Z.M., Takao S. (1994). The Patterns of Human Resource Management: Eight Cases of Chinese-Japanese Joint Ventures and Two Cases of Wholly Japanese Ventures. Journal of Managerial Psychology, 9 (4), 12-22.

Watson, J. and Wright, K. (2000). Consumer Ethnocentrism and Attitudes Toward Domestic and Foreign Products. European Journal of Marketing, 34 (9/10), 1149-1166.

Watson, James. (1990). McDonald's in Hong Kong: Consumerism, Dietary Change, and the Rise of a Children's Culture in Golden Arches East: McDonald's in East Asia by James L. Watson (Eds.). Stanford: Stanford University Press. 78-109.

Watson. E. (2006). Golden Arches East: McDonald's in East Asia. Palo Alto: Stanford University Press.

Wei, L. and Williams, M. (2007). Innovations and Technology Research Laboratory. Sydney, NSW, Australia: University of Technology Press.

Wei, Shou Hua (2002). Dynamics of Competition in Clusters with Reference to a Case. China Industrial Economy, 175(10):27-34.

Wen, Jiabao (2006). Adhere to the Path of Peaceful Development and Promote Peace as well as Prosperity in the World-A Speech at the Welcoming Banquet Held by Australian Prime Minister Howard, China: Beijing Review.

Wen, Jiabao (2011). Government Work Report-The Fourth Session of the Eleventh National People's Congress, Beijing, China: People's Publishing House.

Westbrook, R. A. and Black, W. C. (1985). A Motivation-based Shopper Typology. Journal of Retailing, 61, 78-103.

Westbrook, R. A. and Reilly, M. D. (1983). Value Perception Disparity: An Alternative to the Disconfirmation of Expectation Theory of Consumer Satisfaction in Advances of Consumer Research by Bagozzi, R. P. and Tybout, A. M. (Eds). MI, Ann Arbor: Association of Consumer Research, 256-261.

Western Regions of China and Benefit Compensation. Asian Agricultural Research. (5).

Wilk, R.R. and Cliggett, L. (2007). Economies and Cultures: Foundations of Economic Anthropology (Second Edition). Boulder, CO: Westview Press.

Wittink, D.R., Vriens, M. and Burhenne, W. (1994). Commercial Use of Conjoint Analysis in Europe: Results and Critical Reflections. International Journal of Research in Marketing, 11(1), 41-52.

Wong, A. and Dean, A. (2009). Enhancing Value for Chinese Shoppers: The Contribution of Store and Customer Characteristics. Journal of Retailing and Consumer Sciences, 16, 123-134.

Wong, G.K. and Yu, L. (2003). Consumers' Perception of Store Image of Joint Venture Shopping Centers: First-tier Versus Second-tier Cities in China. Journal of Retailing and Consumer Services, 10, 61-70.

Wong, H.W. (1999). Japanese Bosses, Chinese Workers: Power and Control in a Hong Kong Megastore, England, Curzon Press.

Wong, M. and Hendry, C. (1999). Comparing International Human Resource Management Practices between Yaohan and Jusco in Hong Kong. Asia Pacific Business Review, 6 (1), 104-122.

World Bank (1993). China: Strategy of Supporting the Poor in 1990s, China Finance and Economy Press.

World Health Organization (2007). Global Age – Friendly Cities, A Guide. WHO Press, 5.

Wu, J. and Liu, D. (2007). The Effect of Trust and Enjoyment on Intention to Play Online Games. Journal of Electronic Commerce Research, 8(4): 128-140.

Wu, J., Li, P.T. and Rao, S. (2009). Why They Enjoy Virtual Game Worlds? An Empirical Investigation. Journal of Electronic Commerce Research, 9(3), 219-230.

Wu, Weiqun (2016). The 15th Anniversary of China's WTO Accession | Jumped to the Second from the Sixth Largest Economy in the World and Reduced the Total Tariff Level from 15.3% to 9.8%. Shobserver News. 2016-11-10.

Wu, Y. (2011). Innovation and Economic Growth in China: Evidence at the Provincial Level. Journal of the Asia Pacific Economy, 16(2), 129-142.

Wuchang, Zhang (2000), Economic Interpretation, The Commercial Press.

Xi'an Daily (2007). Firmly oppose education industrialization, October 23, 2011.

Xi'an Daily (2011). Frosty response of expensive medical expenses, April 9, 2011.

Xia, Mingqun (2009). Company Competitiveness Ranking is Released by the Academy of Social Sciences. Sina Finance, 2009-12-14.

Xia, Mingqun (2011). 2011 Top 100 State-owned Enterprises Ranking in China. Sina Finance, 2012-08-15.

Xia, Ya Ming and Lina Chen (2007) Wuhan China Optical Valley of Regional Branding. Contemporary Economics, Vol. 2007 (1): 14-19.

Xia, Ying (1995). Poverty and Development, People's Publishing House.

Xiao, G. and Kim, J. (2009). The Investigation of Chinese Consumer Values, Consumption Values, Life Satisfaction, and Consumption Behavior. Psychology and Marketing, 26, 610-624.

Xiao, Jian (2006). China Becomes the Fourth-largest Economy, http://www.sina.com.cn, Accessed in July 2006

Xiao, Jian (2006). China Becomes the Fourth-largest Economy, http://www.sina.com.cn, Accessed in July 2006

Xiaoqun, He and Shaojie Chen (2000). The Application of Conjoint Analysis in the Inquiry of Apartments. Statistical Research, 10 (12), 10-14.

Xie, Huanchi (2010), "The Audit Reports Present Four Big Attractions This Year", People's Court Daily, 24th June 2010.

Xin, Ling (2009). The National Bureau of Statistics Increases Chinese GDP of 2007, China becomes the third largest economy, The Southern Metropolis Daily, 16th January 2009.

Xinhua (2009). Regulation on Revitalisation of Electronic Information Industry. Available online: http://news.xinhuanet.com/fortune/2009-04/15/content_11191634.htm. accessed on: September 10, 2010.

Xinhua (2011). Investigation on the whopping medical expense owed by one patient after death in Guangdong, April 8, 2011.

Xinhua News Agency (2009). China Aims for 3.3 Trillion Yuan Restaurant Industry by 2013. Available online: http://news.xinhuanet.com/english/2009-01/26/content_10722259.htm. Accessed on August 2010.

Xu, Hongming. (2009). Adivon: Shanzhai Brands' Shanzhai Marketing. New Marketing. (2009)1, 44-46.

Yan, Qiuluwei (2011). Education industrialization, China Social Security, September 9, pp. 56.

Yan, R. (1994). To Reach China's Consumers, Adapt to Guo Qing. Harvard Business Review, September-October 1994, 66-67.

Yan, Xiaohong (2011). China's Textile Industry Will Accelerate the Transformation of Economic Development as the Main Line in the "Twelfth Five-Year Plan". Sohu News, 2011-06-29.

Yan, Xiaohong (2016). The Main Economic Indicators of the Chinese Textile Industry are Relatively Good during the "Twelfth Five-Year Plan". China News Network, 2016-01-14.

Yan, Zhijie (1996), Economics before Adam Smith, Beijing: Peking University Press.

Yang Tingshuo (1995). Interphase Operation Model. Guizhou: Guizhou Minzu Publishing House.

Yang, D., Fryxell, G. E. and Sie, A. K. Y. (2008). Anti-piracy Effectiveness and Managerial Confidence: Insights from Multinationals in China. Journal of World Business, 43(3), 321-339.

Yang, Shiyong (2010). Analysis of the Influence of Economic Globalization on Developing Countries. Knowledge Economy, Volume 7: 81-81.

Yang, Y. (2008). The Perfection of the Employment and Population Policies of China under the Condition of Population Aging. The Finance of China, 7, 46.

Yang, Z.L., Zhou, N. and Chen J. (2005). Brand Choice of Older Chinese Consumers. Journal of International Consumer Marketing, 17, 65-81.

Yau, O.H.M. and Steele, H.C. (2000). China Business: Challenges in the 21st Century. Hong Kong: The Chinese University Press.

Yee, N. (2009). The Norrathian Scrolls: A Study of Ever Quest. Available online: http://www.nickyee. com/eqt/report.html. Accessed on March 21, 2009.

Yin, Lu, and Li, Tianzhu (2010). Study on the General Disciplinarian of Shanzhai Phenomena and Its Policy Suggestion. Studies in Science of Science, 3, 321-328.

Yin, R.K. (2003). Case Study Research: Design and Methods. 3rd ed. CA, Thousand Oaks: Sage.

Zaheer, S. (1995). Overcoming the Liability of Foreignness. Academy of Management Journal, 38 (2), 341-360.

Zahra, S. J. and Covin, J. G. (1993). Business Strategy, Technology Policy and Firm Performance. Strategic Management Journal 14, 451-478.

Zaltman, G., Duncanand, R. and Holbek, J. (1973). Innovations and Organizations, New York: Wiley.

Zang, Y. and J.P. Neelankavil. (1997). The Influence of Culture on Advertising Effectiveness in China and the USA: Cross-cultural Study. European Journal of Marketing, 31(2), 134-149.

Zeithaml, A. Parasuraman and L. L. Berry (1990). Delivering Quality Service: Balancing Customer Perceptions and Expectations. New York: The Free Press.

Zeng, Hu (2008). Roundup: China's development achievement earns world-wide praise, http://news.xinhuanet.com/world/2008-09/23/content_10096738.htm, Accessed in September 23, 2008.

Zhan, W. and Ren, W. H. (2003), What Will the World Gain from China in Twenty Years? The China Business Review, 30 (2), 36-39.

Zhang and Lu, (2018). In 2015, the Total GDP of China exceeded 80 trillion yuan, a year-on year increase of 6.9%. Wangyi News, 2018-01-18.

Zhang, A., Zhang, Y. and Zhao, R. (2003). A Study of the Brand Efficiency and Productivity of Chinese Firms, Journal of Comparative Economics, 31 (3), 443-464.

Zhang, C. (2016). Understand "Supply-side Structural Reform". Economic Herald

Zhang, G. (2016). The Supply-side Reform in Education. Journal of Schooling

Zhang, J. (2004). Cultural Values Reflected in Chinese Advertisements: Self-construal and Persuasion Implications, unpublished doctoral dissertation, University of Illinois at Urbana-Champaign.

Zhang, J. and Shavitt, S. (2003). Cultural Values in Advertisements to the Chinese X-generation: Promoting Modernity and Individualism. Journal of Advertising, 32(1), 23-33.

Zhang, N. (2009). The Influence of the Population Aging on the Labor Resources of China. The Economy of North China, 8, 10.

Zhang, Shu. (2005). Make A Company Localized or Personalized: A Case Study of A Japanese Electric Subsidiary in Shanghai, unpublished master thesis, the University of Hong Kong.

Zhang, W. (2016). The Reform of State-owned Enterprises is the Real Supply-side Reform (In

Zhang, Wuchang (2000), Economic Interpretation, Hong Kong: The Commercial Press.

Zhang, X., Grigoriou, N. and Li, L. (2008). The Myth of China as a Single Market: The Influence of Personal Value Differences on Buying Decisions. International Journal of Market Research, 50, 377-402.

Zhang, Xiaoqing (2018). Industry Picks Up. China's Ship Industry Still Loses 2.3 Billion last Year. Sina Finance, 2018-04-23.

Zhang, Xin (2011). Japan Announced GDP Data of 2010, Fall Back to the Third-largest Economy, http://www.chinanews.com/gj/2011/02-14/2840576.shtml, Accessed in February 2017.

Zhang, Y. (2015). "Supply-side Reform" Is a Strategic Plan for the Overall Situation (In

Zhang, Y. and Khare, A. (2009). The Impact of Accessible Identities on the Evaluation of Global Versus Local Products. Journal of Consumer Research, 36, 524-537.

Zhang, Yi (2011). Ten Years' of China's Entry into the WTO. Automotive Companies are Soaring. Xinhua Net, 2011-12-11.

Zhang, Yong and Gu, Mingming (2011). Cultural Factors in Social and Economic Development. Economic Research Issues, 2008, (1) :22-26.

Zhao, Haijuan (2011), "National People's livelihood Index Is Compiling; the Pattern of Achievement Assessment Changes", China Economic Times, 11th December 2011.

Zhao, Qing (2017). What have Foreign Banks Experienced in Their Ten Years in China? Hexun, 2017-12-16.

Zhao, X. (2016). What does "Supply-side Reform" Reform? . Ningbo Economy.

Zhao, X. and F. Shen (1995). Audience Reaction to Commercial Advertising in China in the 1980s. International Journal of Advertising. 14(4), 374-390.

Zhao, Yongchang (2010). Importance of Non-Economic Factors to the Economic Development, Wenshan Daily, September 3, 2010: B3.

Zhe, Xu, Tingting Fang, Wenping Su. (2004). the Application of the Method of Combination Analysis in the Research on Consumers' Preference of Product Attributes. Quantifiably Economic and Technologically Economic Research, 12, (11), 138-149.

Zheng, Guangguan and XuemeiChen (2006). The Cluster Marketing Formation and Development of Exploration. Commercial Economics Review, 24(7),78-80.

Zhou Ling-qiang and Huang Zhu-hui. (2004). Sustainable Development of Rural Tourism in China: Challenges and Policies. Economic Geography, 4, 4.

Zhou Ying Heng, Lu Ling Xiao, and Geng Xian Hui (2003). The Change of the Fresh Food Purchasing Channels and its Trend: An Investigation on Why Consumers in Nan Jing Select Supermarkets. Journal of Chinese Distribution Economics, 4, 14~17.

Zhou, Daming (2013). Preface// Tian, Guang and Luo, Kanglong, Economic Anthropology, Yinchuan: Ningxia People's Publishing house:1-3.

Zhou, Daming and Liu, Zhaohui (2003). Chinese anthropology review, in Zhou Daming (Ed.) 21 Century Anthropology, Beijing: National Publishing House: 1-13.

Zhou, Ji (2004). Opposition to Education Welfare and Education Industrialization, http://www.chinanews.com/, Accessed in March 2017.

Zhou, L. and Wong, A (2008). Exploring the Influence of Product Conspicuousness and Social Compliance on Purchasing Motives of Young Chinese Consumers for Foreign Brands. Journal of Consumer Behavior, 7, 470-483.

Zhou, X. (2015). The Ideological Root and Governance of "Pan-Marketization"—Comment on Critique of Pan-Marketization . Journal of Tianjin University of Commerce. (4).

Zhu, Jianrong. (2003). Marketing Management of SME Clusters. Journal of Beijing Technology and Business University (Social Science), 18(4), 26.

Zhu, K., Kraemer, K. and Xu, S. (2006). The Process of Innovation Assimilation by Firms in Different Countries: A Technology Diffusion Perspective. Management Science, 52 (10), 1557-1576.

Zhu, Ling and Jiang Zhongyi (1994). Relieving People in Disaster Areas by Giving Them Employment instead of Outright Grant and Alleviating Poverty, Sanlian Bookstore.

Zhu, Y. and Warner, M. (2000). An Emerging Model of Employment Relations in China: A Divergent Path from the Japanese? International business review, 9, 345–361.

Zhu, Zhengqi and Lin Shuzhong (1989), The Development Road of the Federal Republic of Germany: The Practice of Social Market Economy, Beijing: China Social Sciences Press.

Zimmer, L. (2007). How Viable is Virtual Commerce? - Businesses That Understand the Potential of Second Life are Finding Real-World Commercial Opportunities in the Virtual Space, Manhasset, 6(1), 44-48.

Zinkhan, George M. (1994). International Advertising: A Research Agenda. Journal of Advertising, 23(1), 11-16.

Zirger, B. J. and Maidique, M. A. (1990). A Model of New Product Development: An Empirical Test. Management Science, 36(7), 867-883.

Index

D

E

M

N

O

P

R

U

V

W

X

Y

Z

Made in United States
Orlando, FL
04 November 2026

90200104R00243